TALKING WITH THE PAST:
THE ETHNOGRAPHY
OF ROCK ART

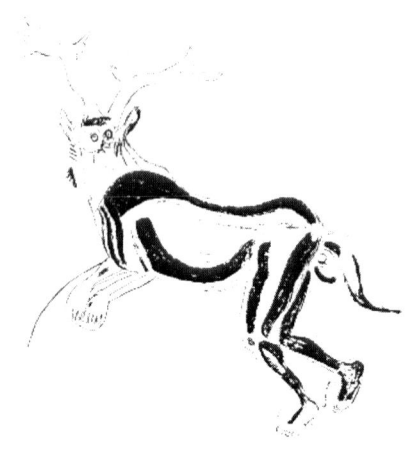

In Appreciation...

This book is published with the generous financial assistance of Ray B. and Jean M. Auel and David Easly. Their contributions have enabled this research to be made available to libraries throughout western North America.

TALKING WITH THE PAST: THE ETHNOGRAPHY OF ROCK ART

James D. Keyser

George Poetschat

Michael W. Taylor

Editors

Oregon Archaeological Society Publication
www.oregonarchaeological.org
Portland, Oregon

57839565

970.6
TAL

Published by
The Oregon Archaeological Society
P.O. Box 13293
Portland, Oregon 97213

Printed by
Maverick Publications
Bend, Oregon 97708

Publication No. 16
Copyright © 2006 by The Oregon Archaeological Society

All rights reserved. No part of this publication may be reproduced, stored in a retrieval system, or transmitted in any form or by any means, electronic, mechanical, photocopying, recording, or otherwise, without the written permission of The Oregon Archaeological Society.

ISBN (paperback) 0-9764804-2-5
ISBN (hardback) 0-9764804-3-3

Keywords
(1) Rock Art, (2) Rock Painting, (3) Cave Art,
(4) Cave Painting, (5) Petroglyphs, (6) Pictographs,
(7) Ethnography, (8) Archaeology, (9) Indians

Printed in the United States of America

TABLE OF CONTENTS

PART 1
  CHAPTER 1
    Editors' Introduction   1
      The Ethnography of Rock Art   2
      Rock Art Ethnography Presented in this Volume   5
PART 2
  Editors' Introduction to the Field Trip Discussions   9
  CHAPTER 2
    Field Trip Discussion   11
PART 3
  THE PRESENTATIONS
    Editors' Introduction to Papers and Discussions   29
  CHAPTER 3
    Rock Art and Ethnography: A Case in Point from Southern Africa   30
    J. David Lewis-Williams
      Discussion   44
  CHAPTER 4
    Reading Between the Lines: Ethnographic Sources and Rock Art Interpretation Approaches to Ethnography and Rock Art   49
    Linea Sundstrom
      Discussion   69
  CHAPTER 5
    Habitus and Narratives of Rock Art   73
    Robert Layton
      Discussion   94
  CHAPTER 6
    After the *Shamans of Prehistory*: Polemics and Responses   100
    Jean Clottes and J. David Lewis-Williams
      Discussion   136
  CHAPTER 7
    Tíim'enin': Indigenous Conceptions of Columbia Plateau Rock-art   143
    Phillip Cash Cash
      Discussion   153
  CHAPTER 8
    The Beaver Bowl: Ethnographic Evidence for a Northwest Coast Shaman's Petroglyph   158
    James D. Keyser, George Poetschat, Helen Hiczun, Pat McCoy, and Betty Tandberg
      Discussion   173

TABLE OF CONTENTS (Continued)

CHAPTER 9
House of the Rising Sun: Using the Ethnographic Record to Illuminate Aspects of Klamath Basin Rock Art — 176
Don Hann and Gordon Bettles
   Discussion — 193

CHAPTER 10
The Blade Cuts Two Ways: Using Ethnographic Analogy to Interpret the Columbia Plateau Scratched Style — 200
James D. Keyser and Michael W. Taylor
   Discussion — 222

CHAPTER 11
Rock Art, Physical Setting, and Ethnographic Context: A Comparative Perspective — 225
Johannes H. N. Loubser
   Discussion — 248

CHAPTER 12
Nymphs, Waterfowl, and Saints: The Role of Ethnography in the Interpretation of the Rupestrian Tradition of Valcamonica, Italy — 254
Angelo Fossati
   Discussion — 281

CHAPTER 13
Fertility and Sexuality in Rock Art of the Southwestern United States: Rock Art Research and Cultural Affiliation — 282
Kelley Hays-Gilpin
   Discussion — 293

CHAPTER 14
Rock Art and Rites of Passage in Far Western North America — 295
David S. Whitley
   Discussion — 326

PART 4
EPILOGUE
Editors' Introduction to the Spilyay Tymoo Articles — 327
Spilyay Tymoo Articles
   New theories shed light on tribal rock art — 327
   Shannon Keaveny
   Shamanistic Rock Art: Tribal Elders from the Columbia River Basin share their knowledge with world scholars. — 328
   Shannon Keaveny

REFERENCES CITED — 333
INDEX — 374
CONTRIBUTING AUTHORS — 378

DEDICATION

We dedicate this book to Viola Kalama, James Selam, Phillip Cash Cash, Táxli Winch, Willie Selam, Brigette Whipple, Lori Watlamet, and Les McConnell. Each of these Indian people participated directly in the 2002 symposium and Phillip and Lori assisted with the fieldwork on which several of the presentations are based. These tribal traditionalists eeach have a deep and abiding knowledge of their peoples' customs, folklore, and traditions; but, equally importantly, they also have a willingness to share that knowledge with others so that we all may understand a little better the lives of the original inhabitants of the Columbia River. Without their participation and their desire to share, to teach, and to learn together, this book and the gathering on which it is based, could not have happened.

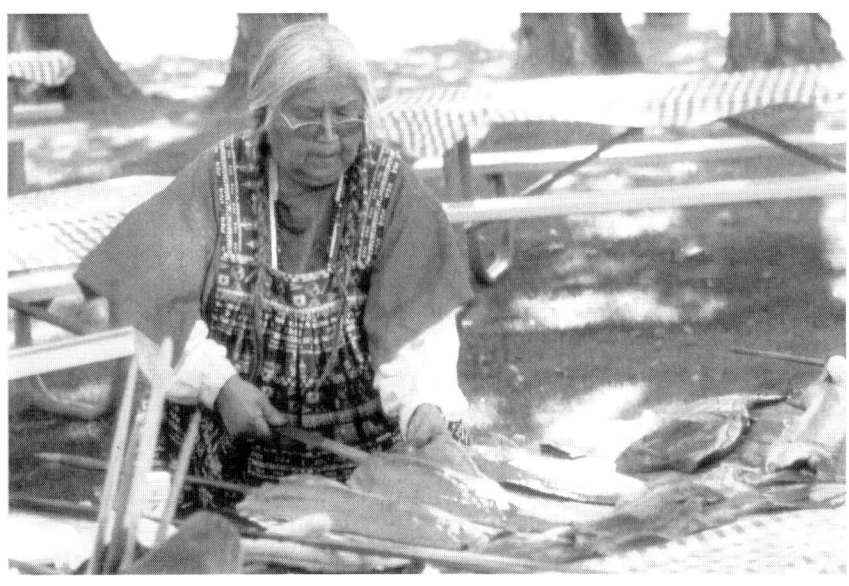

Nola Queahpama, Warm Springs tribal traditionalist, preparing salmon for the salmon bake that followed our symposium field trip.

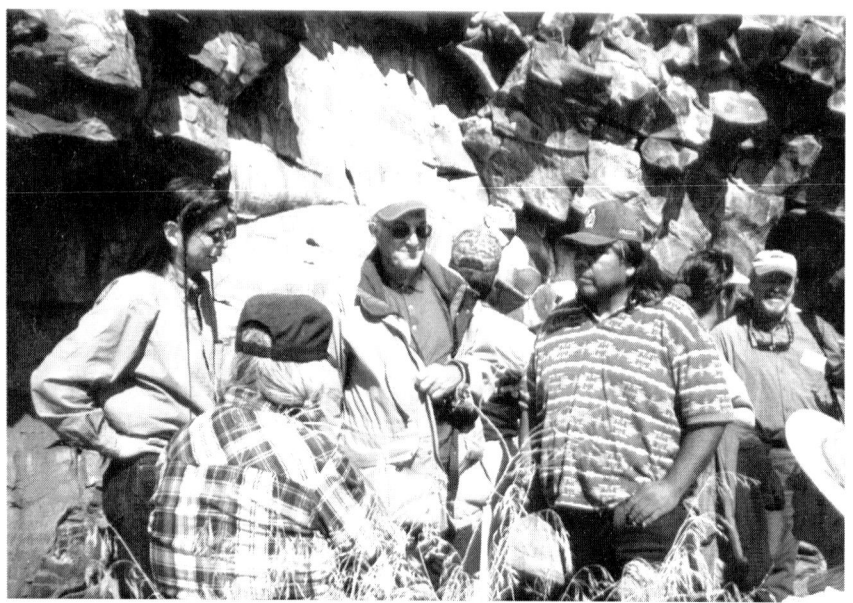

Scholars and Indians discussing rock art during the symposium field trip. From left: Phillip Cash Cash, James Selam (with back to photographer), Jean Clottes, Willie Selam, and David Whitley.

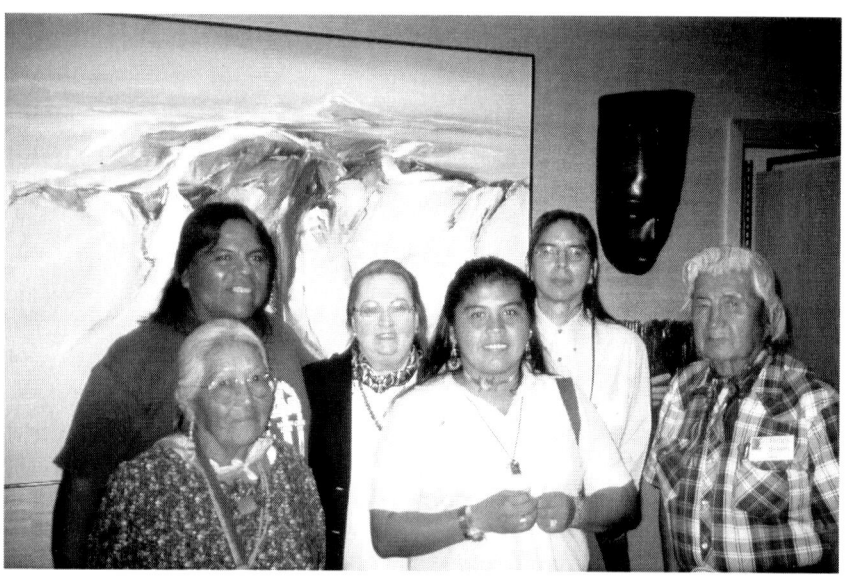

Symposium participants with sponsor Jean M. Auel. From left: Viola Kalama, Willie Selam, Jean M. Auel, Brigette Whipple, Phillip Cash Cash, and James Selam.

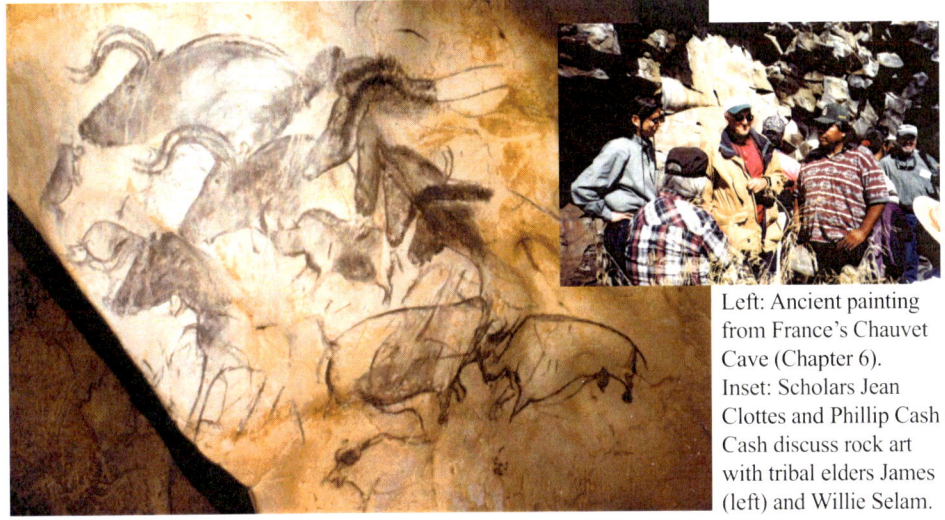

Left: Ancient painting from France's Chauvet Cave (Chapter 6).
Inset: Scholars Jean Clottes and Phillip Cash Cash discuss rock art with tribal elders James (left) and Willie Selam.

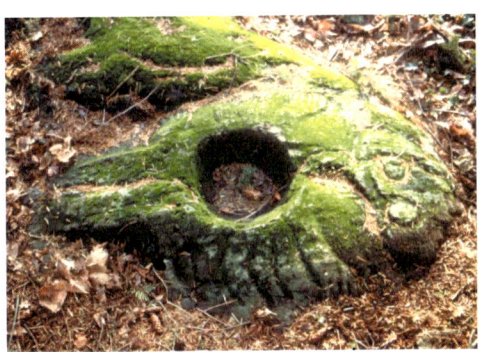

Bedrock carving of a shaman's bowl in the shape of a beaver (Chapter 8).

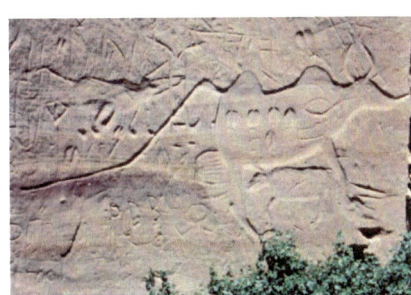

Intaglio of bison cow and calf from the Northern U. S. Great Plains (Chapter 4).

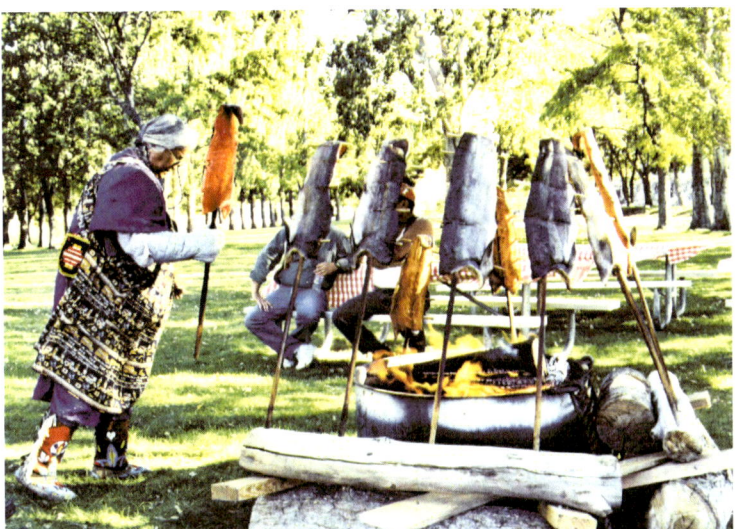

Columbia River Salmon prepared using traditional American Indian methods.

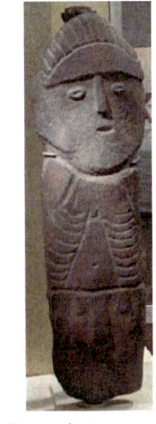

Carved stone sculpture from the Columbia Plateau (Chapter 8).

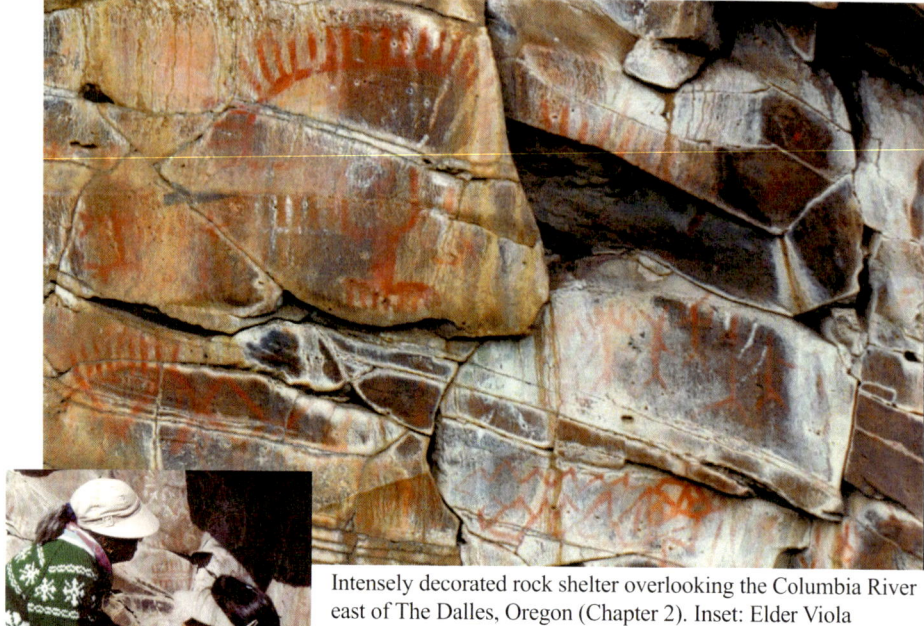

Intensely decorated rock shelter overlooking the Columbia River east of The Dalles, Oregon (Chapter 2). Inset: Elder Viola Kalama and granddaughter Brigette Whipple examine images in the rock shelter.

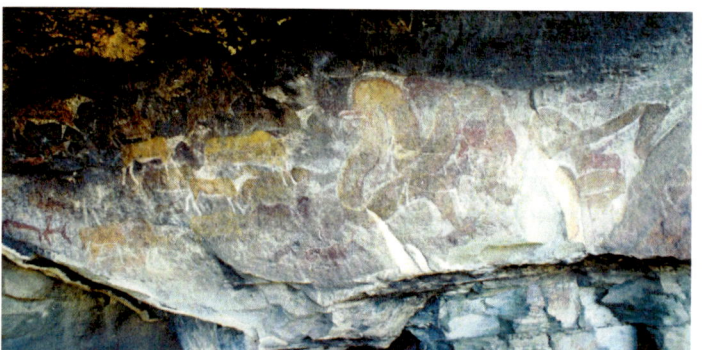

South African painted rock shelter (Chapter 11).

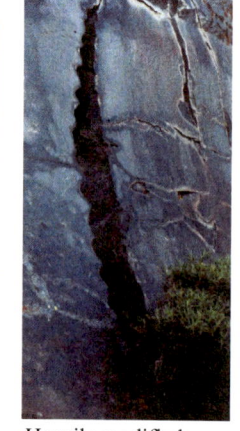

Heavily modified Basalt crack on the Columbia Plateau (Chapter 10).

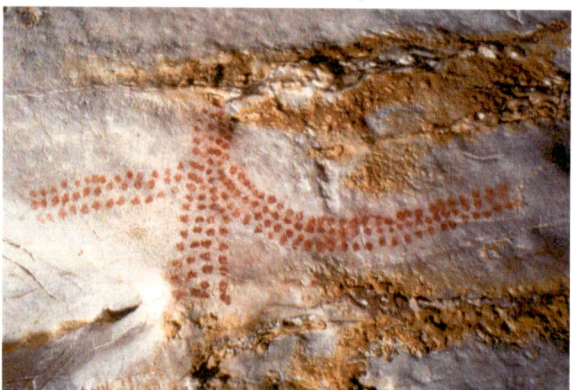

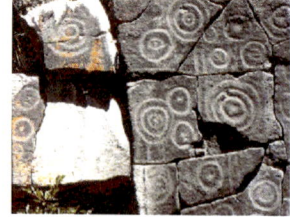

Concentric circle motifs in the Klamath Basin (Chapter 9).

An ancient sign of unknown meaning found in El Castillo Cave in Spain (Chapter 6).

PART 1
CHAPTER 1
Editors' Introduction

During the course of a multi-year rock art recording project in the Dalles-Deschutes area of the Columbia River Gorge (see Keyser et al 2004), Phillip Cash Cash, one participating researcher, told us of his desire to do some primary ethnographic fieldwork with tribal elders from the Lower Columbia River area. Phillip's idea was to record information about traditional places and activities along this stretch of river that could be provided to both tribes and federal and state agencies to help with the area's management. About two years later (in late 2001) the Civil Rights staff of the Washington Office of the US Department of Agriculture-Forest Service (USDA-FS) made available some funding for studying the "Heritage of Diversity." Based on Keyser's discussions with Phillip he prepared a proposal and was awarded a small USDA-FS grant for a study entitled "Traditional Places of the River People." Phillip, who speaks Sahaptin-Nez Perce and is traditionally trained to deal with several different classes of sites, items, and knowledge whose use and discussion is somewhat restricted in Columbia Plateau cultures, was selected to conduct this research (see Cash Cash 2004 for part of the results).

In discussing how this project would be conducted, Phillip suggested that it might present a unique opportunity for tribal traditionalists to share their knowledge of rock art with international scholars interested in ethnographic approaches to the subject, while at the same time providing the chance for the traditionalists to learn about rock art from other areas of the world. Given Phillip's willingness to mediate such an intellectual exchange, Keyser spoke with the other two editors of this volume about the feasibility of cooperating with the Oregon Archaeological Society to organize such an event.

Based on our discussions, and the success of a series of lectures and workshops we had organized the year before (Fossati 2001a, 2002a), we agreed to seek the additional sponsorship and funding necessary to organize and conduct such an event. Over the next few months we obtained additional sponsorship from the Oregon Archaeological Society, Ray B. and Jean M. Auel, Donna Tallman—State Farm Insurance, Le Orme dell'Uomo, the US Fish and Wildlife Service, and the USDA-FS.

At that point we selected a group of scholars who would be invited to participate in the symposium. Following discussions with a few professional colleagues, our effort was oriented toward inviting senior rock art scholars from around the world who had demonstrated an interest in studying rock art ethnography, and had experience working with native traditionalists knowledgeable about rock art and related subjects. Ultimately, we received commitment from fourteen scholars to participate in the symposium. One of these, David Lewis-Williams, was forced to miss the conference at the last minute for health reasons, but his paper was presented by David Whitley (who spent two years working with Lewis-Williams in South Africa as a Fullbright Scholar in the mid 1980s), and it is published here. The twelve papers presented by these scholars were selected to emphasize Columbia Plateau rock art (three papers), a broad international view of rock art ethnography (five papers), and theoretical and methodological issues (four papers).

In addition to the symposium papers (which are presented in Part 3; Chapters 3 through 14), scholars and Indian traditionalists together visited a group of rock art sites for discussion about the art. The discussions, during and after the visits, are presented in Part 2; Chapter 2. During the symposium, the OAS sponsored a public evening program entitled "Shamans of Prehistory" with presentations by Jean Clottes on Chauvet Cave and David Whitley on the "Shamanic Model" as expressed in the rock art of South Africa and the Coso Range in southern California's Great Basin region. Although not published here, these public presentations were attended by more than 800 people. Finally, following the symposium, "Spilyay Tymoo," tribal newspaper for the Confederated Tribes of the Warm Springs Reservation of Oregon, published a pair of articles describing the participation of Indian people in both the field trip and the paper presentations. These articles are contained in Part 4, the Epilog.

The Ethnography of Rock Art

The use of ethnography to understand and interpret rock art has a spotty history both in North America and around the world. Probably the earliest efforts to use ethnography to study North American rock art (Schoolcraft 1851-1857; Mallery 1893; Teit 1896, 1900) were based on the notion that native people in various areas could provide direct insight into the use and meaning of the rock art in their territory. Mallery's work, the earliest comprehensive study of North American rock art, provided some notable ethnographic insights into meaning, even though the work as a whole was based on the ultimately faulty premise that rock art was in fact the earliest beginnings of a written language. In his work, Mallery recounts many of Schoolcraft's interpretations, derived directly from oral traditions of Ojibwa informants—interpretations that have been expanded and reinforced by researchers using various informants and other primary ethnographic sources over the ensuing century and a half (Conway 1993; Conway and Conway 1990; Dewdney and Kidd 1962;

Rajnovich 1994). In addition, Mallery was the first researcher to summarize the rich ethnographic information concerning the incised Micmac rock art of Kejimkujik Nova Scotia, and the Biographic robe and ledger art of the Northern Plains. Both of these sections of his work remain primary sources for researchers even today (e.g. Keyser and Cash Cash 2002).

Following Mallery's lead, many American ethnographers took up the interest in questioning native informants about their knowledge of rock art—including who made it, for what purposes, and how it was done. For more than half a century—from 1890 to 1950, dozens of ethnographers throughout western North America regularly obtained detailed information about rock art from numerous traditionally-trained members of many different ethnic groups (Barbeau 1960; Cline 1938; Driver 1937; Gayton 1948; Lowie 1924; Malouf and White 1953; Simmons 1942; Stephen 1936; Steward 1943; Teit 1896, 1900, 1906, 1918, 1930; Voegelin 1938). This information ranges from incredibly detailed, straightforward explanations of the rock art's symbolism and meaning, to culturally-conditioned, metaphoric references couched in terms of Little People, Water Babies, or *Maymaygwayshi* making marks at their "houses of power."

For some entire regions, and specific sites or areas within other regions, this information was easily transferred into the study of rock art—even though the researchers were often avocational scholars rather than formally trained anthropologists or archaeologists.[1] In the Columbia Plateau and Plains regions and the Canadian Shield area of the Eastern Woodlands, both avocational and archaeological scholars routinely incorporated ethnographic information into the archaeological study of rock art (e.g. Conway and Conway 1990; Conner and Conner 1971; Corner 1968; Dewdney and Kidd 1962; Jones 1981; Keyser and Knight 1976; Leechman et al 1955; Wellman 1979). Likewise, in the American Southwest, one particular rock art site associated with a sacred spring has long been known to be the clan symbols of those who make pilgrimages to the site for ceremonial purposes (Simmons 1942). In all these instances there never has been an actual gap between ethnography and rock art.

However, in other regions or areas, where the ethnographic references to rock art are less direct, or couched in more metaphoric terms, both archaeologists and avocationalists often failed to comprehend the meaning of this information, and routinely argued that references to Little People, Rock Babies, or Ancient Ones making the art meant that it predated the cultures currently living in the area and was thus beyond the "reach" of ethnography. Arguments that ethnography is of little or no use in understanding the function or meaning of rock art are found in some of the best known early works in several areas (e.g. Grant et al

1968; Heizer and Baumhoff 1962; Malouf and White 1953; Over 1943:3; Steward 1937). Unfortunately, this failure to understand the essence of the ethnographic record, and thus to appreciate the information encoded therein, left the door open for self-ordained "experts" to promulgate all manner of interpretations purporting to explain the art. These ranged from the wildly speculative and fancifully foolish arguments suggesting ancient spacemen, Celtic monks writing Ogam (Fell 1976, 1982; McGlone et al 1993), or Indian cryptographers (Martineau 1973), to more plausible—yet still not anthropologically or archaeologically well-supported—hypotheses of solar alignments, ancient hunting cults, Mesoamerican influences, or fertility rituals (e.g. Grant et al 1968; Green and Holmes 2001; Hayden 2001; Holmes and Cramer 2002; McLane and Frock 2001; O'Connor 2002; Sprague and Grasse 2001).

Although such speculative explanations have been proposed throughout North America, one of the first places where they were effectively challenged was in the Great Basin. Blessed with a wealth of detailed ethnography, David Whitley began a critical re-examination of these sources, which led him to a deeper understanding of the metaphors employed in reference to rock art, and thus to some startling reinterpretations of the rock art record in light of both archaeological and ethnographic evidence (Whitley 1992, 1994a, 1994b, 1998, 2000b). This continues today as some of the liveliest debate in North American rock art research (Gilreath and Hildebrandt 2003; Hedges 2001, 2002; Keyser and Whitley 2006; Quinlan 2000; Whitley 2001, 2003), and one whose last words have certainly not yet been written.

The last quarter century has seen a resurgence of rock art scholarship based on analysis of the ethnographic record. Across North America, scholars from the Eastern Woodlands (Diaz-Granados and Duncan 2000; Loubser et al 2004; Salzer 1987) to the Pacific Northwest (Boreson 1998; Keyser 1990, 1992) and Alaska (Poetschat et al 2002) have used various types of evidence from the ethnographic record to interpret rock art. Other areas where such well-documented, ethnographically-based interpretive efforts are common in the rock art literature include the Canadian Shield (Conway and Conway 1990; Rajnovich 1994), the Great Plains (Francis and Loendorf 2002; Keyser 1977, 1979, 1987, 1991; Keyser and Klassen 2001, 2002; Keyser and Mitchell 2000, 2001; Parsons 1987; Sundstrom 2002; Sundstrom and Keyser 1998), the greater Southwest (Bostwick 2001; Boyd 1998, 2003; Brugge 2001), and California (Whitley 2000b). Based on primary ethnographic and ethnohistoric sources, current oral traditions, and ethnographically-collected material culture items and artworks, these interpretations have enabled a much more complete understanding of North American Rock art than could have been envisioned in 1970, and new evidence leads to additional interpretations every year.

Outside North America, ethnographic research into the origin and meaning of rock art has an equally spotty history. Current research in the last two decades in South Africa has shown that a rich rock art record can be significantly better understood using clues available from all sorts of ethnographic and ethnohistoric contexts (Lewis-Williams 1981, 1992a, 1996, 2001; Lewis-Williams and Dowson 1989, 1990). Although rock art research in much of Asia has only recently been available to a worldwide audience, there are many examples of direct ethnographic evidence known that help interpret rock art from Siberia (Devlet 2001) through China and into the republics of central Asia around the Caspian Sea (Chen 2001). Certainly there is much more that can be learned from the rock art ethnography of these and many other Asian countries. In Australia a rich ethnographic record is augmented in several areas by the oral traditions of people who have made or refreshed traditional rock art in their own lifetimes (Taçon 2001).

Even in Europe, where for years the age of the most striking art—that of the Paleolithic caves—precluded a strong focus on ethnographic interpretation, and focused interpretive efforts more toward technical, archaeological, and structural interpretations, scholars have recently used models derived from ethnographic research on other continents to subject this ancient art to "ethnographic" analyses (Clottes and Lewis-Williams 1996; Lewis-Williams 2002). More recently, ethnographic evidence relating to other art in Scandinavia and the Alps has been studied and found to contain interesting bits of evidence that provide significant aids to interpretation (Bradley et al 2001; Chippindale 2001:254-258; see also Fossati, chapter 12, this volume).

In summary, ethnography has proven its usefulness around the world, and the source material—ranging from written ethnographic and ethnohistoric documents to oral histories and interviews of informants living today—has much new and often surprising information to provide (Keyser and Whitley 2006, Cash Cash 2004, see also Cash Cash, chapter 7, this volume) and promises to be the genesis of new models (Sundstrom 2002) that will be refined, debated, and used into the foreseeable future.

Rock Art Ethnography Presented in this Volume

This volume contains papers that contribute key new data to rock art interpretation in several areas of the world. For North America, papers by Cash Cash, Hann and Bettles, and Keyser and Taylor focus primarily on Columbia Plateau rock art. Cash Cash's contribution (chapter 7), written in both his native language—Sahaptin-Nez Perce—and English, interprets a group of Biographic tradition drawings at the Steiwer Ranch site in north-central Oregon (see Keyser et al 1998a) by reference to previously unpublished 1930s field notes from a Cayuse elder who provided first-hand identification of symbols and events that are portrayed in the art. This incredibly exciting paper combines Cash Cash's knowledge and talent as a linguist with his knowledge of rock art in his first effort of what one hopes will be a series of others designed to obtain rock art ethnography from field notes on file in several archives. In this same vein, the work of Hann and Bettles (chapter 9) also represents a similar effort. Spending many hours transcribing the ethnographic notes of Jeremiah and Alma Curtin, these scholars discovered a wealth of information about rock art of the Klamath and Modoc tribes. Their work has already been used in several publications (Hann et al 2004; Loubser and Whitley 1999; Whitley et al 2004) and promises to be a rich source for scholars in the Klamath Basin area for years to come (e.g. David 2004). Finally, Keyser and Taylor (chapter 10) define a new scratched rock art style within the Columbia Plateau tradition, and then use extensive ethnographic analogy to suggest that it functioned in the rituals of a specific type of Columbia Plateau shaman.

Three other papers discuss rock art elsewhere in North America. Keyser et al (chapter 8) report on a Northwest Coast petroglyph with a striking Classic Conventionalized style motif, and utilize previously unanalyzed ethnographic information to identify it as a shaman's site. One of this paper's main strengths is its comparison of rock art to the wealth of mobiliary art from the lower Columbia River area. Kelley Hayes-Gilpin (chapter 13), in accord with her recent research emphasis (Hayes-Gilpin 2004), focuses on rock art in the American Southwest and shows that even indirect ethnographic evidence can enable us to better understand gendered rock art imagery relevant to Puebloan concepts of fertility, sexuality, and gender roles. Whitley (chapter 14) summarizes the rock art associated with puberty rituals in southern California—a topic that has recently received considerable attention and debate in the literature (Hedges 2001; Whitley 2003). This work is a long-needed summary that promises to put to rest many of the primary questions in the debates about California rock art.

Two papers are case studies involving mostly rock art outside North America. That by Jannie Loubser (chapter 11) is a broadly-based comparison using ethnographic and structural data to highlight similarities and differences in rock art from Africa and the Pacific Northwest. His model differentiating between shamanic and shamanistic imagery provides some intriguing avenues for future rock art research in all areas. Angelo Fossati, one of the principals of Le Orme dell'Uomo, summarizes a rich record of ethnographic and ethnohistoric information that has enabled him to make some startlingly new interpretations of the Alpine petroglyphs of Italy's Valcamonica (chapter 12). Using ethnohistoric records, linguistic clues, mythology, and modern oral tradition, Fossati shows that ethnographic methods can help us understand some rock art that was made as much as two millennia ago. His work establishes a research approach that promises to yield exciting results for future efforts.

The first four papers in the volume stress more theoretical or methodological issues than site-specific approaches. David Lewis-Williams (chapter 3) provides another in his long sequence of papers that relate the ethnography of the San people of South Africa to their magnificent rock art. Pointing out the inherent difficulties of using the ethnographic record, he illustrates the principles of parallelism and synecdoche that allow us, as researchers, to interpret the rock art record. Linea Sundstrom, a North American Plains rock art expert, discusses the direct ethnographic approach to rock art study, utilizing sites in and near Ludlow Cave, South Dakota, as a case in point. Her work (chapter 4) is in fact, a discussion of methodological advantages and pitfalls inherent in ethnographic approaches to rock art research.

Bob Layton (chapter 5) looks at the validity of ethnographic information, using case studies from Australia, the American Southwest, and the Columbia Plateau area of British Columbia. Layton's analysis of the strengths and weaknesses of these cases, and how their information has been used, is clear and concise. His discussion of Annie York's testimony about Columbia Plateau tradition pictographs is a "must read" for anyone using ethnography in the Pacific Northwest. Finally, Jean Clottes and David Lewis-Williams publish here (chapter 6) for the first time in English their analysis of the criticisms directed toward their groundbreaking work in "The Shamans of Prehistory" (Clottes and Lewis-Williams 1996). After their initial publication of this work, they carefully compiled all critical responses leveled for and against it—both published and unpublished. They then analyze these critiques as a test of whether such sorts of interpretation are appropriate for rock art beyond the reach of direct ethnography. These theoretically and methodologically oriented chapters form a corpus of work directly relevant to any interpretation of the prehistoric record. Any rock art scholar would benefit by reading them, but it is a body of literature with which all archaeologists should be familiar.

Although there are several perspectives on the use of ethnographic information contained in these collected papers, and frequent cautionary notes that ethnography is more than simply taking previous writings at face value, the papers in this volume provide another example of what Whitley (Whitley and Loendorf 1994) so cogently summarized just a decade ago. The scholars published herein are rock art specialists—not simply archaeologists who, as a respite from real research, publish a descriptive summary of a flashy petroglyph site. Defining methods, exploring the extensive archives of unpublished field notes, and showing how the appropriate use of various anthropological techniques (from ethnohistoric research and linguistics, through art history, to comparison with mobiliary art) can yield striking interpretive breakthroughs, these scholars are at the forefront of a new focus on rock art as a primary archaeological resource. As the most visible and most easily studied manifestation of ritual behavior in many prehistoric cultures, rock art can no longer be thought of as outside the main stream of archeological research. As these papers show, its study can yield information and inferences about the past that are not as easily accessible (if accessible at all) using traditional archaeological data sets. In summary, if we wish to have an integrated understanding and interpretation of prehistoric cultures—both hunter-gatherer and horticulturalist—these papers demonstrate that rock art must be incorporated into archaeological study wherever it exists.

---

[1] The shift away from the study of rock art by most professional archaeologists and the subsequent filling of this void by a variety of avocational scholars from many different backgrounds is well summarized by Keyser (2005) and Francis (2005).

PART 2
Editors' Introduction to Field Trip Discussions

As part of the 2002 symposium, scholars and Indian traditionalists visited a group of rock art sites in the least developed part of the Dalles-Deschutes area of the Columbia River Gorge. The visit, on the symposium's first day, served to introduce scholars and tribal traditionalists to one another, and also to familiarize several scholars with Columbia Plateau rock art, which they had not previously seen. For the elder traditionalists it was also an opportunity to once again see a relatively unspoiled part of the river—an experience somewhat akin to the days of their youth. Field trip participants included all of the symposium scholars and Eugene Hunn, author of "Nch'i-Wána, The Big River" (Hunn 1990), and tribal traditionalists James Selam, Willie Selam, and Gregg Kiona from the Yakama Nation and Viola Kalama, Brigette Whipple, and Táxli Winch (Tule Mat Man) from the Warm Springs Reservation.

After personal introductions and a traditional welcome to the area, we visited three rock art sites. At each site the participants had unstructured discussions, often in the form of scholars' questions that were broadly discussed and answered (in whole or in part) by one or more traditionalists. In some cases a question would elicit one elder's response and that response would then lead others into topics only loosely related to the original. At least two elders later remarked to us how the visit had brought back memories from their youth, and that had led them to talk of many things in addition to rock art.

These wide-ranging discussions were videotaped for later transcription and editing. Our editing pared these discussions down to a focus on rock art and related topics. For brevity, discussions of current events, tribal politics, and natural history have been omitted from this summary. Otherwise, however, we have attempted to maintain the wording, cadence, and sentence structure of the traditionalists' responses as closely as possible—within guidelines for clarity of communication, which corrected grammatical errors and omitted interlocutory expressions and similar utterances.[1]

Following the day-long field trip, we met in Portland for formal presentations of symposium papers. We started the session with a round-robin discussion of what had been talked about on the field trip. That discussion is presented here as the field trip follow-up, with the same editing guidelines as summarized for the field trip discussions.

10   Field Trip Discussion

[1] Throughout these discussions, and those that occurred after each paper, we have used parentheses to enclose material or information supplied in some form by the speaker at that time or later. We use brackets to set off information that is provided by us as editors.

CHAPTER 2
Field Trip Discussion

Editors' Note: After arriving at the first of three rock art sites we visited as a group, Phillip Cash Cash made a statement in his Nez Perce language and sang a short song. He began the discussion by asking if any of the elders who were with us would like to talk. The following is an edited summary of the discussions that took place at the three sites.

Táxli Winch: Memories of the past, Memories that are only with the older ones today. Sometimes it is hard for an elder to share information about things like this, the paintings and carvings, as we go along. But I believe in my heart and her [Viola's] heart that she is glad to be here and I'm glad to be here. This is something in my life I thought that I'd never see, that I'd never be with people like you, experienced people who have gone on to educate yourselves about the past, and help revive some of the information of the past.

The (young people) back in the past they'd leave signs on the walls, like she [Viola] said,[1] to keep that information for those people. The river played a big deal for our tribe, the Chinook people.

This is new to me and I want to thank everybody. I was just explaining to her [Viola] what I am doing for myself, for my benefit. I'm going to record songs I was taught, but now I'm losing. She [Viola] says that she's losing Wasco songs too. This is because we never have the chance to Wasco dance anymore, for ten years or better, because of powwows.

They used to have a social gathering at powwows where different groups came in and did their things. But now they won't even let the Wasco people do the grand entry, because we'd have to have a number on our regalia. My uncle, who is her [Viola's] brother, is the Wasco chief of this area, and he was told that we couldn't dance so we never participate in powwows anymore. The number is competition and we are not competition people.

The way I was taught and was told was that this area was almost all spiritual. People believed everything was put here by the creator. They prayed everyday, whether it was for the water, the fish, the deer, the roots, the rocks, whatever. Everything here is life.

I'm a person who looks for knowledge. I want to learn this.

Viola: When people made these [pictographs] I don't believe they ever imagined there would be a group of people, especially *bushtons* here. *Bushtons* was a name they gave to non-Indians. When the White people first came, they said they were from Boston. So today we still use that word, *bushton* for White people.

Like I say, the old people who painted these never thought that today's people would be looking at them. This might have been the place where they came to seek their spirit helper. From the great spirits. They painted these with big hearts. They were earnest in their painting. They didn't just come up here to scribble or just to pass time. They did it because there was meaning in it. All of that had a message in it, the pictographs and the petroglyphs. We go quite a way into central Oregon up past John Day and all over and everywhere they [the rock art images] seem to be similar. The same kind of messages left.

They were seeking their helper in their life. Sometimes they stayed for days. The people down at the village, if they (the seeker) got home with no sign of anything, they would send them again. So they'd have to go again, maybe to another spot.

Usually they piled rocks. Below The Dalles they found piles of rocks and no one knew what they were. They thought they were some kind of barricade in order to go to war or fight. But they're not. They were places where the boys were sent to seek their (spirit helper). That's what those were.

There are other signs [rock art] like this further up, (near) Mosier.

(To have their vision they would go) way out a treacherous trail, or way up a hill, or into the forest, wherever that they were away from camp.

Táxli Winch: I think it was similar to the vision quest for a young man.

Viola: That's what that was.

Táxli Winch: (A young man went) to seek his vision and seek himself. What he is to be or how he is to be. Whatever life was going to be prepared for him in the future. A lot of the younger men went out to different areas. There were certain areas that were all over, not just one area. They were sent on their journey themselves. Like she [Viola] said, maybe it took a week or longer. They had to stay there until they saw what they were seeking.

Mike Taylor: Do you think this is still going on?

Viola: It's not done anymore. No one does it any more, not like those days. They don't go seek their spirit any longer. The way it is being carried now, it's being passed down. Somebody's song—old songs that are handed down. Nobody goes out to seek anything anymore.

(The rock piles) we find are old, old ones. But there are some people yet that still carry that old religion of the river. The Chinook people were great ones for that. That was their religion. The medicine songs.

It is a powerful religion. It only occurs when the first frost comes and they start like a revival or something. Then it goes on all winter. Like Coyote followed the people clear to the mouth of the Columbia. Both sides of the river—he attended every gathering, every song festival. When the spring comes and the frost goes away they lay aside their winter things and go out for the summer to rustle food and whatnot.

Our church at home, we kind of laugh about it, but it's an Indian religion too, but is kind of mixed with the modern.

It started across there—at Wots'qus—where that old shaker church used to be. That's where their religion hit first, from 1910. That's late. That's a late religion. This religion, it gets powerful too. We kind of don't know what we're doing when we're participating. You get carried into the spirits, you know. We know what we're doing but I mean the spirit hits. It's really powerful. Powerful for prayer and healing.

That's the medicine society religion.

Táxli Winch: They actually call two of them now on the reservation of Warm Springs. They call them the *Wasklicks* and the *Twatees*. *Twatees* are medicine people that either do both, they heal and undertake. The *Wasklicks* are actually feather people. They have two feathers, one in each hand, and they spin the individual they're healing round and round. They beat with a drum fast, and they sing. But they are slowly changing. They are taking the drums away now. They are starting to use the sticks and *shi-shis*, or deer-hoof rattles. Those were used to drive out spiritual evils. The *Washkookums* [Wascos] or Chinooks they would use that. They never had the drums at that time.

James Keyser: You were speaking of the mortuary rituals happening at home. I have read that red paint was used in the mortuary ritual. Is that still practiced?

Viola: That was one of the sacred things that happened. The Chinook people used a lot of red paint. The red paint was very important. Even being out in some kind of a celebration or any kind of activity people painted. My mother used to paint a lot. She painted (each cheek.) When they gambled, they'd paint real bad, red faced.

When there was death they painted their faces and they sprinkled paint on them. We were the red people too, but this is not done anymore.

Brigette [her granddaughter, who accompanied her] and I practice that yet. "Paint," I tell her, "To help you." So she does it. I do it.

James Keyser: Does it bring good luck?

Viola: It staves off bad thought and bad spirits.

Táxli Winch: The same way they used otter for when they did spiritual things. They used them as headbands. It was like a shield. If people had bad thoughts for you, that otter would flick those thoughts back to the individual. When I'm healing or singing I always wear an otter headband or I've got a belt that's an otter, or my medicine stick will have an otter on it. It's a shield. The *Wasklicks* have a little tiny mirror, a medallion. The mirror, that's to reflect bad thoughts from other people. You can tell when you see a medallion with a mirror on it.

Viola: Years ago I think it was a shell, an abalone shell. That was used instead of the modern glass today. That's why you find them in burial sites—abalone shells polished to shine. They always wore that on their wampum. [Showing her beads, she continues] These are old beads you know. They find a lot of these in the sites. Well before, people used to dig them up. We went to the Burke museum in Seattle and we handled a lot of burial material. The wampum. And that seal skin they used to wrap bodies in, (it came) from this island.

Táxli Winch: Yes, they [seals] came up here.

Viola: This is as far as the seal came. (This area was) just shining, my mother said it used to be. Shining is what her mother told her. Just shining with seals resting and lounging around. So the people came here to get the sealskin. Shoot the seal or spear it. That's what we saw [in the museum] so I believe it. They did use seal to wrap the bodies.

James Keyser: There is the red color and the white color. Often these two colors happen together. Is it important when those colors are together?

Viola: I've just seen the red. I don't know what they used for the white paint. It might have been that warrior paint, that white chalk. They made paint out of that too. The Paiute people.[2]

We use the white paint. There is a lot of it over in central Oregon. The men do too, the warriors use all kinds of paints. But she [Brigette, her granddaughter] and I, we use it to whiten our buckskin and to clean it. Like an outfit—a buckskin dress.

(When a person dies) they are dressed all in white. The buckskin dress, and moccasins, even the headband. All in buckskin. They don't put anything fancy on those clothes like beadwork or anything.

James Keyser: Did you ever hear what the paint might be mixed with?

Viola: What I heard was they used urine to mix the paints. I don't know how it would work, but one of the ingredients was urine.

James Keyser: When a person would come or be sent to a place like this to find a spirit helper, would they come here because the paintings are here? Or would they come here and make paintings to find that spirit helper.

Viola: They'd make one themselves.

James Keyser: How did a young person know it was time to go find a spirit helper?

Viola: Well, they became a certain age. When they were so old, they sent them up. They had to stay there the length of time it took for something to speak to them, to sing to them. It could be a bird, it could be an animal, it could be anything that was going to help them throughout their life. Then they knew it was time to go home.

James Keyser: So they were sent maybe by a grandparent?

Viola: By the spiritual people already down in camp.

James Keyser: So a person who came to a site like this might make a painting then as a remembrance of their experience or as an offering?

Viola: As he was directed to do.

James Keyser: Oh, by the spirit helper.

Viola: Yes.

James Keyser: Would that picture have special meaning to that person?

Viola: Yes.

James Keyser: Would he come back?

Viola: Yes he could come back to visit. To renew his strength.

James Keyser: Was this only young men, or was this also young women who went and had these visions?

Viola: I never heard of women, but maybe they did. There were women *Twatees*. I don't know how they got to be, but I never heard of women going [to have a vision]. Maybe they inherited it.

Angelo Fossati: When they came back to the site another time, did they have a vision again?

Viola: Probably they'd get more strength if they come visit, from that painting they made. It's like looking in a bible and refreshing yourself. Reading spiritual scriptures and getting strength from it.

Les McConnell:[3] Do you know, when the people came up here did they bring any food?

Viola: No, they never ate in all those days they sat. No water. No food. Until they got their vision and went down and drank everything dry I guess.

James Keyser: Those people who were healers, they would come and have a vision. Would they have more than one spirit helper or one main spirit helper?

Viola: I haven't heard of anybody having more than one. We just believe in one spirit, the Great Spirit. But there can be water spirits, that's what the Chinooks often prayed. We were sun people too. We pray when the sun comes up. We follow the sun in a certain way that we turn. We never let the sun get away from us. We are sun people too.

James Keyser: The Indians who lived here before the Peyote religion, did they use peyote or any of these things?

Viola: Peyote. It's not ours. Tobacco was the only thing. The Indian tobacco. That was really important. The Tobacco with the pipe. When anything went on, that was the first thing, the great prayer with the pipe. The pipe service and the song. Today no one knows the pipe songs. They're lost. They don't do that.

Táxli Winch: I don't know if you remember, but Nelson was telling me that, one time when we were coming down the river he was telling me too. Like on a vision quest. Back in time, he was telling me a young man would go out and seek a vision quest. They didn't have tobacco at that time. They smoked human remains. Pounded up the bones and smoked the people themselves. That's what he was telling me. Because he asked me at one time if we should do that. He watched me to see what I would do. I never did do it.

David Whitley: Would a young boy that was going on a vision quest, might they go to the same place as a medicine person or would they go to different places?

Viola: Different sites. Different places. That's why they find them all the way down the river. Different places all over the hillside. I don't think they've discovered all of them. There's a lot yet to be discovered.

James Keyser: That must be an awfully powerful thing - for a person to smoke a crushed up old bone.

Viola: I've never heard of that.

Táxli Winch: That's what he was telling me that one day when we were coming by here.

Viola: My brother is five years younger than I,[4] and I often wonder if he knows anything. I wonder if he remembers. I always think that. So I think he kind of concocts things sometimes.

When we were growing up over here my family lived on that side of the river and on this side of the river, what they used to call Spearfish. Just below Horsethief Park around where the village used to be. That was Spearfish we called it.

We were just little tykes after we were left alone. My father passed on when we were little. We had to fend for ourselves, my Mother. So she came to her brother who used to live at Spearfish. He used to fish just down there. There used to be a rock right down at the fishing sites where my uncle and some of the other fishermen fished. Their scaffolds were overlooking the river, right down deep. Before you get there on the trail going there, there used to be an old water channel or something just layered with sand. On that cliff like this there was picture that looked just like Tsagiglalal. We used to play with her. We would run up that way and she would look at us. We would run down this way and she would look at us. But yet that picture was just straight. We just had fun playing with that. I often wonder if it was a second Tsagiglalal or if it was the same picture. It must have gone under.[5] It was right down where the fishing places were. I just wonder who knows what happened to it. I never really talked with Clifford or Nelson [Viola's younger brothers] about it. They played there all their lives. I just wonder what they think about that face that played tricks on us.

James Keyser: At some sites there are petroglyph faces with lines that flowed out from the mouths and big faces with big eyes. Some of the old people back then said that those were spirits in the water. You mentioned spirits in the water

Viola: Water Spirits.

James Keyser: So those would be made as the rock art pictures on the cliffs by the water?

Viola: I don't know who made them. Must have been the camp people who lived right there, near the beach. That one village was pretty near, they called it [indistinct]. Where the Ida White family used to live, near the Big Eddy.

Táxli Winch: (As we have talked about these sites) I have learned a lot too.

James Keyser: I think it's good for people who know these old things to pass them on because it's the way young people and people in the future will know what the old people knew.

Robert Layton: In Australia, where I've worked, there is a problem on the east coast. When young people lost interest in their own traditions, the older people didn't teach them anything because they said they weren't respectful of their own traditions. Now the next generation wants to go back to the traditions but they can't because the generation before never listened.

Viola: That's the way it goes. That's how we are. That one gap in there they didn't care about nothing. Now we have schools trying to teach the Indian language but they are not teaching our language right. I always say I wish someone would get in there and straighten them out. I tell my family, "This is the right way to say it. It's hard. It sounds ugly, you know, but its our language. It comes from way down and comes out." They say, "But our way sounds pretty." But that's not right though.

Phillip Cash Cash: I would ask that you all meet someone. One of the respected elders in Yakima is this man here, James Selam, and also his son Willie Selam has come.

Editors' note: Phillip then asked James Selam to recall his boyhood on the river.

James Selam: Indians didn't live in permanent structures. They lived in homes that were built, then torn down and stored away. Its kind of hard to explain. They were tule mat lodges. We followed the seasons, going up and down the river.

My area of the river where I grew up was from John Day and Roosevelt down to the falls, they call that Wishram now.

James Keyser: In those times did people live here on Miller Island?

James Selam: My time? No.

Maybe there's an explanation, at least from my—my people's—point of view. The channel here [Hells Gate Gorge] it was forbidden for people to go near it, or go fishing in it, or ride their boat through it. There is a deep hole up at the head of it—it goes more than a hundred feet below sea level. There is a legend about Coyote and the *Naisla*—the one who would swallow all the people in the legend. He would lure them—maybe hypnotize them in some way to come near this place, and he would take them in. Coyote got the word somewhere up there [up river] that something bad was happening to our people down here. So he asked his little sisters and they told him what was happening. On his way down he gathered dry twigs, sagebrush and other things and bundled them up in a BIG bundle. Then he turned them into small bundle, but with wood--he had the power to do this. He went on the other side [gesturing to indicate the Hells Gate Gorge] where there was a little slide [a scree slope above the river]. He sat up there and started calling the monster down there [in Hells Gate Gorge] those names. After four days, five days, six days the monster got tired of this. He took that whole hillside down—swallowed it. After he [Coyote] got inside he saw all the animals: deer, grizzly bears, rattlesnakes. He looked at them and said, "What are you guys doing here?" He thought he was tough so he decided to kill him [*Naisla*, the swallowing monster] to save all the animals. So he took out his bundle. He said "Don't you ever get cold or anything? Its cold in here." He took that bundle and started a fire right under his [*Naisla's*] heart. The fire got bigger—the fat from the heart started dripping down and in time it got so hot the heart just burned up. Then the monster spit them all out. So for that reason my people never come up that channel [Hells Gate Gorge]. So this place was very seldom used by people.

James Keyser: They came here to make these paintings.

James Selam: I was looking at them. I can't tell for sure, but there are some plants that can be used to make the markings. I can only think of the one plant that my people use for coloring buckskin moccasins. It helps them, when it got wet it didn't shrivel up. That plant turns kind of red. That might have been what they used.

Of course a lot of markings identify something that happened or something that was here, or somebody who got something[6] that was outstanding. They put that record on the rock. Or you identified one person maybe having family. There was a lot of things I could talk about from life, not what I learned in school. What I learned in my time. My experiences. The way my people lived.

Eels run all summer long. Salmon change in the spring. All winter long you can catch steelheads. In the spring the spring salmon would come up. It would only last maybe two weeks at the longest. When the water got too high there would be no more salmon. We'd go up into the hills. Around June we'd go back down. When the water would be down far enough the bluebacks would come up. We'd have thousands of them coming up. Then the summer Chinook. After the summer Chinook we would go huckleberrying. Our time was with the seasons. We didn't plan it. Indians know when to go and where to go and why.

James Keyser: When young people went out to have their visions was that also seasonal thing or did they go whenever they got old enough?

James Selam: No. When they are small, four or five years old, maybe older, we'd send them out. A certain place was selected for these kids to go. A lot of the kids were able to get this power by just being alone. Something would come speak to them. Give them the power.

After they grew up, as a man, the power they had would help them in times of war. It is kind of hard to explain. A lot of people from the river here fought with the cavalry. They were recruited by a guy named Captain McKay. Seventy-six Indians from along the river here fought in that war against the Shoshone, the Paiute. Only one got killed. The rest of them had this power I was talking about.

Mike Taylor: Protective power?

James Selam: Bullets would never touch them.

Mike Taylor: Almost like a shield.

James Selam: Like a deer when I'm shooting at it.

James Keyser: Well, I've seen the word written and I don't really know how to say it, but the word would sound something like *"Tahmanawis"*.

James Selam: It's two things. *Tahmanawis* is the law. And it's like *Shooka*, spiritual power. Like you said, gained by a child going out and searching for a spiritual power.

James Keyser: You mentioned that one of those words was also *Shooka*, that word would mean the spirit power?

James Selam: Yeah.

Willie Selam: You asked if there was a season for sending them out but each child has his own timeline by the Great Law. Some children receive it, like he said at four or five, and some of them don't go out until they are ten or eleven years old. But each child shows his propensity, I guess you would say. His creativeness or his strength. It is hard to find words to say what you mean. When a child is ready there are people with the eyes to see. They take hold of the child and favor them with words or teachings that come from the Great Law. Then they just naturally gather their momentum in life and you know when they are ready to send them out onto the water or send them up into the mountains.

Mike Taylor: It's a very individual thing.

Willie Selam: Right. There's a teacher and a student.

James Keyser: So there is always, for the young person, a teacher—a mentor who helps them understand?

Willie Selam: A lot of times it is parents. A lot of time it will be relatives, uncles, grandparents. Sometimes it's friends.

James Keyser: When a young person goes out and finds the power does the young person know what it is that he has found right away? Or does he have to discuss that with someone?

Willie Selam: It takes time to understand.

Mike Taylor: So he would talk with this person who was his teacher, it might be his parent or it may be a relative, to understand what happened?

Willie Selam: Meditate. Some people it takes a lot of years to figure out their purpose in life. Some people have their calling right away.

Editors' Note: The day after the field trip the group had a discussion in the symposium of some of the things that were discussed in the field.

James Keyser: James [Selam], I would like to ask you a question. This is speaking of rock art in the landscape. You told the story yesterday of swallowing monster and Coyote. Coyote went inside swallowing monster and all the people came forth from that. Where you talked about that, is a very narrow channel and filled full of rapids before it was a reservoir. It is very deep. James mentioned yesterday, speaking with Eugene Hunn, that that place is several hundred feet deep. The bottom is below sea level. It's the deepest place on the river right there. That deep hole had a part of that story about the swallowing monster being in there. Right above that deep hole is a major rock art site. It is very different structurally than the rock shelter where we first went. It is not composed of little small paintings with little humans with rayed arcs and little animals. Instead it has great big faces.

When Phillip Cash Cash and I were talking about the rock art in that area, it is right above that very dangerous place. It's a very dangerous place to get to. It's on a very narrow ledge. You have to climb up. It is very hard to get there. Phillip noted that, to him, it seemed more like public art that you can see from a distance away—that stands out on the landscape. I guess the question I would like to ask, James, do you think that rock art is associated with that story of swallowing monster? Or is it just accidental that all of those things come together at that place?

James Selam: Everything has an explanation. The place you are talking about was a probably witness to what happened. Probably became a witness. That water in that channel is down so deep below the sea level, 180-some feet I believe. Where the swallowing monster lives. On the [Washington state] side, near the beginning [upstream end] of channel, there is a big slide. That's where the Coyote sat up and teased that monster until the monster got tired and swallowed him. That's the legend. We tell that legend all the time.

That channel, people are forbidden to enter from either side, because if you went up or down in a canoe the water would start to whirl and take you down. That place [the rock art site] was probably a witness to that time.[7] It wasn't seen by anyone living, but it is part of nature's identifying there were people there. The animals were people. Coyote turned himself back into coyote. Of course a lot of animals were people that were swallowed by the monster.

So these legends, these stories, were more of a lecture to the children to understand the foundation and form of the land and water, whatever was there. Even the [Celilo] falls. There are legends about the falls. The story is interesting. I believe the face on the rock is something to identify that place as being dangerous.

James Keyser: Thank you. I was thinking in that same way. Interestingly, at the other end of that channel, visible when you come up the river is another great big site. This one is another great big rayed arc that was painted red and white. It would have stood out from down on the river. From what you say I think maybe that painting on the downstream end was also to warn people that this was a dangerous place.

David Whitley: But all sacred places are, by definition, dangerous in the sense that supernatural potency, good or bad, is dangerous unless you know how to use it.

James Keyser: Yes, but this is clearly public art on both ends of that dangerous channel. It's made to be seen from some distance away. Whereas none of the other art we saw yesterday really is.

Jannie Loubser: Its like Buffalo Eddy in Hells Canyon. There was quite a big rapid there and they cleared that. The Corps of Engineers did the clearing of the channel. It is a transfer point from a wide, open valley to a more closed valley. On both sides of the river you can see quite conspicuous pecked images. As you go up the river at Class Four Rapids you see stuff from the river as well, maybe less public [than the art at Hells Gate Gorge] and less well executed but nevertheless quite big figures high up against the cliffs.

Phillip Cash Cash: Just to follow up on Jimmy's [Selam] statement, he said a word that was really crucial to understanding the role of the rock art. He said the image may be a witness. In our way of life a witness was a really important figure in the life history of an individual, in the history of a people, and in the time of the myths. When the laws were made on the earth, as Jimmy explained yesterday, a witness was always proclaimed as being a witness to an event that occurred in the creation or in the formation of the world as we know it now. These witnesses then stood for all time and some were actual land formations or rocks. In the creation of the world when everything was put in order, what we call the natural law, these markers then stood witness for all time, as to how the world was brought into being. They were a reminder to the people that those times have ended and now we are in the world of the human being. They stood as a marker, a reminder to the people that the law will always be, to stand for all time.

One of the unfortunate things about today, is that when they build the dams and other developments, many of these markers were destroyed, (markers) that were witness to remind us of when the world was put into order and the laws made. We lost a lot of those when the dams were made. It covered up many of these landscapes. So all along the river, down the Columbia River up to the Snake River and in various other areas there are landmarks like that.

Mike Taylor: Would these markers have been known by different groups of river people?

Phillip Cash Cash: Each group, the area that they live in, would have that as part of their tradition.

Mike Taylor: I was wondering, in particular, at the upstream entrance to the Hells Gate landing channel. There are those very large, red-and-white, bull's-eye-like concentric circles. I was wondering if people who came from farther away would have recognized any of those symbols as providing any information to them?

David Whitley: Other tribal groups?

Mike Taylor: Yes. If there was a tribal group that came down the river from the Snake into the Columbia and saw these red and white circles above what looked like a particularly bad stretch of water would that tell them then that this is a warning and I should not go there? Or would it mostly have just pertained to the people who lived around the area?

Willie Selam: I believe that for the visitors who came in it would be up to their lineage and their training to be able recognize certain aspects of the marks. Like the older people of the world—the animals. They mark their territory. They know which tree they go to. They don't go beyond it. A bear won't go beyond into another bear's area. They're the older people of the world that my dad referred to. They've been here a lot longer than human beings so our people have learned how to adopt trainings and teachings from that world.

He spoke of the witness. The witness stands as the recognizer. He knows the truth. And our people are told the truth is always there for us to see. So when a young child goes into a search, when he comes back he speaks only truth because he knows the witness was there, watching him. If he doesn't speak true it will come out.

David Whitley: Is She Who Watches also one of these witnesses too, in this sense?

Willie Selam: It's probably a portion of its teaching. That it was a witness to the gorge and to the falls. Even Mount Adams, Mount Hood, Mount Jefferson are ones who watch over. They look over us and we recognize that. They are the spires, the temples of our world.

David Whitley: Let me ask a question from what I've learned from native peoples in California. We don't have rivers. We don't have rapids. We don't have rock painting and engravings on rivers as a result. But they did make many paintings and engravings. For example, often we'll find in the desert engravings that are near springs. So a lot of people immediately say, "Oh, well these mark the places where there are springs." In the same way we could say when we get to a big rapid and there is a big painting there, so it would be possible for us to interpret that to mean that the painting were there to tell people there were rapids or there were springs. But I've come to be taught and understood that that is sort of missing the point.

The native peoples, and people today, if there is a spring there they can see the spring. If there is a rapid there they can see the rapid. They don't need a rock painting or engraving to tell them that there is spring water. In the desert you can actually smell that from half a mile away. The point is the thing that creates the spring, or creates the rapids, in the desert in California it is called *poha*, supernatural power or potency. That causes the spring and that is why the rock art is there. Medicine people would go and be interested in that power or potency. Not just because it was a sign to tell people there is water here or there are rapids coming up. Does that make sense here?

Phillip Cash Cash: I think in our area people were very knowledgeable about the land. Everyone carried a map in their personal experience about their family's area or their band territory, and other people's territory. That knowledge was really very critical to how you gathered food for your livelihood. So your knowledge was very detailed and encyclopedic. I think the role of what you were describing might not be so critical because we all had that knowledge.

David Whitley: You didn't need a signpost to tell you.

Phillip Cash Cash: Yes. Like Jimmy [Selam] was describing the particular places on the river, that might play a role for other purposes.

Linea Sundstrom: I have to say I agree as far as the mental map. I've studied Indian maps quite a bit. It's interesting that all the ones that we have, with the exception of those that are the picture record of an actual event or series of events,[8] all the things that we would normally consider a map were made for outsiders. They were made for white people. The Indians, if they were planning an expedition, might draw some lines in the dirt. That was enough that everybody knew they were "on the same page" as it were. I think children learned this geographic competence at a very young age and built, and built upon it. So when the Hudson's Bay traders came in they obtained maps from Blackfeet people that showed everything from the Missouri River west to the Pacific Ocean—all the drainages, all the mountain ranges. They just took a piece of paper and like that, gave it to them. So I think it's a little hard for us to even imagine it because we don't have that kind of competence. We don't place a value on really knowing the landscape that we are moving through.

There is a map story about when General Custer was being sent to investigate the Black Hills, to find out if there was really any gold there. Of course the Black Hills were part of the great Sioux reservation at that time. He was stationed at Fort Lincoln in North Dakota and he made friends with a man named Goose who was half Lakota and half Arikara. They were planning their expedition. They got out the only map he had, which was terrible. No white people had ever made maps of the area. Goose came up and looked at it and took a pen and corrected it here and there and everywhere and handed it back to Custer. Custer said, "Goose I really want you to come along with us and correct this map along the way. If you'll do that for me I'll get you a copy of the map when we get back." Goose just looked at him and said, "My map is here" [Sundstrom made a gesture indicating that Goose pointed to his head]. He liked Custer personally but he had complete contempt for the way this man was trying to operate in a place with which he was so clueless.

Editors' Note: This concluded our general discussion about rock art and related subjects. Then the twelve scholars each presented a paper about rock art ethnography. Following each paper there was a discussion in which both scholars and traditionalists participated.

---

[1] A few moments earlier Viola Kalama had said [as an aside to Táxli Winch and a few scholars], that young people made the rock art images as part of their puberty rite vision quests. Unfortunately, this was not recorded, but Viola came back to this observation twice more at the site [see below].

[2] The Paiutes share the Warm Springs Reservation with the Wasco (Chinookan) and Tenino (Sahaptin) tribes.

[3] Les McConnell is tribal liaison for the USDA Forest Service, Pacific Northwest Region.

[4] Between 65 and 75 years old.

[5] The reference here is to being submerged under the reservoir behind The Dalles Dam.

[6] In later, unrecorded, conversation this "got something" was identified as indicating "had a vision." Metaphorically all these expressions could relate to the vision experience.

[7] Here, as can be identified by the rest of the paragraph, James Selam is referring to mythic time, when the Swallowing Monster episode took place.

[8] See Fredlund et al 1996, for discussion of such "biographic" maps.

28   Field Trip Discussion

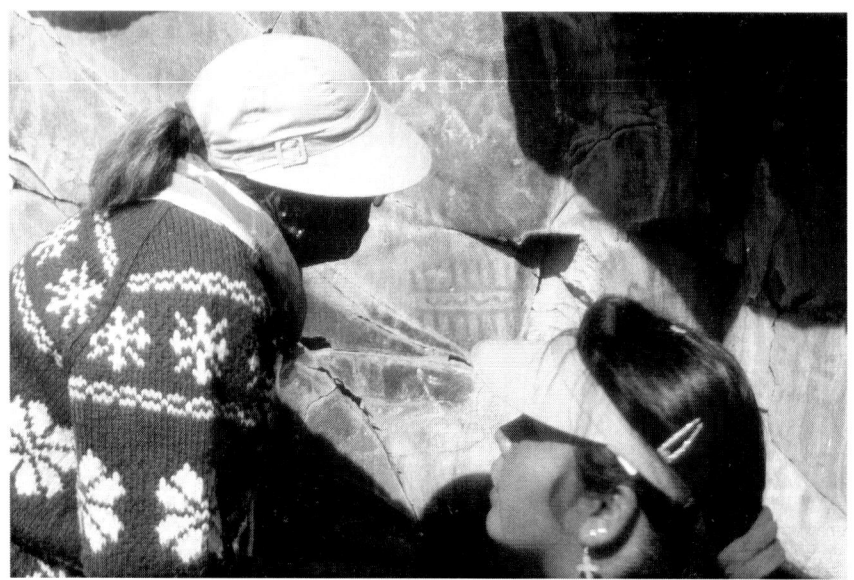

Viola Kalama and her granddaughter Brigette Whipple looking at rock art images during the field trip.

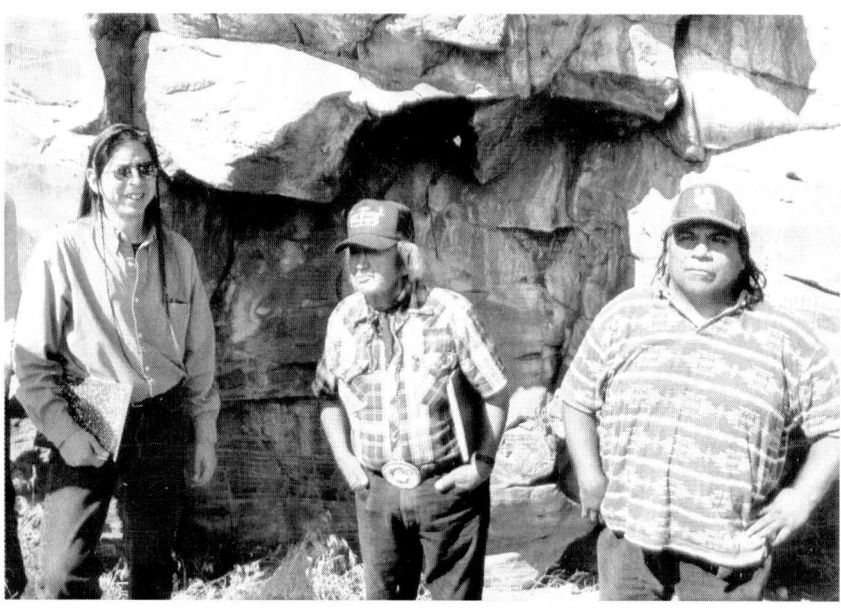

Phillip Cash Cash, James Selam and Willie Selam during the field trip.

PART 3
THE PRESENTATIONS
Editors' Introduction to Papers and Discussions

The symposium presentations were organized to provide an opportunity for significant discussion after each one. Like all discussions done at various times during the three day program, these were intentionally unstructured in order to engender the maximum amount of information that might be shared, and to facilitate exchange between scholars and traditionalists. In this regard, the efforts of Phillip Cash Cash were invaluable because he was the only participant who is both an academic scholar and tribal traditionalist. All of these discussions were recorded with both audiotape and videotape for later transcription.

Our editing of these post-presentation discussions generally follows that of the field trip and follow-up discussions. General statements, asides to other participants, and discussion of meeting administration details have been omitted, as have most extraneous comments (usually by scholars) that can best be considered as "thinking out loud." Only when such commentary clearly adds to the substance of the discussion is it retained. Like the other edited discussions, we have maintained as closely as possible, the wording, cadence, and sentence structure of the traditionalists' responses—within guidelines for clarity of communication, which corrected grammatical errors and omitted interlocutory expressions and similar utterances.

CHAPTER 3
Rock Art and Ethnography:
A Case in Point from Southern Africa
J. David Lewis-Williams

Numerous writers distinguish between, on the one hand, rock art research based on ethnography that is said to 'explain' painted and engraved motifs and, on the other, research on rock arts for which there is no relevant ethnography to guide interpretations. A few seem to believe that research contexts that include ethnography are 'easy', while those that lack such records are much more challenging. While there is an element of truth in this view, those who hold it overlook the many and subtle problems that invest recourse to ethnography to understand rock art images. Indeed, it is sometimes a case of foolish angels rushing in to treacherous territory and discrediting the whole venture in the eyes of those who are more circumspect.

At the same time, writers who believe that they can avoid the problems by eschewing ethnography altogether find themselves in an even worse, but to them invisible, dilemma: though they do not realise it, they too are dependent on ethnography, the 'ethnography' of Western thought. They employ Western notions such as 'picture', 'making pictures', 'representation', and, of course, 'art' and 'artists' unreflectingly, as if they are human universals. They are, of course, socially constructed concepts that are specific to particular times and places. Seemingly ethnography-free research demands methodological and definitional explicitness every bit as much as work that is, apparently comfortably, founded on ethnography.

The difficulties encountered by those who try to relate ethnography to rock art constitute the central theme of this book, though the issues discussed hardly exhaust the topic. Indeed, the very construction and evaluation of ethnographies have exercised the minds of anthropologists in recent decades; rock art researchers would do well to familiarize themselves with this sometimes iconoclastic literature.

In this chapter, I address a practical matter that came to my attention during my work on southern African San (Bushman) rock art. Though the specifics of this issue are geographically and culturally derived, it has, I believe, wide relevance. I then take a San rock art panel and show how nineteenth- and twentieth-century records of San belief and ritual contain clues to the significance of precisely depicted images, though not in any *directly* explanatory way. Identification of the iconography of such images (this is a bowman, that a dancer, though such identifications are themselves misleading) is only an initial step in rock art research. In southern Africa and elsewhere, we need to go further and to investigate the social contexts and consequences of the images. Strictly speaking, it may be true that ethnography can never be said to 'explain' rock art—however one may define that slippery word 'explain'.

Ethnography and San Religious Experience

If researchers have access to a rich ethnographic source, they are able, independently of the art itself, to construct some idea of the belief system of the people who made the images. This has been abundantly demonstrated in southern Africa, where numerous workers in the Kalahari Desert of Namibia and Botswana (Figure 1) have published comprehensive accounts of San belief and ritual (e.g., Thomas 1959; Lee 1979; Marshall 1976, 1999; Katz 1982; Katz et al. 1997; Guenther 1999). The hunter-gatherer linguistic groups (rather than 'tribes') who live in the Kalahari did not make the art farther to the south in South Africa, Zimbabwe and Lesotho (there is next to no rock art in the sandy Kalahari Desert), and the southern San communities that made the art ceased to function towards the end of the nineteenth century.

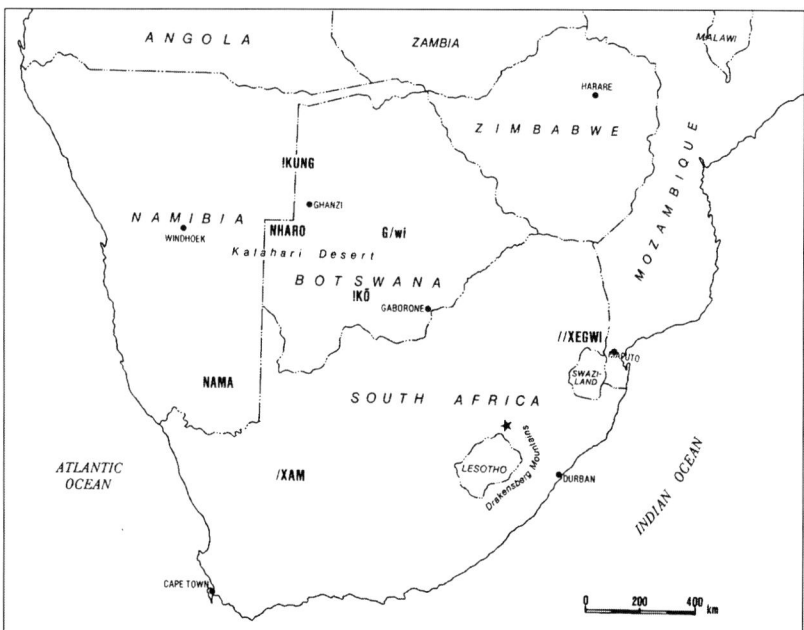

Figure 1 **Map of southern Africa showing San linguistic groups. The star marks the location of the site known as FSA1.**

Nevertheless, the temporal and spatial gap between the Kalahari people and the southern image-makers is bridged by extensive nineteenth-century texts. Point-by-point comparisons between the verbatim /Xam texts of the Bleek & Lloyd Collection, compiled in the 1870s (e.g., Bleek and Lloyd 1911; Lewis-Williams 2000; see also Orpen 1874), and the beliefs and rituals of the Ju'/oan, !Kõ and other Kalahari groups have shown that, whatever differences there may be, there are striking parallels (Lewis-Williams and Biesele 1978; Lewis-Williams 1981): we can form some idea of the cosmology, principal tenets of the image-makers and read contemporary descriptions of their rituals. Then we can turn to the hundreds of thousands of images that enliven thousands of southern African rock shelters.

So far so good. All seems set fair for easy interpretative work. Not so.

One of the first points to strike me when I began the task of linking the ethnography to the rock art was that the art, despite its apparent diversity, was not a comprehensive illustration of daily life. Nor does the whole range of San ritual and belief feature on the walls of the rock shelters. Whatever beliefs and rituals may be obliquely referred to (Lewis-Williams 1998), there is an empirically discernible and overwhelming emphasis on the San's central ritual, the one that brings all the people together and that cleanses and protects everyone (Lewis-Williams and Dowson 1989). This is the healing, trance or medicine dance. Megan Biesele (1993:71) sums up the centrality of the dance:

> Though dreams may happen at any time, the central religious experiences of the Ju/'hoansi are consciously and, as a matter of course, approached through the avenue of trance. . . . Great attention is given to trancers' accounts of what they have experienced, and no one's account of a genuinely altered state is belittled.

She goes on to show how metaphors of transformation derived from the trance dance, together with other related concepts, permeate San folklore. It should therefore come as no surprise to researchers that the dance and its transforming experiences inform the practice of rock art (Lewis-Williams 1981, 2003; Lewis-Williams and Pearce 2004).

Still performed in the Kalahari, and well documented, the dance entails co-operation between men and women, and between ritual specialists and the whole community (Lee 1968; Marshall 1969; Katz 1982; Guenther 1999). Whatever 'spirituality' it may possess, it is socially situated. I use 'shaman' to denote the San ritual specialists. Other writers prefer 'healer' or 'doctor'; a few may still use 'medicine man'; none retains 'sorcerer', the word that Wilhelm Bleek and Lucy Lloyd used. These English words are, of course, just as much approximate translations of the indigenous words as 'shaman'; they are no more neutral than 'shaman'. Why then use 'shaman'? It seems to me that the word usefully highlights common shamanistic elements in San belief and ritual without obscuring particularities, any more than 'Christian' obscures differences between Russian Orthodox, Roman Catholic, Episcopalian, Methodist, Southern Baptist, African Zionist, liberal, fundamentalist and charismatic house-church believers (Lewis-Williams 1992a).

Briefly, the all-night trance dance in the Kalahari today is circular. Focusing on a central fire, seated women sing powerful medicine songs and clap their intricate rhythms. The men dance in a circle around them. Sometimes shamans break through the ring of seated women to come closer to the fire, even to plunge their heads into it, and also out of the circle of dancing men to confront malevolent spirits that lurk in the darkness beyond the firelight. As the dance and singing increase in intensity, the shamans, who may number as many as half of the men and a third of the women present, enter an altered state of consciousness: they stagger, tremble violently, bend forward as their stomach muscles contract, and sometimes fall writhing or cataleptic to the ground. Those shamans who have learned to control the level of their 'boiling' potency move from person to person attempting to draw sickness, both physical and supernatural, from them by the laying on of hands. They then expel the sickness through a 'hole' in the back of the neck; it is believed to return to the spirit world and beings whence it came.

There are rock paintings of this dance, both in the now common circular form and in more diverse choreographies. This conclusion results from a fairly direct, though merely initial, recourse to San ethnography. Figure 2 shows a simple painting of a dance, one that does not show the circular form: four cloaked seated figures, presumably women, clap (their fingers are individually drawn just as they are held in the Kalahari today), while two men hold dancing sticks and dance in the bending-forward position. In addition, one presumably male figure sits in the frequently depicted arms-back posture that, Kalahari shamans say, dancers adopt when they wish to increase their 'boiling' potency (Marshall 1969:363–364; Lewis-Williams 1981:88). One male figure dances upright. He and one of the bending forward dancers have erect penises with the enigmatic cross-bar that researchers usually, but strictly speaking incorrectly, call 'infibulation'. The containing line may depict a rock shelter. The multiple parallels between paintings such as this one and what may still be observed in the Kalahari Desert are inescapable.

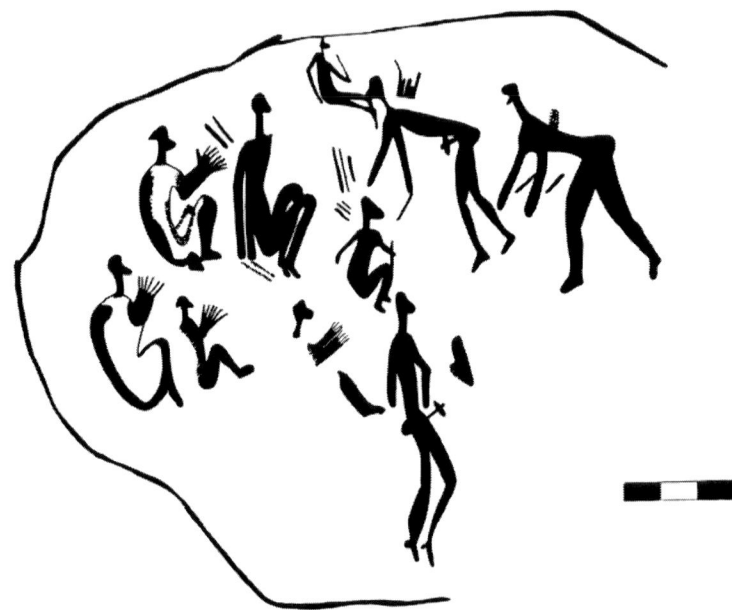

Figure 2 San rock painting of a curing, or trance, dance. Seated women clap while men dance in typical postures. Color: dark maroon/red. Scale is 3 cm.

Other paintings of dances are, by contrast, remarkably detailed. In addition to the elements shown in Figure 2, they depict dancing rattles worn on the legs, flywhisks used to flick away 'arrows of sickness', eared caps worn by shamans who controlled the movements of game, and so forth. Importantly, many paintings also show non-real entities, such as the potency that the dancers activate, expelled sickness and shamans partially transformed into animals. These visions were apprehended by inducing altered states of consciousness (not by ingestion of psychotropic substances but by rhythmic driving and hyperventilation) and consequently experiencing visual, somatic, aural and olfactory hallucinations. The paintings thus present a privileged view of the dance; they show what the shamans, not merely ordinary people, saw. Such images suggest that much, not necessarily all, of the art was made by people who depicted their own visions and insights—the shamans themselves.

Synecdoche

Given the vast number of rock art images in southern Africa, paintings of complete dances are comparatively rare. Yet the dance is ever-present on the walls of rock shelters. It suffuses panels of, perhaps, well over a hundred images, even though there may not be a recognisable 'dance scene', such as that in Figure 2. This level of saturation is achieved by synecdoche—part is used to stand for the whole.

The painters 'dismembered' the dance into what they considered to be significant components (such as only one man bending forward, a set of flywhisks, or a single arms-back figure) and then used these 'fragments of the dance' to stand for the whole enterprise of making contact with what they believed to be a supernatural realm. This is not to say that fragments of the dance did not have their own, more specific, meanings, that they did not highlight certain component experiences and the social significances of those experiences. Indeed, fragments of the dance operated on at least three levels. First, and by synecdoche, they manifested on the rock shelter walls the whole trans-cosmological shamanistic experience. The spirit realm was ever present. Secondly, a fragment focused viewers' attention on part of that all-embracing experience to highlight what was very possibly a particular shaman's special experience. Thirdly, a fragment of the dance could, by focusing on an individual's 'moment of personal truth', act as a statement about his or her status in the community.

In accordance with conventions that we do not fully understand, painters built up, over many years and generations, a reticulation of images, some overlying others, some juxtaposed with others, but all inter-related and situated on a surface which we now know was considered to be the interface between the material and spiritual realms (Lewis-Williams and Dowson 1990). The spiritual realm, with all its complex social implications, seeped through the rock face to permeate daily life. If the rock face was a 'veil' suspended between the spirit and material realms, one could say that the mediating visions and insights of the painters were woven into that veil.

To illustrate these propositions about the ways in which San painters deployed fragments of the dance I turn to a specific rock painting site.

FSA1: A Case in Point

The site is in the eastern part of the Free State Province of South Africa, a few kilometres from the images shown in Figure 2. Its pseudonymic name is FSA1. To protect sites from vandalism and in deference to landowners' wishes researchers withhold more precise locations.

As Figure 3 shows, images are grouped in panels scattered through the rock shelter. Those with which I deal are designated panels

36   J. David Lewis-Williams

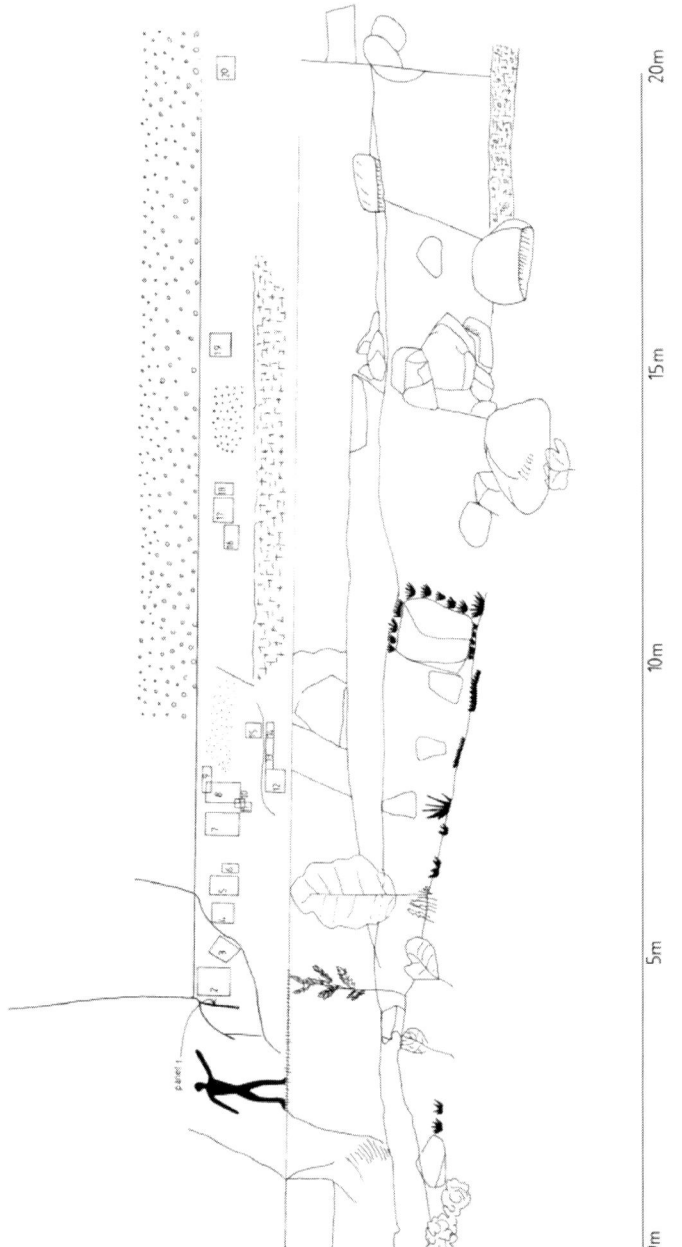

Figure 3.   Diagram of site FSA1 showing locations of painted panels.

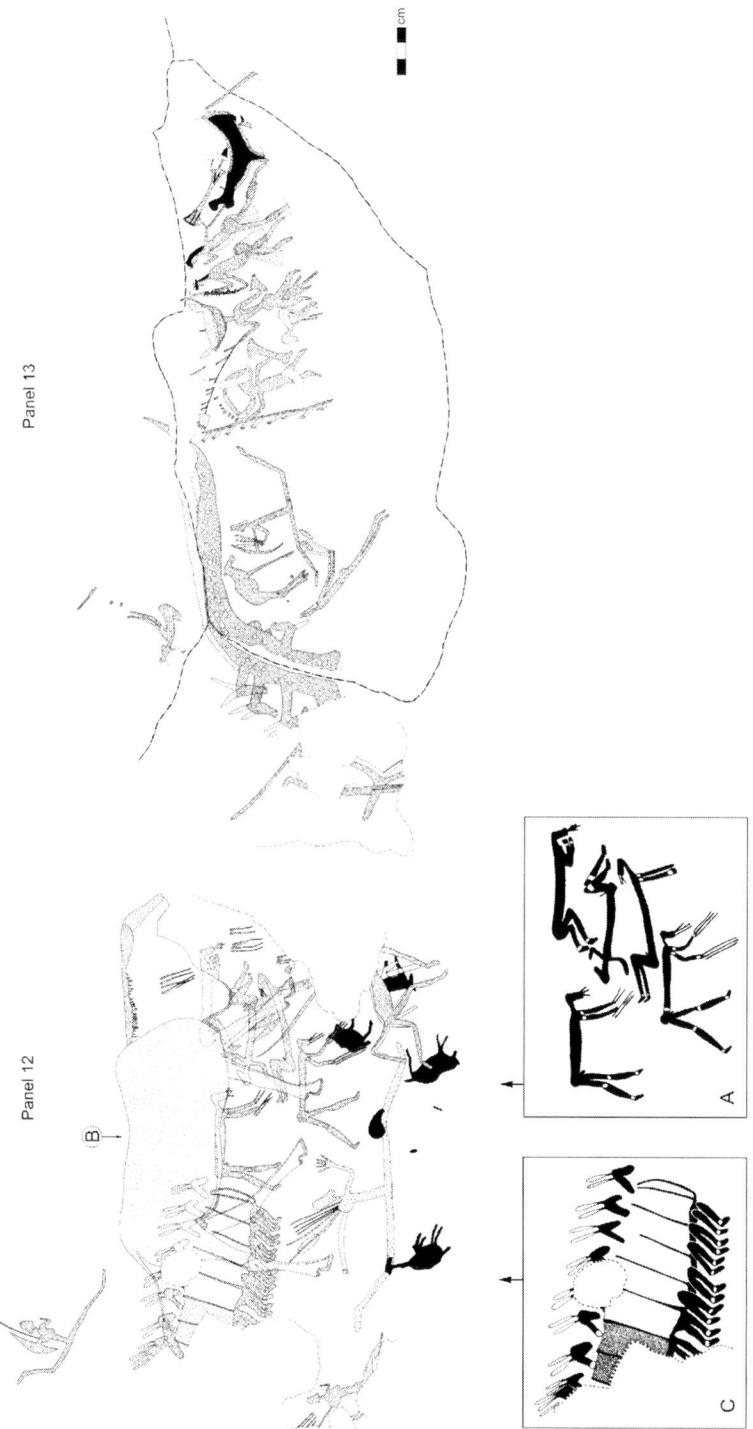

Figure 4. Panels 12 and 13 at FSA1. Colors: black, dark red and light red.

12 and 13 (Figure 4). Explanations of panels such as these two could easily fill a book; they open windows on the complex San belief system and cosmology, let alone the shifting ways in which the images must have constructed, reproduced and contested social relations within the communities that occupied the shelter at different times. For convenience of exposition, I begin with the group on the left, panel 12 in Figure 3.

Panel 12

Within this densely painted concentration of images (Figure 4), there is a sequence of three painting 'episodes', groups of images that a combination of style, paint colour and quality, composition and subject matter suggest were painted at a single time (Lewis-Williams 1992b). To clarify further the tangle of superimposed images, two of the episodes are isolated below the main panel. Episode A, a dance group, is the oldest; episode B comprises one image only, the large depiction of an eland; and episode C, the most recent, is a group of buck-headed figures. (Constraints of space mean that I must omit reference to other images, including the partially preserved baboon with human legs, down right.)

Episode A

In this fragment of the dance, five figures are shown in various postures. Two dance with sticks and bend forward; one lies supine; one appears to lie back with arms in the backward posture; one kneels. All have white decorative bands (probably animal skin or ostrich eggshell beads) at their ankles, wrists, biceps, waists or above their calves. Four of the figures have short lines emanating from their faces. These lines, a diagnostic and commonly painted feature, represent the nasal bleeding that frequently accompanied a San shamanic altered state of consciousness. Four are clearly male; the other probably so, although its primary sexual characteristic is not shown.

Episode A thus shows men entering, or already in, altered states of consciousness and engaged in transition to the spirit realm; the supportive role of women is omitted. Writers on gender relations in San rock art have not noted this important point. San ethnography shows that some women were recognized as shamans in their own right, but the art seldom depicts them in this role. Usually they are shown supporting the men's dancing, or perhaps apparently controlling a rain-snake. Never, as far as I am aware, do fragments of the dance focus exclusively to the role of women: depictions of clapping women are always associated with other images.

Writers who seek the negotiation of gender in the art seem to concentrate on gender discrimination in economic activities—hunting and gathering. But the art is not principally an economic panorama. Rather, such gender construction as took place did so in the dance and, through this arena, reached the rock face. The spirit realm and differential gender access to it is where researchers should look for gender negotiation. It would be more profitable to study the ways in which the dance is fragmented and represented.

Episode A thus makes a statement about the centrality of the men's role in the dance, the throes that they suffer on behalf of their communities, and the healing and protection that their work affords.

Episode B

The next addition to the growing panel was the eland that partially overlaps the male dancers. This animal, the largest of all African antelope, was, for the painters, a central, polysemic symbol. Its referents include: girls' puberty (during which rituals an Eland Bull Dance is performed), boys' first-kill observances (boys' desire to kill, specifically, an eland, though they are not always successful), marriage (during which a bride is anointed with eland fat), and the shamanic dance (more than any other creature, the eland has the potency that shamans desire and that takes them into the spirit world) (Lewis-Williams 1981; Vinnicombe 1976; Lewis-Williams and Dowson 1989). Did the painted eland 'deal with' all these referents simultaneously?

To answer this question we need to note that the context of a polysemic symbol focuses on a segment of its semantic spectrum. For example, a lamb in an ecclesiastical stained glass window refers to a different segment of associations from those of a lamb painted on a nursery wall. In a cathedral, the sacrificial lamb stands for Christ; in a nursery, a lamb signifies innocence and gentleness. The context of the wall of a rock shelter (the 'veil' between this world and the spirit realm) similarly highlighted a segment of the eland's associations. It seems likely that the painter who added the eland to the panel so that it overlapped the shamanic dancers had in mind the supernatural potency that San shamans harness to pass through the veil into the spirit world; all the other rich associations of the eland symbol were probably penumbral and added complex affective impact. This is not to say that the polysemic eland symbol was a consciously formulated San concept. When painters fashioned depictions of eland, they were probably not making a 'symbol', or, for that matter, a 'picture'. They were rather constructing an intrinsically potent *object* that did not 'stand for' potency but that *contained* potency. Nor did it 'depict' a vision: it *was* a vision, a glimpse of the spirit realm made tangible.

Episode C

The painter who added episode C took the shamanic focus of the panel further. These images show at least nine cloaked figures with human legs but antelope heads. Each has two enlarged ears, or, less probably, horns. Their flexed legs suggest that they are dancing.

Transformation into an animal is a commonly depicted and painted San experience. The wearing of an antelope skin cloak was associated with transformation. 'Getting into' an animal skin (in certain myths also in the form of a leather bag) was like getting into an animal and absorbing its potency (Lewis-Williams 1996).

Episode C thus depicts a shaman's insider's view of what happens during a dance (transformation), while episode A shows what everyone could see (men dancing and falling in an altered state of consciousness). Episode C highlights the visionary component of the shamans' privileged experience and thus goes deeper into the exclusivity of shamanic experience than episode A. Over time, the content of the panel moved from what everyone saw to what only special people saw; there was a growing esoteric element and a concomitantly tightening social focus (cf. Lewis-Williams 1992b).

Panel 13

This panel is at once more allusive and more enigmatic than panel 12. Most importantly, it exemplifies how painters used inequalities in the rock face to make statements about access to the spirit realm. In this reproduction, the broken line indicates a rough but fairly sharp edged depression in the rock face. Because there is no overlapping, it is not possible to be sure about the sequence of painting episodes; most of the images seem to be parts of a single episode.

The overall shamanic context of panel 13 is initially suggested by two fragments of the dance placed towards the left. Above the depression in the rock is a kneeling figure in the arms-back posture. Below it, and inside the hollow, is a standing figure in the same posture; it holds two flywhisks. In the absence of a penis, its slender body suggests that it is male. Unlike the related images in episodes A and C in panel 12, its very solitude points to an individual's experience and his social role, rather than to a group of people.

Above the arms-back man are an antelope and an associated running figure with bow and arrows. This is the sort of grouping that early researchers took to illustrate a completely mundane activity. At that time they did not know about the significance of the arms-back posture and the other fragments of the dance to which I have referred. They therefore did not have to explain the proximity of the supposed 'hunting scene' to a shaman. Is there any connection between hunting and San shamanism?

During a dance, and sometimes in dreams, San shamans are believed go on extra-corporeal travel. Such journeys, they say, take them to God's village in the sky and to other parts of the desert where they find out how their friends and relatives are faring. They also seek out, control the movements of and hunt game. One shaman told how he killed an antelope during the dance and then took his family to the carcass the next morning. Again, we see that the spirit world, into which shamans penetrate, was believed to interdigitate with the material world. Dances may be held if hunting has been poor, and the giraffe potency song may be sung 'so that whenever they go out hunting they will be successful'. 'An unsuccessful hunter may be treated during a dance so that when he next goes out to look for game he will be successful' (England 1968:401; Marshall 1999:65). There is therefore nothing incompatible in the juxtaposition of a 'hunting scene' with images of the spirit realm.

The other paintings in panel 13 explore that realm in a number of ways. To the left, an only partially preserved snake is painted around the edge of the depression in the rock face. It has spots, and antelope heads seem to protrude from it. Although its head is not preserved, its tail is clear; it was painted to suggest that it goes behind the rock face and emerges above the hollow where it tapers to a point. Snakes were closely associated with shamans. Both were believed to travel underground, and snakes shed their skins as shamans were believed to escape from their bodies. The snake may therefore be a transformed shaman; on the other hand, it may be an inhabitant of the spirit realm. Either way, it is closely associated with the edge of the hollow in the rock face: it curves round the rough edge of the depression.

The four (there were originally probably more) antelope heads that appear to protrude from the snake are more enigmatic than the snake itself. It may be that the heads are actually coming through the crack in the rock face and that the rest of their bodies are still in the spirit world. Such mediating paintings, half in and half out of the spirit realm, are not uncommon (Lewis-Williams and Dowson 1990).

Many similar paintings, together with San beliefs about a subterranean spirit realm, reinforce the conclusion that the rock face was itself a focusing context, every bit as much as a stained glass window in a cathedral. Every image placed on it was immediately given a shamanic context.

Mediation and transformation also characterise the group of images to the right. Here four elaborately painted figures walk towards the left; it is not clear if they are male or female, though, in terms of San rock art, the one second from the right seems to have a female body. Another, smaller, bending-forward figure may relate to another painting episode. Three of the figures wear antelope skin aprons; the apron of the second figure from the left is clearly in the shape of an antelope skin. All the large figures carry unidentifiable objects, three of which may be plants. Two have large heads. One of these appears to have antelope ears and thus to imply zoomorphic transformation. No exactly similar head transformations are known, but, in broad terms, distortions of the human head are common (Blundell 2004). Shamans all had their own ideas of how they looked in the spirit world, and such idiosyncratic paintings were personal statements (Dowson 1988, 1994).

All in all, panels 12 and 13 show how fragments of the dance, rather than complete representations are routinely, but always imaginatively, deployed in San rock art. Each fragment points to a particular shamanic experience; each invokes the whole shamanic enterprise, but at the same time each draws distinctions within it. Particularity, rather than generality, was high on the painters' list of priorities.

The Power of Spirituality

Near the beginning of this chapter, I said that I doubted if ethnography ever explains rock art images. What I meant was that ethnographic texts, especially those recorded verbatim, express beliefs and experiences according to conventions and in the idioms and contexts of the spoken word. Rock art, on the other hand, expresses *some* of those beliefs and experiences in its own conventions; it is its own meaningful context. Thus ethnographic texts do not directly explain the images—any more than paintings simply illustrate myths. Each expresses, in its own way, beliefs based on the existence of a non-material realm. The ethnography and the images are *partially* parallel texts: one does not duplicate the other. Interpretation, or explanation, is a practice performed, not by ethnography, but by researchers who attempt to move back and forth between the two texts to allow one to illuminate the other. In doing so, they show how metaphors and symbols are 'translated' from verbal to graphic form and how complex, multicomponent rituals are fragmented to suit the purposes of a particular painter.

For the rock painters themselves, moving from experiences and beliefs to graphic images necessarily entailed selectivity: they could not produce facsimiles of their entire experiences. At this point, we see the power of 'spirituality'. Today spiritual beliefs, widely acknowledged to be sacrosanct and not open to debate, are sometimes invoked in attempts to use rock art images in political disputes. The same was, I argue, the case in prehistoric times; not much has changed. Rock painters consciously selected fragments of the shamanic dance and its associated experiences to make statements about their own power and social statuses. They thus placed themselves within the overall category of shamans vis à vis other people: shamans were different from ordinary people. A nineteenth-century San man put it thus: 'For these are not people who are like other Bushmen' (Bleek 1935:14). Sometimes shamans went further and asserted their individuality and personal accomplishments and social influence. But why did San people take any notice of these paintings and what they implied?

For the San, rock art images were not mere 'pictures'. Rather, they were manifestations—recreations—of spiritual experiences. As I have pointed out, they were not records of visions; they *were* visions. Actively and visibly, they weaved their way in and out of the rock face. Some contained potent eland blood and the supernatural energy that it implied. These potency-impregnated images were also divisive: 'good' people (however defined) were able to draw on this stored-up potency; 'bad' people who tried to touch the images were in danger of adhering to the rock and eventually wasting away and dying (Lewis-Williams 1986). Even though it expressed group sentiments, spiritual rock art was socially divisive. The two functions are not incompatible. Indeed, social cohesion is inevitably built on the distinction of groups from other groups.

It was to their imputed spirituality that the images owed their social impact: you can't argue with a vision manifested before your eyes on the interface between the material and spiritual realms. In the absence of the very possibility of disbelief in spirituality (such as we have today), the image ruled supreme. It could be challenged only on its own terms—not by destroying it (that would be too dangerous) but by creating different and yet more potent spiritual images (Lewis-Williams and Pearce 2004). The discourse of imagery had its own rules and conventions, its own social implications.

Acknowledgements

I am grateful to the organizers of the Portland 2002 International Symposium: The Ethnography of World Rock Art, for inviting me to attend, and to the sponsors who provided financial support for the gathering. In the event, I was unable to be present. I thank colleagues who kindly commented on drafts of this chapter: Geoff Blundell, Jeremy Hollmann, David Pearce and Ben Smith. The illustrations were prepared by Zac Kingdon, Paul den Hoed and Justine Olaffson; digital processing of their copies was undertaken by Willem Steyn. The Rock Art Research Institute is funded by the University of the Witwatersrand, the National Research Foundation, and Anglo American; the views expressed here are not necessarily those of the funders.

Discussion

James Keyser: What we have done with these papers is to provide time for a discussion following each that gives an opportunity for any of us to comment on what may have piqued our interest or that relates to our own knowledge or research.

David Whitley: This paper struck me, because I have been thinking about some of the issues that are subtexts in David's paper; issues that may not be obvious to those of you who aren't obsessed with rock art the way that we specialists are. There has been a lot of criticism in certain circles recently of using the ethnographic record to interpret rock art. After reading what Kelley has written (Hays-Gilpin 2004) and noting that David states it again here, I realize that the criticism results from methodological confusion about how we [rock art scholars] use ethnography and how we interpret symbols. The basis for the criticism is neither that ethnography is unusable nor that we have interpreted it incorrectly. Instead, it is one of context. The point that David makes here is that we know all symbols have many meanings—David talks about the lamb and that's a good one. Following Victor Turner (1967), who has as good an approach for symbolic analysis as currently exists, we see that he emphasizes that each culture has a dominant symbol. Among the San its probably the eland, among the Great Basin Numic speakers it's the bighorn sheep—it is certainly other things in other regions. That dominant symbol means very many different things, but it is contexualized—it is given one of it's specific meanings in a particular case—by what Turner calls an instrumental symbol. That instrumental symbol, to someone that understands the symbolic systems, says "okay you are looking at the symbol here, it's going to mean this particular range of meanings." In rock art our instrumental symbol is always the rock face itself. That has a particular meaning and it is from that meaning that we can pull out the specific meaning intended by the individual making the art. And it happens to be the same for the San as for most people in the California and the Great Basin where I study. The rock face is that impermeable barrier between the natural and the supernatural realms. Thus, when we see a rock art bighorn sheep in California or the Great Basin, we know it symbolizes the spirit bighorn. We know it's not talking about the bighorn sheep song circle or a named Southern Paiute clan.

But the criticisms that people have been raising, particularly about some of David's work, essentially say "well, you've ignored the fact that eland also means these other things in mythology" and so on. But he *hasn't* ignored that. The point is that the rock face gives a particular meaning to the image and it's that context that he studies. Those criticisms are in fact decontextualizing and generalizing, when David is actually going towards the particular meaning.

Robert Layton: I would like to note a couple of other small points about ethnography. One is that David's ethnography is not just the spoken ethnography, it's also the "visual ethnography"—the postures in the dance, for example. This is something that could be observed ethnographically and then identified in the rock art. The other thing (and David [Lewis-Williams] says, it very clearly—I just want to reiterate it) is that it's one thing to say that the rock art can tell you something in itself that the ethnography can't, but we shouldn't lose sight of the fact that that rock art is culturally specific and that you have to read the rock art in the idiom of the culture. That understanding comes from the spoken and the visual ethnography of that particular culture.

Kelley Hayes-Gilpin: I'll say a little bit more about this debate for those who aren't familiar with it. In the paper, David [Lewis-Williams] refers to scholars discussing gender negotiation. He's referring there to Ann Solomon and certain other people, and I decided I needed to deal with this debate because I'm writing about rock art and gender and I wanted to try to figure out what each side was saying. I think they both have something to contribute. Although third parties have characterized the debate as, "is the rock art about trance or is it about gender," I want to point out that nobody who is actually in the debate seems to have ever said that. What they say is that "of course, trance can be a metaphor for sexual intercourse and of course there are complimentary gender roles in the trance dance and so of course if you are talking about trance you really can't ignore gender." But those people who are talking about negotiating gender aren't really negating trance experience either. What I think is interesting, that I haven't seen anybody really emphasizing before is that David [Lewis-Williams] has, from a scientific point of view, looked at how much rock art is there and quantified what things are depicted and how they link up. And I like his focus on "fragments" not only because at a lot of sites there's only fragments of that dance within some of these large panels, but also because a lot of rock art sites are just a fragment of the dance and those are all over the landscape. So he has said, because of numerical preponderance, this is what most of it's about. This is really important. But I also think, on Ann Solomon's side—and I don't mean to speak for her, but I am getting this out of her writing—that she has a different goal. Instead of trying to understand the rock art and using the ethnography to do that, I think she is saying she wants to understand gender dynamics in San Society, and wants to see if using rock art helps her understand that. She maintains that we can no longer observe some of these things and that ethnographers have not written much about them. So I think she's approaching it from a different direction, and she'll say "are there particular rock art sites somewhere, even if they are very rare, that can tell me something about gender?" And there is one picture I've seen of female shamans performing, and she has a couple,[1] but you can find hundreds of males. And she's picked out about eight mythic women paintings, all in Zimbabwe, and that's interesting because then you are looking at differences among San groups—different groups, different time periods, or different dynamics. So I think that what she's trying to get at is sort of a history of gender relations, and can rock art be used as line of evidence.

Jannie Loubser: Well she shifted her argument in later articles towards saying that it's not so much an issue of gender, but more the spirits of the dead. She reinterpreted the original Orpen documents and then argued that those really say instead of Shamans being metaphorically dead, it really is the spirits of the dead—the ancestral spirits. But there, I think, is a mistake, because we know that the San don't have ancestral spirits like the Bantu-speaking people have. There is no ancestral cult. And really, if you go back to the original documents, you do see that if you take all the information together they are referring to death as a metaphor for trance rather than actually dead spirits. As you say, I agree with the possibility of studying gender. In the beginning, Salomon argued that gender was part of a shamanic explanation. But then her argument morphed from that more toward the gender, and then finally toward ancestral veneration. And that's where the argument now lies.

Kelley Hayes-Gilpin: I see, but because I don't know the ethnography, I was just following the structure of how she's using feminist theory. And she's not using that in the ancestral veneration argument.

Jannie Loubser: And there are depictions—actually more than we think there are—of women doing trance dance. I think that the way women are situated within a society is not really material as to what might be contested thinking between shamans within the spirit world.

Kelley Hayes-Gilpin: One thing that I have been following in world-wide rock art studies is that a lot of people in the far north are looking at Siberia and Scandinavia and talking about gender transformation. They are not just human/animal transformations, but instead the male shaman may disguise himself as a woman in a sense. And a female shaman may put on men's clothing or experience a transformation of sex and gender in trance. So maybe its that you're both, and that's very powerful, but it's also crossing a boundary or a barrier—it's a kind of transcendence to transform gender. And sometimes you hear of people cross-dressing the dead and sometimes you get the explanation "oh, that's so bad spirits in the next world won't recognize them." But I think there is a lot more to it than that. And I haven't seen that come out in David's [Lewis-Williams] rock art study.

Jannie Loubser: There are engravings of elands that are double sex as far as being both bull and cow.

Kelley Hayes-Gilpin: Yes, that's included. One other question. What is the crossbar across the penis?

Jannie Loubser: Well, we really don't know. But some have suggested that it relates to the eland. From the ethnography, when a person does wound an eland with his arrow, the arrow point breaks off in the eland; they designed that specifically so the poisoning works its way into the eland's bloodstream. That hunter then, in effect, is in the eland (by way of his arrow), so whatever he does affects the eland. If that person urinates, he gets rid of the poison—like the eland would do. Or if he indulges in sex—you know that's vitality—then the eland would live longer. So they have taboos concerned with a person, and this penis crossbar might be an explanation of that. Sort of a sympathetic magic, if you like. You often get this [penis crossbar] depicted on people in association with an eland in the background.

David Whitley: But, in a material sense, there is no ethnographic explanation.

Kelley Hayes-Gilpin: Yes, but it might be simply a metaphorical indicator of continence.

David Whitley: Yes, or something of that order.

---

[1] David Lewis-Williams published one in his earliest book (Lewis-Williams 1981).

CHAPTER 4
Reading Between the Lines: Ethnographic Sources and Rock Art Interpretation Approaches to Ethnography and Rock Art
Linea Sundstrom

Ethnography has entered rock art research in several ways. Some researchers have sought to apply broad anthropological theories derived from ethnography as a whole to the problem of understanding rock art. For example, they may start with an assumption that nonurban societies generally have shamanic or shamanistic religions, and that such societies will therefore have produced rock art linked to shamanism. Some researchers seek universal symbolism in rock art. They believe that all humans share certain symbols, because human populations share a remote history, because they experience the visual world in the same way, or because brain structure and chemistry determine how people produce symbols. Other researchers may apply observations from one culture to another that is similar in some way. Comparing modern hunter-gatherer art from southern Africa with European Paleolithic art is an example of this type of ethnographic approach. Even though the cultures being compared are remote in time and space, they are assumed to share basic use of symbols because their purportedly similar economic and social systems dictate which ideas are important and how they are expressed symbolically.

Other scholars limit their application of comparative ethnographic data to cultures linked to the rock art spatially, temporally, or both. For example, a symbol might be traced back in time from historic or modern contexts to prehistoric rock art. Assuming cultural continuity between the historic and prehistoric people who created the symbols, the modern or historic meaning of the symbol can reasonably be projected onto the older art. Some researchers avoid applying any ethnographic data to rock art except information that comes from the group known or hypothesized to have produced the rock art. Others argue that even this limited application of ethnographic data is problematic, because cultures constantly change as new elements are introduced and older ones drop away. According to this view, the meaning of prehistoric art is beyond our reach, because we can never accurately reconstruct the cultural context in which it was produced.

Each of these uses of ethnographic data has pros and cons. Broad applications of ethnographic analogy often fail because the cultures being compared are not truly analogous. Certainly, such an approach has little to recommend it in attempting to recognize the meaning of particular images or symbols, because symbolism, except on the most graphic level, is culturally specific. While a picture of a four-legged animal with branched antlers may represent "deer" in many cultures, any more obscure symbolism will not likely transfer between cultures. To the extent that deer behavior is the same everywhere, the image of the deer might be used in more than one culture to symbolize a concept associated with observable deer traits, such as fleetness. But even such interpretations can easily go astray, because fleetness, for example, is just one of many concepts that might reasonably be linked to deer. Others might be palatability, the action of running or leaping, maleness (assuming a male deer is depicted), identification of a particular place as deer habitat (and thus hunting territory), a record of an actual hunt or an unusual animal, the ability of a person to transform into a deerlike state, or illustration of a myth or event involving deer. Attempts to define a lexicon of universal symbols have failed because of this great individuality and flexibility in human use of symbols.

Comparison of purportedly similar cultures may prove more manageable in that the types of experiences typical of those cultures limits the potential range of meaning assigned to a particular symbol. For example, cultures whose economy is based exclusively on hunting and gathering are not likely to develop symbols related to farming. In such cultures, the image of a deer might still represent a deer, transformation to a deerlike state, or a myth involving deer, but the deer would not likely represent a cultigen or a brand of tractors. One problem with this approach is that the number of potential meanings of a symbol is still very large, as Nancy Munn's (1973) study of Walbiri symbolism so aptly demonstrates. Sometimes materially or economically simple cultures develop extremely complex systems of mythology and religious beliefs.

The identification of universal symbols based on neurological research is more accurate in the sense that certain images can be demonstrated to be perceived during particular mental states, such as those induced by fatigue, fasting, migraine, blows to the head, use of hallucinogenic drugs, and the like (cf. Kellogg et al. 1965; Reichel-Dolmatoff 1978). This approach is ultimately limiting, however, because we already know that all humans have the potential to experience and reproduce these images. Most such images can be experienced either within or outside a given mental state. For example, a person can imagine and reproduce a black-and-white checkerboard pattern during a normal state of mental alertness, as well as during certain types of altered consciousness. Thus, although a predominance of such visual images in a rock art style can argue for its production during an altered state of consciousness, it by no means proves such a connection. States of altered consciousness produce different perceived images, depending on the way in which the altered state is induced (Helvenston and Bahn 2002). All religions include activities through which adherents seek to achieve a mental state that makes them extraordinarily receptive to religious messages or feelings of enlightenment. Ethnographic records demonstrate that most rock art in North America was produced in a religious context. Thus, identifying rock art images as shamanic tells us little we did not already know, especially when shamanism is loosely defined. One important contribution of this school of thought, however, is the recognition of visual symbols linked to widespread religious experiences, such as human figures with wings or other indicators of a flying sensation and humans with rays or halos extending from their heads or entire bodies.

One standard definition of *shaman* is a person who has special religious power acquired through his or her own initiative and is thought to possess certain special abilities to deal with supernatural beings and powers. By this definition, it is hard to identify a culture that does not include shamans. *Shaman* is frequently contrasted with *priest*, a full-time religious specialist who has undergone formal training for the role. Again, most cultures include this role. For example, while American Indian healers would generally be classified as shamans, men and women who act as keepers of sacred bundles, such as the Lakota's Sacred Calf Pipe Keeper, typically inherit the position, undergo a long period of formal training for their role, and carry out the obligations of the role at all times. At the same time, it is unlikely that a person would be chosen as a sacred bundle keeper unless his or her spiritual potential had been validated by powerful visions. The bundle keepers are thus more like priests than shamans, but no clear line can be drawn between the two.

The concept of shamanism is itself problematic. Virtually all religions involve public and private ritual, communally held and individual beliefs, and openness to receiving signs, messages, or enlightenment from the supernatural realm. If we identify an anthropomorphic petroglyph with wings and a rayed head as shamanic, then we must logically identify a Medieval painting of a winged and haloed angel the same way, even though the social contexts of the two vary greatly. Is a horned serpent shamanic, but a gargoyle not? Can we say that the Flagellant cults of the Middle Ages were not following a shamanic religion, but the Sun Dancers of the Great Plains were? Is the Lakota Bear Dreamer who sings over a sick patient a shaman, while the Pentecostal faith healer--or for that matter the Roman Catholic priest-- who prays over a sick patient is not? Both are in fact acting as interveners between the person in crisis and the supernatural world, whether through transforming into a spirit being that controls healing or through achieving a state of grace through repetition of a chant or prayer. Both are specialists in certain types of ritual, and both have undergone selection (by self and community) and specialized training. Members of fundamentalist sects who handle poisonous snakes and speak in tongues perceive themselves in direct contact with the supernatural world, just as do native healers in a trance state. Thus, rather than a clear dichotomy between shamanic and nonshamanic (or priestly) religion, it appears that most religions have some elements of each. This makes the conclusions one can draw from a "shamanic" rock art image even more limited, as it may reflect just one part of a more complex religious system.

While the problems of ethnographic approaches to rock art studies will never be fully resolved, it may be instructive to begin with the most straightforward and easily defended kind of application: the direct ethnographic approach.

The Direct Ethnographic Approach in Rock Art Studies

One of the most influential voices in American anthropology was that of Franz Boas, who taught at Columbia University from 1896 to 1936 (Willey and Sabloff 1980). Reacting to some patently false ideas being put forth by followers of cultural evolutionism, Boas trained an entire generation of ethnologists to toe a line called historical particularism. Boas insisted on the uniqueness of each culture and its historical development. Each culture was viewed in terms of its own values and history, not as an accident of universal stages of cultural evolution or psychic unity.

One disciple of historical particularism was William Duncan Strong. In creating the Nebraska Archaeological Survey in 1929, Strong established two goals: the first was to survey the state to find out what archaeological remains were there. The second was to organize this material into a cultural sequence (Wedel 1938:1). He hoped to accomplish this by tracing known historic and protohistoric Indian cultures back in time through the archaeological record. He would extend the archaeological sequence "from the known historic into the unknown prehistoric" (Wedel 1938:1; Strong 1935). Under the competent hands of Strong's colleague, Waldo Wedel, this approach became known as the direct historical approach. Strong's and Wedel's research laid the groundwork for Plains archaeology (Wedel 1938; Willey and Sabloff 1980:108-109). This was not the first time that archaeologists had called on ethnology (Willey and Sabloff 1980:108), but it was certainly one of the most successful marriages of the two disciplines.

Problems with the Direct Ethnographic Approach

This paper focuses on problems inherent in the direct ethnographic research—that is, applying ethnographic information about a particular group to rock art made or used by the same group. More specifically, it focuses on some pitfalls of using information recorded or reinterpreted by those outside the culture. Many ethnographic sources suffer from bias or misunderstanding on the part of the writer. Those non-Indians who first encountered and recorded Indian cultures found themselves in a novel cultural environment, one whose rules they knew only vaguely at best. Because such records are inevitably incomplete, they allow researchers to view precontact Indian culture only as if through a glass, darkly. But because most ethnographers tried to fit their observations into contexts that made sense in terms of Euroamerican culture, the glass is not just darkened, but tinted in Victorian hues. Only through careful examination of ethnographic sources can one reconstruct what the Indians were trying to tell the ethnographers. It is this information—what the Indians themselves said—and not the ethnographer's (mis)interpretation of it, that provides insight into the use and meaning of rock art sites.

Another problem is that many of the outsiders who first described Indian cultures were actively trying to change them. Fur traders wished to maximize profits and minimize the complications of obtaining hides and pelts. Missionaries wanted to replace native religions with European ones. Together, they sought to restructure native societies around the church and trading post. Their writings inevitably reflect the tensions of trying to force Indians to adopt new ways of life. These ethnographies either record a period of sudden and often traumatic change or fail to distinguish between cultural ideals and cultural reality. Ironically, the records of white captives and semiliterate trappers and explorers sometimes offer the most straightforward view of Indian customs, simply because those writers were not carrying out an economic or religious agenda.

Strong theoretical bias has sometimes compromised later accounts by anthropologists. In marshalling data to support a particular theory, researchers sometimes neglected or omitted other information. Even those anthropologists with no theoretical bias were not immune to more subtle cultural bias. Most Euroamerican anthropologists sought out male informants, because it was assumed that they, not the women, were the experts on native religion, politics, and history. Further, anthropology has long tended to use Western technology as the yardstick for measuring cultural complexity or advancement. Technologically simple cultures were thought of as less complex in all areas. This type of thinking often expressed itself in terms that were supposed to dichotomize between the culture of the ethnographer and the native

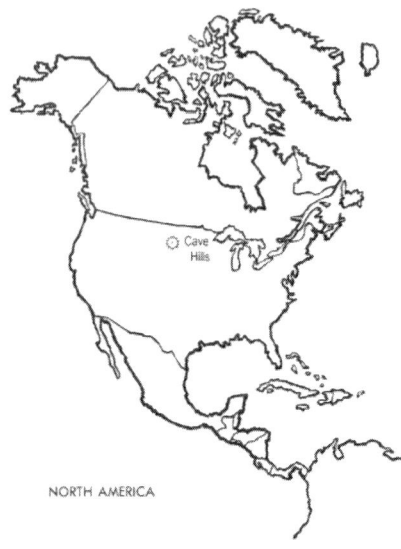

Figure 1. Approximate location of the Cave Hills, northwestern South Dakota.

cultures being studied. Terms such as primitive, tribal, underdeveloped, and nonmodern both exaggerated differences between "us" and "them" and created poorly defined categories in which vastly diverse cultures were lumped together.

Ludlow Cave and the Ethnographic Record

Ludlow Cave in the Cave Hills of northwestern South Dakota is one of the most important sacred sites in the northern Great Plains of North America (Figure 1). Ethnographic sources state that the cave was sacred to the Lakota, Hidatsa, and Mandan people. Archaeological evidence points to Cheyenne use of the cave, as well, and the close association of the Crow people with the Hidatsas strongly suggests that they, too, knew of and used the cave (Sundstrom 1996). Ludlow Cave is more rockshelter than cave, but a narrow crevice extends back into the sandstone for several hundred feet from the cave opening. This feature and the north-facing opening impart a true cave-like coolness and dampness (Figure 2).

Two accounts of Lakota traditions about Ludlow Cave will serve as examples of the problems of native accounts carried over into non-Indian discourse. The first is from the diary of a cavalryman on the 1874 Black Hills expedition. The second is from a group of Arikara scouts who accompanied Lt. Colonel George Armstrong Custer on the same exploratory expedition to the Black Hills in 1874. North Dakota state historian Orin Libby interviewed the Arikara scouts in 1912.

In the first account, Private Theodore Ewert, a white soldier on the 1874 Black Hills Expedition, relates what Lakota scouts told him about Ludlow Cave:

"The Sioux say that in years past an old white man inhabited this cave. He wore long, snow-white hair, and his beard, also snow-white, reached below his waist. It was believed that he held intercourse with the 'Great Spirit' and that he was proof against steel and bullets, as a great many warriors had, at different times, fired upon him even at short range and yet without hitting him.

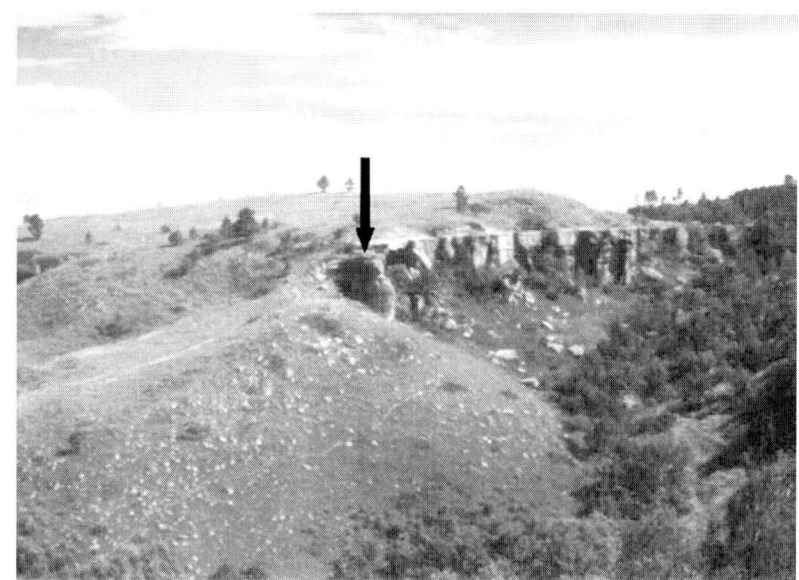

Figure 2. View of Ludlow Cave, opening in rimrock at left center indicated by arrow.

The oldest inhabitants of their camps spoke of the same figure, always looking as it did now, as having been there when they were children." (Carroll and Frost 1976:18)

Ewert then added, "Of course, a great portion, if not all, of this story is untrue, and yet it might be possible that some criminal, flying from justice, had come out here to drag out his remaining few years in a dull, monotonous, dangerous existence. Who knows?" (Carroll and Frost 1976:18).

Two Arikara scouts who accompanied the 1874 expedition, Strikes Two and Bear's Belly, recalled this Lakota account of its discovery:

"When the Lakotas first found this cave, they saw on the flat rock near the cave opening a woman taking the hair off a deer hide with an old-fashioned scraper. She ran away and they could not find her. They thought she hid in the cave, far in. Beyond the flat rock was a spring. Here was a large hollow rock full of water like a trough in a pasture and the tracks of the deer were all about like cow tracks at a watering place." (Libby 1998:164)

The Lakota called Ludlow Cave simply "the cave," "the big cave," or "the place where the cow killed a man." The latter name referred to an accident in which a young hunter was gored to death by a buffalo cow protecting her calf in the draw below the cave (Krause and Olson 1974:110). One version of the story says the cow had two calves

(Carroll and Frost 1976:18). Twin buffalo are extremely rare (Schult 1979:21) and thus in Lakota terms were *wakaŋ*, sacred or mysterious. A bison killing a skilled young hunter was also a very unusual event.

What do these strange stories have to do with rock art, specifically the rock art that once covered the walls and ceiling of the cave and that still covers the cliffs of the draw opposite the cave entrance? Without an understanding of Lakota religion, the stories seem to have no common theme--a bearded white man who cannot be killed, a woman dwelling in the cave, an accident with a buffalo cow. Once the stories are placed in their cultural context, however, a common theme emerges, and it is this theme that the most prominent petroglyph at the site expresses. The common theme is the renewal of the bison herds, the mainstay of human life and a metaphor for the Indians' own survival.

In Lakota tradition, all facets of the natural and supernatural world have both visible and invisible expressions. Thus, Wind, Rock, Sun, Moon, Earth, Movement, the Whirlwind, and the various animals have both a visible aspect perceived by human senses and an invisible aspect—a spirit, if you will—that is not visible but that is embodied by (or is the force behind) the visible object (Walker 1980). As in virtually all religions, natural and supernatural forces are symbolized by humanlike beings. For example, Wind is personified by four grown brothers, one for each direction; the Whirlwind is their restless little brother who has no direction of his own. Both large and small forces or energies are symbolized by various spirit beings in the form of animals or humans. This symbolism is informed by observable characteristics of the particular force or energy. The Elk symbolizes the power of men to attract women, because bull elk seem easily to attract female elk by bugling. The Bear symbolizes healing power, because these beasts were observed to be carefully selecting their food from among the various plants, roots, and berries (Densmore 1918:195). Thunder is conceived as a great winged creature that shoots lightning from its wingtips, or as a warriorlike being riding a horse that thunders across the sky hurling down spears of lightning.

Two such spirit beings symbolize the powers of the north and of womanhood, respectively. The energy of the north is visualized as a cruel, selfish man, dressed in furs and covered in snow and frost. His name, *Waziya*, refers to pine trees, literally "green in the white [snow]." In mythology, he can never be completely defeated, but hides in the caves and crevices and in the northern regions, returning each fall to bring back the hardships of winter (Walker 1980:120-121; 108-109). His association with caves is twofold. First, because caves emit cold air and sometimes even have frost or ice inside them well into the summer, and Waziya is the source of the cold, he is believed to dwell deep inside the caves. Second, he sometimes hides the bison inside this underground world, especially in winter. In winter, the huge herds disperse into small groups or seem to disappear altogether, leaving the people hungry and cold. The clouds of condensation seen around the entrances to caves and deep crevices in winter are identical to the clouds of steam by which the Indians could sometimes locate herds of bison during times of bitter cold. Waziya starves the people, especially little children, in his stingy hoarding of the bison. He, in the form of cold and snow, also depletes their fat, so that even if hunters can locate bison, their meat may be too poor to sustain human life.

The other spirit being associated with caves and rocky places is called Double Woman (Walker 1980:165-166; Wissler 1912:92-94; Sundstrom 2002). This being is visualized as two very tall women, with a cord or membrane between them from which dangles a doll. Double Woman represents both the good and evil aspects of womanhood. She is the inventor of the women's arts and crafts, but she has sacrificed normal family life in pursuit of the arts. The doll that dangles from her cord is remote and lifeless, symbolizing that she cannot achieve the ideal of Lakota womanhood: the bearing and rearing of children. Double Woman is said to dwell in the rocks and to create the rock art seen there. Those who dreamed of her were given the choice between a virtuous life as a wife and mother or a disconnected life of promiscuity and isolation. Great artistic skill might come to those who chose the latter path, although their personal sacrifices might be considerable. Double Woman gave women the skills and designs they needed to create beautiful quilled robes and other clothing.

Double Woman is closely associated with another female spirit being, Deer Woman. Often the two are conflated in stories and symbols. Deer Woman is a dangerous seducer of men (and sometimes of women). The individual who is overcome by her beauty and the perfume of her hoofprints is led to insanity or death. She represents womanhood gone wrong. Like the doe, Deer Woman is promiscuous in mating and leaves her children alone to pursue her own selfish interests. The opposing force or energy—that of the stable, careful mother—is represented by the bison. The buffalo cow, unlike the deer, chooses her mate carefully, accepting the advances of only the most powerful and protective bulls. She carefully guards her calf, never leaving it alone until it can fend for itself. At puberty, Lakota girls were instructed to emulate the bison cow—to attain the most honored position within the group, that of the mother of its future generation (Walker 1980:241-255).

With this context, it is not difficult to interpret the story of the woman living at Ludlow Cave. She is the Double Woman—visualized in this case, not as two separate women, but as the woman who transforms between human and deer form. This is expressed in the Indians' assertion that she disappeared into the rock and could not be found again, except in the form of animal tracks around a watering hole. In Plains Indian tradition, bison and deer tracks and places where water collects are symbols of women's vulvas and thus of their reproductive or seductive potential. The mysterious woman is scraping a deer hide with a bone tool, symbolizing the role of Double Woman in the women's arts. I have hypothesized elsewhere that the stone tools composing the women's tool kit were made at cliffs associated with Double Woman (Sundstrom 2002). This explains the occurrence of tool grooves both at rock art sites and at tiny, isolated places that would certainly not be the most convenient for making tools. The area around Ludlow Cave contains many sites with abraded grooves, tracks, and vulvaforms, the types of petroglyphs created in shaping and sharpening bone tools on the sandstone cliffs (Figure 3).

The first story—about the old man with the snow-white hair and beard—makes little sense if taken literally, but not when taken as an attempt to explain the Lakota concept of winter. The white of the

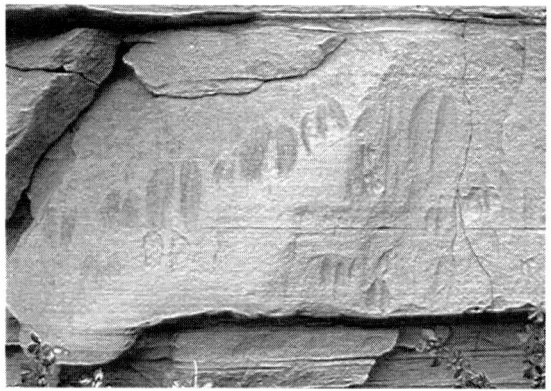

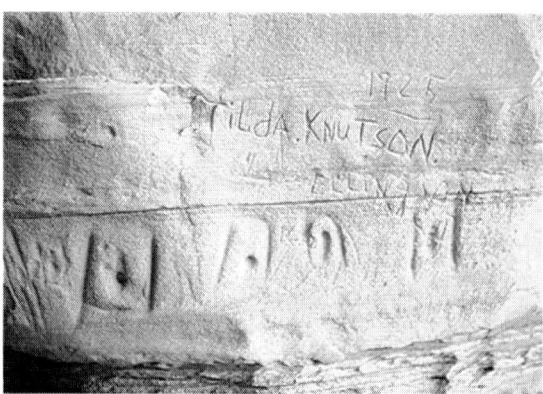

Figure 3. Abraded rock art from the Cave Hills: top, deer and bison tracks, 39HN205; bottom, vulvas, 39HN150.

hermit's hair and beard is that of snow and frost. He cannot be killed and never dies or changes. And he is one of countless aspects of the "Great Spirit"—the energy that informs all things in the earth and sky.

In the mid-1800s, a Lakota man called The Grindstone frequently talked to Henry Boller about a

> "white hermit in the pines among the Black Hills. He had a hut on the summit of some towering rocks. No one had seen him, but they knew him to be a very tall man because they (the Sioux) found a deer that he had killed and hung up in the top of a lofty pine tree. He is the person, they think, who poisoned all the creeks and streams, causing such distress among the wild animals. There had been no thunder this spring, and it was currently believed that he had killed the thunder-bird." (Boller 1972:327)

Again, this passage is puzzling only until we realize that Grindstone was speaking of Waziya. He is, literally, dwelling among the pines—that is, in the north or the high mountains. He is white like frost and snow. His blizzards cause snow to pile up so high that the deer can find no food. In Lakota tradition, the beginning of spring is marked by the return of the thunder—and only winter's persistence can prevent the thunder's return.

In Lakota, the term for non-Indians, especially Euroamericans, is the same word used for the intangible aspects of north and winter—that is the force or energy of the cold, ice, snow, and wind of winter. This term, *wasicu*, is sometimes translated as "the one who takes the fat"—a translation that derives not from the root words (*wa*, the color white, and *sicun*, the unseen aspect of something), but from a metaphorical term for the hardships of winter. Besides being white in color, covered with frosty-looking hair and beards, and wearing furs like Waziya, the white men seemed to embody the greedy, stingy behavior of the spirit of winter, taking for themselves and ignoring the needs of the larger community (Walker 1980:108-109). Thus, when the scouts and Grindstone referred to "white" hermits, they meant not Euroamericans, but spirits associated with cold and snow.

These stories, as well as the account for the name of "where the cow killed the man," all connect bison with Ludlow Cave. Waziya takes the bison herds into the below world in winter. Double Woman, her dual aspects symbolized by deer and bison, dwells in the cliffs there. And a bison cow kills a hunter to protect her young at the cave. At this place, at least, the power of the mother bison is greater than that of the hunter. Ethnographic data suggest that Ludlow Cave was one of several "buffalo home buttes" of the Mandan and Hidatsa long before Lakota people entered the area (Bowers 1950:171-172, 1963:369; Beckwith 1938:304). Bison spirits were believed to emerge from caves or crevices in these buttes to replenish the herds. People fasted and made offerings of dressed hides, eagle feathers, and buffalo skulls at these buttes to encourage the renewal of the herds upon which they depended for sustenance (Bowers 1950:90, 1963:53-54, 127, 255, 436). Lakota, Cheyenne, and Arapaho groups also believed that bison spirits lived under the ground and that caves were the entrances to this underground world (cf. Bass 1966:43; Hoebel 1978:19, 89; LaPointe 1976:73-85).

The largest petroglyph near Ludlow Cave, certainly one of the most elaborate in the northern plains, depicts a bison cow, her back still humped in labor and her newborn calf beneath her (Figure 4). She has a very long tail and extensions from each horn to show that she is not an

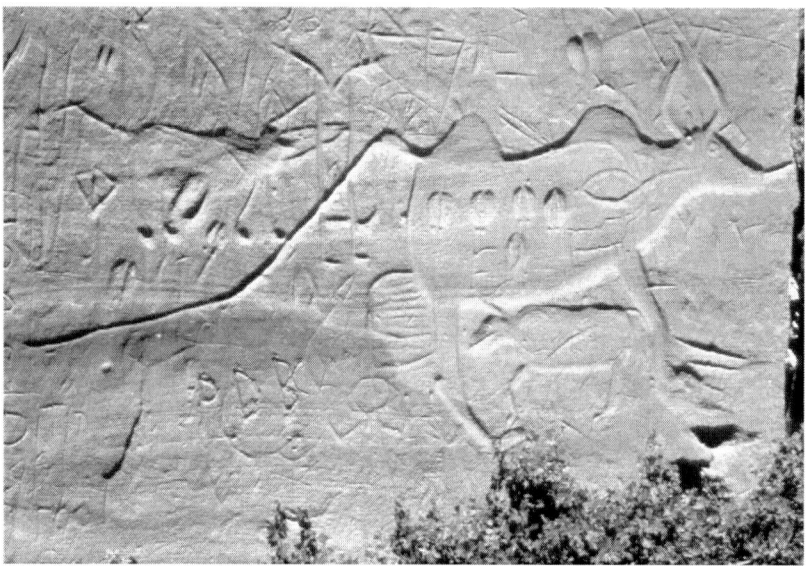

Figure 4. Abraded bison cow and calf petroglyph on rimrock facing Ludlow Cave entrance, 39HN17.

ordinary bison, but one of the spirit bison that dwell in the underground places (cf. Hultkrantz 1979:63). The five hoofprints deeply carved across her side represent the essence of the bison, as well as that of human reproduction. As noted, the bison or deer hoofprint is a metaphor for the human vulva throughout much of North America. A snare carved across the animal's neck is a symbol for capture among the Mandan and Hidatsa. Thus, this petroglyph is a visual prayer for the renewal of the herds and that the people can take the animals needed to sustain the life of the tribe. It is a plea that Waziya—the spirit of winter—release his hold on the spirit bison, that spring and the herds return, that the men be successful in their hunt, and that the women be good mothers. This image, in this place in the landscape, thus symbolizes a complex set of ideas related to the most fundamental aspects of life. Although we cannot know for certain which of the tribes first created the great bison carving, nor when exactly it was made, its meaning is clear from the strong connection between Ludlow Cave, bison, and women's reproductive potential expressed in the various ethnographic accounts about the cave.

Ethnography and Rock Art

This example illustrates several points about the use of ethnography in rock art studies.

First, ethnographic sources are most useful when applied to the group or groups most likely to have produced or used the rock art. In this case, it is the Lakota, Hidatsa, and Mandan ethnographic material that is the key to understanding the bison petroglyph and the significance of Ludlow Cave. Direct historical and archaeological evidence of use of Ludlow Cave is strongest for these groups. Although it is likely that Crow and Cheyenne groups, at least, also used the cave, ethnographic materials related to those groups contain no specific references to it.

Second, it is important to focus on what the native people actually said, rather than what the outsiders said they said. Both of the accounts of Waziya given above give a clear description of a supernatural being associated with the north and with mountains or caves, but both outside recorders took them as accounts of white men living in the area. Similarly, outsiders recorded that Dakota people said that the rock art in the country around Pipestone, Minnesota, was made by "two women" (Catlin 1973II:164; Bray and Bray 1976:72-77; North Dakota Writers Project 1938:289; Sioux Falls *Argus-Leader*, ca. 1931; Landes 1968:73; US Court of Claims 1927:157-158). In the Dakota language, however, the same phrase is used for "two women" and for the name of the supernatural being Double Woman. It was Double Woman, not any actual women, who was believed to make the designs.

This brings up a third point: when the native text was recorded, it is important to return to it to make sure the English translation is accurate. For example, many ethnographic references mistranslate the terms for Bear Butte and Bear Lodge Butte (two sacred mountains in the Black Hills), but the two terms are distinct in Lakota. Where the native text was not recorded, the researcher may have to reconstruct it from the context of the passage, substituting a translation that is likely to be correct for one that is likely false, as in the two women versus Double Woman terms discussed above. The potential confusion in Lakota between "white" people as an ethnic group and as the spirits of cold and snow was discussed above. In Cheyenne, the same term is used for Spider, the trickster being, and for non-Indians. Again, the researcher must be aware both of the potential for mistranslation and the highly metaphorical forms of Plains Indian speech.

Fourth, researchers must account for the gender biases of those who recorded the information. In accordance with their essentially Victorian worldview, some white male anthropologists interpreted the exclusion of women from some rituals as meaning that women were considered a polluting influence. They further interpreted it as meaning that men's role in religion as a whole was more important than that of women. Conforming to the Judeo-Christian tradition, these writers viewed women as nonessential to religious ceremonies; however, the Indians' own statements give a different picture. Few, if any, ceremonies could be conducted without women (cf. Walker 1980; Brown 1953; Grinnell 1923; Schlesier 1987; Ewers 1958; Landes 1968:50; Bowers 1950:226, 248). Women might sponsor or conduct ceremonies, including both the large annual ceremonies and the semi-private healing rituals, such as the *Yuwipi* ritual, and frequently acted as healers, especially regarding disease and childbirth. Female Double Woman dreamers enacted their visions, just as male Elk or Buffalo dreamers enacted theirs. In fact, no dream society was exclusively male or female, at least in theory. Several important medicine bundles originated in the dreams or visions of women (Ewers 1958; Irwin 1994).

Making rock art has sometimes been assumed to be a male activity. But a closer look at ethnographic sources shows that the Indians did not assign all of it to men. Many Indian historians said they simply did not know who made it (cf. LaPointe 1976:5; DeMallie 1984:376; Stone 1982:76; Lewis 1980:76; Dempsey 1994:125). Blackfoot, Hidatsa, Mandan, and Pawnee warriors are known to have recorded combat scenes on rocks and trees (Beckwith 1938:306-307; McGee 1897:169; Hyde 1968:54; Grinnell 1926:31-34; Barbeau 1960:69). The Cheyenne, Crow and Wind River Shoshone said rock art was made by spirits, gender not specified (Hultkrantz 1979:60, 1981:35; Bradley 1961:52-53; Grinnell 1923II:148). According to a Lakota informant, the rock art at Deer Medicine Rock, Montana, was made by "generations of Indians" (Lame Deer and Erdoes 1972:113-114). That at Painted Rock Creek was said to be the work of "medicine men" recording visions (Clark 1885:320). The old Ponca historians stated that their "medicine men" made rock art at various locales to mark the route of the tribe's migrations (Howard 1965:17-18, 71). Considering that the term "medicine men" is that of the non-Indian ethnographers, a gender-neutral term may have been turned into a gender specific one in this case. In other words, "medicine man" may refer to women as well as men. Cheyenne and Assiniboin sources stated that some rock art appeared of its own accord, but some was made by fasters to record their visions (Grinnell 1923II:96, 148; Stands in Timber and Liberty 1967:104;

Barbeau 1960:207-209). The Cree stated that rock art was made by the Little People, a race of tiny but fierce humanoids that included both sexes (Wormington and Forbis 1965:170-171). Blackfoot people attributed the markings at Writing-On-Stone in southern Alberta, Canada, to spirit beings dwelling in a lodge-shaped butte there (Klassen et al. 2000). Apart from the biographic combat scenes, none of this rock art was said to have been an exclusively male endeavor.

In the Siouan country east of the Missouri, traditions are more consistent. Nearly all rock art in this area was said to have been made by spirits. Several boulders with rather amorphous bird-tracks were said by numerous Dakota sources to have been created by the Thunders (Lewis 1886, 1887). These thunderbird track rocks are stylistically similar to the hoofprint rock art found along and west of the Missouri and probably are their immediate precursors. These thunderbird tracks presumably included female Thunderbirds because the imprints of their eggs are also sometimes found at these places. The Prayer Rock now at Britton, South Dakota, is one such Thunder nest, according to the Dakota. George Catlin recorded a Dakota tradition that another Thunder Nest near the pipestone quarries was that of a *female* thunder spirit (Catlin 1973II:164). As noted above, several sources, when correctly translated, refer to Double Woman creating the rock art in western Minnesota and the eastern Dakotas. When a woman dreamed of Double Woman, she might enact the spirit being to fulfill the vision. The above accounts strongly indicate that making rock art was one way in which women recreated the Double Woman spirit. They worked at night, chipping or abrading designs into the rock, imitating Double Woman's flagrant laughter. In this sense, spirits *did* make the rock art—through the agency of those whom they visited in visions. As a whole, the ethnographic literature suggests that both men and women—and male and female spirits—were associated with rock art.

Fourth, visual information may be as important as written records in understanding rock art. Historic Plains Indian ledger art and painted robes have provided a key to rock art showing warriors' deeds, because they are historically linked and similar in function (Rodee 1965; Keyser 1979, 1987, 1996; Keyser and Klassen 2001). The connection between Double Woman and spiders is most clearly seen in historic ledger drawings and decorated objects (cf. Maurer 1992:159; Penney 1992:290-291). The use of a long tail and "ears" on top of the head to designate a spirit or underworld bison, as seen at Ludlow Cave, is best documented through similar images in other rock art and portable objects (Sundstrom 2003). Characteristic shield designs have been recognized in rock art by comparing them with actual historic shields and ledger art (Sundstrom and Keyser 1998).

Finally, different cultures have different ways of viewing the world. One problem in interpreting native statements is that in our Western worldview, we tend to recognize strict dichotomies between sacred and secular, the human world and the natural world, and the biological (living) and physical (nonliving) world. These dichotomies make little sense in the Plains Indian worldview in which all things, seen and unseen, are sacred, alive, interconnected, and constantly changing. This includes rock art. Most rock art researchers notice different glyphs when they revisit a site. They attribute this to changes in lighting, more careful examination of the rock surface, or the amount of time spent at the site. From the Indian point of view, it is the message carried by the rock art that changes. It is meant to change so that each time one views it he or she receives a message relevant at that time. Whether the petroglyph actually physically changes is not important—either it does, or the spirits change the way the individual perceives it. Either way, the glyph communicates something new to the person viewing it. Western culture views petroglyphs as art, something made to be viewed for enjoyment or emotional enrichment, not as a medium of communication from the spirit world. Most adherents of modern Western religions, in fact, do not expect to be confronted with tangible supernatural communication ever, much less in response to a deliberate quest on the part of the individual. Western science largely disallows the idea that the image on a rock can change significantly without human intervention, although erosion, lighting, and other physical forces may be called on to explain different perceptions. Researchers need not, and should not, abandon Western cultural tenets, including scientific approaches, in attempting to understand rock art, but, at the same time, should not let these tenets obscure the very different way other cultures have of looking at things.

Ethnography: The Good, the Bad, and the Nonexistent

Not all ethnography was created equal. In the northern Great Plains, some ethnographic information about rock art sites is straightforward and easy to understand. For example, Nicholas Black Elk, famous as the voice of *Black Elk Speaks*, told John Neihardt that:

"There is a place in the Black Hills, also on the Little Big Horn, a bank of solid rock where there are inscriptions that only a medicine man can read. It is a mystery. There is one in the Black Hills that only a medicine man can read. We don't know who wrote it, but a medicine man can decode it and get the meaning. We would camp and when we would come back there would be more writing." (DeMallie 1984:376)

Other references are more difficult to interpret, but nonetheless accurate. These require a more complete knowledge of the culture in question. For example, in relating his religious vision to Garrick Mallery, the Brule Lakota Battiste Good (or Brown Hat) speaks of seeing the prints of a man's hands and horses' hooves on the rock walls. Mallery notes that this refers to petroglyphs (Mallery 1893:290). Without this footnote, one might easily overlook this reference to rock art, but if one were familiar with the rock art of the Black Hills—where Brown Hat fasted—the connection would be easier to find. The rock art of this area contains many representations of animal tracks and human hand and footprints. But it is equally important to understand the significance of petroglyphs and of tracks in Lakota culture. Petroglyphs are viewed as messages from the spirit world. For that reason, vision seekers often fasted at rock art sites. Throughout Lakota pictography and art, horse tracks were a symbol of earned wealth and prestige—specifically, the horses a person had obtained through raiding enemies.

Just as understanding a work of art, a past event, or a person's actions requires a historic context, the research must take into account the historic context in which ethnographic statements were recorded. Did the person have first-hand knowledge of the practice or belief being described? Did he or she have a reason to bowdlerize the information (as frequently happened after missionaries tabooed talk of human reproduction and certain religious practices that were deemed barbaric or "heathenish")? Did the person have an incentive to obscure or fabricate information, either for financial gain or to protect a traditional practice? Was the person coerced into sharing the information or was it freely given? What was the relationship between the person speaking and the ethnographer? Did the ethnographer talk only to people of one gender, age group, or social class, and if so, why? All these factors will affect the reliability of a statement.

Good ethnography has several characteristics. It is clearly attributed to a specific person or persons. Either the native text is provided or the passage is well translated. Interlineal translations are ideal, so that the reader can explore the degree to which the speaker was employing metaphorical terms or idioms, rather than a more literal rendering of the passage. The ethnographer should provide information on the age and expertise of the speaker, as well as the context in which the information was given. Most importantly, it should be clear where the speaker's text and comments leave off and the ethnographer's interpretation begins. Good ethnography does not put words or concepts into the mouths of native speakers.

Bad ethnography lacks these characteristics. It does not state what the Indians actually said, but how the anthropologist or diarist interpreted it. Bad translations are not necessarily a problem, if the original phrase or a word-by-word translation is included. As long as the writer makes his or her biases clear, even prejudiced statements can be useful. For example, when William Ludlow wrote in 1874 that Ludlow Cave "proved to possess no special interest other than that imparted to it by the superstition of the Indians" (Ludlow 1875:10) and the expedition naturalist, George Bird Grinnell stated that the cave was "altogether…a fraud" (Grinnell n.d.:69), it is not difficult to understand that a cultural gulf separated their views and those of the Indians. They were perturbed by the impulsiveness and lack of discipline of the expedition leader, George Custer, who had diverted the expedition to look at the cave, and were hot, thirsty, and exhausted from Custer's grueling schedule. Both sets of notes, if carefully examined, do record that the cave was important to several Indian tribes and that it was well known to Custer's scouts. But Ludlow and Grinnell were looking for geological resources and fossils, and in that respect, the Indians' enthusiasm for the cave made no sense to them. In this case, the ethnography is salvageable, because it is an easy matter to reconstruct the mindset of both the Indians and the people writing about them. Ironically, Custer's own notes and letters are much more positive (Custer 1874). He clearly states the religious significance of the cave and identifies the materials inside it as offerings—something that subsequent archaeological studies failed entirely to do.

It is common for nonanthropologists to view rock art through their own experiences, rather than those of the people who created it. For example, in describing the petroglyphs of Ludlow Cave, Custer said he "could not satisfactorily account for" pictures of ships there (Custer 1885:299). These "ships" in all probability were animals. In the Cave Hills, animal petroglyphs are described as either boat-form style or mature style (Keyser and Sundstrom 1984:10); thus, Custer seems to have mistaken boat-form animals for actual boats. Indians in this region neither produced nor imported boats except for expedient rafts and short-lived "bull boats" made of buffalo hide stretched over a bowl-shaped framework of willow poles. This type of mistake is easily corrected by considering the cultural context in which the art was made—one that clearly would support the animal interpretation and not the boat interpretation. More problematic is bias on the part of the researcher. Professionals and amateurs alike can be prone to seeing what they want to see in rock art. Petroglyphs representing vulvas are common in the Cave Hills and much of the northern plains. These have variously been interpreted as plants, buffalo trails, abstract designs, butterflies, and even faces, although the same designs occur as part of larger human figures where their meaning is unambiguous (Figure 5). The failure to correctly identify vulva pictures seems to result from two cultural biases. First, images of genitalia are taboo in modern American society. Second, a Victorian bias persists that everything important or publicly visible is male. This carries over in rock art research to the extent that at least one

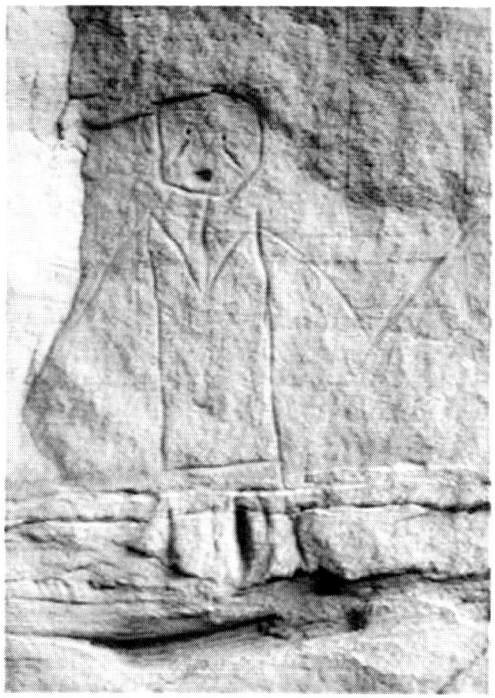

Figure 5. Petroglyph of crying woman, Cave Hills, 39HN165. The tears on her face suggest she is undergoing a vision quest, often called "crying for a vision."

explicitly female figure has been interpreted as male. A Plains anthropologist once insisted to me that the vulva glyphs were actually "coup counts" made by men, because, he wrote, we could surely agree that women were not making rock art. As noted above, the assumption that women did not create rock art, as well as the assumption that images of women must be referenced to the actions of men, lacks any support in the ethnographic literature.

The "nonexistent" refers to those parts of the story that simply are not available. As noted, many women's religious traditions were not recorded, or were recorded only sketchily, because anthropologists either did not have access to women for conversation or assumed the women had nothing to say. In the case of Vulva-Track-Groove style rock art, no ethnography states directly that women created the art by abrading their hide-working tools against the sandstone cliffs, however, several ethnographic sources can be drawn together to make this argument indirectly (Sundstrom 2002). Just because a custom was not recorded does not mean it did not exist. For example, as far as I can determine no source mentions the creation of rock art as part of Hidatsa and Mandan eagle trapping (cf. Bowers 1950, 1963; Wilson 1928; Beckwith 1938).

But the Cave Hills contain numerous sites with visual images directly linked to eagle trapping and the myths that gave this activity a deeply religious meaning. Although they never specifically mention this type of rock art, the ethnographies provide the context in which these images can be understood.

Other information is nonexistent because the people who knew it died. For example, it appears that a large body of Cheyenne star knowledge was lost entirely during the epidemics and massacres of the last quarter of the nineteenth century (Schlesier 1987; Petter 1915:1009). Of the seven major ceremonies of the Lakota nation, only five are still practiced today. In this case, descriptions of all seven exist, but these pertain primarily to the Oglala division. The exact rites followed by the other six Lakota tribes are not known today. Although some rock art can be interpreted from ethnographic information, researchers must accept that some will remain beyond their reach.

Summary and Conclusions

The direct ethnographic approach can be an effective path to understanding rock art from the contact era and the centuries preceding European contact. The extent to which interpretations can be carried back in time depends in large part on the cultural stability of the region. Some symbols and practices are geographically widespread and have a very long history, while others are more restricted in time and space. Several caveats should guide researchers' attempts to apply ethnographic data to rock art.

First, focus on what the Indians said, not what the anthropologists say they said. Second, use competent translations of the native accounts, and consider alternative translations of words that may be used metaphorically or have multiple meanings. Third, distinguish between the fluid, religious meaning and the original or historic meaning of the rock art. Because traditionalists believe that rock art changes to convey new messages from the spirit world, researchers should not expect recent interpretations of a glyph to mesh with its original significance or meaning. Fourth, when possible, include "visual" ethnography, such as ledger drawings and portable artworks. The information contained in such items is often very detailed and does not suffer from the problems of bias and poor translation inherent in written ethnography. Fifth, learn the symbols used in a particular culture or in a larger culture region. Every detail of a story or drawing carries meaning.

Lastly, place the rock art in as specific a cultural and historic context as possible. This requires knowledge of the myths, religious beliefs, and material culture of the cultures likely to have made the rock art. In addition, researchers must consider the landscape, site setting, and relation of the site or glyphs to other rock art, as well as reconstructing the spatial and temporal distribution of the rock art style. Although this emphasis on context is standard in history and art history, it has frequently been neglected in archaeological rock art studies. Although some degree of conjecture is inevitable in archaeology, placing one's interpretations in a plausible historic and cultural context will greatly increase their validity. For example, vision questing either at a very secluded location or at a site associated with strong supernatural power was a pattern typical of all northern Plains Indian groups. This allows one to hypothesize that a style of rock art that co-occurs in secluded locations and in prominent places with evidence of repeated use over a period of centuries or millennia is associated with the vision quest. If the images contained in the rock art are similar to historic drawings of visions, then the hypothesis is further supported. Archaeological materials may also aid in identifying the significance of rock art. For example, virtually all the sites in western South Dakota that contain bone awls also contain abraded grooves, alone or with abraded tracks and vulvas. Because the bone awl was the most important item in the historic women's tool kit, the creation of this kind of rock art is hypothesized to taken place during women's vision quests (Sundstrom 2002).

The direct ethnographic approach links images in rock art to the ethnography of people likely to have produced them. In this way, researchers can propose specific interpretations of rock art. Researchers have identified religious symbols and mythological beings in this way and have recognized specific ceremonies and rites shown in rock art. The biographic rock art of the late prehistoric and early contact periods can be interpreted by using conventions and symbols from painted hides and ledger drawings to "read" the events depicted in the rock art. Ethnography can also clarify the significance of a particular site containing rock art. This may, in turn, bear on the meaning of the rock art itself.

To effectively employ the direct ethnographic approach, it is necessary to cull out bias, misconceptions, and mistranslations in the historic documents and to place the information within its original historic and cultural context. Historic Plains Indian speech and art were highly metaphorical, especially when referring to religious concepts. Only by reading between the lines can one begin to understand the ethnographic information and to begin to see patterns within it that illuminate the rock art.

Discussion

James Keyser: One comment on this paper that those of you who aren't familiar with the North Cave Hills wouldn't realize is that the big intaglio of the bison and the calf is visible from the mouth of Ludlow Cave. Linea knows better than I that it's intimately associated with Ludlow Cave, but she didn't mention it. So, it's important to realize that that site and Ludlow Cave are in essence the same place in the world.

Mike Taylor: The grooves are interesting. And I will suggest in my paper tomorrow that one very important thing about the grooves is the by-product—rock powder—that is produced when you make them. Because they wanted to acquire part of the power place. Is there any ethnography to support that on the Plains?

Linea Sundstrom: Not in the Plains that I know of, but I wouldn't be surprised to find it. Because there is—probably across the continent—a lot of use of special kinds of earth or sand. So, for example, when you create an altar, you take the dirt and you kind of clean it through your hand. You pick out every little rootlet, every little worm, so that you've got an area that is neutral—it doesn't have any living thing in it. Well, the rock is sort of a living thing, but maybe that process of scraping it off gives it that same neutral quality. But there's no direct evidence that they were actually collecting the dust. My feeling is that girls and women would go to what I identify as Double Woman sites and make their durable tool kit so that they could get some essence of—some of the power of—that place. Then when you sewed the clothing and made the things for your family, the power transfers into that and is protective for them.

So, in the last paper that I just published about this (Sundstrom 2002), I noted that these tool grooves do not occur with historic era rock art. They stop very abruptly sometime around the time that a lot of trade goods started coming in. I think what happened, is that the hide trade (as a kind of a vicious circle) demanded more and more hides and the women demanded more and more metal tools that didn't have to be sharpened as often. Finally, they are just mass producing these hides. Well of course if you are going to create something and send it down river to the enemy, you don't want it to have power in it. But this tradition [of making tool grooves] falls apart at that time and there are no ethnographic records as to women making their tools that way. This is all something that I've concluded from putting together different pieces of it. I did so much work on the tool grooves because there are so many of them on the plains, yet they tended to be dismissed as merely tool grooves, so nobody considered them to have any particular cultural or religious significance.

Mike Taylor: Were they called tool grooves in the ethnography or by the ethnographers?

Linea Sundstrom: No, it's always been kind of an informal term. But I have one piece of evidence, which illustrates another lesson about rock art research—look everywhere, because evidence comes in many forms. My grandmother was a reporter for one of the newspapers in the Black Hills and she used to do feature stories from time to time. I was burrowing through a box of her old photographs and found one showing a set of tool grooves in the Black Hills which I have not found yet—I think the site is probably gone. But, I turned the photograph over and on the back was written "rock where the Indian squaws made their tools." I don't know who she talked to—who told her that information—but it specifically said that was where the women made their tools.

Jean Auel: Would the introduction of metal needles as opposed to bone needles have had something to do with this?

Linea Sundstrom: Yes, also needles. The awl is the one they talk about most because that was so symbolic, that was the main tool and even today at the powwow the girl wears an awl case to symbolize industriousness. There's no awl inside it, but it really symbolizes the girl's good qualities. It's like a badge, of sorts. But, yes, needles were imported by the millions. Awl tips were also imported. It was really interesting, that after I came up with this idea, I looked for the lists of what was being carried in [by traders]. So, I got this list of trade goods, and it was amazing how many of those things—a gross of awls here, 500 awls there—were brought in early on.

And, there's been one archaeological study of bone tools along the Missouri River that shows that the first bone tool to fade away when metal tools come in is the women's sewing awl. So, there is some archaeological evidence for this process.

Another thing that happens with the trade goods, philosophically speaking, is a change in "power." Originally you've got the awl, it's made out of the leg of an animal; you've got sinew, it's part of the animal. You've got the quills, which either came from porcupines or bird feathers. Sometimes they use a black grass for black edges around the design. What do all these things have in common? They're all living things. And when you made the quill work, you had to soak the quills in your mouth. So the woman was actually putting some of herself— literally her body—into the item because she had saliva from her mouth on the quill. Well, all of a sudden you've got metal needles and awls, glass beads, cotton thread—you know, that connection is lost. I think the materials didn't have to be treated as carefully because they didn't have this sort of living spirit as part of them.

David Whitley: I would support your comment about the need to pay attention to what the native is saying in addition to what the anthropologist says. I think that's important. I know in California, when I summarized the statements by Native Americans, I had 150 years where Indians were saying exactly the same thing. For about 125 years, the archaeologists were just misinterpreting it.

Kelley Hayes-Gilpin: According to the latest theoretical fashion.

David Whitley: Yes, that plays a part.

Linea Sundstrom: While we are discussing archaeologists, I'll add this. The material taken from Ludlow cave—all those things were left there as offerings. Some were taken out by the Custer expedition. And we all know what happened to them two years later.

Jean Auel: Bad luck came to them.

Linea Sundstrom: That's right and that's what the Indians say even today.
 The rest of the collection was taken out by a person who fancied himself an archaeologist but really wasn't, and he just kind of scooped everything up. It's in the state museum, at the state archaeologist's office now. That collection contains more than 300 unused arrowheads, dozens of arrow shafts, strings of beads on sinew, hundreds of dentalium shells, lots of bone and shell beads, and hundreds of feathers, including eagle feathers that have been trimmed to signify a person's status. So that's the assemblage from this site. Want to guess how the excavator interpreted this?

MikeTaylor: As a cache?

Linea Sundstrom: No, as a camp! Now, the Indians that I know are not so stupid as to leave 300 unused arrows behind in their campsite. You could buy a horse for 10 arrows. So, yes, you get in a particular kind of mindset—that was the category they had; caves that had artifacts in them were campsites.
 But now we know that a lot of them were sacred sites and we can recognize this by taking a little more careful look at the assemblage. Of course the ideal would be for the items to still be there. It shouldn't have been disturbed in the first place, but there's nothing we can do about that.

CHAPTER 5
Habitus and Narratives of Rock Art
Robert Layton

Culture Versus Habitus

There are a few cases where an anthropologist has been able to speak directly to the person who engraved or painted a figure on rock (e.g. Turner 1973; Chaloupka 1982:30; Douglas 1987:187-189; Layton 1992:22, 27). Instances where the art then becomes part of a local cultural tradition are equally, if not more interesting for anthropology. This paper will examine the ways in which people who are competent in a cultural tradition construe rock art that was produced by members of earlier generations in that tradition. I will look at four case studies, two from Australia and two from the United States. Examples of discussion, alternative opinions and disagreement are particularly interesting, because they reveal the criteria people use to interpret figures. All four case studies are of communities radically affected by colonization, and the impact of colonization is a major factor in the transmission of traditional culture.

Anthropologists now appreciate that "culture" is not a monolithic collective consciousness in which every member of the community is equally immersed. The French Structuralist Durkheim advocated the concept of the collective consciousness (Durkheim 1915). Bourdieu (1977) objected that structural analysis in the Durkheimian tradition tends to render variation in individual performances as deviations from an unwritten score (culture) that is, in fact, an artificial construct built by the analyst. Bourdieu devised the concept of *habitus* to bridge structure and action. Each individual internalizes what they understand to be the way that meanings and values are organized in their community, and then express that understanding through their own actions. *Habitus* is the individual's reconstruction of rules and tactics deduced from others' actions. Each person's *habitus* can be seen as a structural variant of those learned by other members of the community.

For communication to succeed, each participant must share similar, if not identical, understandings of each other's intended meanings. Artists learn how to read the style and iconography of existing performances and use their knowledge to create new performances within the cultural idiom. These new works are in turn "read" by an audience, whose expectations are shaped by their experiences. Where artist and audience share a similar habitus, readings will be more or less consistent, but we cannot assume this, as a Structuralist would. The degree of consistency of readings needs to be verified and explained through fieldwork.

Bourdieu's most famous example of how the *habitus* of each community member converges with others is the case of the Kabyle (Berber) house. Children grow up associating men with the higher, more prestigious part of the house and therefore come to think of men as superior to women. When, as adults, they build their own houses, they re-embody this perception. Bourdieu (1977:60) also shows that the Berber lineage has a practical unity based on its members' mutual dependence. Since many activities would be impossible without the help of the group, ostracism is a terrible sanction. Hence *habitus* is "constantly reinforced by calls to order from the group, that is. . .the aggregate of individuals endowed with the same dispositions" (Bourdieu 1977:15).

Extrapolating from Bourdieu, it could be said that there are three preconditions for the persistence of a cultural system (a congeries of habituses?):

    It must be mutually intelligible and transmissible
    It must make sense of experience
    It must generate behavior appropriate to the environment

Within these constraints a number of possible worlds can co-exist. The preconditions do not determine the content of a cultural tradition, but they provide points of anchorage for inter-cultural understanding and explanation.

If we consider the commonalities and variation between the habitus of people in a community whom one might want to consult about rock art, it is clear these will vary according to the way knowledge is held and transmitted. The type of shamanism found in the Kalahari and Central Africa, open to any adult, where particular cults spread and replace each other quite frequently (Marshall 1969; Tsuru 1998), is different than shamanism on the NW Coast of North America. On the Northwest Coast, shamans have passed through a second stage of initiation open only to the gifted (e.g. Garfield and Wingert 1966, Jonaitis 1988). In clan totemism each clan holds a unique body of specialist knowledge within the regional tradition known to all adult men and/or women (see Evans et al. 1993 on right to knowledge among the Hopi). Everyday stories about incidents that befell one's parents and grandparents are different again. Related in an anecdotal fashion they capture the light-hearted or traumatic experiences of the recent past (Turner 1973), but are either forgotten within two or three generations, or incorporated into enduring legend. The extent of indigenous information available about rock art will therefore depend on the following factors:

1. The status of the person providing the information in relation to,

2. The particular way in which the art is embedded in a distinctive body of knowledge, and how access to that knowledge is gained.
3. The rules governing how, when and how much of that knowledge can be divulged to an outsider.
4. The empathy, training and theoretical orientation of the person receiving and recording that knowledge.
5. The manner in which the primary ethnographic record is construed when conducting secondary and probably more general analyses.

The four case studies exemplify a range of possible situations.

The Case Studies
Mulvaney: Reminiscences of Mirriuwung and Gadjerong Artists

Mulvaney's case study comes from the Keep River region, in the monsoon zone of northern Australia. His paper (Mulvaney 1996) documents the recollections of elderly Aboriginal people concerning rock art produced between 1920s and 1940s. These people were in their 70s and 80s when Mulvaney interviewed them; one of the youngest was born in 1929, and the paintings were made by members of their parents' generation. The region was colonized by pastoralists in the 1880s, followed by a gold rush in the first decade of the twentieth century. Aboriginal people were repeatedly rounded up to work on the stations; there are many stories of killings, of escapes and recaptures. Some families remained living in the bush until the Second World War, and cattle station workers were paid off, to return to the bush, during the monsoon season. Mulvaney's instructors participated in this way of life, and the paper deals only with paintings attributed to named people who were witnessed painting by Mulvaney's instructors. Paintings that were already in existence when the instructors were children are said by them to be "much earlier." Individuals used recognizable, personal styles and favored particular themes (cf. Hascovec and Sullivan 1989). Garndiwul produced multicoloured, striped anthropomorphs with helmet-shaped heads, no necks and large eyes. His younger brother Larngoorok painted in monochrome, usually white. "The art of Paddy Carlton's father and Peter Newry's father are less distinctive in style, though in a general sense the subjects painted correspond to Dreaming associations of the site or in the local area" (Mulvaney 1996:18). Rock shelters were favored camping places in the wet season. The paper describes paintings in seven shelters.

By the 1960s many Aboriginal people had moved into towns and when Aboriginal stockmen were awarded wage parity with white stockmen, Aboriginal employment fell sharply. During the 1970s, the Federal Government protected communities who were turned off cattle stations through unemployment by providing them with small areas excised from cattle station leases. The people Mulvaney worked with live on an excision from one of the pastoral stations.

Four categories of rock painting were recognised, of which the first is sorcery painting. Paddy Carlton's father produced two sorcery paintings to kill his first wife and the man she had run off with. They were placed high on the shelter wall; the height increased their potency. The choice of site and materials was important but based on restricted knowledge (see Mulvaney 1996:9 and addendum).

The second category consists of ancestral and legendary beings. These are typically large, and placed in shelters associated with the travels of the ancestor in question. Pee Wee Junbun painted several snake figures during one visit to a rock shelter; these are linked to local dreaming figures. Carlton Andy Wurditgarri painted many figures at Kaljapi; the predominant motif is the blackheaded python, the Dreaming associated with this site. Garndiwul painted the Dreaming figure Moorali at Goorungenim shelter. Mulvaney does not state whether Goorungenim lay on Moorali's route, but writes that Moorali is prominent in Gadjerong and Mirriuwung mythology, and traversed the territory of both communities with his wives while pursued by a pack of dingoes. Gandiwul painted Moorali after dreaming of him. Mulvaney explains this can be interpreted in three ways, either a dream in the European sense, a mental visualisation, or a spiritual encounter during a ceremony. After he had been struck by lightning and paralysed for a while, Gandiwul's younger brother Larngoorok painted a figure of the Lightning Man, in the same shelter. I am not certain whether the Lightning Man is a totemic ancestor in the Keep River district, as he is in the region discussed in the second case study, or a trickster being, as he is in Western Arnhem Land (Chaloupka 1993:56-58; Gillespie 1982). The Lightning Man became Larngoorok's personal spirit and he painted him again in another shelter.

Bilunbilum, the "Devil Dog" is certainly a trickster. Garniwul had a personal encounter with this being, but managed to scare him away. Garndiwul painted Bilunbilum at two sites, depicting him as a four-legged, but somewhat human-like, rather hunchbacked and with prominent eyes. In one of these shelters, a more naturalistic red ochre figure of a dog with a white outline was identified as a memorial to a good hunting dog buried nearby. In Goorungenim shelter, Larngoorok also painted a large number of goannas in white. These are smaller and rather crude compared to the anthropomorphs. The goannas were painted to record a very successful hunt; they were cooked and eaten in this rock shelter. Paddy Carlton's father painted a bullock at Kaljapi so people could recount the time when he speared a bullock that ran, wounded, into the gorge before collapsing near the shelter. A painting at Largun of a snake superimposed on a man with upraised arms records a trick played on a sleeping man. He had a dead snake placed on his body and was so frightened when he woke that he jumped into a nearby waterhole known to contain crocodiles.

Mulvaney documents examples of hand stencils, placed by known people as markers of ownership or as a record of their presence, at several sites (this motive for hand stencilling is widespread in Australia: see, for example, Layton 1992:74, 75, 138).

One of the most appealing aspects of Mulvaney's paper is the number of intimate personal insights provided by people who were present as children when the events portrayed took place and were recorded (compare Turner 1973). Mulvaney states that while rock art is framed in the mythico-religious sphere of Aboriginal life, some paintings relate to more mundane events. The paintings are "memory triggers for whole stories, events and remembering people of the past" (Mulvaney 1996:18). Mulvaney seems to have concentrated on the more anecdotal aspects of these memories and concludes: "without the direct information supplied by the artist (or people present when the paintings were done) understanding the original meaning in the painting is uncertain" (Mulvaney 1996:19). Note that Mulvaney did *not* talk to any of the artists. What he was told had already become part of the memories of their children. How much can be transmitted to succeeding generations depends on the context and the idiosyncrasy of the subject. Where the theme of rock art is unique and individual cases of hunting success, little can be said by succeeding generations other than general remarks on traditional hunting techniques and the importance of particular species in the diet (see Layton 1992:124-126, 1995).

Mulvaney provides some information on the kind of contextual clues that help to reduce potential uncertainty. Most importantly, painting was only ever practised within one's own country. Coupled with the tendency to depict ancestral beings at sites on their track, this circumscribes potential interpretation. Ancestral figures appear usually to be larger than other paintings. The painting of Moorali is 329 cm. long, the Lightning Man figures are 300 and 341 cm. high. One of the ancestral Blackheaded Pythons is 270 cm. long. Garndiwul's paintings of Bilunbilum the Devil Dog are, by comparison, 130 and 146 cm. long. The hunting dog's memorial picture is 100 cm. long and the goannas cooked at Goorungenim c. 45 cm. On the other hand, one of the largest paintings measured by Mulvaney is the bullock speared near Kaljapi, at 340 cm.

Merlan and the Interpretative Framework of Wardaman Rock Art

The significance of contextual clues to interpretation is highlighted in the second Australian case study. Willeroo Station lies some 200 miles to the east of the Keep River, closer to the Stuart

Highway and Overland Telegraph line that formed the backbone of pastoral colonization.

Mulvaney cited Macintosh's (1977) argument that one would need to talk to the artist to discover the original meaning of rock art. Merlan objects: "if taken to an extreme, (that) would deny the significant social dimension of the art" (Merlan 1989:22; cf. Layton 2000a). Stylistic analysis, she argues, may allow us to go some way toward recovering, or at least suggesting, some of the constitutive conventions of the iconography, such as the species represented by animal figures and whether the paintings are secular or totemic. But "anything we would want to call the 'meaning' of the art lies in the relationship between images and their understood interpretation or sense within the terms of the *contemporary narrative tradition"* (Merlan 1989:14 [my italics]).

Wardaman territory was also colonized in the 1880s, with the establishment of Willeroo cattle station. Wardaman contact history was one of considerable violence through into the 1930s, although Davidson (1935) recorded that rock shelters were still inhabited during Wet Season when pastoral work was impossible. The rock art site best known to Euro-Australians is the Lightning Brothers site on the neighbouring Delamere Station. The anthropologist Arndt was first told the Lightning Brothers had "left their own shades on the rock". Later his instructor Kulumpit explained that the human artist Emu Jack had dreamed or visualised the design and placed it on the rock after pastoralists prevented Wardaman people from returning to the site to which the Brothers properly belonged (Arndt 1962:169-170, 179). Emu Jack (and possibly other artists) worked on the paintings over a lengthy period from the 1930s to 1950s (sources reviewed in Layton 1992:13, 21-22).

The dislocation of Wardaman people made return visits to some sites impossible for long periods, with the consequence that knowledge is now fragmented. People rely on the style and iconography of the art, their knowledge of the totemic landscape in which the art is placed, and the legends describing the ancestors' travels. Clan totemism is a territorial system, and paintings of totemic ancestors are an assertion of control over the land of the clan estate. Wardaman interpretation of rock art rests fundamentally on the distinction between *buwarraja* (Dreaming) and man-made *bulawula* (drawings) or engravings (Merlan 1989:16). A minority of the man-made figures are attributed to named individuals or categories of people, but the majority are not; and simply attributed to "old people", perhaps before the birth of living people (compare Mulvaney 1996:6).

Merlan found that Dreamings are described as becoming placed in the landscape by "falling." While emphasising such paintings were not man-made, Wardaman say they should be repainted to make them good and colourful. Those who are related to the site by descent from the father are primarily responsible for repainting, but it may be done by others. Merlan's instructors shared certain ideas about how to deduce whether paintings are Dreaming or man-made. Major paintings are generally agreed to be Dreaming, even if the identity of the Dreaming is disputed. At the Lightning Brothers site two legendary Gecko (small lizard) brothers are represented in human form, as large striped figures. A small male figure nearby is said to be their unnamed younger brother, and two small female figures their wives (Merlan 1989:20). Whether or not minor figures are identified as Dreamings seemed, to Merlan, to depend on whether they feature in the verbal narratives. The song cycle describing the fight between the Lightning Brothers mentions that they owned two dogs. There is only one dog painted at the site, but this is identified as one of the dogs of the Dreaming. Paintings of "bush potatoes" (wild yams) on the opposite side of the rock are said to be Dreaming, because they were the brother's food. However some rock abradings around the site are said to be human-made; one woman reminded Merlan they had seen her son make some of them in 1978. Other unspecified paintings at the Lightning Brothers site were said to be human-made, and were not incorporated into the legend. At all sites visited, paintings of subjects from the colonial era such as cowboys and horses were said to be man made, although aspects of colonial history have been incorporated into legend.

  The central part of Merlan's paper describes a disagreement that arose over the interpretation of engravings at sites near Yingalarri (Ingaladdi). Yingalarri has a pair of painted figures in the same style as the Lightning Brothers. A couple of years previously, a senior informant had told Merlan the engraved figures were Lightning Brothers, like those at Delamere. In 1988, when detailed work was undertaken at Yingalarri, all other senior informants said this identification was incorrect. Although stylistically similar to the Delamere figures, "the single informant's identification of the large figures here as Lightning Brothers is viewed by other Wardaman as tantamount to ignoring and collapsing important differences among Wardaman sub-areas" (Merlan 1989:18). As soon as they arrived at the site, one senior man said the figures were *gulirrida* or peewees (*Grallina cyanocleuca,* a black and white bird 25-28 cm. long). The peewee dreaming/ancestral figure is one of the defining features of a clan estate that includes sites in the Yingalarri area, where the peewee motif is common. The site is, however, separated from the other peewee sites by sites belonging to another patriclan, whose principal Dreamings are White Cockatoo, Death Adder and Marsupial Mouse. The engraved figures also look very different from the usual peewee figures in the neighbouring estate, which all have a characteristic headdress, like those worn by Lightning Brothers.

Merlan describes how, in the course of the debate, a woman linked to the intervening estate through her father made a series of remarks to the effect that peewee is not found everywhere (in other words, it is specific to one, or certain clans). A woman who was unable to come on the trip had suggested, based on a general understanding of the location of the site, that the engravings might be Masked Owl. It was eventually agreed that Masked Owl is located at another site, in another patriclan estate. Three senior people then suggested one after another that the engravings were White Cockatoo, linked to the nearest known major site, a waterhole a few miles away, and this was agreed. People repeated several times that the oldest man in the party had actually been to the site years ago, and that the site had long been identified with White Cockatoo.

The little-known site was, in other words, discussed in terms of certain conventions, especially relationship to known dreaming sites nearby and the patriclan affiliation of the surrounding country, which both limit the number of possible interpretations and identify particular people as best authorised to make an assessment. Paintings and engravings are Dreamings if actively linked to contemporary mythological tradition. Large/monumental figures are considered Dreamings, while small scenes of colonial contact or conventional Aboriginal figures are not, although there are no precise rules.

Annie York and Rock Paintings in the Stein River Valley, British Columbia

The Columbia Plateau of North America has a longer history of colonial contact and settlement than northern Australia. Permanent trading posts were constructed by the Hudson Bay and other companies from the 1830s. The discovery of gold on Queen Charlotte Island in 1852 and the Fraser River in 1857 started large-scale colonial settlement (Jonaitis 1991:46). The Stein is a tributary of the Fraser.

'Nlaka'pamux religious knowledge is partitioned in two ways. The majority of young people were sent out into the forest after receiving stories and instructions from their elders. Annie explained: "They go up there [in the mountains], and they sleep, and this dream tells them. Then he writes his dream on the rock. That's left there forever" (York et al. 1993:xv, brackets in original). Few were selected to undergo the further training to become a shaman, which took four years, but both men and women could become shamans. Each family had its own body of knowledge handed on during the higher levels of training, providing a second way of partitioning access. The protection of this exclusive body of knowledge remains an aspect of ranking in the region, and becomes more formal as one approaches the coast, where clan totemism co-exists with shamanism. Daly writes that "the families of gifted hunters, warriors, shamans, weavers, carvers and dancers tended to elaborate the training of their descendants, and maintain the most complete tellings of the ancient narratives and teachings" (York et al. 1993:227).

Annie (Zex'tko) was born in 1904 and learned the traditional stories of the 'Nlaka'pamux as a child. Being of mixed descent, she was not sent away to boarding school to have her native culture eradicated. As a young girl, Annie had a dream about one of her older relatives, correctly divining that he had lost his rifle on a hunting expedition. After that, older people took a special interest in her training. She had other spiritual experiences later. She was encouraged to embark on her own dream quest and was trained by older relatives and other elders. Annie describes her own initiation in the mountains, "When I went to sleep it sounded like if I had lots of friends talking to me" (York et al. 1993:240-241).

In the early twentieth century James Teit interviewed native people in British Columbia, including two 'Nlaka'pamux elders, about rock art (Teit 1918[1]). Some artists were still alive at that time (Teit 1918:4). Teit recorded several motives for rock painting. He learned that "At the expiration of the training (or sometimes also during the same if they had any vision or experience considered extraordinary or especially important) the novice painted pictures on cliffs or boulders…. By writing these things on the rocks the novice hoped to facilitate the acquisition of power and make it stronger and more permanent: people usually made their paintings in secret and alone" (Teit 1918:1-2). Teit also recorded other reasons for painting. Paintings were occasionally made to ward off disaster foreseen in a dream. Paintings of guardian spirits were painted near camps or overlooking walking routes, to deflect enemies or evil. Some paintings were historical records, for example, at sites of battles. The largest and oldest paintings were "pictures made and shown by the mysteries, or powers, or spirits of the places where they are to be seen" (Teit 1918:4).

Teit's information is corroborated by what we were told of paintings on the Columbia River in September 2002. We visited Miller Island with Viola (Atumani) Kalama and Táxli Winch. Viola said the following about painted rock shelters (this is a paraphrase based on the notes I made at the time): Might be places where people came for a spiritual experience; they weren't painting for fun. Seeking their helper. Sometimes they stayed for days. If they didn't find anything the people down in the village might send them to another place. When they came here they might make a painting themselves, a painting of the animal that was going to help them through their lives. The spiritual people that were already in the village would send them up. They painted what they were directed to by their spirit helper. He (the young man) would come back to renew his strength. Táxli Winch amplified: a vision quest; seeking out their future. Later in the day, Willie Selam explained, each child has his own time line, his own creative power. Willie said: "when a child is ready, there's people to see. They gather their momentum and when they're ready they send them out into the mountain. Some people take a lot of years to figure out their purpose in life, others find it right away.... You have to go on your own. If there's two of you, you get talking." Philip Cash Cash's paper (see chapter 6, this volume) and recent work at Butte Creek (Keyser et al 1998:63-75) corroborate Teit's statement that some other paintings were records of historical events.

Annie never visited the Stein River paintings herself; they lie some 50 miles up-river from her home town of Spuzzum. Instead, she worked with detailed drawings made by Chris Arnett. Working with drawings is not ideal, but it has been done before, by Elkin in eastern Australia using questionable material and, more productively by Bleek in South Africa (Elkin 1949; Lewis-Williams 1981:32-34). A number of themes run through Annie's explanations. Paintings of animals and people prompt her to relate legends: the story of beaver, of the raven and bear, the boy who went up to the moon, and so forth. Zigzags and short strokes are measures of time. Animal tracks, particularly bear tracks, appear in a number of sites. Many compositions are interpreted as dreams of hunting success; sometimes the desires of individuals slide into records of the World's creation. Of one panel, Annie says "that's an animal. A deer. The man dreamed the deer. It's his hunting dream. It's also God's messenger, giving humans the ways of hunting. . . .That means that in his dream the first hunter woulda liked to have something to kill the deer with" (York et al. 1993:70-71; compare 136). Of another painting, she comments: "In his dream, the man sees God's messenger drawing the bow and arrow for him" (York et al. 1993:75). A number of panels contain artifacts such as snares and traps, baskets and a smoke house.

It is not clear whether hunting dreams are the dreams of shamans, or ordinary (initiated) adults. However, Annie interprets a torso with outstretched arms, three curved lines from top of head and square object at one hand (Figure 1) as a shaman healing. "He's got a head-dress and his cup or bowl." Daly compares the panel to picture of a headdressed shaman painted on a shaman's hat that was documented by Boas. The similarity is notable. Annie's

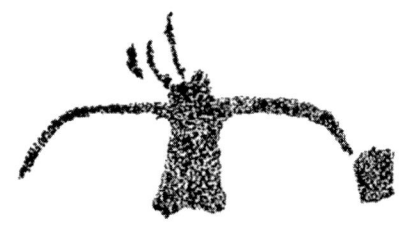

Figure 1. Pictograph at EbRk b, identified by Annie York as a type of shaman carrying a cup or bowl for healing. Adapted from York et al 1993:171.

grandfather let her watch a woman shaman once. She had a thing in her hand that she said was "this spiritual life thing, her friend." She put it in a bowl of water and sprayed the water over the sick man (York et al. 1993:171). Two panels are apparently identified as records of the adolescent spirit quest. Of one (Figure 2), she says: "down below the man is his sweathouse. . . .You can even see the tie in the middle there. . . .This is the first tipi the young man is going to sleep in. . . .In his dream he walked toward it and as he walked he learned more things about it" (York et al. 1993:79). Of another, "After a while he gets hungry in his dream. The little animal in his dream tells him, 'Now you can eat.' He has nothing to eat, so he shoots a squirrel or something – a bird. . . .But that little animal, when he eats it that time, that becomes part of his power" (York et al. 1993:77).

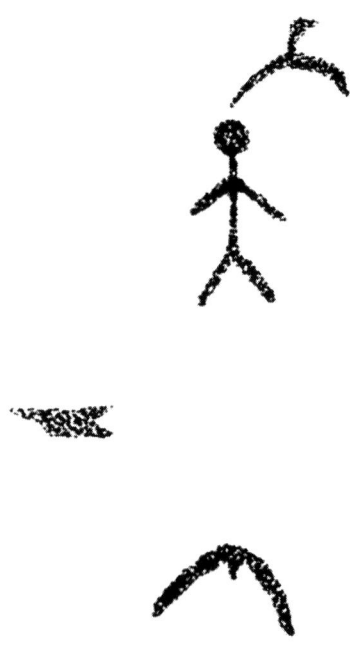

Figure 2. Vision quest pictograph at EbRj62. Adapted from York et al 1993:78

Unlike the people with whom Mulvaney and Merlan worked, Annie provided her readings of rock art on her own, without the opportunity for discussion and reflection with peers. In a few cases, discussion between Annie and Richard Daly is recorded. When she interprets a triangle with five short lines attached to the top edge as a snare rather than a bear footprint, Daly asks "what's the difference between the pit snare and the bear paw?" Annie replies, "the bear paw has a heel. When it's footprints it's more than one usually" (York et al. 1993:98). Daly is able to compare Annie's interpretations of some sites with two records obtained in the late nineteenth century by Harlan Smith and Teit. Harlan Smith was a member of the American Museum of Natural History's Jesup North Pacific Expedition, which was led by Boas. Teit owned a ranch near Spences Bridge, only 20 miles from the confluence of the Stein and Fraser rivers, where he lived with his native wife Lucy Artko (Jonaitis 1991:160). Teit was responsible for outfitting the Jessup Expedition team (Jonaitis 1991:161). Boas, and others who worked with him on the Northwest Coast, did not consider Harlan Smith an able fieldworker (Jonaitis 1991:193-197). Teit, on the other hand, was highly respected by Boas. Boas inspired him to start collecting ethnographic data. In Jonaitis's assessment, "Teit's writings on Indian culture were scientifically accurate, thorough, and extremely informative" (Jonaitis 1991:190).

Harlan Smith was shown the rock shelter at Nzikzak'wxn by his 'Nlaka'pamux guide, who said it was a place where boys and girls went to fast during the puberty rituals. The guide "Jimmy" showed Smith a painting of deer or mountain goats connected by two lines to a three metre vertical line marked by short diagonal dashes. He explained that the line represented a trail over the hill where the animal goes (York et al. 1993:81). Teit showed two of Smith's drawings of this site to his 'Nlaka'pamux instructors who told him a large bulbous human figure with antlers represented a vision. The pair of horizontal lines behind the figures were trails, and the two circles connected by a single line were lakes connected by a river. The game animals were mountain goats (York et al. 1993:82).

Annie construed the two circles joined by a line as a snare, with a mountain goat standing below it. The small animals at lower right corner are a doe, a buck and a fawn. The line running off above the buck [Harlan Smith's trail over the hill] is the stick to cook it with. The bulbous figure with horns is "a man, yet he has a deer horn on his head. He's a deer in the time of that legend life…. In the beginning he just walks like a human being. Some people don't eat deer meat on a Friday because he used to be a man. Walked upright" (York et al. 1993:91).

Harlan Smith was told that Ts'ets'ékw, a second site, is a place where girls washed with fir branches during their puberty ceremonies. His instructor identified bear and bear-cub tracks, and a figure that represented a rattle. There is a natural ochre stain which Smith thought was a painting, so included it in his drawing. Teit also showed this drawing to his instructors. They also interpreted the circles and triangular tracks as the tracks of bear and bear cubs. The two circles joined by a bar which Smith's instructor thought was a rattle were identified as lakes connected by a river. The four curving lines falling from the line of natural iron oxide were said to represent a cascade. Smith thought a "frontal" human figure represented a woman, but Teit's instructors interpreted it as "a vision" (York et al. 1993:95).

Annie had difficulty with the "frontal" human figure at Ts'ets'ékw. At first she identified it as the man who was turned into the sun. The circle between its legs showed there will be a difference between man and woman. Later she identified it as a beaver (the circle becomes its tail), and told the legend of beaver. Annie recognised three types of footprint. The rounded ones are black bear, above is a grizzly print, on the left a brown bear. She construed the four curving lines below the natural stain as a sweathouse; the adjacent circles show the shaman in the sweathouse waited three days (York et al. 1993:105-108).

Compared with Mulvaney and Merlan's instructors, Annie has several disadvantages. At least one shamanic site was different to those used by initiates (York et al. 1993:114, see also 216) but Annie is unlikely to have been sufficiently familiar with the geography of the valley to have known which sites were which. While expertly competent in 'Nlaka'pamux culture, Annie does not have personal knowledge of the artists, nor are paintings of the legendary themes geographically partitioned as they are in a system of clan totemism. Daly concludes Annie's readings and those obtained by Teit and Harlan Smith are equally plausible. Everyone was familiar with trail talk and sign language, recording of historical events (and marking time), but only the individual dreamer would know of their specific revelation. The dreams of one initiate, or seasoned healer or hunter, are unique and cannot be conveyed in their entirety to others (especially, as Teit [1918:4] points out, the painter was alone at the time). Daly argues that the most informed readers, shamans, would understand a painting in terms of the general theme or story portrayed. All adults shared a common foraging tradition, regional culture and artistic tradition. The gestural sign language, iconography of artifacts, and exposure to psychic training would have enabled the art to be read "in a meaningful way" (York et al. 1993:230). However, "in such a system… no two readers will arrive at exactly the same interpretation of the writings, even though the general theme and iconography may be known to both" (York et al. 1993:229). Teit gives two hypothetical but illuminating examples of what the artist might depict, and how much others might be able to infer (Teit 1918:3).

Stoffle et al.: Paiute Paintings at Kanab Creek

The paper by Stoffle et al. (2000) is an exemplary example of joint authorship between native experts and academics of European descent. It is admirable for the space it gives to alternative ideas (as, for example, on the durability of oral tradition). It nonetheless raises the issue of where native explanation ends and academic inference takes over, making it appropriate as the final case study before the paper concludes with some general points.

The paper discusses a Southern Paiute rock art site in Kanab Creek, which gives onto the outer edge of the Grand Canyon. The crucial panel consists of white paintings of humans, geometric shapes and a horse. In 1976 a number of Paiute stated that the panel was associated with a Ghost Dance ceremony. Four Southern Paiute elders contributed to the Stoffle et al. (2000) paper. All four believed the panel was made by Paiutes. One commented, "It was all white [paint] for a reason. When they used red paint, they used it for special reasons also" (Stoffle et al.

2000:21 [my brackets]). One woman said she had visited the panel as a child, with her parents, but they had not told her its meaning, just given her lessons about life in general. The elders associated the site with an adjacent source of white pigment, and with Indian residence across and up the canyon. They identified the art as a record of event and things seen, a part of history, a record of traditional beliefs. One said it was "an overwhelming experience to see these are still here… and touch the white paint source" (Stoffle et al. 2000:20). The panel includes at least one headless human figure and one of the elders said "the headless people are about Paiutes that were killed by white people" (Stoffle et al. 2000:20). Stoffle (personal communication) notes that native instructors in the southwest of the U.S. prefer to read the cultural landscape in which rock art sites are situated in order to place them in context, rather than answer questions about the "meaning" of the art itself. He reminds me that the paper (Stoffle et al. 2000) is jointly authored, and that the several authors sometimes reached different conclusions. Stoffle also points out that there are many reasons why instructors may not wish to divulge the significance of particular paintings. The questioner may not, for example, be entitled to know, or the instructor may fear that the information will become public knowledge through publication, and fall into the hands of people untrained to use it safely.

Stoffle et al. (2000) state that Southern Paiute participation in the Ghost Dance is recorded largely in oral traditions told to Kroeber and his students in 1929, supported by newspaper reports published at the time of the Ghost Dance in 1889. The paper elucidates the Kanab Creek paintings further by drawing on these records. At the right hand end of the panel is a white-painted figure made up of two concentric circles, with a line running away from the outer edge. A Hualapai elder interviewed by Kroeber told him that in the Ghost Dance, people danced around a pole with a spiral painted on it. Some of the human figures have double vertical lines on their arms, legs and bodies, suggesting clothing. A late nineteenth century observer recorded that white clothing was worn at the Ghost Dance. The paper also draws on wider contemporary Paiute traditions. On the ceiling, immediately about the principle row of figures, are humans with their arms and legs stretched out at right angles to their bodies. These are very similar to those on the ceiling of a shelter at a site called Whitmore Wash, which two knowledgeable Southern Paiute identified as a Ghost Dance site. Many Paiute believe rocks are alive and powerful, therefore none would mark a rock casually. To mark a rock is also the place a human desire upon it. Pigment sources also treated cautiously because of their power. Painting or pecking may be done for good or evil reasons.

The paper concludes that it is uncertain whether the paintings at Kanab Creek depict a Ghost Dance held there, or elsewhere, and whether they were painted as a reminder, or public validation of supernatural journeys undertaken by participants, or as a mnemonic device for shamans learning the dance (Stoffle et al. 2000:23). When Southern Paiute visit the site they offer prayers and tobacco in a traditional manner, and teach their children, transforming and further empowering the already sacred place, and empowering themselves by reaffirming their identity. Stoffle and the other authors then present some further interpretations derived from the existing literature on rock art and shamanism, which I return to in the final section of this paper.

Is Art a Visual Language?

The authors of all four case studies discuss the messages communicated by the art itself, and the extent to which the art depends on collateral information in the indigenous oral tradition. In itself, all of this rock art is highly ambiguous. To the informed viewer, there are some clues that help to reduce ambiguity in the art: iconography, size and style, location in the landscape and materials used. In all four case studies, however, verbal narratives (stories) are important. They provide a parallel discourse that further removes ambiguity.

To what extent, if at all, can rock art therefore be treated as a medium of communication? In his posthumous book *Art and Agency* Alfred Gell argues provocatively against art as visual communication. He asserts that nothing except language itself has "meaning" (Gell 1998:6). The need for verbal exegesis partly supports Gell's argument that art is not like language. Mulvaney's comment that paintings are memory triggers for stories applies equally to the Stein River, but although Annie uses personal anecdotes to elucidate her interpretations, much is based on her reasonable assumption that she and the makers of the paintings share a body of knowledge about legendary beings. Daly treats Stein River art as a proto-language which is "read" by those literate enough to appreciate it, but Schmidt's objection (quoted by Daly) seems valid. Schmidt argued "I think it is more useful to see your rock 'writings' as rock 'art' with a specific set of literary functions: to act as a prompt for oral performance, interpretation or creation" (York et al. 1993:225). Merlan writes that the dependence of Wardaman art on spoken tradition probably existed from the moment the art was created. What we call meaning lies in the relationship between figures and the narrative frame (Merlan 1989:21). To take another example, Klassen (1998) argues that the structure of rock art of Writing-On-Stone, Alberta, changed from an assemblage of "iconic," unrelated figures depicting the spirits and beings encountered in dreams, to "narrative" compositions paralleling the development of ledger art during the period of conflict on the colonial border. This case suggests the structure of rock art may depend on the type of verbal discourse with which it is associated.

Far from dismissing the idea that art is devoid of impact on the viewer (the "patient"), however, Gell argues art directly transports the artist's agency. Paintings and engravings look like what they stand for; the materials with which art is constructed are (according to traditional, non-Western communities) intrinsically powerful. Gell's explicit aim is to understand how art works in terms of the worldview or theory of being of non-Western peoples. This leads him (unfortunately, in my view) to revive Frazer's theory of magic. The power of the icon is exemplified through what Frazer called homeopathic magic. Homeopathic magic aims to destroy an enemy by destroying an image of him (Frazer 1994:29). The power of the index (for example the pigment, or wood used in carving) is exemplified by contagious magic. Contagious magic works on fragments a person gives off, such as hair or nail clippings (Frazer 1994:37). This theory may convey why people attribute power to art, or to the sites where art is placed. (See for example, Mulvaney 1996:9 on the selection of site and materials for sorcery painting, or Stoffle et al. 2000:22 on the power of place in Paiute country.)

Gell is right to argue that icon and index are less arbitrary than language. Annie York's readings depend on construing the Stein Valley paintings as iconic, and thus keying them into her considerable body of traditional knowledge. Nonetheless, the need to be familiar with local cultural codes to interpret rock art greatly weakens Gell's theory that art has an intrinsic power of agency. Gell in fact gives a number of examples that show an art object must be interpreted according to the appropriate cultural discourse. He criticises, for example, western misunderstandings of West African nail fetishes (Gell 1998:59).

Two Lessons for Shamanic Readings of Art
The Art Isn't Necessarily All Shamanic

The Australian case studies show that not all north Australian rock art is totemic, and that indigenous people rely on cues such as subject, size and style to discriminate between secular and totemic art. Even in regions where rock art is demonstrably associated with shamanism, not all rock art is shamanic. Can native instructors tell us about similar cues? Hill-Tout began fieldwork on the Stein River in 1895. His chief instructor was a chief of the 'Nlaka'pamux. Hill-Tout reported that the Stein River paintings had been "made in the past by noted shamans" (quoted in York et al.1993:13). However, in a letter written in 1925, he wrote "we know that Indian boys and girls undergoing their solitary preparation for the acquisition of a guardian spirit or personal totem often recorded their dreams on rock faces" (York et al. 1993:14). The much better informed Teit identified five contexts for rock painting in British Columbia. Teit also records that pits were hollowed out by boys during initiation, using a stone adze, while seeking strength in their arms (York et al. 1993:216).

Both Lewis and Hultkrantz define the shaman as a ritual expert, and this accords with the role of shaman in North America.[2]

> "a shaman is a person of either sex who has mastered spirits and who can at will introduce them into his own body. . . .by his power over the spirits which he incarnates the shaman is able to treat and control afflictions caused by pathogenic spirits in others" (Lewis 1971:51).

> "the shaman [is] a social functionary who attains ecstasy with the help of guardian or helping spirits, and who through his ecstasy creates a rapport with the supernatural world—all this on behalf of members of his group" (Hultkrantz 1989:46).

It may seem trivial to insist that the initiation of children is not shamanism. But while guides showed early researchers two rock art sites in the Stein Valley where young people trained, they did not show them the largest rock art site in the valley, nearby, which oral tradition today says was "associated with the activities of Indian doctors" (York et al. 1993:114). The distinction was evidently important to them. It takes four years to train to become a shaman in the area of the Stein Valley.

Chinook elders made it clear that the art of adolescents on the spirit quest must be distinguished from the art of shamans on the Columbia River (see also Loubser, this volume). Táxli Winch said medicine people had different sites to those young people going on the vision quest. James Selam told us tahmanawis is the word for spirit helper in Chinook jargon. The tahmanawis is given to a person when he's young and he carries it with him. He uses it to heal people. Only he knows where it is, no one else is allowed to see it, because if another doctor found it, he could destroy it. Willie Selam, James's son, added: a person of power would place his mark in a certain place and that would take care of his power; that's a personal thing and it's not generally discussed in public.

The issue has also been raised in recent debate about rock art in Southern California. Whitley points out that there are two rock art traditions in Southern (coastal) California: art associated with the initiation of all adolescents, and the art of specialist shamans (Whitley 1992:94-95). Quinlan notes that the most detailed ethnographic accounts of rock art in Southern California describe its use in Luiseño and Cupeño girls' initiation rituals. He argues the figures portrayed in rock and sand paintings were the supernatural agencies who punished social transgression, such as the rattlesnake, rather than spirit familiars (Quinlan 2000:97). Whitley, however, argues that Luiseño and Cupeño girls' initiation is fundamentally shamanistic, since it involved attaining an altered state of consciousness (Whitley 1992:94, Whitley 2001:110).

The Ghost Dance is not a form of shamanism in the sense defined by Lewis and Hultkrantz. While created by shamans, it was a millennial resistance movement that La Barre compares with Melanesian Cargo Cults and movements in other parts of the world prompted by colonial dispossession. The first Ghost dance was brought by a Paiute called Tävibo who had many visions (La Barre 1972:227). Tävibo was succeeded by Wovoka, who had a vision in which God taught him the second Ghost Dance, which would speed the reunion of the living and the dead (La Barre 1972:229). He was also given five songs through which he controlled the weather. Stoffle et al. (2000:13) comment that the Ghost Dance is best understood as a response by Indian people to the stresses of Euro-American encroachment. Stoffle (personal communication) states that the headless figures are symbolic of death and generally believed his instructors to be Indian people who were killed by whites. He confirms that the Kanab Creek panel is consistently associated with the Ghost Dance, although pointing out there are many other paintings at the same site. He comments that while the Ghost Dance was in some ways unusual, it grew out of indigenous rituals associated with shamanism.

Any comparative theory of shamanism seeking to define the distinctive attributes of shamanistic rock art will need to discriminate between the defining traits of shamanism and other practices which may be taken up within its intellectual umbrella. Discovering the criteria that native people use to discriminate between shamanic and other rock art will be a helpful step in this direction.

During the first half of the nineteenth century, the French sociologist Comte argued that humankind's intellectual development could be divided into three stages: from magic to religion, to science. Magical thought imputed a direct link between sticking a pin in a wax model and the bodily pains suffered by the victim, whereas religion acknowledged the intervention of non-human agencies. This theory of non-Western thought entered anthropology and archaeology through the work of Frazer and Levy-Bruhl. Frazer considered Australian Aboriginal increase rites (striking a stone to increase numbers of a totemic species) a form of magic because, seemingly followed by Gell, he failed to realise increase rites are framed within a totemic theory of being. Keyser has argued that the art of hunting magic could be distinguished from shamanic art on the Columbia Plateau (see Hann et al. 2004:11-14). While Annie York's interpretations leave it unclear whether the hunters who dream of their desired prey are ordinary (albeit initiated) adults or shamans, it is not magic in Frazer's sense, because it *is* mediated by a theory of being. Australian sorcery may harness the power of totemic beings (Mulvaney 1996:9, and see Layton 1992:84-86 on sorcery in the Kimberleys) but it does so in an anti-social manner and usually in a distinctive style of art. Securing successful hunting, on the other hand, can be an intrinsic part of the shaman's role (see Reichel-Dolmatoff 1967 on the Tukano; Ray 1967; and Seidelman and Turner 1994 on Inuit). Is hunting "magic" therefore less likely to be visually distinguishable as a category of art in a shamanic tradition, than sorcery painting in a totemic tradition?

Not Much Sign of Entoptics

One aspect of the growing literature on shamanic rock art that concerns me is the tendency for an aspect of art well-attested in one part of the world to be incorporated into a global model which is then used to interpret art elsewhere. The Western United States have, I believe, contributed the notion of rock art sites as centres of power to the comparative study of shamanism (e.g. Whitley 1992). Clottes and Lewis-Williams (1996:33) list the concept of rock shelters as entrances to the other world, as one of the characteristics of shamanism. Both York et al. (1993) and Stoffle et al. (2000) include a section arguing that entoptic forms can be identified in their rock art. The ethnographic evidence that art depicting trance states incorporates simple geometric forms experienced cross-culturally comes from Reichel-Dolmatoff's work with the Tukano of Colombia (Reichel-Dolmatoff 1978). Demonstrated on portable art, it can be extended, by inference, to the region's rock art (Reichel-Dolmatoff 1967).[3]

Stoffle et al. (2000:21) suggest the "spiral" at the right hand end of the Kanab Creek panel can be linked to the spiral on the centre pole used in the Ghost Dance, "presumably a representation of the route used to enter a trance". In his work on Southern African shamanism Lewis-Williams' interpreted paintings of "flying buck" in the Drakensberg through the ethnography of other San communities who describe a sense of flying while in trance (Lewis-Williams 1981:95-100). Apparently drawing on this parallel, Stoffle et al. (2000:22) suggest the figures on the ceiling at Kanab Creek, with arms and legs outstretched, are flying. "Flying figures are often the vehicle used by shamans to explore other worlds." Lewis-Williams showed how the explanations of Qing, the Maluti survivor in the Drakensberg itself, could be construed as references to "death" as trance (Lewis-Williams 1981:81). Stoffle et al. note several figures at Kanab Creek are headless, suggesting a possible representation of "death" associated with trance. This interpretation contradicts the Paiute elder's statement that "the headless people are about Paiutes that were killed by White people". Stoffle has generously drawn my attention to the comments of NcNeil (2001) and Patterson (2001), who question whether shamanic dancing was part of the

Southern Paiute Ghost Dance. Both query whether the geometric shapes are appropriately construed as entoptics. Patterson, citing local ethnography, suggests the headless figures are probably dead people.

Daly draws on the influential paper by Lewis-Williams and Dowson (1988) to argue for the presence of entoptic forms in the rock art of the Stein Valley: rows of parallel strokes, circles, zigzags, catenary curves and undulating lines (York et al. 1993:232-240). In almost every case, Annie construed these shapes as iconic. Two vertical zigzags are lightning; a little quasi-human figure adjacent is "running away from the bad weather" (York et al. 1993:117, for another example, see 154). Another pair of zigzags show the number of days of a man's dream (York et al. 1993:102). Rows of parallel strokes are also measures of time. Strokes record number of days a person spent fasting in the mountains (York et al. 1993:73). Three parallel lines mark the three days it took to create the earth (York et al. 1993:132). Nine parallel lines show how long the shaman spent fasting in the mountains (York et al. 1993:156). Every family used to keep a length of knotted string to record the passage of the days, with a special knot for Sunday (York et al. 1993:118). Circles depict a hailstorm; four curving lines represent the frame of a sweat lodge (York et al. 1993:108). Lest readers take the easy way out and infer that Annie's readings correspond to the "third stage" of trance when all these shapes are said to be re-envisioned as iconic, Annie has something very interesting to say about the single or double chevrons

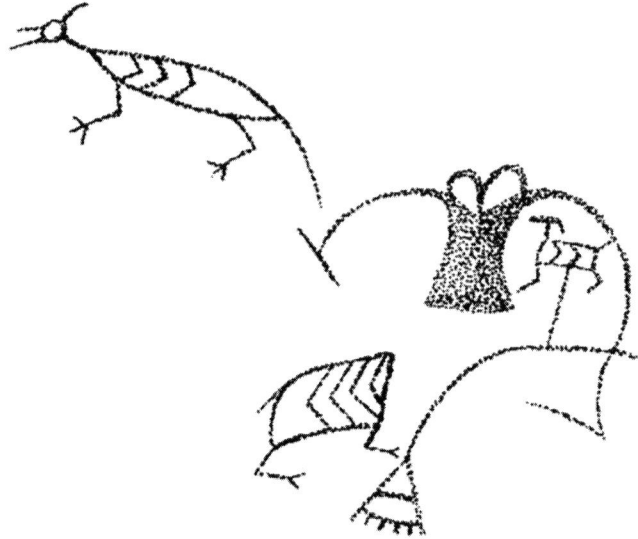

Figure 3. Chevrons on the bodies of these animals, painted at EbRk2, may be derived from entoptic imagery. Adapted from York et al 1993:153.

that often appear on paintings of game animals (Figure 3). "When they were created they had different colours and stripes. The stripes show that it was coloured. Different markings from now" (York et al. 1993:111). Later, she says chevrons on the bodies of two goats "show the markings the goats used to have a long time ago. Women who wove the goat blankets went up in the mountains and dreamed the old life of goats and they wrote their dream in their blanket" (York et al. 1993:152). If one were inclined to interpret that as a vision of entoptic forms, then one would have to give equal credit to Annie's explanation of another panel: "The long line is all about crossing a swamp. The four vees or sergeant stripes show the way to go" (York et al. 1993:204). We can't put our native instructors in the witness box when they say what we want to hear, yet overrule them when they don't. Rather than construct a kind of generic shamanic "shopping list" we must be as sensitive to variability as to common themes if we are to appreciate the rich ethnographic data on rock art provided by native instructors in Australia and North America. We need to appreciate the circumstances that contribute to what people know and are allowed to say about rock art in order to value the information they have given us.

---

[1] Further information recorded elsewhere by Teit is republished in York et al. 1993:241 and 264-265.

[2] Clottes and Lewis-Williams use a broader definition of the shaman: "those who, in hunter-gatherer cultures, practice particular rites. They pass into an altered state of consciousness to achieve a multiplicity of goals, such as treating illness, predicting the future, meeting animal spirits, modifying the weather or controlling real animals by supernatural means" (Clottes and Lewis-Williams 1996:19).

[3] Philip Cash Cash commented at this point in the presentation of my paper that entoptics or geometric shapes would be a distraction to the healer's clear vision. Willie Selam also noted the purity of vision. He said: you see in your mind's eye the power in everything, even in a blade of grass. That's why people become singers. The world is too beautiful for even our language to describe.

Discussion

Jannie Loubser: Was Mulvaney a trained ethnographer?

Robert Layton: Yes, he studied anthropology and archaeology, he is a trained ethnographer.

Jannie Loubser: So, the statements he made about the person with the snake swallowing it—that was a literal event?

Robert Layton: Yes, that befell an older man, and the aboriginal people who took Mulvaney to the rock shelter witnessed that as children. And they saw the painting being made, so there is no doubt in those cases.

James Keyser: One thing about Annie York's work, and I've read it very carefully and closely……

Robert Layton: Yes, there's a lot in there.

James Keyser: Well, her work is a little bit like the encyclopedia—it goes from A to Z. You can get about anything you want if you look at only some specific, individual things. And consistency was not Annie's strong suit when she described those images. I guess the comment that I would make is that I agree with you, Bob. I've always felt a little uneasy about those who say "oh yes, we believe this Indian who says this, but we don't believe him when he says something else, or we don't believe this other one who says something else." But we need to look carefully at how these ethnographic sources are reported and quoted. I get the feeling that sometimes Annie York was filling in some gaps for the people who were recording her. And I suspect that there was some pressure on her—probably unintentional pressure—to say something because she was the "expert." I also noticed that in a couple of places her reported words were diametrically opposed. She discusses almost the same image in three or four places, and she identifies the primary figure as a dreamer of hunting power—and in several places she identifies animals associated with him as caught in a snare or corral. But in one place she is quoted (from the taped conversation) as saying "the deer and [mountain] goat are *not* in a snare. That's the way you write it. It shows he has caught them in his mind."(York et al 1993:160-161, emphasis ours) When I first read that, I thought it was an example where she was saying one thing for one image and a different thing for another painting that is almost exactly the same.

But when you read her whole quote and you fully understand it, you realize that the transcriptionist misheard "*caught* in a net" and wrote "*not* in a net." Annie was consistent in this case, the transcriptionist made an error. So with any ethnographic reference, and especially with Annie York, you really must read beyond just the little statement and understand the greater whole.

David Whitley: Yes, that's one thing, and you must also check your translations.

Robert Layton: Yes, I think that's right. And I should point out that Annie York was working under severe constraints. It's not an ideal situation, and she's doing her best. If she's working with pictures, she's not at the site. And she doesn't have the option of going to ask other members of her culture: You know—"What do you think? Let's discuss this and agree on what's the most likely interpretation."

James Keyser: But it *is* an incredibly rich source of information. And I think one of the most important things about that work—and we are getting some similar things here at this meeting—is that what Annie York is saying can be duplicated by what James Teit's informants said 100 years before almost to the year—that's cultural continuity.

Robert Layton Yes, exactly.

David Whitley: And remember, Teit's informants were elders when he interviewed them.

James Keyser: And, we heard very similar things yesterday. Viola [Kalama—a Wasco elder who attended the entire symposium] told us some things that fit exactly with what people on the Columbia Plateau have been saying about this art for more than a century.

David Whitley: Let me make a comment about entoptics on the plateau in general. If you look more widely, there are in fact a whole series of clear references to what you would interpret as statements that an entoptic was occurring during the vision. It starts out as a flash of light and then becomes something else. So it's there.

Robert Layton: Yes, I'm not disputing it's there. I think that her [Annie York's] comments about the chevron are that (see Figure 3 in Layton's paper). But, what I'm disputing is that we can therefore infer that all geometric shapes are entoptics. What would be nice to be able to work towards would be an understanding of the criteria by which native people make one interpretation or the other.

Jean Clottes: That's a big problem.

Robert Layton: Yes, and we need to be aware that it's a problem.

Jean Clottes: Yes, because there have been lots of neuropsychological studies on altered states of consciousness and entoptics. People do see entoptics, not only during the first stage of trance, as has been said, but also during the later stages of trance. When people talk of the three stages of trance, that is an idealized model. I have talked to quite a number of psychologists, and they say "well I have seen maybe three thousand people in my practice and none of them goes exactly through these three stages." Of course not. Some of them will stay in the first stage, others in the second, others straight to the third and most of them will never go through all three stages. But, one thing that they say is that they see those entoptics and in the third stage of trance generally those mental images—dots, zigzags, whatever—are there. But they are in the background, they are not as prominent as the images of levitating or other things are. But the entoptics are still there. So the problem is, do the people—let's say the shamans—who experience a lot of those visions, do they pay much attention or not to those entoptics. Do they fill them with meaning or not. That is a cultural choice and it's my opinion that it is absolutely impossible to say why they make one decision or another. For example, one group might give a lot of importance to them, because for them it's the Milky Way or the spirit of the shaman. In other cases, people will not pay any attention. It's a cultural decision that may vary widely from one culture to another, from one group to the next.

Phillip Cash Cash: Entoptics is a very specialized word, and some of our guests may not be familiar with it. Could we give an explanation of what entoptics are so that all of us can better understand?

Robert Layton: Yes, of course. It's little light flashes, zigzags, spirals, that people see in their mind's eye when they are in an altered state of consciousness.

Jean Auel: Or what people see when they have migraine headaches.

Robert Layton: Yes, indeed, and the question is, are these characteristic of rock art traditions which relate to trance experiences—to visions? But all I want to say, and I take Jean's (Clottes) point, is that I'm persuaded that tally marks and other simple geometrics are a characteristic of native rock art in North America, and they appear in many Stein River sites. Annie doesn't identify these as entoptic phenomena, and therefore I think there can be alternative meanings or explanations for such simple geometric shapes. We just have to be on our guard in how we construe them.

Jannie Loubser: The flipside of that, I think, is in Africa, among the Bantu-speaking agriculturists where a lot of ethnographies have been done. For instance among the Venda where we get rings and zigzags on the Venda chief's gates and doors. Those things are carved as a result of the chief diviner's dreams and visions. And those are all being interpreted by what the informants tell the anthropologist they mean. For instance, the concentric rings are said to be a pool and the zigzags a python. But how those things were generated was never really followed up. So, I would suggest, perhaps, the ethnography just fell short of pursuing it a bit further; of taking it maybe to a neuropsychological basis. The anthropologists stopped at a certain point. Reichel-Dolmatoff, among the Tukano, took it further and tried to reconstruct what lies behind it. So, perhaps there is more ethnography potentially out there, but we just haven't looked at it. So absence of evidence for entoptic phenomena may not mean that they didn't play a part.

Robert Layton: Of course, but on the contrary, evidence of another interpretation must be considered. If people offer another interpretation of simple geometric forms, then we also have to respect those.

Phillip Cash Cash: I want to give another view on this idea of seeing geometric shapes or abstract imagery as part of the trance state. In our area, great value is placed upon sight and the ability to see, and there are gifted people in our community who have the gift of sight to see the future—to see sickness and illness, life and death. And these people are relied upon by our Indian communities to help them and guide them. As Willie [Selam] mentioned earlier [in the summary discussion of the previous day's field trip], there's a basic truth in that belief system—the belief that these people had obtained something in their lifetime that gave them that ability. As part of this, to be truly coherent, one always strived to be truthful. So, if there were rock art images, relating just to simple geometric patterns and things of that nature, that would be almost incoherent in reference to one's ability to see. It would almost be meaningless in a sense because it didn't give us the gift to help our fellow man, to be healed of the sickness. In other words, the gift of vision was truly significant because it gave us the truth of the great mysteries in life and those kinds of states were really important to people who you call shamans. The coherence of the seeing was really critical. If you didn't have that, you were not considered—how I should say—a helper of the people. So, as I'm trying to understand the discussion, I think maybe there is an element of that—I'm sure entoptics probably exist—but in our way, I guess, seeing is very, very important to this element of truth. It goes back to the idea that when you see these large images—like the one we saw at Hells Gate Gorge, with the diamond eyes. It is a very large image, and you note that there's a real emphasis on the eyes themselves as being the key component of the image. Its similar to "She Who Watches," where there's a focus on the eyes. I think that's just kind of touching upon the idea that sight is real crucial. Seeing is an experience.

David Whitley: Let me give an example of one way that this works in my part of the world, which is in the Mojave territory along the lower Colorado River. The primary creation point is at *Avikwa'ame*, Spirit Mountain, which is where the creator deity, Mastamho, lives. The Mojave shaman goes to Spirit Mountain to conduct a vision quest, and there, at that location, he re-experiences a dream that he had before he was born. And that dream is reexperiencing the mythic creation of the world with *Mastamho*—seeing that event. Now the Mojave shaman is said to get from that experience his curing song, which is in fact the creation story. And the creation story is so closely associated with the shaman, and with his curing, that the creation story is called the shaman's song. But, among the Mojave if you look at the written versions of the shaman's song, they don't provide any kind of narrative sequence of events that would identify *Avikwa'ame* or the myth of *Mastamho* and his relationship with his evil twin brother *Kataar*, and so on. The anthropologist's explanation of the song would be "well, these are almost nonsense syllables that don't make up a story." The Mojave response when that is expressed to them is "of course that's true," because everyone knows the creation story. No one needs to be told the creation story during the shaman's singing of his song. So what is being sung is the essence for the pattern of creation that the shaman realized during his reenactment. Well, the same thing appears to occur in the rock art. The rock art is depicting the shaman's re-experiencing of the mythic creation and what we see there are not images that look like the creator deity *Mastamho*.[1] In the shamans' art, the images are just complex geometric patterns, which again are the essence or the pattern of the creation. I have tried to understand it in this way: In our own scientific mythology we believe the creation of the world began with a big bang. You could define that—write it—in some kind of physics equation, or in words, or you could draw a picture of colors moving. Each of these could be the essence, or the pattern of it.

Phillip Cash Cash: That makes better sense to me than just saying it's an almost arbitrary state of vision. That makes much better sense, because an elder of mine, she gifted me with a bag and said she had a dream of death and the design is what she saw. It was a series of red, white, and black stripes. And she said that was to help me with my work while I was at the Smithsonian working with human remains on a daily basis.[2] She said "That's to help you" and she gave me this beaded bag with the image on there and that image was the reference to her sight at what death represented—this series of lines. And, of course, we see that at the Steiwer Ranch site where there is a whole wall of just linear red and white elements.[3] So, that makes better sense when it has a purpose. In the vision it's almost like the Mojave shaman came to the end of his ability to see—to the very end of sight—so, he ended his journey. And that's the farthest extent he could see. I'm just trying to put the explanation into my own context, my own experience, to relate that to entoptics.

---

[1] In other circumstances—not shamans' art—there are depictions of these beings, done as geoglyphs—earth figures—which are placed on mythic locations on the landscape and used in a ritual pilgrimage that follows the mythic events, but shamans' art is different.
[2] Phillip was formerly repatriation curator at the Smithsonian Institution in Washington DC.
[3] Keyser et al 1998a:40-41

CHAPTER 6
After the *Shamans of Prehistory*: Polemics and Responses
Jean Clottes and J. David Lewis-Williams

The ideas we expressed in our book on shamanism in Paleolithic cave art (Clottes and Lewis-Williams 1996) were occasionally cited in the press as having caused numerous controversies or having "been heavily criticized in France" (*Libération*, 30/3/99). As a matter of fact, this happened relatively rarely, at least explicitly. A number of the objections to our work had already been raised when the first article on the subject was published (see discussion in Lewis-Williams and Dowson 1988) and they were answered then and in later papers.[1]

The fact, however, that various specialists felt they should reaffirm or rediscover them made it necessary for us to quote their positions as objectively and completely as possible before discussing them. This is what we did some time ago at more length in French (Clottes and Lewis-Williams 2001). We referred to all the criticisms that we could find from the publication of our earlier work until mid 2000. This article presents and discusses the same data, this time in English.

As will be apparent, we wonder if many of our critics actually read what we wrote. We are also amazed by the vehemence and emotionally charged language of so many of them. Is the unknowability of Upper Paleolithic art for them a 'sacred' cornerstone of archaeology?

The arguments advanced by our critics fall under five different headings. We examine them successively.

1. The Supposed Impossibility to Access Meanings

This is the first and main argument. We could call it the pessimistic stance. A few authors do not go any further than unqualified statements, as though the impossibility were so obvious that it would brook no discussion: "The meaning of cave art lies beyond our comprehension" (Vialou 1998:81); "the motivations of that art are obviously out of reach" and "meanings have vanished for ever" (Valentin 1999:103). For some, this does not matter much because "not to know what those long vanished structured messages mean is far less serious than persisting to ignore that Paleolithic art is coded and symbolic" (Vialou 1998:19). This is why "a growing number of researchers have decided to abandon the fruitless search for meaning" (Bahn 1998:171), "to concentrate on other aspects of its study. . .and abandon any serious attempt at interpretation as a waste of effort" (Bahn and Vertut 1997:211; also see Chakravarty and Bednarik 1997:195-196). Such pessimism is even said to be a methodological necessity, because "theoretical excesses, all amounting to 'single answers,' need restraint" (Steinbring 1998:52).

The main reason for the inaccessibility of meaning is said to reside in the lack of proof for any hypothesis about the art and, consequently, for the inherent subjectivity of all hypotheses. "What it comes down to, basically, is whether one is content to work with the art as a body of markings that cannot be read or whether one wants to have stories made up about it" (Bahn 1998:247), because then "one has to become subjective and make extraordinary assumptions. All is hypothesis and claim; nothing is proven at all" (Bahn 1998:249).

"No doubt the idea of shamanism in the Paleolithic is alluring, because it is linked - at least in its beginnings - to a hunters' economy. . . .Thus there is nothing impossible in the supposition that it existed in the Paleolithic. But this is at present totally unprovable" and the hypothesis "cannot be falsified" (Beaune 1998:215), which would be contrary to the necessities of a really scientific research. Leroi-Gourhan, despite being tempted by the shamanistic hypothesis (see below), had in fact resisted it because of the lack of formal proof: "This is why the prehistorian cannot follow the path of shamanism, unless he changes his methods" (Leroi-Gourhan 1977:25).

Bednarik forcefully stressed this point, as did other specialists. "Empirical knowledge is the only form available to us about the physical world," "it is therefore complete nonsense to say that an alien observer, from a totally different culture, can objectively identify objects in an ancient, prehistoric art." "Interpretation of the art lies outside of science's capabilities, and will presumably always remain there" (Chakravarty and Bednarik 1997:195-196).

By nature our hypothesis would then be impossible to prove, because it is "beyond the reach of any kind of demonstration" (Francfort 1998:313), so that "lacking any clear documentary proofs, we must limit our efforts to. . .exhaustively collect all the available evidence so that our successors may check the [Paleolithic] code and decipher its meaning" (Ripoll López et al. 1999:97).

White also challenges the scientific character of our hypotheses. According to him they cannot be verified because "they are fortified by highly selected examples and they are not evaluated statistically" (White 1997:104; see also below).

So, pessimistic colleagues challenge the very fact of trying to understand meanings. And yet, "the study of material culture is an irrelevant distraction if it merely becomes a study of things for the sake of things" (Tilley 1999:338). More generally, we think that the aim of archaeology, as that of all sciences, is to understand and to explain phenomena. To record and describe them is just a series of steps towards that aim. The most complete attainable knowledge is what we are striving for. The history of science is full of pessimists who were proved wrong by progress and by the evolution of disciplines. Hardly one century ago (and in some cases far less), it was unthinkable to contemplate precisely dating a minute piece of charcoal lifted from a cave drawing, or disintegrating atoms, or curing some dire diseases, or again sending an inhabited vessel to the moon. And yet all this happened.

The alternative that our critics propose is that specialists should be content to describe facts "objectively" and draw the simplest possible conclusions from them, i.e. those that meet the eye. This is not only unsatisfying for lack of ambition; it can also be downright dangerous because of its naive empiricism. Empiricists pretend to be objective and to keep free of any hypotheses, but - as has often been demonstrated - they are mistaken. When we are facing the infinite possibilities of material reality, it is impossible for us to make a choice from amongst the innumerable parameters we are presented with without having first decided what is relevant and what is not. As philosophers of science have repeatedly shown, the relevance of data can be assessed only in relation to a hypothesis. For example, when we describe the painted or engraved animals in a cave, we do so in terms of their species (horses, bison, deer, etc.). Now, how can we be 100% certain that species was the prime criterion for Magdalenians or Aurignacians? After all, what was most important for them could well have been sex or attitude (Clottes *et al.* 1994), in which case it would be preferable to list female and male animals or again those involved in such and such an action (Figure 1). The important point is that those choices are never or very rarely discussed and made explicit; they are taken as self-evident. In fact, they correspond to the general opinion of the time and thus they do not shock anybody and are perfectly safe. A shared opinion, however, has never been accepted as a formal proof and the most famous scientists were occasionally mistaken because they relied on "self-evident" descriptions. This was recently said once more with force by the late Steven Jay Gould: "Utterly unbiased observation must rank as a primary myth and shibboleth of science, for we can only see what fits into our mental space, and all description includes interpretation as well as sensory reporting" (Gould 1998:72).

This is all the more true when one tries to give a supposedly simple and literal interpretation: it cannot but stem from the personal ideas of the author and from the criteria and admitted "truths" of our culture. For example, one of our most extreme critics, writing about the two famous Magdalenian carvings known as "fawn with birds" (or "bird"), both discovered in the Ariège (Figure 2), asserts "Few would

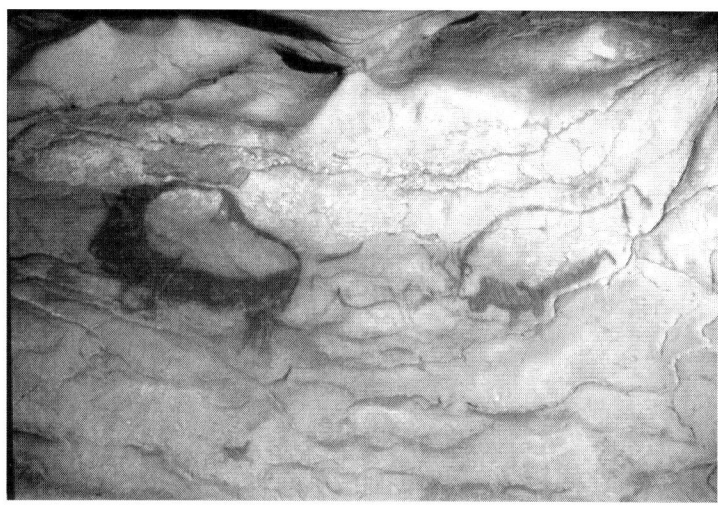

Figure 1. In Le Portel Cave (Ariège, France) three bison are represented in a scene: the one to the right is a female facing her calf (middle), while the the one to the left is an old male whom she has chased off. Merely registering three bison in statistics would be misleading as we have no way of evaluating the real importance of age, sex, attitudes, seasonality, myths, power, and probably other things for such images. *Photo L. de Seille.*

doubt that the Mas d'Azil and Bédeilhac fawn/bird spear-throwers...were by the same artist or, at least, two artists, one of whom had studied the other's work" (Bahn and Vertut 1997:201). This is possible, but there is another possibility which went unmentioned even though it is far more likely: it is that this theme, also known elsewhere in the Pyrenees (Simonnet et al 1991), may have materialized a myth or a legendary story for the Pyrenean Magdalenians, in which case it would have been represented independently in different locations and perhaps at different times by artists who did not know one another but who shared the same cultural background (Clottes 2001).

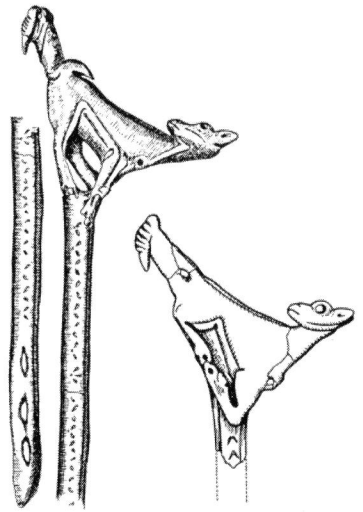

Figure 2. The famous "Fawns with Birds" from the Ariège Pyrenees caves in France. The one to the left is from Mas d'Azil (*drawing St-J. Péquart*), the one to the right is from Bédeilhac (*drawing R. Robert*).

On the other hand, when we are told that the shamanistic hypothesis for Paleolithic art does not explain everything and in particular the exact meaning of the figures, this is perfectly true. We acknowledged this several times in our book and other authors have done the same: "Efforts at interpretation are often dismissed and disavowed as fruitless speculation, but of course it depends on the level of interpretation that is sought" (Coles 1995:182).

It is true that attempting to access meaning(s) can only be done through various steps or stages (see Panofsky 1962). To reach the highest stage, that of detailed explanations, requires an informant perfectly aware of all the subtleties of significations in the framework of his (or her) culture. Even then one can never be sure that one knows all there is to know. Some explanations may be meant for men and others for women, or they may vary with the degrees of initiation and status. They may also change (and will) change with time when we are dealing with ancient art. That degree of knowledge will truly be inaccessible to us with the tools at our disposal. Much more modestly, we attempted to discover the *conceptual framework* within which art was made. This is a far from negligible aim. It is indeed possible to explain some things without attempting to explain everything. Otherwise there would be no archaeology.

Pessimism concerning meaning is based upon the history of our discipline. The grand theories of Breuil and Leroi-Gourhan collapsed after new discoveries were made and paradigms changed. Does this mean that the same fate awaits all interpretive hypotheses and that the shamanism hypothesis will necessarily be a fad among others, condemned like them to vanish within a generation or so (Bahn 1997:66)? The same dire prediction could have been made when all sorts of explanations were proposed in various domains (among others, cases in point are astronomy and evolution). Everybody knows that this was not the case (Clottes and Lewis-Williams 2001). There is no intrinsic reason why cave art cannot be explained, at least partly. In our domain as in others the partial failure of preceding theories does not necessarily entail the same fate for *all* other theories.

As we have shown, the lack of formal "proofs" is the main criticism we encountered. It is said that our hypotheses are neither provable nor falsifiable, and are therefore outside the scope of science. This is in a way true, as it is also true for all human sciences - what are called the "soft" sciences - because on this point they are distinct from the "hard" sciences where one can re-do equations or experiments, i.e. where hypotheses can be experimentally checked. This is why, in archaeology as in other human sciences, the process of knowledge is not - and cannot be - exactly the same as in mathematics and physics. Whenever something is asserted and even if it looks obvious, a hypothesis is underlying the assertion, whether it is clearly formulated or - as is more often the case - whether it remains implicit.

Let us take an example of this. When an archaeologist carefully excavates a hearth and the remains around it, he/she may prove that the fire reached 650°C if he/she correctly used the right kind of measuring equipment. Charcoal analysis will demonstrate that, say, Silvester Pine was used as fuel and some radiocarbon dates may possibly be obtained. The artifacts collected will be determined as being Magdalenian and the fire will be said to belong to that culture. At this stage, we are already making an assumption, undoubtedly very plausible but by no means formally proven: that is, that the artifacts discovered around the fire belonged to those who made the fire initially and not, for instance, that they had been picked on an earlier habitation site for some unknown reason and brought there. The archaeologist will notice the presence of numerous animal bones, some burnt, others not. It will be possible to determine that 80% came from ibex, 10% from lagopedes and another 10% from salmon. The logical conclusion will be that those Magdalenians mainly hunted and ate ibex and that they supplemented their diet with a few birds and fish. All this is most likely but nothing is as certain as hard science would have it. After all, they could have killed and eaten many more birds and fish elsewhere (or other animals) and just have brought the ibex to the fire in order to make an offering to their gods or for any other reason. If the hypothesis that they ate them is by far the more probable, it still lies beyond any scientific possibility of proof or falsification. And yet this will invariably be mentioned by all as a scientific objective hard fact.

This is why the concept of "proof" which we find so often these days in papers and books, as though archaeology needs a scientific boost in order for it to join the exclusive club of the "real" sciences, is properly speaking misleading. On the other hand, hypotheses are - as we have just seen - constantly presented as hard data, and, on the other hand, real proof can only be obtained for a very low level of elementary knowledge. As a consequence, "certainly, archaeology diminishes itself when asserting that the only valid contributions are those which are 'testable'" (Feliks 1998:129).

Statistics play a similar role. They are a tool, not a panacea. When our hypotheses are taken to task for explaining relatively few images or for not being supported by statistics, this means that the type of images that the critic deems significant should necessarily be more numerous than the others. Now, we know from well-known religious contexts that the most numerous motifs are not always the most important or significant ones. For example, in Islamic art the human form (or that of any other living being) is not represented, neither are Mohammed or Allah. In Roman Catholic churches, the images of the

Virgin Mary, those of Saints and of angels are statistically far more numerous than those of Christ, not to mention God the Father and the Holy Ghost, who for believers are the most important personages by far. In an undisputably shamanic culture, the counting of therianthropes at Ndedema (KwaZulu-Natal), only reached a bare 0.85% for more than 10,000 figures. Similarly, shamans are seldom represented by the Tukanos of Columbia, another shamanic culture (Lewis-Williams and Dowson 1988:233).

Rather than relying on statistics - which can be useful when they are used without lumping together "different levels of signification" (Schefer 1997:28), we chose to establish links between numerous and diverse, even apparently unrelated kinds of data. Those various clues then reinforce one another, and each takes its place in a logical and solid framework.

In so doing, we have not applied the methods of the "hard" sciences, which would be inappropriate, but those which have been defined by science philosophers. An analogy with a rope with multiple strands has often been employed and rightly so. Each separate strand can withstand just so much strain. Everybody knows, however, that twisting and combining those components together will create a rope that will bear a far heavier load and withstand a much greater strain than the mere adding up of each separate strand. This may be the reason why our critics have invariably attacked distinct separate elements of our hypotheses or remained fairly vague, and why no other hypothesis has been put forward to replace ours. Rather than checking the strength of the rope itself, a few of its strands and their components were attacked, but a rope that would be stronger than ours has never been proposed.[2]

When we are dealing with human sciences, we should reject the illusory and misleading concept of "proof" and substitute the notion of the best-fit hypothesis. It is the one that must be adopted, at least provisionnally until another one fills (if it ever does) its conditions better. Basically, those conditions are: to explain the greatest number of facts; to explain the widest range or diversity of data; to be checkable; not to run against well-established facts and to be wholly compatible with solidly established former observations; to have predictive value, i.e. to be corroborated rather than contradicted by subsequent discoveries.

About his theory of evolution, Darwin wrote a long time ago: "I believe in the truth of the theory, because it collects, under one point of view, and gives a rational explanation of, many apparently independent classes of facts" (Darwin 1893:13-14). More modestly, this is exactly what we tried to do, as can easily be checked by reading our book with an open mind (also see below).

To end our discussion of this fundamental problem, we stress the fact that hypotheses about various aspects of prehistoric life are constantly being expressed without eliciting any reaction. They are implicitly accepted without discussion. Let us examine three examples of this.

The recent discovery of open-air Paleolithic art in Spain and Portugal (Figure 3) was interpreted as pointing to the fact that the art inside deep caves must have been a marginal sort of phenomenon, because the physical conditions inside those caverns were much better suited to the preservation of the art. As a consequence, the art in the open must have been far more widespread. Similarly, in most books and articles about life during Paleolithic times, all authors devote at least one or two paragraphs to what could not last for long and must be missing, i.e. artifacts made out of wood or leather, and nobody ever forgets to mention wild plants, fruit and mushrooms as having played a great part in the Pleistocene diet. And yet all these are obviously nothing but hypotheses.

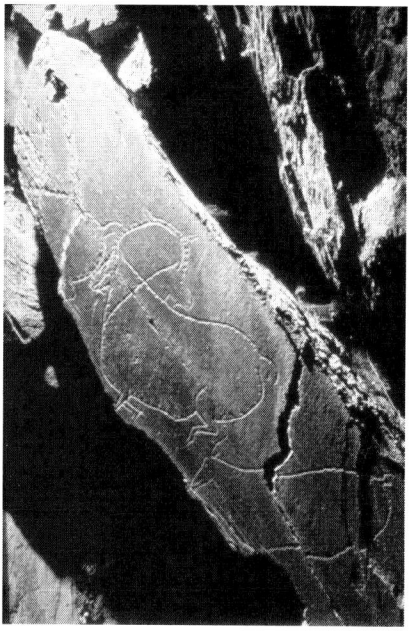

Figure 3. Several ibex engraved on a rock in the open at Quinta da Barca (Foz Côa, Portugal). *Photo A. Martinho Baptista, Centro Nacional de Arte Rupestre.*

The last two are quite likely - even though formally unproved and unfalsifiable - because taphonomic phenomena do exist and above all because those hypotheses are based (however implicitly) upon ethnographic analogies: the major role played by wood, leather and vegetable foods has been established in innumerable ethnographic cases (see below for more on ethnographic analogy).

As for the first example, even though the hypothesis is probable, it remains wholly speculative. This is because it is at present as impossible to quantify the disappearance of art in the open as it is to quantify the destruction of cave art. In that case, comparisons and assessments are based on two unkown variables.

All this does not prevent some authors who are among the most pessimistic and who most often invoke "proof" from drawing conclusions about those aspects and to hypothesize about them (Bahn 1995:231; Bahn and Vertut 1997:133; Bednarik 1994:74).

If those examples, just as those we cited previously, do not cause adverse reactions and if the hypotheses about them are generally accepted without any difficulty, this is probably because they deal with the *material* aspects of the prehistoric world and of Paleolithic life. On the other hand, everything which related to the *spiritual and religious* world, for example the interpretation of the art, is an obviously far more sensitive matter and is not dealt with in the same way. Not only is this unscientific, but in this case it is also illogical and paradoxical, because it is well-known that in traditional societies the material and religious worlds are inextricably mixed and indissociable.

2. Vanity of Ethnographic Comparisons?

Criticism of our use of ethnography has been founded on two major points. The first is that our work is "based entirely on recent research on southern African rock art" (Bahn and Vertut 1997:181). Critics add that it has not been proved that the San made their art within the framework of a shamanic religion: "there is nothing in the ethnographic record to prove any connection between shamanism and the execution of the art" (Bahn and Vertut 1997:183).[3]

Since the ill-fated attempt by the Abbé Breuil during the first half of the 20th century and the warnings of celebrated ethnologists such as Claude Lévi-Strauss and above all André Leroi-Gourhan who was both an ethnologist and a prehistorian, all specialists have been very wary about hasty ethnographic analogies. And yet, this is exactly what we have been charged with doing: "It would seem that more caution and rigour are needed to avoid the abuses of ethnography seen earlier this century, as well as the simplistic wholesale transfer of specific interpretations from one body of evidence to the other in what has been called 'ethnographic snap'" (Bahn and Vertut 1997:211).

Moreover, that the Southern African San practiced rock art within a shamanistic religion would not necessarily mean that their own ancestors had done the same nor that one could deduce from that fact that Paleolithic people had the same conceptual and religious framework. "Supposing . . .we admitted that Southern African art were linked to shamanism, this would not make it clear why Paleolithic Franco-Cantabrian art should also be" (Beaune 1997:235). "It is helpful to resort to universalistic concepts of supposed primitive mentality" because of the "unpredictable variations in behaviour" of those people (Bahn and Vertut 1997: 211). As a consequence, rather than launch into wild theories, "when ethnographic evidence is absent. . .*interpretations of prehistoric art are far safer*"[4] than more symbolic ones (Bahn 1998:222).

Our method would thus have been doubly at fault, first because of our supposedly exclusive South African base, second because of the fundamental impossibility of using any formal analogy between different cultures.

The Value of Ethnographic Comparatism

Detailed specific articles have been devoted to the subject (Lewis-Williams 1991; Lewis-Williams and Dowson 1988:235-236, 1992). It would thus be useless to rehash their arguments once more. We shall content ourselves with discussing the main two objections that were raised and with examining André Leroi-Gourhan's position because his views have been relied upon.

To state that we only based our hypothesis upon Southern African shamanism and that we transferred a San model on to the Paleolithic is plainly not the truth, as we have already said (Lewis-Williams and Clottes 1998:a48) and as a careful reading of our book shows. The difference of approach is the one between two distinct concepts: *analogous* and *argument by analogy*. The part about the San in our book is an important example *and not* the starting point of a chain of reasoning or the basis of a hypothesis. As regards ethnographic examples, we mentioned many others, from Siberia to Colombia, California and other places.

We are as persuaded as anybody else that it is impossible to transfer and thrust the ideas or the images belonging to an African, Australian, Polynesian or Indian context onto the Paleolithic world. The problem is in some ways comparable to the one we broached above about the different stages or degrees of interpretation: the upper degree is unattainable. Similarly, any exact, complete analogy is impossible; there are no Ice Age hunter-gatherers left. The variability of beliefs and concepts all over the world is such that exact ethnographic analogy would fail.

It is against that type of excess, far too common during the first half of the 20th century, that Leroi-Gourhan fought and he was right to do so. And yet, as Catherine Perlès clearly established: "Leroi-Gourhan's reaction was fully as violent as the excess he denounced: from the sixties on, he just refused any form of ethnographic comparison. Far from solving the problem, he just refused and rejected it. And then he found himself in a paradoxical blocked situation" (Perlès 1992:47). His situation was paradoxical because he made abundant use of ethnographic comparisons without saying so explicity: when, in order to support his interpretation of Paleolithic images, he insisted on the universality of a vision of the world that divided it into the male and female principles he drew an implicit ethnographic comparison. He placed himself, said Perlès, in a situation scientifically blocked because the "structures" that he saw in the symbolic constructions of the cave were "no more directly interpretable in themselves than the individual elements that made them up," whereas "a comparison between analogous structures. . .would have enabled him, from a partial knowledge of ancient symbolical structures. . ., in a controlled manner to deduce the different forms that the vanished elements could have had" (Perlès 1992:47).

Ethnographic comparisons are different from analogies[5] in so far as they point to the possibilities of social and mental concepts and structures, or else to their frequent occurrence within certain contexts. It is then valuable to use them, while being once again extremely careful not to switch a modern model onto a fossil reality. This is exactly what we have done, as was acknowledged by some[6]. This way of proceeding will be all the more fruitful when applied to societies that have a comparable way of life, in this case to hunter-gatherers.

Numerous ethnologists have noted that shamanism is the type of religion most frequently found among hunter-gatherers (Vitebsky 1995:29, 30; Vazeilles 1991:39). "Shamanism appears to be particularly adapted to egalitarian societies. This is the case of hunter-gatherers" (Perrin 1995: 93). "Many authors have noticed that link, acknowledging that hunting lies at the basis of shamanism, which from the facts seems to be self-evident" (Hamayon 1990:289). This does not mean either that other cultures with different economies could not be shamanistic, nor that hunter-gatherers have always and necessarily had exclusively shamanistic practices, if any. When dealing with hunting-gathering cultures such as those in the Paleolithic, however, this ethnographic observation considerably reinforces the possibility that that type of belief may have been entertained in the Ice Age. At the very least, it makes it desirable to check whether this was or was not the case.[7]

Naturally, we do not look for a "so-called primitive mentality" as has been claimed, but rather for convergent ways of thinking, of interpreting the world and acting upon it, i.e. to look for "universals" which can - if not "explain" Paleolithic art in all its details - at least provide us with possible keys to its interpretation. This way of proceeding is far more logical and scientific than "letting facts speak for themselves," which they of course never do, or to interpret them "in a literal way," because in that case interpretation necessarily stems from the particular concepts that are prevalent in the society to which we belong. Without running any risk of error we can postulate that the ways of thinking of Magdalenians and of other Paleolithic cultures were closer to those of hunter-gatherers on other continents, because of the similarities in their ways of life, than to those of materialistic Westerners living in a complex industrial society at the beginning of the 21st century.

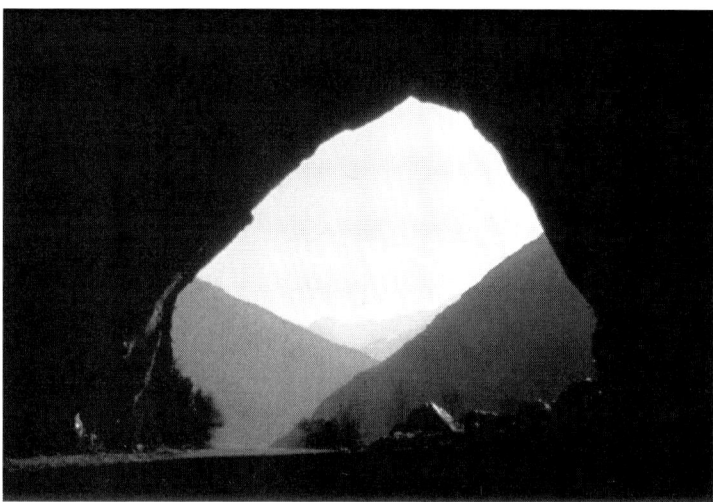

Figure 4. Everywhere, caverns have been considered to be the realm of the supernatural. This is the entrance to Niaux Cave (Ariège, France). *Photo J. Clottes.*

When, for example, we see that numerous shamanistic cultures - and others - consider the subterranean world to be the realm of spirits, gods or the dead, i.e. as a supernatural world (Figure 4), it is quite admissible to take this explanation into account when dealing with the mysterious Paleolithic explorations, for more than twenty millenia, of the deep caves where nobody lived.

3. An Erroneous Conception of Shamanism?

Our account of shamanism was also criticized by some authors. They raised four different points.

"They presume a generalized, almost universally applicable notion of shamanism that few if any ethnologists would accept" (White 1997:104). In this case, it is the global character of the religious phenomenon known as shamanism which is challenged.

The other three problems were raised by a French specialist of Siberian shamanism, Roberte Hamayon (1997). After her, the latter two, the most important ones, were quoted by various authors (Demoule 1997; Beaune 1997; Bahn 1997, 1998; Bahn and Vertut 1997).

We were wrong, she said, to write about a tiered cosmos, even though the notion was

"frequently mentioned in the literature and was made popular by Mircea Eliade. Anthropological analysis shows that on the contrary the structure of the universe appears as horizontal to the hunter (while) the tiering of the world seems to be correlated with the development of an organized economy and a hierarchical social organization. Often, it is also linked to a 'great' religion or to a centalized state" (Hamayon 1997:67, note 8).

Much worse, she says, is our association of shamanism with trance and altered states of consciousness. According to her, we started "from a ready made idea of shamanism as the exploitation of altered states of consciousness" (Hamayon 1997:66). Such a concept "is akin to the one spread by the neo-shamanic movements that developed on the Californian coast at the end of the sixties. . . .It turns shamanism into a spiritual quest model working through the search of states of consciousness defined by trance and favoring the use of hallucinogens" (Hamayon 1997). The "primary role" attributed to trance in the origins of shamanism would be a mere speculation that would reduce "religious life to religious experience and the latter to neurology" (Hamayon 1997). Now, "that all the productions of the human mind should have a neurological basis is both indisputable and meaningless," because "about such obvious truths one can say everything and anything." It is "as senseless to try and give a fixed form and evolution to the variations of those states of consciousness as to try and find in them a basis for cultural and social phenomena." In any case, "no serious neurologist believes in the kind of (trance) experience mentioned, nor will accept to study those phenomena, because they deem them to be of a symbolic order. . . .For the same reason, neither are anthropologists convinced by them: 'it is akin to analyzing marriage solely as a function of reproductive biology' as says Atkinson (1992, p. 311)" (Hamayon 1997).

In an interview with a journalist, Hamayon made her position more precise and went even further: "Shamanism has got nothing to do with trance. It is a system of beliefs and practices . . . .[The shaman] remains as self-possessed as an actor in a theatre. This is all symbolical." "Nobody could scientifically demonstrate what trance is. It belongs to individual experience, its manifestations are quite variable according to people, moments and circumstances: what common ground is there between the ecstasy of a whirling dervish and the catalepsy of somebody under the influence of hallucinogenic drugs?" (*La Croix*, 20/12/1996).

Sophie de Beaune deliberately takes to extremes our supposed association of shamanism with trance: "If one followed that type of logic to its end, one should invoke shamanism every time one talked of an art associating both geometric signs and therianthropes. We would thus have shamanism in Greek art, shamanism in the Romanesque, etc." (Beaune 1998:215).

Finally, we were accused of having established too close a relationship between trance and hallucinogens, despite the fact that "the consumption of hallucinogens for shamanic purposes hardly spreads beyond the Americas where it is mostly used as a sort of process of qualification, to qualify for the function, and then it stops (or at least it diminishes) when the function is exercised" (Hamayon 1997:66). Let us do away with this criticism now before addressing the others: each time in our book we mentioned the means used to enter trance, we said quite explicitly that they were numerous and varied. We did quote hallucinogens occasionally and with precautions (Clottes and Lewis-Williams 1996:109), not only to say that their use was a widespread practice and that it was thus possible in Paleolithic times but also and above all to rectify the commonly-held idea that this mode of getting into trance was a priviledged one (Clottes and Lewis-Williams 1996:14, 22-23).

Shamanism and Trance

Would it be mistaken to refer to shamanism as a global concept? A few authors truly prefer to talk of shamanisms in the plural but they are rare (Atkinson 1991). By so doing they choose to insist on the indisputable diversity of shamanistic sociological and cultural manifestations in various milieus rather than on what links those shamanisms one to the other, those links being disputed by none. This is a classic case: that of the bottle or the glass of wine felt to be half empty or half full depending on the point of view. If shamanism were not a universal phenomenon the word would not have been used all over the world for such a long time (Perrin 1995). Modern ethnologists keep using it, not only for the Siberian cultures where it originated (Hamayon 1990), but also for the peoples of the Arctic (Robert-Lamblin 1996, 1997), of the Americas (Chaumeil 1999), of Southern Africa and of Asia (Walsh 1989). They all acknowledge both "its disconcerting diversity and paradoxically the impression of deep unity of a phenomenon that dates back several millennia" (Vazeilles 1991:71).

"The word 'shamanism' applies to phenomena of the same type all over the world" (Hultkranz 1995:166). According to Vitebsky (1995, p. 46), the striking similarities between South American shamanism and the forms of shamanism in Siberia "are perhaps the strongest evidence for the basic durability of shamanic ideas over the widest range of environments, social structures and historical periods" (Vitebsky 1995:46). "Shamanic beliefs do not constitute a single religion or doctrinal system, although worldwide shamanic traditions approach reality and human experience in similar ways" (Vitebsky 1997:34; the same idea is expressed in Walsh 1989:4). It is that universality that allowed us - following many other writers - to suppose that the concepts and attitudes of shamanism were extremely ancient and that they go as far back as the Paleolithic.

In the definition we gave of it, we insisted without any ambiguity upon the "complexity of the concept, of its rites and its practices" It is also important to note that shamanism is, in itself, a multi-component belief system. Shamanism comprises healing techniques, control of animals, weather-changing rites, prediction, vision quests, sorcery, out-of-body journeys, and other activities, each of which has its own appropriate rituals, symbols, and myths." (Clottes and Lewis-Williams 1996:112; also see Lewis-Williams 1997:31-32).

As for the notion of a "tiered cosmos" that Roberte Hamayon denies in hunter-gatherer contexts, it still exists in such cultures and is frequently described by ethnographers: the sentence with which she was not happy specifically referred to the hunting-gathering San, about whom definite testimonies are known. As for other hunting-gathering or other cultures, we merely said that "throughout the world, the shamanic cosmos is usually tiered" (Clottes and Lewis-Williams 1996:29), and we gave a few examples. We also expressed the hypothesis that the structuring of the cosmos, which can be found anywhere (and not only in shamanic societies) may have stemmed from the reactions of the human nervous system during altered states of consciousness. After our book was published, Piers Vitebsky gave the following summary: "The soul journeys of the shamans take place, people think, within a tiered cosmos, in which the earth is in the middle of various upper and lower worlds" (Vitebsky 1997:34). In any case, whether those diverse worlds - acknowledged by everybody - were tiered, parallel or juxtaposed for Paleolithic people would be irrelevant to our main argument which is that the subterranean world was most probably considered one of them.

Much more serious is our supposed identification of shamanism with trance states, with which, according to Hamayon, it "has nothing to do." Her view is exaggerated and erroneous. Our definition of shamanism, as quoted above, is enough to show that her interpretation of our book is an abusive caricature. As for shamanism, it most certainly cannot be reduced to trance (we never argued for that simplification), but trance lies at the basis of its traditions and plays a most important role, as so many ethnographic examples show. We quote a few.

Other modern ethnographers, even if they do not refer to Mircea Eliade and his successors, still insist - and with good reason - upon the importance of altered states of consciousness. Thus trance is "an essential part of much shamanic activity around the world" (Vitebsky 1995:64). "Shamanism is mainly characterized by the travel of the shaman pursuing the spirits to another world...The shaman acts through trance, or at least through a state of altered consciousness" (Vazeilles 1991:10; see also Hultkrantz 1995). The Greenland shamans also practiced altered states of consciousness (Robert-Lamblin 1997:285). Nowadays, "one of the most salient features of Amazonian shamanism is the use of a wide range of hallucinogenic plants" to induce trance (Chaumeil 1999:43). Those few examples - there are many others - are enough to show that what we said about shamanism and trance is in fact perfectly correct.

We can also point out that in Chaumeil's article, published in 1999 (after our book), the description of the visions he mentioned is quite close to the model proposed by Lewis-Williams and Dowson (1988) that we took up in our work.

"A distinction needs to be made between two categories of visions, as is clear from shamanic tales. The first one, originating in neurophysiology, is made up of geometrical non-figurative feelings of light (burning candles, sparks, etc.), technically called phosphenes. That set of geometrical motifs for example plays a very large part in the Shipibo Indians' shamanism in Peruvian Amazonia. . . .The other category of hallucinogenic visions is made up of figurative images." (Chaumeil 1999:45).

Hamayon claims that the shamans of traditional societies, exactly as the mystics who practise fasting and sensory deprivation, are unconscious of trying "to alter their state of consciousness" (Hamayon 1997:66), because they are fully persuaded that by so doing they are getting into touch with another world. And yet, this is exactly what they do (Lemaire 1993). As to those who just pretend to be in trance and thus enact a role, they do exist but this does not contradict in any way the existence of the phenomenon of trance. If, in our society, some people pretend to be in love when they are not, this does not mean that true love does not exist.

We find Hamayon's remark about the supposed refusal of "serious neurologists" to study that kind of phenomena, exceedingly strange. Accidental or provoked visions, i.e. trance, are known to have happened at all times and to happen in all cultures (also see Lemaire 1993 and for an extensive bibliography see earlier articles cited in Lewis-Williams and Dowson 1988). It seems difficult to believe that in order to be "serious" one would have to refuse to study a particular phenomenon out of preconceived prejudices against it. Such an attitude would obviously be anything but scientific.

Hamayon, quoting Atkinson (1992), accuses us of seeing shamanism through trance, which would be "akin to analyzing marriage only as a biological function of reproduction" (Hamayon 1997:66). This is certainly not what we did. Her comparison, however, is excellent in so far as in both cases she stresses one of the most basic features of those institutions. Shamanism is not trance only (see above), but trance plays an essential role in it[8], just as marriage is not sex only, even though sex is at the basis of it and without sex it would not exist.

4. Contradictions with Paleolithic Art Itself?

Our hypotheses about Paleolithic art as a whole have occasionally been said to contradict the existing data as regards three points: the diversity of art would not be consistent with our "global" theory; our explanations would be too limited; various features of the art would remain outside our scheme.

Here again some statements were made without any support, as though they were self-evident:

"It is impossible to have a global interpretation of Paleolithic art. Magdalenians are not Aurignacians, no more than the French are Gauls, Romans or Celts !" (Vialou 1998:19).

"I do not believe for a second that there would have been a unique religion and even less that Paleolithic art would testify to it. On the contrary, I believe in the diversity of beliefs, which is apparent in the diversity of the works of art. . . .Those that propose that hypothesis give it far too much importance. Once more, it is wrong to look for a unique explanation" (Lorblanchet 1999:109).

"Like all attempts at global interpretation, this one can be criticized" (Beaune 1997:234).

"Strict adherence to a single theory is a prophylactic against thought. It limits potential explanations and imposes a bogus, reductionist and utterly hypothetical homogeneity on a vast array of different motifs. It suppresses the consideration of any other motivation such as the human urge to create, and what has been called 'the exercise of the normal, undrugged conscious imagination'. . .Prehistoric artists, like those of more recent times, were people like ourselves, <u>and their art can therefore be expected to reflect every facet of life</u>."[9] (Bahn 1997:66).

The diversity of images was the reason why, a long time ago, Luquet, approvingly quoted by White, "steadfastly refused to paint all Upper Paleolithic imagery with the same interpretive brush and insisted on an image-by-image, site-by-site evaluation!" (White 1997:101). Cohen agrees when she says that our interpretation "cannot but be fragile, because of the very universality it presupposes, as it excludes the interpretations of the art that would take its particular context and its own symbolism into account" (Cohen 1999:74).

Other authors have evoked the immensity of Quaternary times, which would make such a long continuation of beliefs unlikely. This is why Dobres admits "to having many reservations about a shamanic explanation to account for so many different forms and contexts of visual imagery production over such a great expanse of time" (Dobres 1999:91). This is an argument which has been used several times: "Uniformity and continuity in ideology and art, with concepts which were structurally unchanged for thousands if not tens of thousands of years" is "a scenario that is *a priori* extremely improbable" (Bahn 1998:247). As a consequence,

"in view of the time span and vast area through which Paleolithic art is spread, it is probable that all these theories contain some truths, and that there were many other motivations which may never be known. . . . (the) basic function (of the images) was probably to affect the knowledge or the behaviour of those who could read them" (Bahn and Vertut 1997:213).

Contrary to these authors, Layton expresses the opinion that we have noted "some interesting and important aspects of variability in Upper Paleolithic art," but he remarks that we "tend to construe these as signalling different aspects of shamanism rather than distinct aspects of culture" (Layton 2000b:179). For example, some signs, according to Leroi-Gourhan, could have been "ethnic markers." Consequently, "the criterion for judging the appropriateness of alternative interpretations of Upper Paleolithic art should not be which hypothesis works best as a blanket explanation, but which hypotheses together most closely match the variability of the art" (Layton 2000b:184), and he proposes to use such a method.

Our interpretations, according to some commentators, would have a limited interpretive potential. "As seductive as it may appear, that positivist hypothesis, based on neuropsychology, can in no way explain the meaning of the drawings" (Gibeault and Uhl 1998:33). It "leaves many questions unanswered - whether the shamans were artists, whether they were the only artists, what the pictures meant, how they were used, and what percentage of the art could conceivably be interpreted in this way." (Bahn 1997:66).

Composite creatures, also called therianthropes or anthropozoomorphs and often improperly named "sorcerers", are generally considered as often being part of shamanic religions (Francfort 1998:312). But, as it so happens, they are quite rare in Paleolithic art in which "no more than a dozen 'sorcerers' are known" (Beaune 1998:208) (Figure 5). "If fantastic, composite animals represent the last stage in visual hallucination, this is an argument against trance as a common factor in Paleolithic art since. . .there are few of these. It is possible, however, that in Pergouset we have one of the exceptions to the rule" (Sieveking *in* Lorblanchet and Sieveking 1997:54). As a consequence, our "model" "explain(s) nothing but a tiny fraction of the images at our fingertips" (White 1997:111). It was even constructed thanks to a "handful of often highly unrepresentative examples that have been carefully selected from a wide array of sites" (Bahn 1997:66).

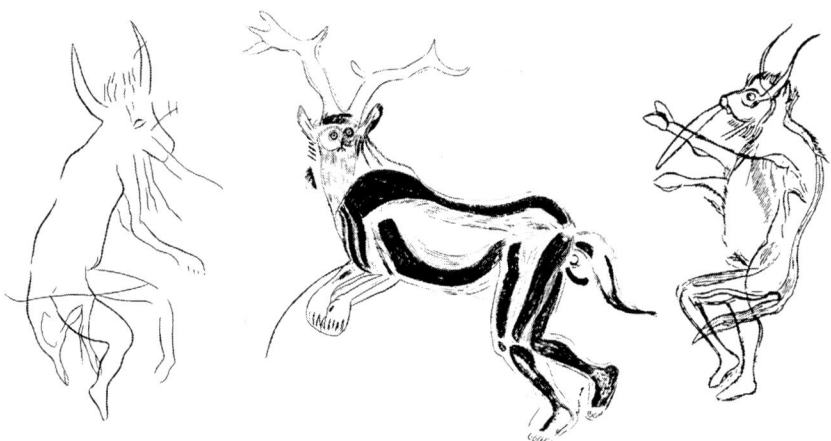

Figure 5. Three of the most famous therianthropes in European Paleolithic cave art. Left, Gabillou, Dordogne (*drawing J. Gaussen*); middle and right, Les Trois-Frères, Ariège (*drawing H. Breuil. From Gaussen 1964, Bégouën & Breuil 1958).*

In addition, our explanation would be contradictory with the "structured" character of the art and with the long duration of its themes. The panels with paintings and engravings testify to an organized way of thinking and not to psychedelic divagations:

"How could an art as structured and permanent correspond to such an inherently personal experience as trance? On the cave walls we see a coherent discourse, nearly a 'grammar' which necessitated teaching and technical mastery, not altered states of consciousness. If they had painted under the influence of visions, we would have had frescoes without any relationship to each other, without inner coherency" (Yvette Taborin in an interview to *La Croix*, 20/12/1996).

Therefore, "one can only say that cave art tells a mythology. The rest is pure fancy" (Taborin, *La Croix*). Others tried to refute our hypotheses with arguments of the same ilk, based on the "restricted bestiary" represented and on the structured assemblages of animals belonging to different species:

"All this implies the existence of a system of thoughts responsible for the conception and the making of the works of art, and also the existence of a social organization that made for the persistence of the tradition. The hypothesis that the images would be intimately linked to sacred stories and myths appears to be the best in order to take into account the inherent coherence of cave art" (Sauvet and Tosello 1998:89).

Finally, whole spans of Paleolithic art would be left outside our explanations. Thus, if "such a hypothesis can partly explain the origins of beliefs and the sacralisation of the subterranean world . . ., it in no way explains the existence of an art in the light. . .and that of a mobiliary art. . .that would refer to the same beliefs" (Sauvet and Tosello 1998:90). We should have realized that our "arguments were shaken" by the existence of the same motifs inside the deep caves and in the daylight (Hamayon 1997:66).

Paleolithic Art and Its Various Aspects

Is our hypothesis really "globalizing" and does it impose an artificial unity over a very diverse art? That objection includes two ideas: the nature of Paleolithic art and our attitude concerning it.

Specialists in Paleolithic art, like those in other disciplines, are more sensitive to differences - because they may betray chronological or spatial stylistic evolution - than to resemblances. The latter are generally so well known that authors do not bother mentioning them. And yet there does exist a Paleolithic "style" which evinces a very strong unity from beginning to end over more than twenty thousand years (Clottes 1998; Clottes and Lewis-Williams 1997a).

We detailed the components of that unity in our book. We now sum them up thus:
- at the same time, deep caves and shelters were used for art,

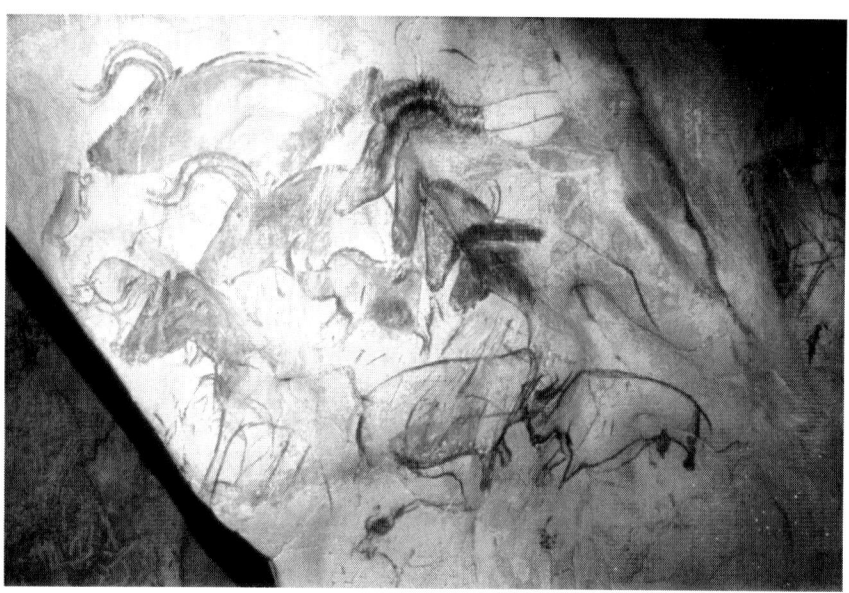

Figure 6. From beginning to the end of the Upper Paleolithic, large herbivores were often drawn inside the deep caves. Here are horses, aurochs, bison and rhinoceroses from Chauvet Cave, so far the oldest dated painted cave in the world. *Photo J. Clottes.*

and probably, too, rocks in the open, like Foz Côa in Portugal or Siega Verde, Domingo Garcia and others in Spain. While painting or engraving on cave walls in the absolute dark is exceptional in the history of humankind, such a tradition went on for more than twenty millenia in Europe. Such a long uninterrupted tradition can only be possible because the same beliefs and practices were transmitted from generation to generation;

- on the whole, certain themes were used throughout the period: animals, particularly big herbivores, were given priority and prominence (Figure 6). They were accompanied with many geometric signs and indeterminate lines, with very rare humans and a few obvious therianthropes;

- the way they were drawn is also very constant: human life and natural landscapes are absent, scenes are very scarce, the animals are represented in profile, without any care for their scale, as though they were floating on the walls in various postures, and many of them are precisely characterized as to their sex and postures;

- in the caves, Paleolithic people acted in similar ways: they explored them in their entirety; they chose big chambers but also very restricted recesses; the walls played a great part in their making of the art, with their reliefs and cracks (Figure 7), the opening of passages and of deep shafts that influenced the placing of images; bone fragments were stuck into fissures (Figure 8).

None of those characteristics were compulsory for people frequenting deep caves. They were all chosen and deliberate. Their persistence over so many millenia testifies to a conceptual framework that remained basically unchanged.

As we wrote in our book (p. 112), "despite all the diversity of the art, there is a long term unity (see Chapter Two) that testifies to some sort of common framework. It is that framework that we have tried to uncover."[10] Our attempt is therefore quite different from a global explanation, as we have been accused. Over the past two thousand years, Christianity also developed within the same framework while undergoing all sorts of mutations and to an outside observer appearing far more diverse than Paleolithic art. And yet, the many Christian churches and chapels of all centuries still fundamentally belong to the same conceptual set of beliefs.

Is it unlikely that beliefs would have persisted for so many millenia in the Upper Paleolithic, when material cultures changed and replaced one another from the Aurignacian to the Gravettian to the Solutrean and to the Magdalenian? The answer is a clear "of course not," substantiated by many examples all over the world. Religious ideas, whatever their nature, change at a much slower pace than material

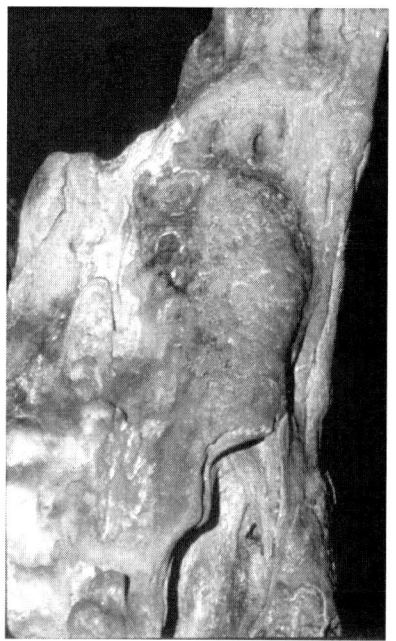 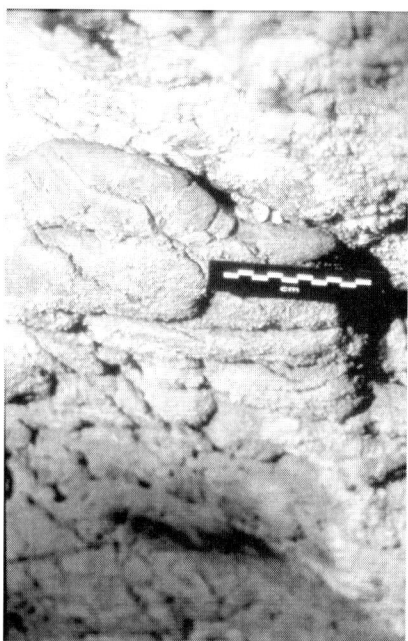

Figure 7. Natural reliefs have often been used to materialize the images of animals. Here a vertically-oriented bison with a human leg was painted in black on a huge stalagmite in El Castillo Cave (Cantabria, Spain). *Photo L. de Seille.*

Figure 8. In various painted or engraved French and Spanish caves, fragments of bones were stuck into cracks, as here in Gargas (Hautes-Pyrénées), where one was radiocarbon dated to 26,860 ± 460 BP (Gif-A-92.369). *Photo J. Clottes.*

cultures. This is obvious from the great religions that not only go on but are flourishing in a world that has dramatically changed over the last centuries. But the best example is from the Upper Paleolithic itself. In Spain, the Parpalló cave, in the province of Valencia, has an entrance that is strongly evocative of female genitalia. Be it for that reason or for any other, the same cultural practices took place in it for more than thirteen thousand years. We know this as more than five thousand engraved or painted stone plaquettes (Figure 9) were deposited there and recovered from layers well dated from the Gravettian to the Late Magdalenian (Villaverde Bonilla 1994). This case gives convincing proof of the continuity of cultural practices over an enormous length of time.

The argument against a conceptual shamanic framework because of the immensity of time is thus irrelevant. The argument that the immensity of distances would have entailed multiple differentiated

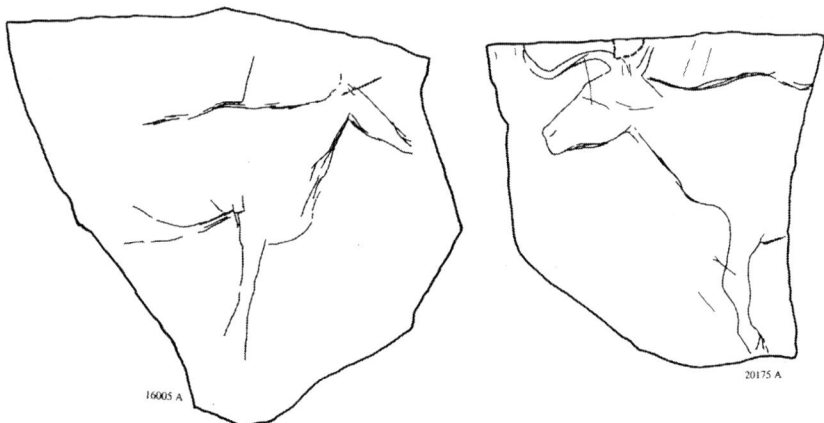

Figure 9. In Parpalló Cave, near Valencia (Spain), thousands of engraved or painted stone plaquettes were discovered in archaeological layers ranging from the Gravettian (left) to the Upper Magdalenian (right), thus testifying to a rite that went on for more than 13,000 years in the same place. *From V. Villaverde Bonilla 1994.*

conceptions of the world is even more fallacious. The European continent is less spacious than Australia or North America and we know for a fact that at the time of contact aboriginal religions on those continents presented a number of common basic characteristics over distances that ranged for thousands of miles. Practices and details often differed on many points but the structures of their fundamental beliefs were continuous. When, in the Upper Paleolithic, we notice the regular recurrence of the features we mentioned, it is then legitimate to propose the hypothesis of one conceptual interpretive framework with - naturally - some variations in time and space.

Another objection is that shamanic practices with their attending hallucinations would be incompatible with the long duration of the art, of its themes and of its techniques, as well as with its structured character. We shall not labour the fact that the first part of this objection contradicts the preceding one: the stress has now shifted to the unity of the art over Paleolithic times. At first sight, the argument may seem strong and well- founded, but only in so far as it is based on what happens in *our* society and not on the constant universal practices of shamanic cultures. In *our* society, visions and hallucinations are generally idiosyncratic, personal and distinct from one person to another, because they are mostly caused by pathologies, physical or emotional accidents or by hallucinogenic drugs, in the absence of a constraining framework, so that the fantasies and individual experiences of each person are given free reign. The case is quite different with shamanic societies. The future shamans or even the individuals that are trying to receive a vision, for example in the course of their rites of passage, are instructed - generally over a long period - into all the details of the myths and sacred stories of the group, on the geography of the supernatural world where they will travel, on the fantastic spirit creatures that they may meet and on the dangers they will have to face so that they can come back safely from their perilous voyage. "Hallucinations are culturally determined" (Sieveking in Lorblanchet and Sieveking 1997:54)." "Trances are ritualized, i.e. they take place in a permitted time/space and they conform to local geography and to the beliefs of the Invisible world" (Lemaire 1993:149). "Shamanic trances are undertaken in the context of a body of knowledge and beliefs handed down from generation to generation through an apprenticeship that ensures contemplative rather than psychedelic states" (Turpin 1994:80).

It goes without saying that, contrary to modern psychedelic hallucinations, to which our critics refer, this implies the existence of structures, those shaping the beliefs of the tribe. The dreams do not take place in a vacuum but in one or several restricted frameworks which are necessarily structured. Among the themes informing the visions, some are predominant or linked to others; there are also prohibitions or taboos that the would-be shamans would already have learned about. To find those structures in an art that is the result of such practices is therefore to be expected. As a consequence, "to consider the structure of the works of art and other testimonies is not an analysis of the contents; from it a form is deduced; such an analysis is in no way incompatible with the concept of a religious function or of shamanistic practices concerning Paleolithic art: it just gives them a form" (Schefer 1997:5).

Finally, according to some authors, our hypotheses do not explain the majority of images (only the scarce therianthropes), nor even the meaning of images in general and many questions remain unanswered.

We must first recall once more that a hypothesis, in order to be the best, does not need to explain everything. It is enough that it should meet the conditions we quoted, i.e. explain more varied and more numerous facts than all others, have a predictive potential and not be in contradiction with well-established facts. This is indisputably the case (Lewis-Williams and Dowson 1988:238). It even clarifies many more images and facts than formerly, but at different levels.

For example, the number of composite beings (therianthropes), whether they were partially transformed shamans, animal spirits, gods or legendary creatures, was no doubt reckoned to be far fewer than it really is. This is due to honest motives on the part of the researchers: in their statistics, they counted only those that were 100% obvious and incontrovertible and not the others. Now, when the figures are studied in more depth, it appears that there is a whole range of ambiguous representations. Some human figures may be given distinct animal features, in which case they are not classified among therianthropes but are generally said to be "bestialized." Conversely, human characteristics may be associated with animals (Figure 10), or else other animals may be given body parts belonging to diverse species (Clottes *in press*). This betrays a conception of the world (or of *a* world) in which reality is more complex and unstable than in ours: "Hybrid animals or composite creatures also correspond to a shamanic view of the world. Composite animals show the metamorphosis and constant transformation of Nature. Composite anthropomorphic creatures express the interpenetration of the natural and supernatural worlds" (Francfort 1998:312). Then we can wonder how many of the apparently fully recognizable animals could in fact be entirely transformed creatures or spirit-helpers with whom shamans identify and whose role is so important in shamanism. If it is not possible to answer this question scientifically, this does not mean that we should ignore the problem and refrain from mentioning it.

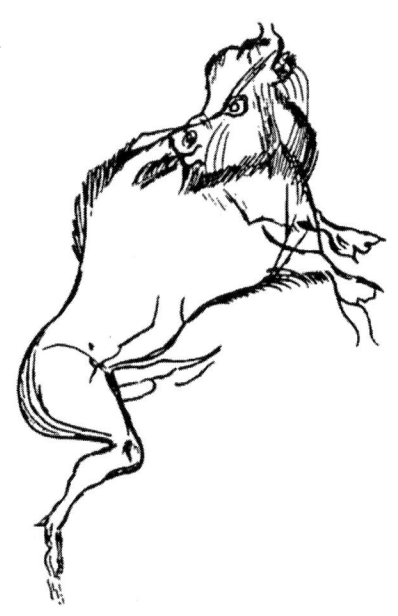

Figure 10. Magdalenian engraving of a bison with distinct but unobtrusive human features (shape of the leg and location of the penis). Les Trois-Frères, Ariège, France. (*drawing H. Breuil. From Bégouën & Breuil 1958*).

Spirit helpers "are supposed to have an animal form in hunting societies" (Hamayon 1990:433), and "everything in the behaviour of shamans supports the idea that he identifies with an animal - and that is exactly what he is supposed to do: he must couple with an animal-shaped supernatural being, he must fight against other animal-shaped supernatural creatures; therefore he is expected to change his own essence" (Hamayon 1990:533). This is why, despite her strong reservations about trance and its role, Hamayon stated: "I have always been convinced that cave art was related to shamanism - real shamanism: there is a fundamental link between the shaman and hunting. It seems to me quite likely that those societies whose living depended so much upon animals should have had recourse to shamanism" (*La Croix,*

20/12/1996). She thus clearly contradicts all her own strictures on our use of the word 'shamanism'.

The existence of portable art, as that of an art in the open, both discussed at length in our book, were felt by some to be contradictory with the arguments we used concerning cave art (see, for instance, Taborin 2000 :59), despite some obvious links between the themes represented in portable art and in wall art (Figure 11). This way of exclusive thinking is strange. Nowadays and in a different context, does the existence of cathedrals and churches make it impossible for priests to celebrate mass in the open? If we dealt at much more length with the art in the depths and the dark rather than with the art in the light, it is because the art in caves is so much better preserved and has such a better archaeological context. We have much more data on which to rely and thus we can understand far more about the motives of its creators. Just as a cross on the top of a hill, another in a church, or even another on the sword or the breast of a crusader stem from the same beliefs while having different functions, nothing makes it impossible that the shamanic framework glimpsed inside the deep caves could apply to both the mobiliary art and to the engravings on the rocks in the open. In any case, there are differences of motifs and techniques between the art in the caves and the art outside, as was noticed long ago (Laming-Emperaire 1962).

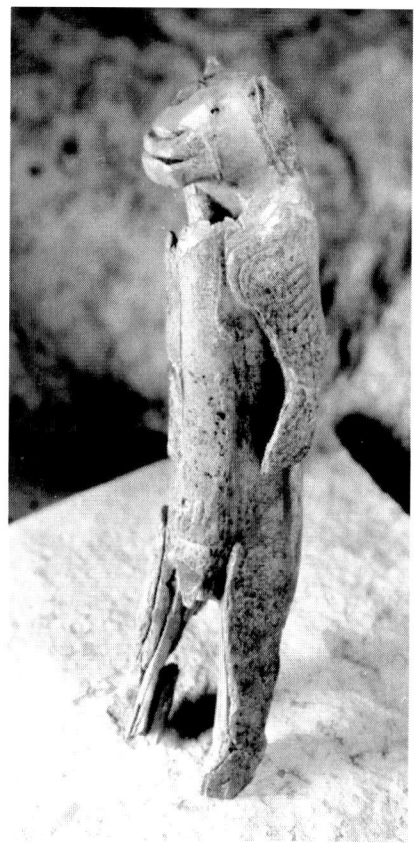

Figure 11. A therianthrope (human with the head of a lion) made out of mammoth ivory. Portable art dated to ca. 30,000 BP from Hohlenstein-Stadel (Germany). *Photo T. Stephan, Ulmer Museum.*

Importantly, we did not say that *all* images came from visions and that *all* visions were bound to have occurred inside caves. Caves were priviledged places, in which enough clues were preserved *in situ* for us to understand better the motivations of those who made those images. It is certain that their beliefs and practices must have been fully as complex as those of the hunter-gatherers studied by ethnologists in recent times. All the different aspects and forms of Paleolithic art, however, appear to the observer to be sufficiently related to one another for us to conclude that the different ceremonies which took place in different environments or the use of various decorated artifacts, had at their root the same conception of the world and the same beliefs. About portable art, we even gave a number of examples to show how those diverse elements could be integrated into a wider whole.

Since our book was published, various information has come our way which reinforced the coherency of our hypotheses, thereby confirming its predictive potential, which is one of the main conditions for a best-fit hypothesis. We cite one about the caves themselves and another about portable art.

In articles or books (Renault 1995-1996; Simonnet 1996:343; Fénies 1965:39-43) or through the direct testimonies of cave-explorers, we gathered a number of undisputable examples of the hallucinogenic character of deep caves. Naturally, those hallucinations, always uncalled for and even feared because of their potential danger in such an environment, are different from one person to the next (see above). They just show that the reactions of the nervous system of very different spelunkers may escape their control in prolonged darkness, in conditions of weariness and sensory deprivation. Taking into account the universality of the perception that the subterranean world belongs to the supernatural and the beyond, it is virtually certain that, when Paleolithic people went into the deeper galleries, they must have been persuaded that they were venturing into the world of the spirits. As a consequence they must have expected to meet them there. Such a state of mind, reinforced by previous teaching, could only stimulate visions. In fact, visions would have been welcomed rather than fought against. The caves could thus play a double role, the aspects of which were fundamentally linked: they facilitated the induction of altered states of consciousness and they allowed people to get directly in touch with the spirits through the walls.

Coincidentally, at the time when our book was published, a Czech colleague published a detailed paper about an old discovery, that of the Gravettian tomb of a man at Brno II. Cautiously, the author expressed his surprise at the analogy the tomb presented with historically known shamanism. As a consequence, he interpreted the tomb as that of a shaman, because "if the man had been a mere Gravettian hunter, why would he alone have been buried in the open outside the habitation site, only equiped for the world of beyond with useless objects, whether weapons or ornaments?" (Oliva 1996:383). In this case, in addition to the localization of the burial, the major support for an argument in favor of shamanic practices and beliefs is based upon portable artifacts.

5. Any Other Interpretive Hypotheses?

The hypothesis that the art of the caves and shelters reflect a shamanistic religion was proposed long before we did, as we explicitly said (Clottes and Lewis-Williams 1996:78). That relative antiquity of the theory has at times been considered as self-condemnatory, because we "recently wanted to revive an old theory that interpreted certain works for shamanistic practices" (Valentin 1999:103). "It seems to me futile to go back to the general models of the beginning of the century, already abandoned" (White 1997:111). "The shamanistic theory has undergone important criticism" (Cohen 1999:74), and even worse "that theory was unanimously criticized" (Mohen and Taborin 1998:73), to the point that "the shamanistic interpretation of Paleolithic cave art was decisively and for ever rejected both by Leroi-Gourhan (1977) and Lévi-Strauss (1973:389), because it was unprovable in any way" (Francfort 1998:313).

This implicitly means that a theory should fundamentally enjoy a limited life span. If it is old, it is *a priori* suspect. If it has been criticized and rejected in the past, then it must be considered as truly dead and must not be "revived" on any account. The argument of authority ("Leroi-Gourhan and Lévi-Strauss said it, thus…") is then the main prop of the reasoning. In this case, this is ironic, as the argument of authority was the one used mostly in medieval scholastic. Like those that were called "The Modern" in that very ancient quarrel, we prefer to examine the validity of arguments in the light of *present-day* knowledge and discoveries rather than rely on opinions - however illustrious and respectable - that were expressed in a different context.

At present, there is no other solidly argued interpretive hypothesis that would apply to the conceptual framework of Paleolithic art. A few proposals have however been made in a few short sentences and presented as alternatives to our ideas. Thus writers mentioned the human urge to create and the possibility that art reflected all the facets of life and that its aim would have been to influence the knowledge and behavior of people (Bahn 1997: see above).

That the creation of images by Paleolithic artists would betray a certain quest for perfection and even artistic enjoyment is possible and even probable judging from the extraordinary excellence of some works. We know, however, that art for art's sake did not exist in traditional societies. For example, in Australia, the concept of "art" was absent from the vocabulary of aboriginal groups. The images were produced within and for the collectivity in which the author lived, nor for his personal enjoyment or for the expression of his personal cravings. A need for novelties and individual creations aiming at escaping from existing rules and constricting schemes in order to express a personal conception of the world is a feeling peculiar to our own culture.

Traditional creation took place - and is still taking place - within a strict framework, its themes and its methods being established and consecrated by custom. This did not prevent what we would call real "artists" from existing, i.e. individuals that were not only gifted for the observation and transposition of the animal world into two or three dimensions, but who could also interpret it in their own personal way, through their talent and originality. The "Master" who worked at Chauvet, if we may make such an overly simple comparison, drew in a different manner from the "Master" in Lascaux, not only for cultural or chronological reasons.

To say that Upper Paleolithic people were like us and that, as a consequence, one should expect them to have represented whatever was constitutive of their lives is a specious argument: false conclusions are derived from an incontrovertible fact. That Upper Paleolithic people had the same intellectual and artistic abilities as we have is an accepted fact. But it is as obvious that their culture was extremely different from ours, that the art of hunter-gatherers is always the product of a complex culture, and that the ways of thinking of present-day Westerners living in an industrial era are not necessarily the same as theirs. Analogies and comparisons can only be made at the level of universals, which is not the case here. Even in Pre-Renaissance Europe, art did not deal with all the aspects of daily life; it was highly specialized. In fact, we would be hard put to find anything in cave art that would directly evoke the daily life of Paleolithic men and women.

As to the art influencing the knowledge and behavior of people, this is indeed possible. It is in fact one of the roles we explicitly suggested for the large painted halls. Yet, art is not necessarily meant for humans alone. It may have been made for the supernatural world in order to draw upon its power in one way or another. The social impact of images is too well-known to need elaborating (Bégouën 1924, 1939).

Far more interesting is the proposal that cave art would have transcribed myths (Sauvet and Tosello 1998, Taborin, 2000), as no culture can do without myths. Artistic creations are not isolated from the world in which they are made. This hypothesis was sometimes presented as a statement, as if it were self-evident: "One can only say that the art in the cave tells about a mythology. All the rest is imagination" (Taborin in *La Croix*, 20/12/1996). Such short-cuts are misleading: one should not deduce from the necessity of myths and sacred stories that all cultures represent them in their art. In some cases they do not, as has been made plain by ethnology. Thus, in the American South West, "the art does not depict myths or their principal actors; indeed, the art has no direct connection with mythology whatsoever (with one very specific exception)" (Whitley 1994a:6).

Sauvet and Tosello (1998:89) proposed the same hypothesis with more caution and a few arguments, the main one being that an intimate link between the cave images and sacred stories or myths would be "more apt to explain the internal coherence of the art." The North American example we quoted shows that their hypothesis would admit of exceptions and would thus necessitate more elaboration (for example, which myths would have been represented?) and more logical support. Leroi-Gourhan had tried to do just that with his interpretations of animals and signs according to the principles of femaleness and maleness, but he failed and acknowledged it towards the end of his life.

In addition, that hypothesis is contradicted in one major respect, as Leroi-Gourhan had himself observed: "One fact struck prehistorians (most prominently the Abbé H. Breuil), it is that the cave sanctuaries were not all intensely frequented, as the traces found inside them show. Some, - not the least elaborate, like Niaux - even seem to have had very few visits" (Leroi-Gourhan 1977:23). This fact concurs with the localization of so many images in restricted places inaccessible to even few persons and it contradicts the idea of myths being represented with a didactic aim, i.e. to perpetuate a sacred knowledge or to transmit it to a collectivity.

This is exactly why Leroi-Gourhan logically came to a shamanic explanation for cave art: "Personally, I often wondered whether the mere knowledge that an organized world existed in the heart of the earth would not have been the most efficient role of the images, and if the competent (not to say initiated) man or men were not the ones who could visit them, either physically or in their minds. From this to imagine shamanic travels would take but a step." But there he added characteristically: "that it is better not to take in order not to conjure up a hodge-podge of the Amerindian mistress of the buffalos freeing the herds from her cavern, Sedna keeping the seals in her underwater retreat, Orpheus charming the animals and recovering Eurydice, Mithra and her sacrificed bull, the shaman and his female statuettes and so many parallel bits of information borrowed from the most diverse cultures" (Leroi-Gourhan 1977:23). Most explicitly, he was then denying the strong temptation of the shamanistic hypothesis to which he had arrived. He did so not because of the merits of the hypothesis nor because it would contradict in any way the Paleolithic data, but solely because of his real phobia (*cf.* Perlès 1992) against ethnographic analogies.

Finally, Layton compared the shamanistic hypothesis to the totemic hypothesis and he strove to evolve a method in order to test them both. At this point, one must remark that they are not mutually exclusive, as can be seen from the knowledge of contemporary cultures. The North-West Canadian Kwakiutl, for example, were essentially totemistic and still practiced shamanism (Rosman and Ruebel 1990). Layton insists more than we did - even though we did it several times - upon the diversity of possibilities. This is more a problem of nuances than of divergence and basically his opinions are fairly close to ours. In fact, after applying his method to Paleolithic art, he concluded: "This test tends to support Clottes and Lewis-Williams' interpretation of the animal art" (Layton 2000b:183).

Other Questions and Tentative Answers by Way of Conclusion

We have been asked a number of questions about different problems, either in published accounts of our book or later, for instance after public lectures. They bear upon:
- the state of consciousness of the artists;
- who they were;
- the unskilfulness of some images;
- the origins of themes (in neurology or not?);
- the scarcity of human representations;
- the double logic of vast chambers and narrow recesses;
- the materialization of visions and its necessity.

Needless to say, we have no formal "scientific" proof that would enable us to solve those problems. We can, however, formulate hypotheses firmly based on facts and logical arguments.

The hypothesis that sophisticated paintings or engravings could have been made in a state of trance is most certainly not ours. A person in trance cannot master the technical and aesthetic subtleties of drawing, particularly in the case of the naturalistic works of art found in the dark of Paleolithic caves. Our answer to that could not be plainer. Out of necessity, the artists were fully conscious when they drew sophisticated figures on the cave walls. There may have been some exceptions, as in Pergouset (Lot), where the engravings become more and more deformed as one is proceeding farther along the narrow crawling passage (Lorblanchet and Sieveking 1997:53), but those exceptions are most rare. When the visions were materialized by drawing this was done after and not when they were taking place.

Would the shamans themselves have been the artists? It seems very likely, at least in a great number of cases. This is because the high quality and sophistication of the works is such that it could not have been so without specialization and training. In the framework we have defined and considering the cultures that produced the art, it would be unlikely that teaching and function would have been kept apart, i.e. that the shaman's soul would have travelled to the supernatural world while an artist would try to get in touch with the spirits of the other world through his or her drawings or would have materialized the visions of someone else. Images held power in themselves and the religious specialists had to master and exercise that power. It is quite possible that the problem was different with portable art, which was created in a quite different context from the art in the caves, and it may also have been different - but not necessarily so (see above) - from the art in the open.

It is even possible to go a few steps further and to use established facts in order to hypothesize about the way the shamans were selected as well as about the teaching they underwent. The so often remarkably high quality of the images drawn on the cave walls raises the question of innate artistic qualities in children. One cannot exclude that children with precocious artistic gifts might have been singled out because people felt that they had thus been favored by the spirits. Those abilities would then have been one of the major criteria in the selection of future shamans. After all, the ability to represents aspects of reality with accuracy - and as a consequence of being able to exercise a form of control over natural and supernatural forces - could well have been perceived as being truly magical.

On the other hand, the lack of skill apparent in other representation (Figure 12), the indeterminate lines and traces on the walls, the hand stencils and hand prints (among which a number of children's hands) might betray the presence of other persons who participated in the rites (for initiation, curing, etc.) in their own way.

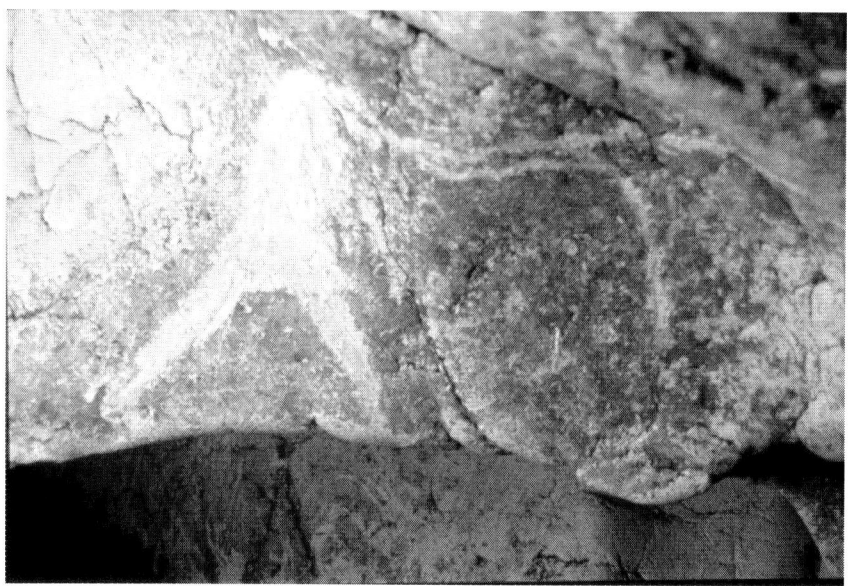

Figure 12. Not all cave art was done by skillful artists. This crude mammoth was engraved in Chauvet Cave (Ardèche, France). *Photo J. Clottes.*

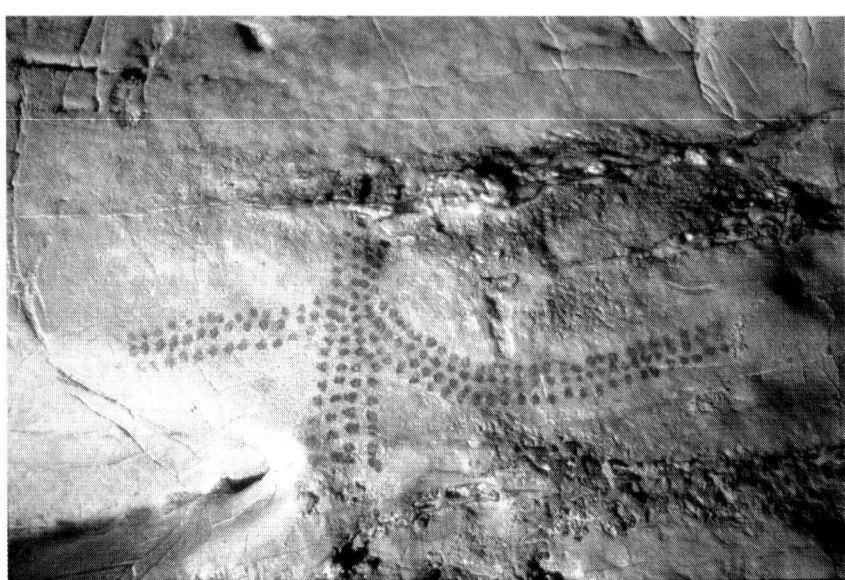

Figure 13. Whatever their meaning, geometric signs such as this one might have had a neurological origin. El Castillo Cave (Cantabria, Spain). *Photo L. de Seille.*

The choice of the themes represented could have had a neurological origin in the case of the simple geometrical signs that are found everywhere and at all times (Figure 13). They would have originated in phosphenes, those images that form within the eye, particularly in the initial stage of trance. A number of the naturalistic painted and engraved images could also have come from the shaman's visions. It is necessary, however, to stress the fact that the contents of those visions had to be controlled, canalized and we might say in great part informed by the training the shaman had undergone and by the cultural beliefs and structures impressed upon him/her in that training. The real origin of those themes was then - and could not be other than - cultural. Their precise meaning, as well as the meaning of geometrical signs,[11] is sure to have varied, too, in different cultures, times and places. One may note that it has been experimentally established that phospenes can play the role of "inductors" for the travels of the mind which they facilitate, somewhat like a catalyt (Lemaire 1993:79, 167). It is therefore not impossible that some geometrical signs might have played that part.

The scarcity of human images in Paleolitithic art has always been intriguing. It is certain that, on all continents and at all periods, humans have always placed themselves - under whatever guise - right in the middle of their stories to explain the world. If they are so rare in

Paleolithic cave art, this choice might result from their natural conditions of living. The world around them was teeming with animal life, and their own groups were so few and scattered. It is understandable that, under those conditions, Upper Paleolithic people should have chosen animal forms for their supernatural spirits, and that those particular images were then drawn inside the caves where they tried to get in touch with the powerful forces that resided there. The extreme scarcity of human representations in the caves is another hint that those animal images, in most cases disconnected from one another, were neither a mere reproduction of their everyday world nor directly tell a particular story. They were drawn for other reasons.

In Paleolithic painted caves, there is a double logic, that of the vast chambers and that of the isolated recesses. The latter, where only one or two persons could be at a time, were not often frequented, as we can tell from the scarcity of traces. In their case, the end result, i.e. the image itself, could not have been the main purpose. What must have counted most was the creation of the image (Figure 14). On the other hand, the drawings in vast chambers such as those at Niaux, Lascaux, Chauvet, Pech-Merle, etc., are often far more elaborate and spectacular, as though they were deliberately meant for spectators. As the tradition's

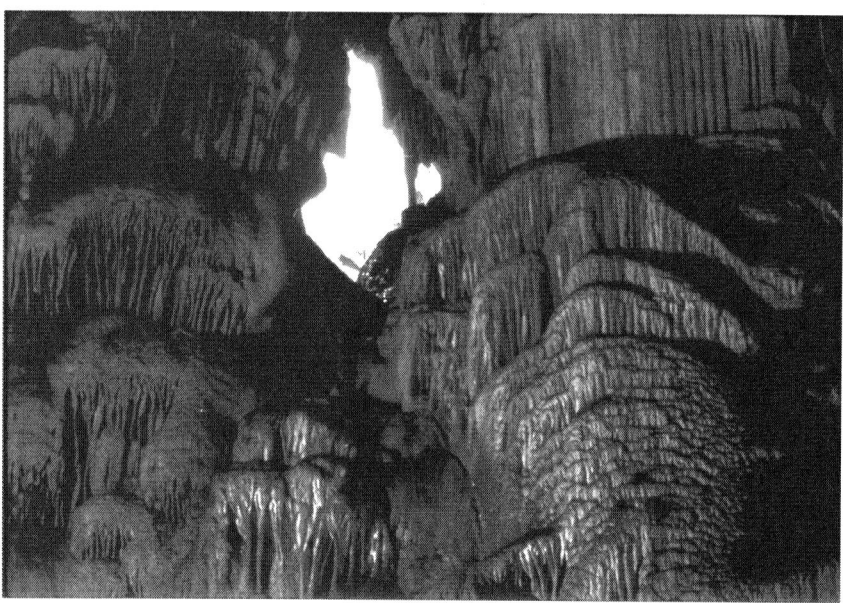

Figure 14. In Candamo Cave (Asturias, Spain), a narrow recess can only be accessed by climbing along the sides of a several meter high stalagmite. A horse and a few other images were nevertheless drawn there. *Photo L. de Seille.*

perpetuation over twenty millenia or more must have necessitated a dogmatic teaching to have lasted so long, it is quite possible that those chambers might occasionally have played a role in the process.

Finally, why materialize visions? Ethnographic examples provide some clues. For example, in California and Nevada, the shamans painted their visions on the rocks the following day. People (and themselves) thought that if they did not do so they would become ill and die. The places thus adorned were loaded with power and they facilitated new "travels" (Whitley 2000a), a role that the big chambers in our caverns may also have played. In the east-central part of the Indonesian island of Celebes, shamans go at night to meet the spirits - often animals that transform themselves into men - in the forest where those spirits reside. There the shamans eat hallucinogenic fruit to induce visions which they then describe to the group: by speaking about them they reinforce their intrinsic power[12]. We can see that, for them, the forest plays a role comparable to that of the cavern or the shelter in a different context. In that case, narrating the visions fulfills the same function as drawing them.

Materializing visions might then have had multiple complementary roles: to concretize them out of vital necessity; to add to their power; to facilitate new visions; to open a door into the world of the spirits with whom one wanted to get in touch; even to have a mnemonic use, comparable to iconography in the Judeo-Christian tradition (Chaumeil 1999:45).

We have read and listened with interest to the criticisms which have been offered. Some surprised us by their vehemence (see Clottes and Lewis-Williams 2001) as well as their content. Still, they helped us in so far as we had to make some of our positions more explicit. The years after our book was first published have given us distance and perspective to reassess our position. New discoveries in rock art, papers and books on Upper Paleolithic art and ethnography, various facts of which we had been unaware but which were later brought to our attention, none of these new elements have contradicted the hypotheses we put forward: on the contrary, they have reinforced them.

---

[1] Lewis-Williams and Dowson 1988, 1992; Lewis-Williams 1991, 1994, 1997; Clottes and Lewis-Williams 1997a, 1997b, 2000; Lewis-Williams and Clottes 1998a, 1998b.
[2] That particular attitude regarding our book is erroneous from a methodological point of view. It (and the state of mind that caused it) were denounced by another of our commentators : "To comprehend this argument in all its complexity I recommend reading the book for yourself, for unlike many others who take sides

in the 'shamanic wars' currently debated among rock art enthusiasts around the world, I am not willing to condense it to a few simplistic sound-bytes." (Dobres 1999:91).

[3] This statement is just not true. As this has been discussed elsewhere and as shamanism in Southern Africa is not our present topic we shall not respond here and will just cite some articles where this was done: Lewis-Williams 1992a; Lewis-Williams and Dowson 1988; Lewis-Williams and Clottes 1998a.

[4] Our emphasis.

[5] Ethnographic analogy, however, is not without defenders in the present day and age: "Although ethnographic analogy is replete with problems, it is much better than not attempting an explanation for the rock art" (Loendorf 1994:130). "Structuralist methods should be supplemented by other explanatory models, e.g. the use of ethnographic and ethnohistoric analogies, as in the case of South Africa" (Mandt 1995:276). Polly Shaasfma, a well-known specialist of rock art in the American South West, interprets the art of the Colorado Plateau from "more or less universal aspects of shamanic phenomena from more remote ethnographic contexts" (Shaasfma 1994:47).

[6] "A careful reading of Chapter 1 makes clear how such observations are being employed while carefully avoiding the pitfalls of simple-minded and superficial ethnographic analogy (a topic Lewis-Williams has been prolific in condemning over the years)" (Dobres 1999:91).

[7] "A survey of 488 ethnic societies found 90% had some form of institutionalized, culturally patterned form of altered states of consciousness (Bourguignon 1973:11, 1977:10) and, in North America, that percentage incread to 97% of the ethnographically documented aboriginal societies" (Turpin 1994:79).

[8] That role is admitted by Atkinson, who, while deploring that the psychological aspects of shamanism are too much stressed as compared to its sociological aspects, writes: "Certainly shifts in consciousness are a key part of shamanic practice," adding "understanding the neurophysiology of trance is valuable" (Atkinson 1992).

[9] Our emphasis

[10] What we tried to do was understood and acknowledged by some authors: "While remaining very prudent and rejecting 'all global system of expanation,' they make us think that shamanism presents a framework that is far more explanatory than all the theories proposed before" (Tcherter 1997:63). On the other hand, others while plainly acknowledging the fundamental unity of the themes and techniques of cave art (Vialou 1998:17-19, 21), still baulk at the logical conclusion that that unity is the consequence of a common way of thinking.

[11] "The neuropsychological model describes only the origins of geometric imagery in rock art - it does not explain the meaning of these images" (Blundell 1998:10).

[12] Information gathered and kindly told to us by Gérard Nougarol, an ethnomusicologist, who has been studying those people since 1991.

Discussion

Angelo Fossati: How do you explain the rock art in the open air?

Jean Clottes: I didn't broach that subject today, but that was also one criticism. They said we weren't talking about open air rock art or mobilary art. Of course, we were talking about the caves, because in the caves we have everything. As such they are an ideal place to try to understand the reasons for the art for several reasons. First, in the caves the paintings are protected, while those done outside were not. You can never find a twenty thousand year old painting outside. And also, in the caves we have the traces of the artists' actions. For example, in many instances we have found bits of bone stuck into the cracks, evidence that people were trying to get in touch with what's behind the wall. It would be almost impossible to find this outside. So we focused our work on the caves.

But that doesn't mean that what was outside was part of a different religion. No. In my opinion they went into the caves relatively rarely because every time a new cave is found—a cave that is well preserved without being trampled—you have evidence of *very few people* going in there. For example, in Chauvet cave there is a small gallery going to the end chamber and the ground is littered with charcoal. Those charcoals were not trampled. We have radiocarbon dates from several of them—half a dozen dates between 30,000 and 32,000 years ago. If that cave had been frequented by lots of people those charcoals would have been trampled obviously. So I think they went into the caves rarely, for very special circumstances, whereas most of their ceremonies took place outside. Probably there was far more rock art outside than we know, because the only Paleolithic rock art—which are carvings—that we know of outside is in Spain and Portugal where the conditions for preservation are much better than in France or England. So I think its all part of the same religion, because they drew the same animals. But, some people have criticized us about that saying that the art outside contradicts that which is underground. It is like saying that if you have churches, its impossible for a priest to give mass outside, or to put a cross on top of a hill. But they do it all the time! You can't restrict people to your own preconceptions. Those cultures were very rich.

Linea Sundstrom: I have two comments. The first concerns the possibility of proof—something I talked about in my dissertation (Sundstrom 1989a) and some other publications (Sundstrom 1989b, 2002) that dealt with the possibility of proving or disproving something that happened in the past. I think a lot of us are trained to think that the only way to study anything is through "science." Most of us [scholars in the audience] have our degrees in anthropology and yet very few of us were required to take a course in history, art history, or historical theory. I suggest that this is our bias. We think were scientific and therefore unbiased, but instead we're scientific and biased in that particular way. There are other ways to study the world.

The second thing is completely unrelated to that. In terms of the kinds of animal images in the caves I recently heard about a study of dreams—regular sleep dreams—and they said that very young children dream about animals, but as they get older their dreams become more diverse and they begin to dream about other things. But the early dreams are almost exclusively about animals.

Jean Auel: How do they know?

Linea Sundstrom: They interviewed children. And they found that over time the focus on animals tapers off. Now I'm not saying that the people who made the cave art were children, but maybe we're somehow hard-wired for that.

Kelley Hays-Gilpin: Or the art is for initiating children—that was one hypothesis for a while—and the images are referring back to that.

Linea Sundstrom: I believe this theory because my children could talk very early and when my son was little he wouldn't wake up easily. I would sit with him and gradually try to awaken him (two or three times a day when he had his nap) and I would always ask him if he had had a dream—if he saw anything in his sleep. He always talked about animals; every single time. That was between the ages of ten months and two years. I thought maybe there was something wrong with him because he didn't dream about people, but this study indicates that's normal.

Jean Clottes: It may be that we're hard-wired that way, because for millions of years people have been living in a world where there were far more animals than humans. Our situation now is reversed, but just for the last few generations—maybe for the past century or two. But for millions of years it was a world with very few humans and lots of animals. And so that makes sense—that those animals would be the powers, the spirit powers would have animal forms. Because we know of many cultures where people consider themselves as just a special kind of animal; and the animals are brothers. There are many examples of this. So it makes complete sense that children should have retained that kind of ancestral memory.

About proof, yes, there has been much discussion about that. We need to build cables with many strands—which I believe in because it makes sense. When dealing with human sciences like archaeology, we cannot use the same methods as when we are dealing with physics or mathematics.

David Whitley: But there is even a more intense elaboration on that if you pay careful attention to what has happened in Philosophy of Science in the last 100 years. It has changed dramatically, and what I see—getting back to Linea's comment about what we were really taught as graduate students—is that there is no question that archaeology adopted the pre-World War II philosophy of science. It got entrenched in the discipline with the hypothetico-deductive model. Meanwhile, philosophers of science went off in other directions and there's a pretty good consensus that (with the exception of mathematics and logic) there's no such thing as proof, and all we ever do is infer to the best hypothesis with the evidence at hand. This really came through to me dealing with the Junior High School science fair in California, in which my daughter was involved and I was a judge. I discovered all of a sudden, that—at least in general terms—no one is teaching scientific method as a philosopher of science today would probably advocate it. (The teachers are) confusing laboratory experimental technique with scientific method which is a means of adjudicating between hypotheses. These kids have to figure out what's the independent and dependent variable and they think that's scientific method. But its not.

The point simply is that this issue of proof is sort of exemplary of intellectual confusion happening everywhere. And it's a big problem for us. My view is that we are robbing children of the single strongest intellectual thing that they can have—the ability to think scientifically. Because we're teaching them the wrong thing about what science is.

One other comment I want to make about the criticism of Jean and David has to do with criticisms like those of Alice Kehoe. She is one of the most vocal critics and she has accused Jean and David quite directly of being racist. That's pretty strange when you remember that Tabo M'beki, the president of South Africa, called up David specifically and asked him to help design the crest for the new republic of South Africa and come up with a new motto for the country. But otherwise, she exemplifies a way of thinking that a lot of the critics are using, and that is quite simply inductive—arguing from the particular to the general. She always takes an anecdote and claims that that's it. In other words, let's criticize Mircea Eliade and show that his synthesis was wrong and then because he was wrong in the general arguments about shamanism, anyone who is talking about shamanism is wrong.

What she fails to recognize is that I've never read Eliade. I read Kroeber and Willard Parks—people like that.

Bob Layton: Jean [Clottes] was very nice about me. I'm one of the people who believe that you can't recover meaning in the Upper Paleolithic. My argument is that its more productive to treat shamanism as a form of political control of knowledge and that that results in particularly appropriate ways of producing paintings.

David Whitley: But that's a kind of meaning.

Bob Layton: No, no it isn't. It is a way of using knowledge but its not in itself a form of meaning. I think that the animal art in the upper Paleolithic has the best case for being shamanic. If you accept that typically in the ethnography certain animal species are the favored vehicles for trance experience, and if you accept that (by definition) trance experience is something that's accessible to people throughout the society—not everyone will get it, but there is no notion that any one local group has the prerogative over that. Whereas totemism, every clan, every group, has its own guardian animal and therefore you will find that the members of a clan will preferentially depict the animals that are appropriate to them.

But, for example, what I suggested was that those large rectangular shapes—tectiforms—are characteristically distinctive to particular places. Although you can have a generalized category of tectiforms, where you find three or four side by side on a panel they're typically variants within a form which is unique to that particular cave and therefore, we might say that what you're looking at there (as Dennis Vialou has suggested) are markers of specific places. And therefore another aspect of the literal use of these images in the Upper Paleolithic.

I'm not saying anything about what they mean, I'm saying how are they used. And I think maybe the mobilary art is something else again. We don't typically find scenes or compositions about foraging practices in the cave art, but we do find them in mobilary art. And therefore, perhaps the mobilary art is more concerned with everyday life than the cave art is.

Fundamentally I agree with Jean and David that on the strength of the evidence, the most plausible hypothesis is that the majority of the cave art was concerned with trance experience.

Phillip Cash Cash: I would like to comment on the use of animal images and the idea that they reflect the power of the people themselves. To follow the logic that I'm most familiar with from my area, when I look at these images, they're animals that possibly were part of the meat supply of the people, and if that was the case, then the powers that they had were carnivorous—meaning that the powers they had craved meat and that these animals constituted that meat supply. That's just the logic that I would apply, because there are certain powers among our people that craved meat. They were carnivorous spirit powers. To satisfy them they ate raw meat.

Linea Sundstrom: So you're saying that they drew the pictures to feed the spirits?

Phillip Cash Cash: To kind of fulfill their craving—the craving of the power itself. That would be close to it.

Jean Clottes: But all the animals that are represented are not those that were hunted. For example, in the first cultures of the upper Paleolithic, like the Aurignacian, the majority of represented animals were not hunted: wooly rhinocerous, mammoth, cave bear, and cave lion.

Phillip Cash Cash: But see—the shamans' *powers* may have been carnivorous. Those powers ate other animals. It wasn't the humans that ate the animals, it would have been the power that fed on other animals.

Jean Clottes: Oh, you mean something spiritual?

Phillip Cash Cash: Yes.

Jean Auel: Jean, how do you know the depicted animals weren't hunted?

Jean Clottes: We infer that from the fact that we don't find their bones.

Jean Auel: Yes, but when hunting something like mammoth, they're not likely to haul many bones back. They're going to haul the meat back.

Jean Clottes: Yes, but if they frequently hunted mammoth, we would find a lot more mammoth bones or ivory than we do. We don't find very much. Probably they scavenged, but I see no proof that they were hunting these animals very often.

James Keyser: I want to come back to Phillip's point, which I think is very important. That is, I don't think what Philip is saying is that this is what regular people eat. This is a different thing.

Jean Clottes: Yes, absolutely.

Phillip Cash Cash: Yes, the particular powers craved meat of some animals they fed on. It wasn't so much what humans crave, but in addition to that.

Linea Sundstrom: This may be somewhat similar to my eagle trapping example [see Sundstrom, chapter 4, this volume] where eagles and snakes are opposed in a certain way. So it's not that people ate either eagles or snakes.

David Whitley: But eagles eat snakes.

Linea Sundstrom: Yes, but for the Mandan-Hidatsa the snakes would help you get the eagles.

Jannie Loubser: I believe the eland was perhaps a case in point—if you look at the former records, which are the early travelers' accounts of what the bushmen said themselves. The bushmen didn't really hunt eland often. They would hunt springbok—medium size antelope—far more and that's borne up by all the archaeological evidence. But what they really liked is the fat from the eland, and medicine men would rub themselves with it to help them journey to the spirit world. There were a lot of analogies drawn between the spiritual journey and the fat. Also bees' honey was a food category, but rather than a general category is was one of supernatural potency.

James Keyser: We have a similar situation in Columbia Plateau rock art, where we see so many mountain sheep; site after site. We excavated sites on the Columbia Plateau, but you could put all the mountain sheep bones that have ever been found right in my hands.

David Whitley: The same thing occurs in the Great Basin.

James Keyser: Yes, and you suggest that in the Great Basin, there's some relationship between shamanism and mountain sheep. Is there any reason known why so many mountain sheep are drawn in Columbia Plateau rock art? Phillip, do you know of any reason why mountain sheep might be important—other than as a food animal?

Phillip Cash Cash: I'm not really sure how to answer. If there were five, then they might be associated with the myth of the legend times.

Don Hann: I'd like to get back to one of the other topics–the term shamanism. I certainly understand one would borrow words, so I personally don't have any baggage about using a term that was specific to one group as a general term. But one of the things our Native American counterparts have brought up is that different groups did have distinctively different religions. There's things that tie them together but there are also differences. We know that scholars have a predisposition to generalize and to focus on similarities rather than the specifics of each group we work with. I've read Kehoe and I disagree with much of her concern, but is there some better terminology that we could use? I certainly haven't found it yet.

David Whitley: I don't think there is. If you have any interest in generalizing beyond the particular, there really isn't. I think Mary Womack (2001) made a very good point in responding to Kehoe's argument that we shouldn't be using the term shaman. Mary basically said that's what we do if we do science and if our goal is generalization. We've got to have terms that have different levels of meaning. And then she used the example of marriage, which we use for a formal institution in a lot of different cultures. But marriage does, in fact, mean slightly different things; it has different implications in California versus in other parts of the country. The point she ultimately made was that anthropologists aren't objecting when we're taking words like marriage which is from old French—a western European language—and generalizing with it. But, if we take an indigenous term like shaman, which is coming out of Siberian Tungu-speaking Evenki, then people are getting upset. Her point is that it appears to be okay to these critics if we only generalize with western European terms, but it's improper to import other terms into our language. I think the answer there is quite obvious.

CHAPTER 7
Tíim'enin': Indigenous Conceptions of Columbia Plateau Rock-art
Phillip Cash Cash

Nez Perce

    Kíi táaqc páayn 'éc'iiqse 'ínim titooqatímtpa. 'Éc'iiqse kínm tíim'enin'.

Kíne pewéeteskin'ix (Figure 1), 'ínim wéetespe we'nikíin "southern Columbia Plateau," 'ilχníiwe hiwsíix waqíiman tíim'enin'. Ke ku'ús núunk'e titóoqanm, hete'ewníx hiwsíix kíime tíim'enin'. 'Imeméeq'umcix núunim híimte'kt kaa núunim wiyéwc'etpeme. Ku'stíite núune péeten'wetetum wéeteskin'iχ.

English

    This day I come talking in my indigenous language. I am speaking of the 'pictograph.'

    Here, throughout this land (Figure 1), in my homeland called the "southern Columbia Plateau," there are many ancient pictographs. To us as indigenous people, these pictographs are very sacred. They hold dear our teachings and our history. In the same way, they continually speak to us from the land.

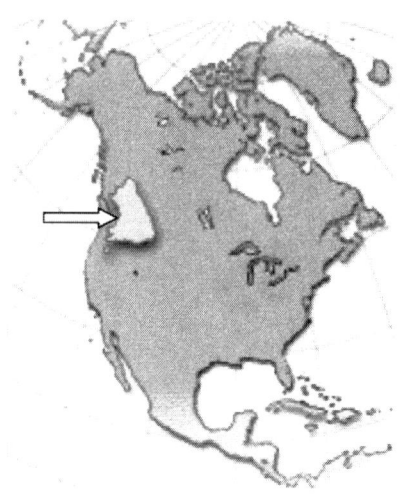

Figure 1 Location of the Columbia Plateau in Northwestern North America.

Táaqc, kíi tim'ées hitqeten'wéesem kíime tim'éenin' kínm "Butte Creek-witáaspa." "Butte Creek-witáas" kúuniχ hí'pewye lu'qíickin'ikeey kaa χuyéełpe "Oregon-pa." 'Ec'íicpe kíi ceptemelíχnikt kinímpa "Butte Creek-witáaspa"'iyáaχnin' pilepúusus waχ púutimt waχ páaχat tim'éenin'. Kinéeme χuyyí hikúuse lepít yóχ wic'enéewitwiteespe. Kíime hiwsíix "Steiwer Ranch-witáaspa" kaa "Rattlesnake Shelter-witáaspa."

Kiné ceptemelíiχnikse ku' mác piswéenm híisemtukt tim'ée kaa koníix 'ew'níise ku'x mac kímti temée'nitne. Ku'ús 'ekúuse kíi *"sepéecuukwen'in wikúut"* (Taçon and Chippindale 1998). Yóχ we, 'ankáaχalpsa wiwaqititóoqanm suqútpeme kaa kúus sapáahaykat keyóχ titóoqanm wiyéecuukwen'in koním yawa "Columbia Plateau-nim" tim'éenin'.

Kí'u wáaqo' 'aw'nakáhtqawna lepítine tim'éenin'e. Kíi kaa 'éete hiwées 'iske c'íiqciqa kikusínm 'anóoqtipx. Kíime hiwsíix núunimkin'ix 'ec'íicpeme eyéewc'etpeme'éetu ke yóχ núunim píiwapc'iyawpama titóoqa.

Kí'u wáaqo' hiwées tim'ée kaa hekípe titóoqa (Figure 2). 'Imé 'éetχ 'esúukiyu' ku' mac wíitim'e kóna 'aqámkin'ika húususnim kaa mitáhampa.

Today, this paper describes the pictographs of the Butte Creek site. The Butte Creek site is located in the southern region beyond the Columbia River of Oregon. A recent investigation at the Butte Creek site found 415 pictographs. From this, two main areas emerged. These are the Steiwer Ranch site and the Rattlesnake Shelter site.

I examine several rock-art images and (from that) I offer several new interpretations. I make use of the *informed method* (Taçon and Chippindale 1998). That is, I draw from ethnohistorical sources and render visible (that which is our) indigenous conceptions concerning Columbia Plateau rock-art.

Here, now I am selecting two pictographs. And surely now, as if speaking, they are coming forward. These (images) are from our recent human history, specifically that which concerns our indigenous warfare.

Here now is a marked grouping of human figures (Figure 2). You will notice a number of markings above each of their heads in three instances.

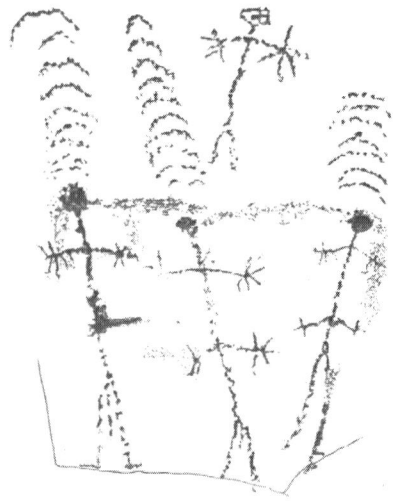 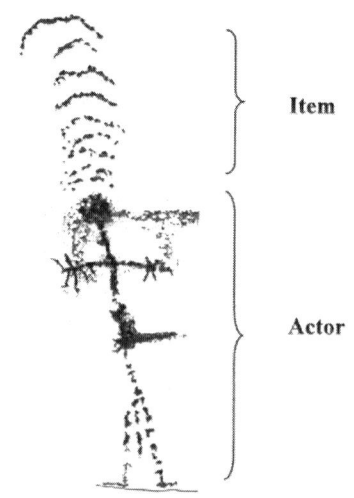

Figure 2 A group of figures from the Steiwer Ranch site 35WH38.

Figure 3 The Actor-Item association.

Kinníx híisemtukt hiwées neke'sníix. Hiwées 'itúunex we'nikíse "wiyekiyew'éet waχ wipe'túu" piwyéetwenin' (after Munn 1973:80). Kíi piwyéetwenin' himscúukweno'qa ke ku'ús hihísaqsa yóχ náaqc wiyekiyew'éetnim 'ipnimnáawit (Figure 3).

Kinkí nekítpe, wáaqo' ceptemelíiχnikse kíime tíim'e ku' 'itúuki hiwées c'úukwenin' titwáatityayanmpa. Kaa núunim wíitim'ee c'íiqin hiwées 'iyáaχnin' titwáatit 1930's-kin'ix.

Kínu' Gilbert Minthorn-nim Weyíiletpu 'eten'wéese (Figure 4).
"Yóχ 'eexnéenitx konma'í tíim'e titóoqanm? Kaa koná wáwya péepe'x téχweyešpe. Koná wáwya kál'a kaa 'itúune šik'éemne huumée

This particular configuration is very significant. It is what I am calling, an "actor--item" association (after Munn 1973:80). This particular association can be understood as increasing the actor's attributes (Figure 3).

With this mind, I now compare each of these markings with what is known in our oral tradition. Found in our language texts is a story from the 1930's.

Gilbert Minthorn, a Cayuse, is speaking (Figure 4).

"See that manner of Indian marking? A "hit" is to strike the enemy in battle.
"The "hit" may be of a horse or a "hit" upon a dead

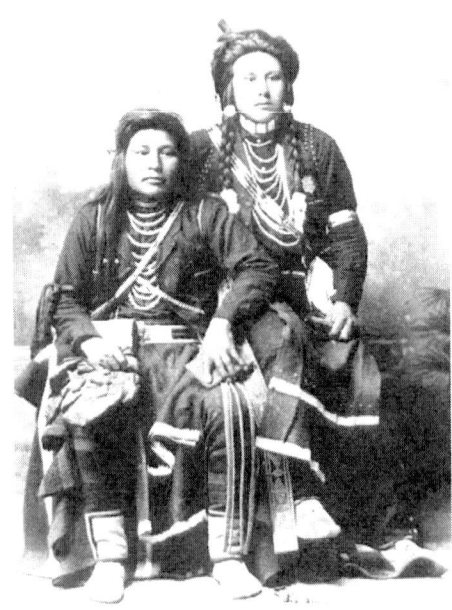

Figure 4 Gilbert Minthorn, a Cayuse, is seated to the right. Photograph courtesy of Tamastslik Cultural Institute.

titóoqana tin'χníišne píiwapciýawpa wáwya huumée waq'íišna wáwya píiwapciýawpa. Kíi ku'úšpeme 'ewšíine tíim'e wáwya haníit. Kíi kínye 'éetx 'óykaloo šooyáapuu 'epemscúukwenu'. Kíi ku'úškin'ix 'awc'aníiqa titóoqan miyóoχatowit píiwapciýawkin'ix."
(Minthorn 1930)

person in war or a "hit" upon the living in war. Concerning this manner (of doing), they had a "hit" mark making. Of this, all of you White people will understand. From thus here, they used to become an Indian leader from war."
(Minthorn 1930)

Ku'ús Gilbert Minthorn-nim péetimee'nise náaqc tíim'e 'iske "WÁWYA" (Figure 5), yóχ wa "péepe'x téχweyešpe." Ku'stíite 'iléχli tíim'e 'ipnáatamapayks yóχ 'ináhinaqin' tilke'ynew'éet kaa náaqc 'isíinm we húume hiwc'éeyu' miyóoχatowit píiwapciýawkin'ix. Kíi witíim'e

Thus, Gilbert Minthorn is interpreting this single marking as a "hit" (Figure 5), that is "to strike with a blunt instrument in battle." Similarly, many markings indicate an accomplished warrior, one who is or will become a leader from war. Here, each image is

Phillip Cash Cash 147

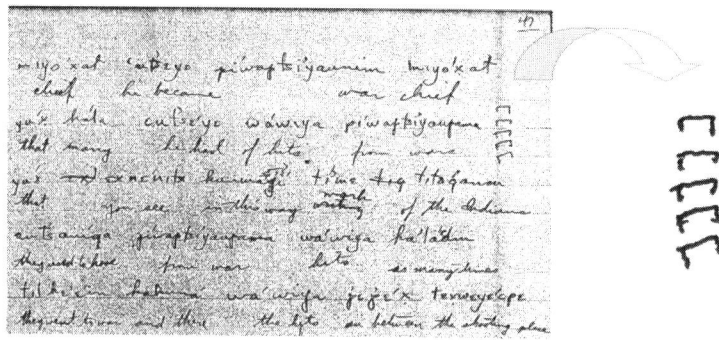

Figure 5 "Wáwya," a hit marking. From a linguistic text collected by Morris Swadesh, 1930.

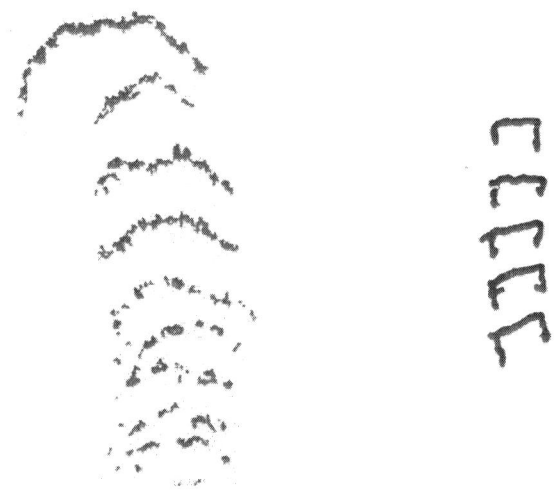

Figure 6 Comparison of "Wáwya" pictographic representations: At left, pictograph at 35WH38; at right illustration from Minthorn linguistic text.

hiwées qo' heci'sníiχ kíne he'kípe (Figure 6). Yóχ wa, wáwya 'ipnatamáapayks 'úylepwene tíim'enin'pe ku'stíite titwáatityayanmpa.

      Kíye nekíin sepíinewyu'qe kíi "wiyekiyew'éet waχ wipe'túu" piwyéetwenin' kíi ko'sanníχ. Kaa Wáwya tíim'e ku'ús hic'íiqtetum yóχ neχce'éce Wikúutpama

strikingly alike in appearance (Figure 6). That is, a "hit" is referenced in both rock-art image and in our oral tradition.

      We can now summarize this particular "actor--item" association in the following manner. A "hit" marking thus describes a set of behavioral keku'ús yóχ titóoqanm 'ewc'éeyu' sukín'. Kíne wa konma'í, Wáwya tíim'e hiwées lawwíit 'ipnimnáawit (Figure 7). Kaa 'ipné kúut'es 'iske sepéecuukwece tamtáaynim. Konma'í hitamtáayca la'ám 'ipnimnáawit kaa kíne 'imíitpa kaa koná 'inéekniktpa.

Kíi temée'nit wa hiwéeke hi'niye yoχniq'ó'c Keyser-pa (et. al 1998a). Kaa lawwitnáawitna pée'níye kíi ku'stíite hi'kúuynektetu yóχ temée'nit. Kaa c'awíin, kíyeχ 'ewéwluqse q'ó' haníiya ko'spayníx yóχ kiné. Henéek'e kakáa kíye tak'áycix kíi híisemtukt tíim'e, 'imé 'éetχ 'esúukiyu' yóχ 'ipc'á'ka titóoqanm héecet penneχsepne'í lukuyníx kaa 'ipnacapatkáaws. Wíitim'e hiwsíix 'aqámkin'ika húususnim ku'ús 'ipnáatamapayks keyóχ lukúylukuynim cuq'úulilamks. Kawatíita híican'aχ hisqu'yúuse náaqcnim ipnimnáawit. Yoχtíita héen'eke

characteristics whereby an individual becomes recognized. In this sense, a "hit" marking is a status indicator (Figure 7). It functions as a means of communicating information. In this manner, it is relating individual status within and among social groups.

This interpretation was first proposed in Keyser (et.al 1998a). The evidence presented thus far confirms this interpretation. However, I want to make an important distinction here. Again when we look at this particular pictographic image, you will notice that the human figures are arranged both vertically and horizontally. The markings located above each of their heads thus indicates its vertical axis. At the same time, it can be said to reference individual status. Again, you will notice the (grouping of)

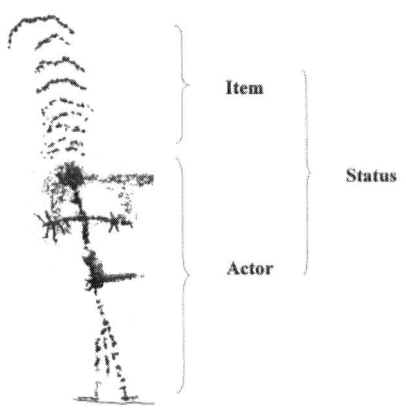

Figure 7   The Actor-Item association as an indicator of status.

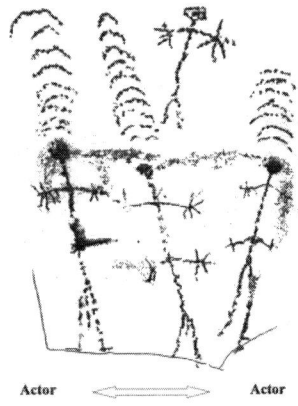

Figure 8   Horizontal alignment of Actor associations.

'imé 'éetχ 'esúukiyu' yóχ titóoqanm héecet hiwsíix 'ipc'á'ka 'ipnacapatkáaws. Kaa ku'stíite ke yóχ hiwées 'ipnacapatkáaws kaa cuq'úulilamks híican'aχ hisqu'yúuye yóχ 'imemnéewit titóoqa 'inéeknikt (Figure 8).

    'Etimée'nis kíi wa c'á'in waχ c'á'in háamanm titóoqanm héecet keyóχ 'iske hisqu'yúuse neké'sniχ telkeke'ykew'éet. Yóχ wa, pakk'o háamanm titóoqanm héecet hiwées miyóoχat. Ku'ús 'iméem 'ipc'á'ka híican'aχ hisqu'yúuye keyóχ titóoqanm píiwyatw'ahtksix.

    Kaa 'úykin'ix piswéenm híisemtuktne 'uuléekiyu' ku'úsu hiwées 'ipc'á'ka penneχsepne'í kinníx 'itúunex we'nikíse "wiyekiyew'éet waχ c'á'in" piwyéetwenin' (Figure 9). Kíi híisemtukt péetwikce titwáatityayana tamtáaycana. Yóχ wa 'ipc'á'ka wihíisemtukt 'iske c'á'in kaa c'á'in.

human figures are arranged horizontally. And, similarly, that which is its horizontal axis can be said to reference social group status (Figure 8).

    I interpret each instance of repetition of figures as referencing a distinct leader. That is, each figurine is a chief, a leader of a group of people. Thus, their arrangement can be said to represent social solidarity.

    The next rock-art image I will look at is arranged variously in what I am calling an "actor-event" association (Figure 9). This imagery follows a narrative mode of expression. That is, each image is arranged as an event sequence.

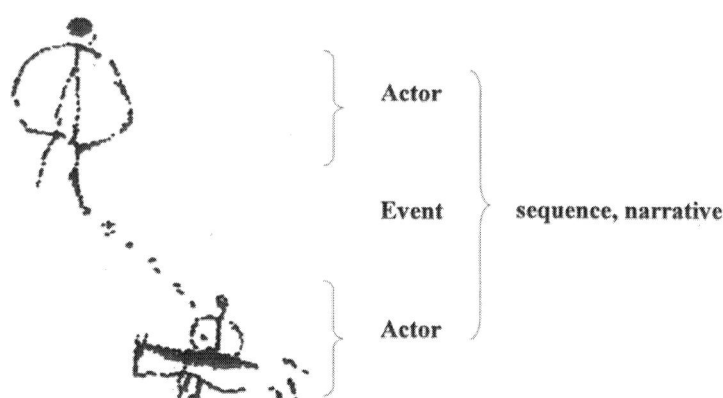

Figure 9 An "Actor-Event" association.

C'a'á hepéey híisemtukt kíne hiwées c'á'in pitaχc'a'kawáat píi'amktat'asíix (Figure 10). Kíne 'imé 'éetχ 'esúukiyu' yóχ hekípe titóoqanm héecet hiwsíix 'ipc'á'ka pellepú' 'inéek'niktpe. Yóχ wa náaqc 'inéek'nikt 'úus mác yik'úupc'eski titóoqanm héecet kaa 'úykin'ix náaqc 'inéek'nikt 'úus mác wece'í titóoqanm héecet. Kinníx tíim'e híisemtukt hiwées neke'sníix. Kíi hiwées 'etke 'ipnáatamapayks yóχ q'o'c c'á'in hiwéeyem sík'em kinéepχ wéetes (Figure 11).

The central image here is a scene of combatants coming together (Figure 10). Here, you will notice that the human figures are arranged in two groups. That is, one group is composed of a set of shield-bearing figures and the other group is composed of a set of human figures on horseback. This particular pictographic image is very significant. This is because it indicates the first stages following the arrival of the horse into this land (Figure 11), the southern Columbia Plateau.

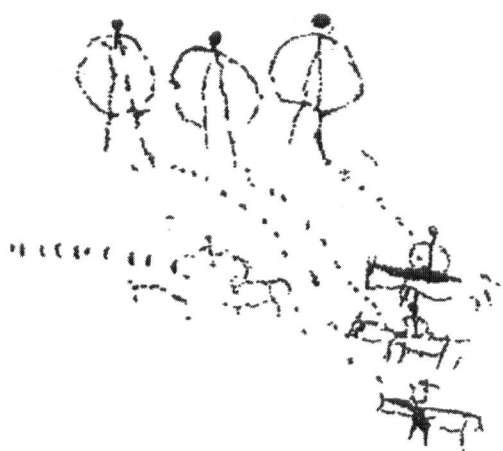

Figure 10 The Steiwer Ranch (35WH38) battle scene.

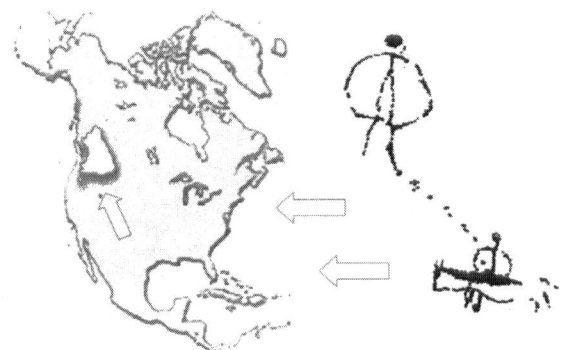

Figure 11 The first stages following the arrival of the horse into the Columbia Plateau.

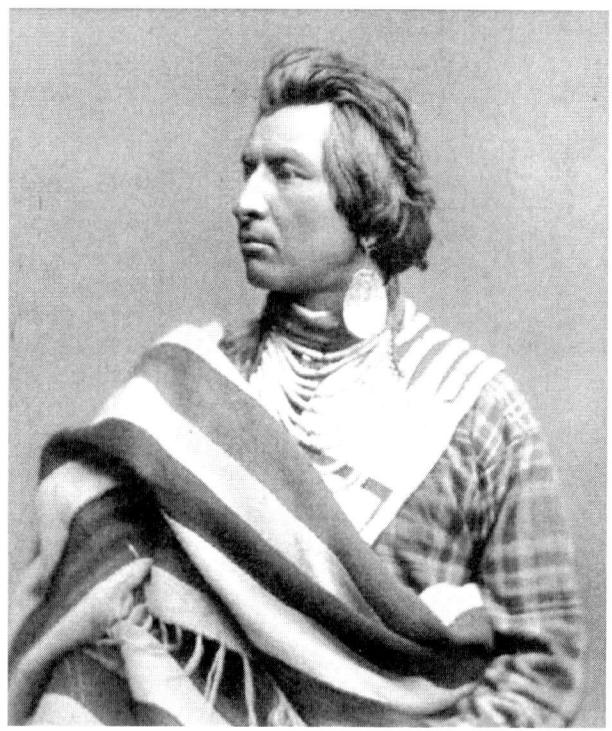

Figure 12 Donald McKay, Tenino. Photograph courtesy of Western History/Geneaology Department, Denver Public Library.

Náaqc c'úukwenin' titwáatityaya 1880's-kin'ix hitamáapayks ku' c'á'in, keyóx hikúuye kóna east-central Oregon-kin'ix.

One oral narrative from the 1880's tells of such an event, that which occurred in the area of east central Oregon.

Kínu' Donald McKay-nim Tenino 'eten'wéese (Figure 12).

Here, Donald McKay, a Tenino (Figure 12), is speaking.

"Kóna náaqc háama we'nik'íin "Ococtuin." Ococtuin-nim péetelkeke'yke pa'aptám tiwélqene. Hitilke'éycine 'ipsqíhamawisa. Kíimet kaa hiwayacikliitoχkika siyekew'éetnim. Hitamáapayciqa 'epehékin

"There was one man named Ococtuin. Ococtuin led a group of warriors against the Bannock. They went to war on foot. Suddenly, the scouts dashed back. They reported seeing the enemy, the Bannock,

tiwélqene hipewéeces ku'itú néχsep wak'íiswitin'. Kál'awnik'ay 'epek'ítne pitimmíyun tiwelqekí. Ococtuin hinéesepn'iye, "pe'npú ke yóx 'iméem!" Tiwélqem péemsteqe'enpse, "Wéet'u!" Q'o' hic'yawksa páa'niksix la'ám tapátka'snim híil'amktpa. Kál'awnik'ay tiwélqem péemsteqe'enpse, "'ehée!" Kaa kóna hipe'níye talohíin sík'em kaa 'áayat sík'em. Kaa k'iyúpcki méet'u yoxmá sík'emki hipackilítoqa." (McKay 1889)

 Ku'ús kaa wal'íim kíne suqútpeme, hiwéeyem sík'em kaa 'iske c'a'ín hiwées 'ipnatamáapayks 'úylepwepe tíim'enin'pe kaa titwáatityayanmpa. Kaa 'iske 'anoqónm c'íiqin, héenek'e kíye siléewsukise ku'úsu tá'c pí'amχna titóoqa 'inéek'niktpe kaa hiwées wéet'u kál'a 'ipnimnáawit titwáatityayanm tamtáaynim.

 Kaa ku'ús hit'éeneksinm kíye nekitkí--ke yóx we witíim'enkin'iχ kaa wititwatityáyanmkin'iχ--hiwées yóχ kíime híimsemtuktnim 'ipnáatamapayks titóoqanm néekt. Hiwées náaqc kinéeme titóoqanm 'inéek'nikt qo' tóosx hipekúuye.

 Kinkí híinaq'is, ke yóχ 'ew'níye koním yawá titóoqanm wiyaka'áwn. Wáaqo' kíi kiwáyl 'ewnéepiniye kíim'e c'íiqin, wéet'u ke manma'í yú'cmene

riding some strange animal. Finally, they decided to deliberate with the enemy. Ococtuin inquired, "We will buy that which is yours!" The enemy answered, "No!" To the very end of nothing, they laid down their weapons in a pile. Finally, the enemy answered, "Yes!" And there they gave them a stallion and a mare. And with nothing but those horses they returned home." (McKay 1889)

 Thus, at a very fundamental level, the arrival of the horse as event is referenced in both in the rock-art image and in our oral tradition. As in the aformentioned, again we begin to see the dynamics of interaction at the group level not just individual biographic forms of expression.

 Thus, the overwhelming impression we have--of each marking and of each oral tradition--is that these images reveal the indigenous worldview. It is one in which the corporate group is most prominent.

 With this I have finished it (the analysis), that which I have given concerning our Indian way of life. Already, thus far, I have brought these words, no matter péetim'eki. Páays kíi kaa wéet'esnim misqíitwece kaa hitk'áyca.

Yóχ kál'o'.

how pitifully they have been written. Perhaps the land is listening, watching.

That is all.

Author's Note:
Writing a paper in Nez Perce is a unique undertaking and the paper presented here may reflect some of the underlying difficulties of trying to effectively communicate between two very different languages. I have attempted to keep my Nez Perce translations of some very abstract rock-art concepts and terminologies as transparent as possible so that readers of Nez Perce may readily recognize the meaning. Also, I adopted a discourse-based style of writing that is more reflective of Nez Perce ways of speaking. This strategy, however, may seem unusual as you read the English translation. In the end, I hope that readers will gain a glimpse of the multilingual character of the native experience thru this brief sample of writing.

Discussion

Jean Clottes: Phillip, you said that those half circles above the heads were communicating the status of those people. Could it also be possible that by drawing them on the rock, it added to the status of the person?

Phillip Cash Cash: Yes, that would make it more visible to people who saw the site—groups that were interacting. That would make sense. It would be like a display to any stranger who would see the image, rather than just [a display] among their own individual group. In this particular area—the John Day River—it was closer to the Columbia River peoples' boundary with the Paiute; so it would make sense that if there was warfare or interaction of that kind then the messages that were displayed would indicate that the enemy would see that there is a powerful people who are residing in this land.

Jean Clottes: But do you think it could also add to the person's individual power—luck—by drawing it on the rock? Not just saying "now you're dealing with powerful people" but also adding to the person's luck. Could that be possible?

Phillip Cash Cash: Yes, yes, very much so because my impression of that image in particular is that there's a red smear all along these three men. And that they were not only indicating their status—but also their relationship with power.

David Whitley: What about the double sets of arms on them—any ideas about that?

Phillip Cash Cash: I'm still not sure about that in particular. It may simply indicate strength. Because a lot of the powers of warriors resided in the body—these physical attributes were significant .

Linea Sundstrom: I wondered if that was some kind of personal or tribal identifier or if there is any identifier in that image. I don't know if they used [name glyph] pictographs to indicate their name, or something else that would say this is a particular person, or these are the best warriors of a particular group. Have you looked at that?

Phillip Cash Cash: No, I don't think we have found those kinds of references.

Linea Sundstrom: So like—Four Arms is not the name of a band.

Phillip Cash Cash: I don't think so.

Jean Auel: What is the extra figure? Do you have any idea?

Phillip Cash Cash: My thought is that it could be a lineage emerging from these warriors.

Robert Layton: Could you say a little bit more about your emphasis on it being an image of a corporate group—the solidarity of the group.

Phillip Cash Cash: The impression that I received was that the Columbia River groups were united at several points in history to fight a common enemy. They weren't separate. And in fact, there's a great deal of inter-tribal relationships between villages. Lineages were connected to various related villages. The impression I get is that they would, in fact, unite to fight a common foe.

Robert Layton: I don't want to push this too far, but are you suggesting there might be a difference here between this and the art associated with the vision quest—which is more individual and less focused on the group as a whole?

Phillip Cash Cash: Yes. I began to think that this kind of imagery wasn't referencing heroic individuals per se. We actually saw groups of individuals as a corporate group interacting with other groups. So that became a core idea rather than individual biographical forms. That's not to say they're not present in this area, but this seems to be a very clear presentation of a corporate group.

Linea Sundstrom: I really enjoyed the connection with the story about how they got the horses. That image is so unusual because, of course, I see dozens and dozens of confrontations [in plains rock art] between people on foot and people with horses. I think that one is the only one I've seen where the people on foot are not obviously getting wiped out by the ones on the horses. It's a very unusual image and I think you're on the right track with it. Its unusual in a sense that the pedestrians are at the top. You know, even in the way its arranged it seems to be saying that they came out ahead.

James Keyser: It seems to me that these images are, in fact, put at a site that had many other pictographs and petroglyphs at it previous to these. These are later in the sequence at that site. When we found these I was looking at them as biographic, but Phillip's research seems to show a more corporately biographic concept—historiographic in a sense— rather than individually biographic. I was having trouble making individual things out of this with my experience with Plains biographic art, but when Phillip first gave his paper, and defined the marks in the ethnography—the exact same marks that are on the rock art; an incredible find—his idea that this is a more corporate sort of entity than an individual thing, seems to make sense.

Linea Sundstrom: That was another thing that struck me about the battle scene—the shield bearing warriors across the top have no identifiers but the horses are each different. So the horses' identities were maybe significant, but normally in that type of rock art there will be a shield design or a different way of showing the warrior's hair or headdress to indicate who that person was—either their social status or their particular individual identity. But in this one, the horses may have that, but it doesn't look like the people do, so I think it fits in really well with what you're saying about the corporate entity.

James Keyser: The only other thing, Phillip, that I can't help but wonder about the picture that shows the coup count marks is that maybe the fellow at the top, who is much smaller and doesn't have the extra set of arms, is a war captive or is a member of another group over which the solidarity group has some domination.

Jannie Loubser: Jim [Keyser] took me to see some imagery on the Plains that seemed to be more individual—sometimes they're tucked away. I was just wondering if the corporate aspect bears any relationship to its visibility. Is this composition readily visible?

Phillip Cash Cash: That was my impression. As you approach this area the site would be very accessible and easily visible from a distance—especially the rock face where these are painted. Anyone who travels through that area would have to pass by there because of the terrain, which creates a narrow passage.

James Keyser: Thank you Phillip, that was excellent. I found the science in your paper fascinating, and the fact that you found exactly the same image that was drawn on the rock in a primary ethnographic source is truly amazing.

But equally importantly, James Selam has told Phillip that he has some stories he would like to share with us about McKay, the Indian scout that told the story about the first horses.

James Selam: What I heard was about this group of men that was recruited to scout by McKay. My understanding is that he was from a place they call McKay Creek. He was not full blood Indian, he was half blood. He lived among the Indians and I believe he was in the cavalry. And they were having hard times with the Bannock, Shoshone, and Paiute. So he recruited men from along the Columbia River all the way from the Nez Perce area down to the Dalles—maybe further down. These men became well-known. There were 76 men that fought through that war. Like Phillip was saying, Indian people were able to find the power by childhood—as a child they received their power. Each man had strong power—he was able to live through all the battles with the Shoshones, Bannock, Paiute.[1] The last place they fought was near Tule Lake [California]—that was the Modoc. As far as I know (Indians had horses for a long time here)—I was telling Phillip that Lewis and Clark's journals (have information) about horses. [Selam read the following from an unidentified source] *"Clark sent out four men to the Indian village at the Grand Falls in order to make the further attempt to procure horses."* That's in 1806. At that time there were already a lot of horses here along the Columbia River. Those men that fought in the war with McKay all had horses.[2] They traveled from place to place. My grandfather was there—my mother's father. His name was Silwah—I'm named after him. He was one of those scouts. I too, was a scout in World War II. So what I'm trying to say is Indians had a different way of understanding nature. They lived by experience and by those stories that were told by their elders. They were not only stories—they actually took them by the hand and showed them. I experienced that. So these men—after the war—came back and they all dispersed. McKay went back—maybe that's why they call it McKay Creek—it's near Pilot Rock, Oregon. This much I remember about stories actually told by my mother from her father. I wish I had a tape recorder for those stories she used to tell us. Thank You.

James Keyser: Thank you, James. It is interesting for all of us to see the first-hand connection to archaeology and rock art.

---

[1] In an earlier, unrecorded discussion on the previous day's field trip, Selam mentioned that only one of these men had been killed. We also have an ethnographic reference to another such scout who, after his military service, was killed by shamanic sorcery. In this reference, an informant talking to McWhorter in the early 1900s said "Sluskin. . . .and *Lesh-hi-hit* killed *Stick Joe*, the Indian scout for the government in the Yakima war. They killed him with bad *tahmahnawis*. (Hines 1993:104)

[2] Hines (1993:between pages 71-73) shows a photo of a mounted Yakima Scout.

CHAPTER 8
The Beaver Bowl: Ethnographic Evidence for a Northwest Coast Shaman's Petroglyph

James D. Keyser, George Poetschat, Helen Hiczun, Pat McCoy, and Betty Tandberg

Introduction

Archaeologists have a long history of evaluating rock art against mobiliary carvings recovered from dated archaeological contexts (Bahn and Vertut 1988:58; Faulkner 1986:67-78; McClure 1979, 1984), most often in the attempt to provide chronological context for images and styles. Others have used paintings and engravings on various sorts of Historic period ethnographic specimens to provide an interpretive framework, ethnic context, and chronological information about North American Plains rock art (Keyser 1987, 1996; Keyser and Cowdrey 2004; Keyser and Cash Cash 2002; Keyser and Klassen 2001, 2003; Parsons 1987; Sundstrom and Keyser 1998; Mitchell 2002; Olson and Loendorf 2002). Even less common is the direct identification of rock art images by reference to ethnographic objects (Keyser 1991, 1996:37; Keyser and Mitchell 2001; Boyd 1998).

Surprisingly, despite a long history of research and some marked similarities between ethnographic carvings and rock art images, Northwest Coast tradition petroglyphs and pictographs have only occasionally been critically compared to the region's well-known mobiliary art (Hill and Hill 1975:273-274; Carlson 1983; McClure 1979, 1984; Poetschat et al 2002). Other than McClure's detailed chronological studies and the well-known Tsagiglalal death cult figures (McClure 1979; Keyser 1990, 1992) most of these comparisons are little more than perfunctory statements of formal similarity.[1]

Given the detailed knowledge of the many levels of symbolism and meaning (both overt and covert) in Northwest Coast tradition mobiliary art (e.g. Duff 1983; Wardwell 1996) it seems evident that there should be significant information still to be learned about Northwest Coast rock art using ethnographic specimens and information as comparative material. Our study of the Beaver Bowl--a Classic Conventionalized Style petroglyph of the Northwest Coast tradition found in the Portland basin--suggests some avenues of research that could be profitably employed both elsewhere in this region and in other areas where there exist significant quantities of mobiliary art.

The Beaver Bowl

Stone sculpture was a significant tradition on the Lower Columbia River (Peterson 1978) and part of a much broader Northwest Coast art tradition that includes both rock art and more common mobiliary sculpted items (Wingert 1952). Mobiliary stone sculpture from the area (Figure 1) includes pestles, net weights, large basalt slabs, boulders with human faces, a variety of smaller modeled animal figures, and effigy bowls--probably the most common stone sculptures on the Northwest Coast. Wilson Duff (1956; see also Ames and Maschner 1999:235) defines four classes of effigy bowls

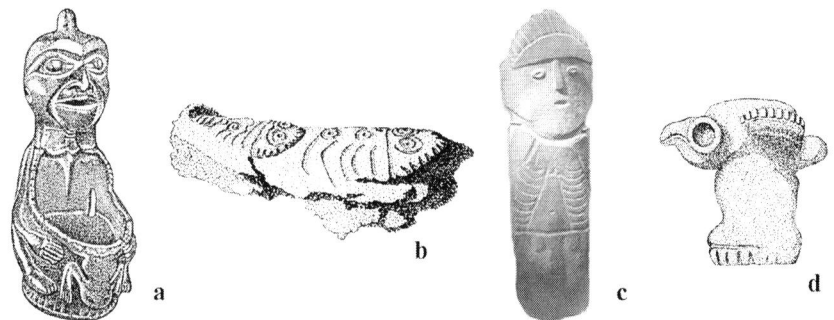

Figure 1 Selected stone sculptures from the Northwest Coast culture areas. a, Marpole phase seated bowl figure (Adapted from Wardwell 1996); b, Bedrock sculpture from Five Mile Locks near The Dalles (Adapted from Schurk 1958); c,d, human figure and bird figure from Portland Basin (Portland Art Museum).

from the Marpole Phase (ca. 600 BC to AD 500) centered in the Fraser River delta of northern Puget Sound. Perhaps the most distinctive and well published are the seated human forms with arms embracing a circular bowl (Duff 1983:57-58; Borden 1983:149-153; Carlson 1983:202; Wardwell 1996:25; Poetschat et al 2003) but other common specimens include zoomorphic forms ranging from bowls with limited animal features to detailed zoomorphic effigies into which relatively large, deep bowls have been carved.

Stone sculptures from the lower Columbia River form a continuum from small mobiliary pieces, to images on large boulders, to carved bedrock forms. These latter are clearly related to the petroglyphs more commonly found from Portland to The Dalles-Deschutes region upstream (McClure 1984). Lower Columbia mobiliary sculptures are often in zoomorphic form and commonly include frogs, toads, turtles, beavers, owls, and other birds. Many of these have bowl depressions heavily stained with red pigment, and are popularly called "paint pots" (Strong 1959a:176). Rock art sculptures(as distinguished from simple petroglyphs) include small and large carved

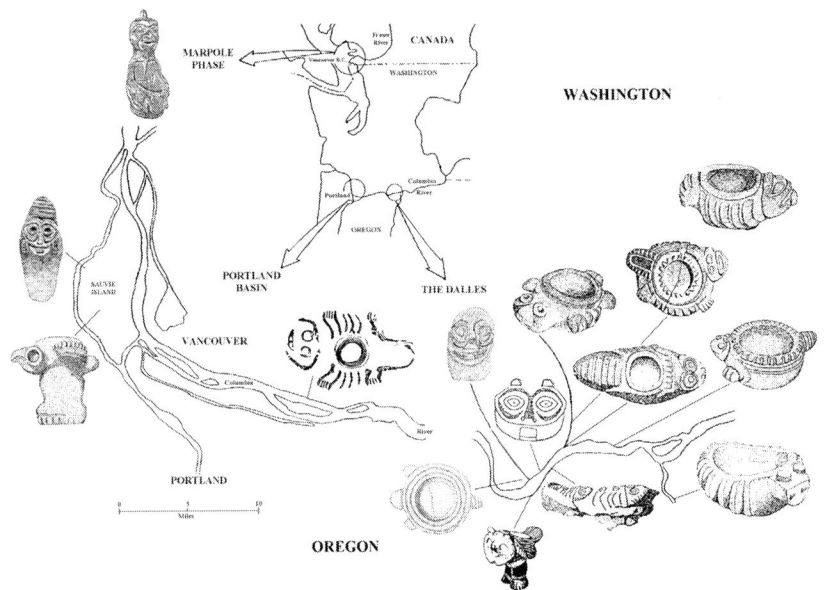

Figure 2 Pacific Northwest region showing areas of significant concentrations of stone sculpture.

effigy boulders. Several of these were found at sites along the lower Columbia River shore (Loring and Loring 1996:3); the two largest are the Beaver Bowl and a nearly two meter long zoomorphic effigy carved on a bedrock outcrop at Five Mile Rapids but now covered by backwater from The Dalles Dam (Schuck 1958).

The Beaver Bowl is located on the north shore of the Columbia River just upstream from the Portland Airport (Figure 2). Originally situated in a dense riverbank woodland dominated by firs, deciduous trees, and rhododendrons, the image was first referenced in 1925 (Strong and Schenck 1925:87; Strong et al 1930:130)[2] and later described in various amateur and professional publications as an effigy bowl in the form of a turtle, frog, or beaver (Richards 1935; Seaman 1946:227; Strong 1959a:36-37; Anonymous 1955; Meade 1971:87; Hill and Hill 1975:248; Wellman 1979:Figure 60; Loring and Loring 1996:4).

The bas-relief effigy bowl (Figure 3) is carved either on a very large boulder deeply buried in flood plain sediment or atop a bedrock outcrop. In either case the carved top of the rock is water worn relatively smooth and round. Numerous other boulders, ranging from basketball to house-sized specimens are scattered for more than three kilometers along the Columbia River shore. More than 100 of these have pecked cupule petroglyphs; some showing hundreds of apparently randomly scattered cupules while others have only a handful. On a few examples the cupules are carefully placed

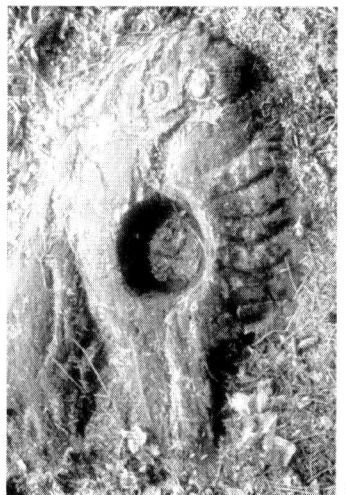 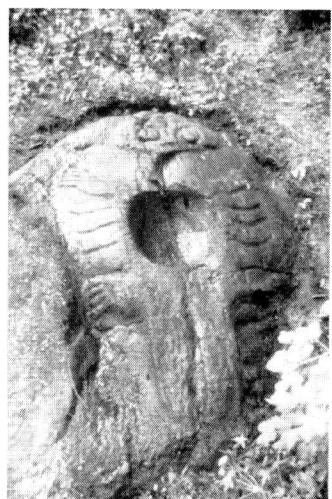

Figure 3 The Beaver Bowl. a., view prior to conservation assessment and recording; b, view of bowl after cleaning and recording. Photographs courtesy of Brad Yazzolino.

in a linear pattern along the boulder's highest spine. At least three and possibly more sculptured boulders were originally located in this boulder field. One of these was removed to a local museum; the remaining two include the Beaver Bowl and another effigy boulder sitting on the tideland beach about 800 meters downstream. All of these petroglyphs are included as part of a large village site which was well known to local Portland area artifact collectors who removed large artifact collections from the general site area in the mid 1900s (Roulette 2001). Due to artifact collection, erosion caused by river fluctuation, commercial use of the shoreline as a steamboat landing in the early 1900's, and home building in the area, most of the village site was destroyed prior to archaeological study.

The Beaver Bowl itself is carved on a rounded basalt outcrop, the top of which is about 30 cm above the present ground surface. The image is oriented east-west with the beaver's tail pointing generally east toward Mt. Hood. Although the carving has been variously identified as a turtle, frog, or beaver, our detailed examination and tracing leaves no question that it represents a beaver. The animal has a flat, round-ended tail and two square front teeth--both attributes that identify beaver in Northwest Coast Chinookan style art. In addition, the animal has well-defined front and back legs that extend straight out from the body and terminate in paws each with four bas-relief digits. Bas-relief ribs occur between the front and rear legs on each side of the body. The legs more likely represent a beaver than a frog since Columbia Plateau and Northwest Coast style frog depictions (Figure 4) have legs that extend out from the body, but bend forward on the foreleg and

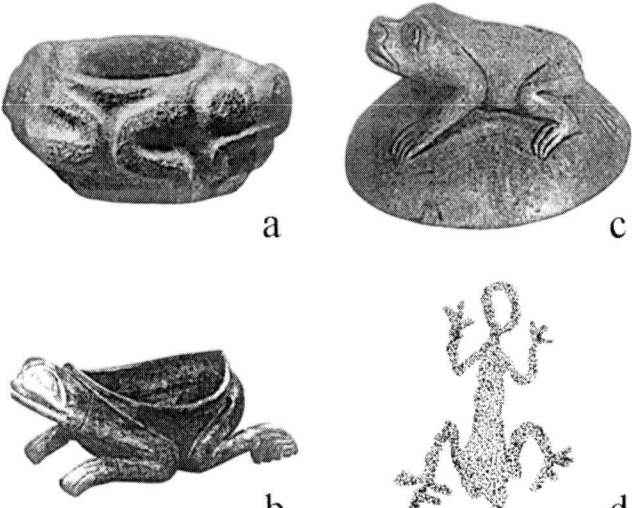

Figure 4 Stone and wood sculptures and a petroglyph of frogs showing leg styles. a, stone sculpture adapted from MacDonald 1983; b, wood sculpture adapted from Sturtevant 1974; c, wood sculpture adapted from Inverarity 1967; d, petroglyph.

backward on the rear (MacDonald 1983:117; Keyser 1992:54; Sturtevant 1974:Plate 19; Inverarity 1967:Plate 211). Certainly there is no indication of a turtle's shell, and no other Columbia River turtle figure has ribs.

In the center of the beaver's back is a large, deeply pecked and polished bowl depression (Figure 3). The bowl is 14 cm deep with an opening 40 cm across and steeply sloping sides tapering to a nearly flat bottom 25 cm across.

The beaver image is pecked using bas-relief to create a shallow three-dimensional animal form with great emphasis on the beaver's anatomical details. The bas-relief technique of pecking away surrounding areas to leave parts of the image raised has been combined with pecking some lines deeper into the removed area so the image itself has three levels. This type of sculpting requires removal of significantly more parent rock than would a more typical pecked petroglyph (even a deeply pecked one). The three level bas-relief further lends itself to rendering intricate detail not otherwise possible in a conventional petroglyph.

The beaver shows a head with eyes and teeth, clearly defined legs with paws and terminal digits, ribs on both sides of the body, and a long flat round-ended bas-relief tail (Figure 5). The eyes are broad circles pecked so that the central part appears in pseudo bas-relief. The legs are true bas-relief carefully carved to include paws with digits and further defined to prevent confusion between legs and ribs. Each paw has four claws or digits although

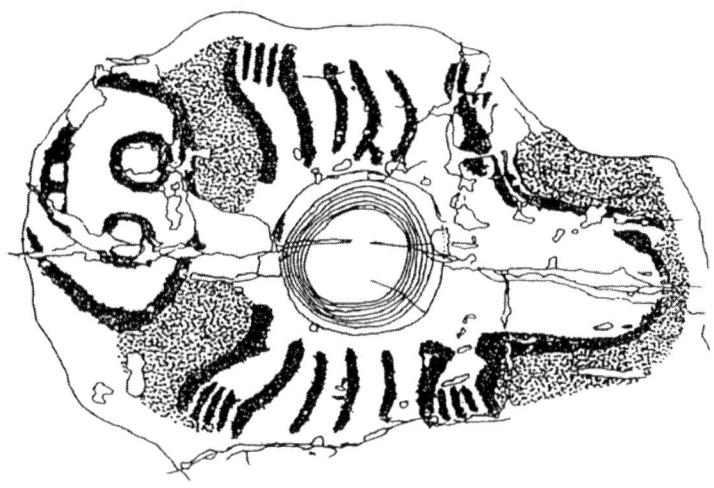

Figure 5 Tracing of the Beaver Bowl. Irregular light lines denote cracks and spalls in rock. Central concentric lines indicate deeply carved bowl depression. Diffuse stippling indicates area removed to create bas-relief carving.

the right rear paw has partly broken away due to root or frost action. Front legs are longer than the rear, producing the illusion that the beaver is moving toward an observer when viewed head on.

A professional conservation assessment and complete recording of the bowl was completed in 2001 (Poetschat et al 2003).

Comparative Analysis

The Beaver Bowl shows classic Northwest Coast Chinookan art tradition features. Specifically it fits within the Northwest Coast Classic Conventionalized Style (Lundy 1974, 1983) characterized by faces with large eyes, teeth, mouths, and bodies that include arms, digits and ribs (Figure 6). Zoomorphic figures are often displayed in a distinctive "spread-eagle" style. The beaver bowl also shows relationships to the Columbia River Conventionalized style (Lundy 1974, 1983; see also McClure 1984:42-44, and Keyser 1992:83) localized in the lower Columbia River region, centered on The Dalles, Oregon.[3] The Columbia River Conventionalized style is a series of highly conventionalized petroglyphs characterized by grotesquely grinning faces and bizarre, elaborately stylized mythical beings. Tsagiglalal (Figure 6f) is probably the best-known Columbia River Conventionalized motif. Supporting the assignment of this figure to a Chinookan art style is the Beaver Bowl's location, in the Portland Basin heartland of the lower Columbia River Chinookan culture area, first observed by Lewis and Clark in 1804 and well described in recent books (Ruby and Brown 1976; Rubin 1999).

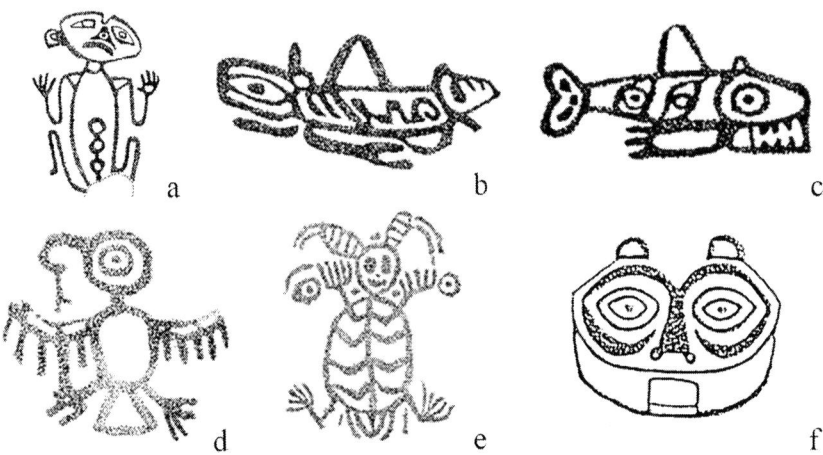

Figure 6 Northwest Coast Classic Conventionalized Style petroglyphs. a-c are found in Coastal Alaska (Adapted from Stevens 1974); d-f are part of the Columbia Plateau Long Narrows (Columbia River Conventionalized) Style found on the Lower Columbia River (d and e Adaped from Keyser 1992, f illustrated by Greg Bettis)

Given the clear stylistic affiliation of this image, and the richness of mobiliary stone sculpture in the Lower Columbia River region (Wingert 1952; Peterson 1978)[4] we were surprised to discover that there had been no formal comparison of the Beaver Bowl to any of this material, let alone to Northwest Coast sculpture from farther afield. Likewise, there had been no investigation of the ethnographic record for the significance of this particular image, or for such bowls in general.

Our research into comparative Northwest Coast stone sculpture involved an initial literature search and visits to four regional museums with significant stone sculpture collections. Library research led us to the Marpole stone sculptures of the Gulf of Georgia/Fraser River Delta region (Duff 1956, 1983:57-58; Ames and Maschner 1999:235; Borden 1983:149-153; Carlson 1983:202; Wardwell 1996:25) but revealed only a few professional references to lower Columbia River stone sculpture. Most of the information on the Lower Columbia River pieces was known only from private collectors' recollections or scant collector's notes on museum specimens. We were, however, able to identify 150 stone bowls from the lower Columbia Region (Table 1). About 80 percent of these were from The Dalles-Deschutes area and the rest from the Portland Basin (Figure 2). Almost 40 percent of the total were effigy bowls, either zoomorphic or anthropomorphic in form. We focused our interest on the 48 sculptured zoomorphic bowls (Table 2) that included effigies representing owls, other birds, beavers, turtles and a bear.

Table 1
Lower Columbia River Bowls by Type of Decoration

	Number	Percent
Undecorated or Geometric	91	61 %
Zoomorphic	48	32 %
Human Form	11	7 %
Totals	150	100%

Table 2
Lower Columbia River Zoomorphic Bowl Types

	Number	Percent
Owl	14	29 %
Other Bird	5	10.5 %
Beaver	8	17 %
Turtle	5	10.5 %
Bear	1	2 %
Total	33	69 %
Unidentified	15	31 %
Total	48	100 %

The eight beaver bowls (Figure 7) are distinguished by large flat tails, paws with claws, ribs, prominent eyes, and sometimes teeth. Two of these beaver bowls originated in Wakemap Mound (Anonymous 1956a:1-2, 1956b:2) and another is from a nearby site in Horse Thief Lake State Park (Strong 1959b:24). Wakemap and nearby sites are an important group of late prehistoric to protohistoric Chinookan settlements.

We also examined 14 owl bowls (Figure 8). One large example, now at the Maryhill Museum, has almost identical owl faces sculpted on each end (Wingert 1952:17) and another is a wonderfully sculptured owl with a small bowl in its back (Strong 1960:1-2). This emphasis on owls is consistent with numerous Spedis

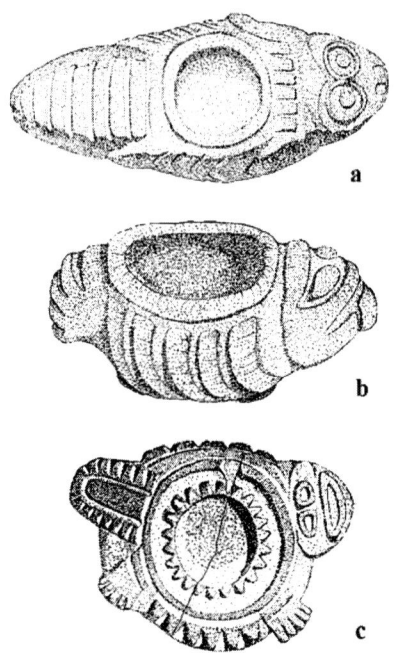

Figure 7 Mobiliary Beaver Bowls from The Dalles Area.

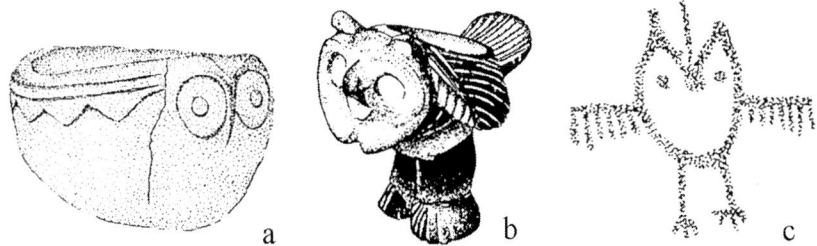

Figure 8 Owls in Lower Columbia River art. a, b, sculpted owl bowls; c, Spedis owl petroglyph, Petroglyph, Canyon (Drawing b is from Ames and Maschner 1999).

owl petroglyphs (Figure 8c) known from sites in The Dalles-Deschutes area and a number of other rock art Barn Owl representations found in the same area (Keyser 1992:90; Keyser et al 1998b:90-91).

A small bear mortar bowl (Figure 9a), currently at Maryhill Museum, was donated by a rancher from the lower Deschutes River, who reported that it had been given to his grandfather in 1910. One of two turtle mortars (Figure 9b) has a bowl carved in its stomach, and appears almost as a real turtle (with its legs touching the ground) when it is on its stomach--bowl side down. This turtle bowl is deeply stained with red pigment. The other example (Figure 9c) has the bowl carved into its back (Strong 1958:1). Neither of these turtle mortars shows ribs.

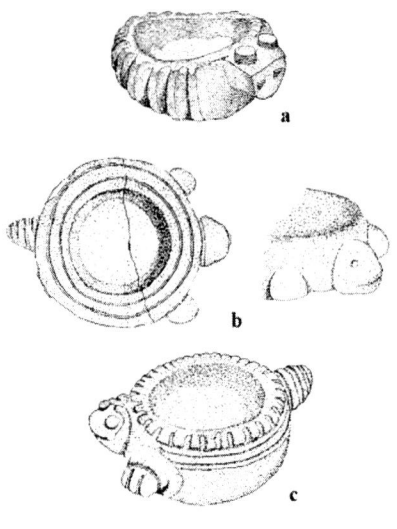

Figure 9 Other mobiliary zoomorphic mortar bowls. a, bear; b, c, turtles. Note obverse side view of head in b.

Following our identification of these zoomorphic bowls (and first-hand examination of many of them), one striking fact crosscuts their specific individual differences of form: More than 75 percent of all Lower Columbia River zoomorphic bowls are of animals considered by Indian cultures throughout western North America to be special spirit helpers because they cross apparent boundaries--land to water (beaver, frog, turtle), air to land (birds), or night to day (owls).[5]

Dating

Specific dates are not currently available for the Beaver Bowl, but circumstantial evidence suggests that it dates from the Late Prehistoric Period. Roullette (2001) identifies the sculpture as part of an undated Late Prehistoric village site, and in 1935 the eminent Pacific Northwest ethnographer, Verne Ray, estimated the age of the carving based on stylistic criteria "in hundreds rather than thousands of years" (Richards 1935). Lewis and Clark in 1804/1805 did not indicate an Indian village at this location (Thwaites 1905), and since they were very exact in noting all active villages it seems likely that this one was no longer in use by 1800.[6] This suggests that the beaver bowl most likely dates before 1800. Similar mobiliary sculptures from The Dalles-Deschutes area date to the last 500 years (McClure 1984:114-115). In summary, this evidence, albeit circumstantial, strongly suggests that the Beaver Bowl dates to the most recent Late Prehistoric Period in the Portland Basin.

Function

Bowls, especially those of human or animal form, are routinely identified as Shamans' paraphernalia associated variously with tobacco ceremonials, curing rituals, pigment production and preparation, and girls' puberty rituals (Carlson 1983:201; Inglis 1998; Strong 1959a:176). All of these activities were also routinely undertaken by Lower Columbia River shamans (Hines 1993). The predominant forms of these effigy bowls in the Lower Columbia River area strongly support a shamanistic function. Most are zoomorphic, but a few have mixed animal and human characters metaphorically suggesting a shaman's transformation into his spirit helper familiar. One particular example found near Sauvie Island in the Portland Basin and currently at the Maryhill Museum shows an obvious owl figure (eyes, beak, wings, and tail) with an equally obvious human mouth below the beak, so that to an observer looking only at the front of the bowl, the beak becomes a human nose (Figure 10). The juxtaposition and blending of these owl and human characters suggests to us an owl mask partially covering a human face--a convention in masking traditions worldwide, and especially common in Northwest Coast ceremonial masks frequently used by shamans. Furthermore, the animals used for effigy bowls also suggest shamanism. In the Lower Columbia River region the most common are beavers, turtles, birds, and owls all of which were thought of as potent shamans' familiars because of their characteristic crossing of boundaries, which was metaphorically associated with shamanic transformation. One other bowl is a bear, also associated with both Northwest Coast and Columbia Plateau shamanism.

Malotki (1998, 2003), in his rock art research in Northern Arizona, identifies both turtles and birds (owls herons, eagles, and hummingbirds) as

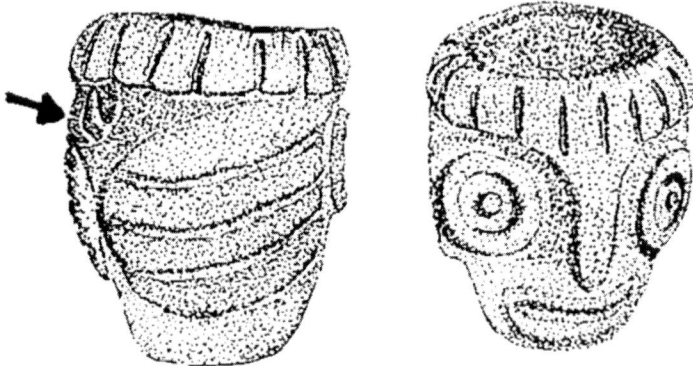

Figure 10 Sculpted mortar bowl showing owl-human transformation. Note wings and tail (arrow) at left.

special shamans' spirit helpers. He suggests that rock art images of these animal familiars are metaphors for the shamanic transition between two states. Shamans commute between the secular and the spirit world just as their spirit familiars commute between two secular states: birds (earth and sky), owls (night and day), turtles (water and land). To this list we would add the beaver who also makes the transition between land and water.

Malotki (2003) argues persuasively that owls are especially well suited to represent shamans because of their nocturnal lifestyle and ability to see to hunt effectively in the dark. These behavioral attributes almost predestine the owl as a shaman's familiar. One could also argue that the beaver, a land animal that controls the flow of water and builds his house with an underwater entrance, might be similarly predisposed to the role of shaman's familiar in Lower Columbia cultures where shamans were particularly concerned with river flows (for salmon migration) and going underwater for their visions (Spier and Sapir 1930:240)

As we were finalizing our analysis of the Beaver Bowl, and had become convinced that it was a piece of shaman's paraphernalia, we stumbled on an ethnohistoric clue that strongly reinforces our conclusion. In an effort to date the village site we obtained a site form that referred to an historic name for one of the petroglyphs in the area as *Temana Wa's Rock* (Anonymous 1979). Originally that name appeared to have been given to the largest cupule boulder located on the beach (Figure 11) near the Beaver Bowl (Keyser and Taylor 2002; Poetschat et al 2003), but an even earlier site form shows that this was the historic name for the Beaver Bowl itself. The importance of this name is that it clearly derives from the word *Tahmanawis*, which means spirit power or spirit helper in Chinook Jargon (Thomas 1970:97-98). The word was also borrowed and used in Sahaptian

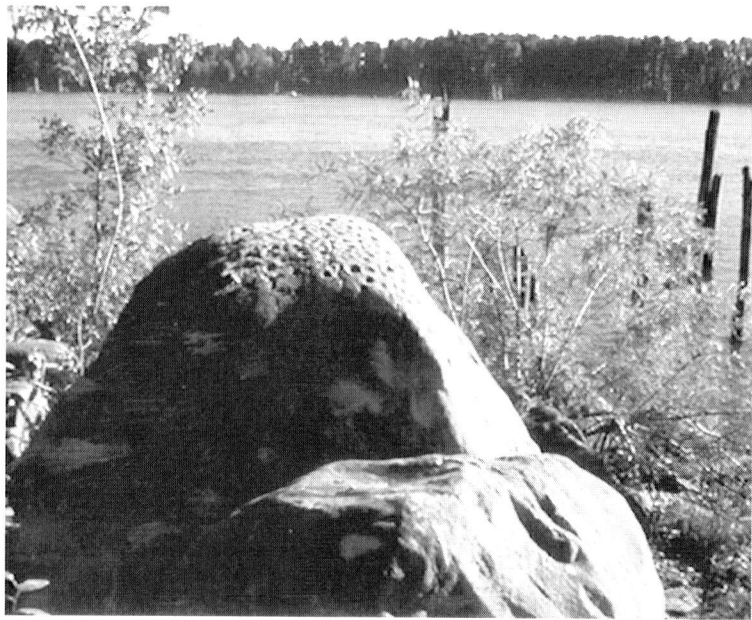

Figure 11 Large boulder covered with cupules at site #45CL258. Photograph courtesy of Brad Yazzolino.

languages (Phillip Cash Cash, personal communication 2002) where it was often associated with shamans' power (Hines 1992, 1993).

Hines (1993:104-105) gives a clear indication of this association with shamanism:

"A remarkable instance of the dread in which 'medicine men' are held came under my observation in April 1912. . . . '*Sluskin* is a medicine man. . . .He said that he and *Lesh-hi-hit* killed *Stick Joe*, the Indian scout for the government in the Yakima War. They killed him with bad *tahmahnawis*. . . .*Sluskin* is bad *tahmahnawis*.'

Possessing the rattlesnake *tahmahnawis*, the shamans, *Wan'-tah* and *We-yal-lup Wa-ya-cika*, had varied powers with which to deal with the serpent."

Shamans and their spirit power also figure prominently in Chinookan references to *tahmanawis*:

"[T]he [Wishram] medicine man . . . .was found, in a trance, at the foot of the rock [a rock art panel]. A ghostly eye was looking down on him and on the people who came to him. All knew that the *tahmanawis* had painted it." (Ranck 1926)

Elsewhere in the southern Portland Basin, the same name--*Tomanowos*[7]-- identified the Willamette Meteorite (Figure 12), an ice-rafted erratic from the Glacial Lake Missoula floods that was originally located

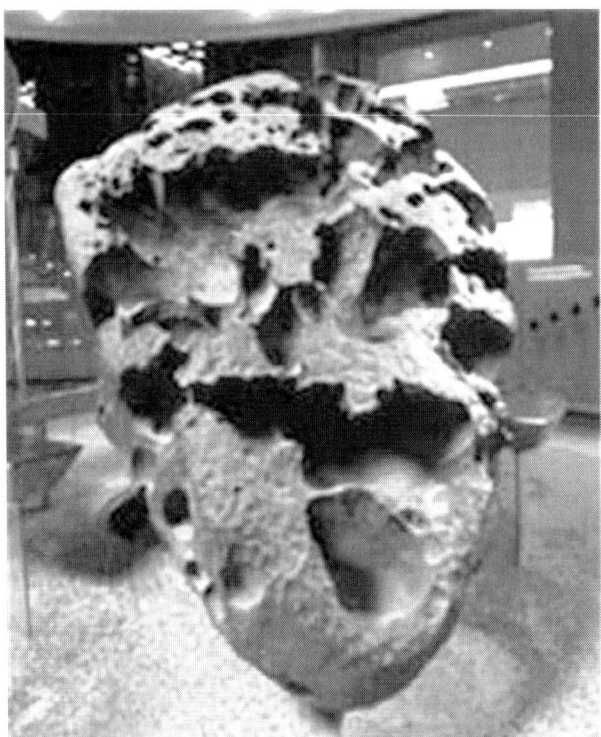

Figure 12 Willamette meteorite. (Photograph reproduced with permission from the American Museum of Natural History Library, New York.)

near Lake Oswego, Oregon. The meteorite, an obvious erratic, even to pre-literate people, is honeycombed with holes and basins typical of iron meteorites. Tribal oral tradition reports that it

"belonged to the Native doctors [shamans] of the Clackamas Tribe who told people how it came from the moon. Native children, approaching adolescence, were often sent by their families to visit the tomanowos in the Dark of night. Young warriors bathed their faces in the water which collected in the caverns carved into the surface of the stone. The water had special healing properties and was used by Native doctors to cure friends and relatives." (Olson 1999)

Clearly, here is another strong association between *Tahmanawis* and the supernatural power of shamans, but this time from a Portland Basin tribe. The emphasis on (and use of) the supernaturally potent water from the meteorite's natural basins further supports our conclusion that the Beaver Bowl's bowl was central to its shamanic function.

After this paper had been written and prepared for publication, but before the delay in its publication due to some unfortunate circumstances, we became aware of another sculpted bowl from the lower Columbia River that strongly supports our assessment that many of these were shamans' paraphernalia. Mercer (2005:26-27) describes and pictures an anthropomorphic sculpture which he says "may represent a shaman." This figure shows a crouched human holding a rattle in its right hand (the bulb of which is a carved human face) and carrying a bowl on its left shoulder supported by its left hand. The figure has a pipe or sucking tube in its mouth and wears an elaborate headdress. Such a figure, using other objects (rattle, pipe/sucking tube) that are certainly shamans' paraphernalia (e.g. Carlson 1983:201-202; Wardwell 1996:239-282, see especially rattles with human faces), is almost certainly a shaman and his bowl can most reasonably be interpreted as another of his ritual objects. In fact, this sculpture is strikingly similar to a series of anthropomorphic bowls found on the southern coast of British Columbia (Borden 1983:149-153; Carlson 1983:202).

Conclusions

Stone sculpture was significant in the art tradition of the Lower Columbia River Chinookans. Many zoomorphic mortar bowls have been found in archaeological sites, most of which are owls, beavers, and turtles--important shamans' spirit helpers. The Beaver Bowl, a bas-relief petroglyph sculpture in the Northwest Coast Art Tradition, is interpreted as a powerful shaman's object, based on various lines of ethnographic evidence including its form, its historic name, and reports of similar, though smaller bowls being used in shamans' rituals throughout Northwest Coast culture.

Acknowledgements

We thank Ann Eichelberg and Bill Mercer of the Portland Art Museum in Portland, Oregon, Betty Long-Scheif of the Maryhill Museum of Art in Goldendale, Washington, David Fenton of the Clark County Museum in Vancouver, Washington, and Sharon Tiffany and Herb Beals of the Columbia Gorge Interpretive Center in Stevenson, Washington for assisting us with access to their collections of stone sculpture. Angelo Fossati was primarily responsible for recording the Beaver Bowl. As always we appreciate the interest of Phillip Cash Cash in our rock art research, and we thank him for his insightful comments that helped us understand the linguistics of Tahmanawis. Finally we thank the Beaver Bowl's owners, originally Carol Shafer and her daughter Julie Bradley and now Grace Siah, who have welcomed us and supported our study. They have always provided access to scholars wishing to see this unique petroglyph, and have also served as excellent stewards for this important site.

[1] Probably the best example of the failure to integrate Northwest Coast rock art into the study of ethnographic (and archaeological) mobiliary art is a volume edited by Carlson (1983). In this volume of eleven contributed papers with more than 200 pages of text and some 200 illustrations and photographs showing Northwest Coast art, only the shortest chapter with the fewest figures (in which there are NO direct comparisons to ethnographic art) is exclusively rock art, and only one other chapter even mentions rock art--describing two sites and generally comparing them to ethnographic specimens. All of this despite the fact that at the time this volume was compiled there were two masters theses, two books, and several key journal articles (Lundy 1974; Stevens 1974; Meade 1971; Hill and Hill 1975; Barrow 1942; McClure 1979) published on the rock art of the region! Certainly Carlson's volume is now a valuable resource for scholars seeking such ethnographic comparisons, but where might we be had this research begun twenty years ago?

[2] Strong was obviously passing along second-hand information, since he erroneously identified the image as a human representation.

[3] The Columbia River Conventionalized style was originally named by Lundy based on a few classic petroglyph forms from The Dalles-Deschutes area of the lower Columbia River. But these images are also part of a broader Long Narrows style when viewed from a Columbia Plateau perspective (Wellman 1979:46; Keyser 1992:83). Clearly, this art is transitional between the more classic Northwest Coast art to the west and northwest and the Columbia Plateau tradition art found throughout the interior Columbia Basin which surrounds The Dalles-Deschutes area on three sides (McClure 1984:42-47). Both Northwest Coast and Columbia Plateau scholars associate the art with the Chinookan-speaking Wasco and Wishram peoples who moved upriver to settle The Dalles-Deschutes area in Late Prehistoric times.

[4] See also various anonymously-authored articles from the period between 1950 and 1970 in "Screenings," the newsletter of the local Oregon Archaeological Society.

[5] Bear was also widely regarded in western North America as an especially powerful shaman's spirit helper, though it was so defined because of its many human-like traits rather than its crossing of apparent boundaries. Tsagiglalal, a shamans' death cult symbol (Keyser 1990, 1992) is often portrayed with bear's ears (see Keyser 1992: Figures 71, 73c).

[6] Nor did any other early explorer note an active village at this location (Anonymous 1955).

[7] Although the spellings are all three different, this is due to the difficulty of rendering native languages in English orthography. Clearly all of these names refer to the same word *Tahmanawis*.

Discussion

Ken Ames:[1]   One thing I noted was a sculpted boulder on which you thought you saw two mouths (see Figure 1b in the paper). There is a tradition along the lower Columbia River here that has a series of skeletalized figurines. With these you have the face, and above it there's a hairdo, and below are the ribs. If you look at that boulder from another angle, you have two of those skeletal figures stacked on top of each other. So, that goes along with your bowl with the owl face and human mouth (see Figure 10). That is typical Northwest Coast art—it's never just one thing. It's three or four, or seven things, all overlaid on each other. And so you've got be real careful with this art. The easy identification may not be all that's there. It could be two or three different things.

James Keyser: You're right, Ken, but unfortunately, that boulder is drowned [by The Dalles Dam Reservoir] and we only have a poor picture of it. I wish I could see that thing in its original form.

Phillip Cash Cash: I would like to ask James [Selam] and Willie [Selam] if they would be willing to share their knowledge of that word *Tahmanawis* that you used. They have more detailed information about that word.

James Selam: My understanding of the word *Tahmanawis* is that it's a power, a spiritual power in a person. It's not in an object or anything. But making faces on an object will bring it—the face is this power. This is *Tahmanawis*. What we call *Tahmanawis* to my understanding is either a creature or an object that has spoken to this child—given him this power.

As maybe a rock, water, a bird, or animal and he carries this power when he gets older and its strong. He picks an object or a place where he will store it, for a time when he might need it to heal a person. If he needs to start working he calls his *tahmanawis*—his special power. We also call it *Pach*. Also the place we're talking about, a place he would select to put his power, is called *ta-wee-ish*. Only he knows where it is, so he can get his power from it, nobody else can see it, nobody else can get it because its spiritual. If another doctor of stronger power could find that, he could destroy the person.

Like some of those objects you were showing made me think back. When I was a kid, I grew up along the [Columbia] River. *Sk'een* was my home. *Wyam*, *Wan-wa-wee*, *Walla-wee-tees*, *Tche-wa-wee* and other places. Back in my father's time, he was raised at *Nish'k*, a village of 50 long houses. When Lewis and Clark were going back up the river there was maybe 15 or more families in each long house. My father used to say, one long house where he lived, there were ten fires. You can figure about 20 feet apart, over 200 feet long. That's how the Indians existed along the river. I grew up in a big longhouse in John Day [at the mouth of the John Day River]. Lot of my relatives, we all lived together. And we experienced all this stuff you're talking about—*tahmanawis*. The small kids were sent out to seek power from nature, or an animal and a lot of these things you see [rock art] was probably put there by someone to hold his power. So that's my understanding of the word *tahmanawis*. I've heard it so many times. But we also call a person who becomes a strong Indian doctor *tahmanawis*[2]—he could tell what's happening, he could tell a person was sick—he could see what's ailing him. Lot of times people tell somebody else and word would get around. They'd hire him to take it [the sickness] out—work on him.

I can speak of that from my own experience. When I was a kid I used to ride horseback a lot. When we moved up to the Yakima valley, I had some buddies—my cousins—who used to ride around a lot. They left me one time with two people—powerful *Twa-tees*—Indian doctors, man and wife. I came out late and I ran to my horse and I was going to jump on, but my horse moved and I fell down. And these two—medicine man and a woman—were watching me. After about a week I got sick. I got weaker, and my mother hired a person who was powerful also. He belonged to the "Feather" religion and became a strong powerful Indian doctor and came down to work on me. On the second day he asked "sometime in the past, somewhere, your horse threw you off. There were two people watching you. I think they scared you—they grabbed you and held you down with their power. That's what's holding you down." So he took that out. Something you can't believe. In a few days I was up and around. That's how Indian doctors worked long ago. We don't have Indian doctors like that any more—except maybe him [indicates Phillip Cash Cash].[3]

James Keyser: James, thank you very much for sharing that story with us. That increased our understanding of that word and how important it is.

Phillip Cash Cash: Jim [Keyser], you say there was more rock art in that area? Right near there—more boulders?

James Keyser: There are additional boulders, not with big bowls in them, but with all the little cupules in them—down along the beach. There is another effigy boulder further down the beach with big eyes and a face that looks like some of the faces in Petroglyph Canyon where they have grins with lines that come out from them.[4] This boulder has a similar face with those big eyes.

Viola Kalama: Well you know, I think to myself that these people that were in the trance drew something, you know, that was just supernatural. We have words in our language that mean an animal or bird but many of us can't determine what kind of thing that is, maybe because it's extinct. For things like that we have just the words, that's all.

Angelo Fossati: Is there any ethnographical reference about the use of beaver meat or the use of something else from beaver?

Viola Kalama: We ate it! It was good.

Angelo Fossati: Was it used for medicine purposes?

Viola Kalama: Oh, I don't know.

James Keyser: Viola, we also thank you for your comments today.

Viola Kalama: I wanted him [indicating James Selam] to talk. I didn't want to talk about it—its man's talk.

---

[1] Ken is an anthropology professor at Portland State University who specializes in Northwest Coast archaeology. He attended the symposium because Portland State University was co-sponsor.

[2] This exactly parallels Yakama informants speaking to McWhorter in 1903 who said in referring to a malevolent shaman "Sluskin is bad *tahmahnawis*." (Hines 1993:104). Elsewhere in the book there is considerable discussion of *tahmanawis*, how it is acquired, possessed, and used.

3 Phillip Cash Cash is recognized by many as a traditional caretaker and a *we'npew'éet* "a singer" in the Columbia Plateau Medicine Society; however, he does not claim to be an Indian Doctor.

[4] Some of these petroglyphs were removed prior to filing of The Dalles Dam Reservoir and are now placed at Horsethief Lake State Park, just downstream from the original Petroglyph Canyon.

CHAPTER 9
House of the Rising Sun: Using the Ethnographic Record to Illuminate Aspects of Klamath Basin Rock Art
Don Hann and Gordon Bettles

Geographic and Cultural Setting

The Klamath Basin is located in south-central Oregon and northeastern California (Figure 1), on the east side of the Cascade Mountain range. It is dominated by a series of large lakes and marshes that drain through the Klamath River system. The internally draining Lost River/Tule Lake/Clear Lake Basin, now cut off from the Klamath River although it was once connected through Lower Klamath Lake during periods of high water (Dicken and Dicken 1985), is also considered part of the Klamath Basin (Sampson 1985). The extensive wetlands provided a wide range of resources used by Indians including salmon, sucker, waterfowl, tule, and wocus (yellow pond lily). These were supplemented by forest and land resources including deer, elk antelope, small game animals, yampa, onion, lily, lomatium, huckleberry and wild plum. These rich and relatively consistent resources allowed for the development of the semi-sedentary cultures of the Klamath and Modoc people (Gatschet 1890; Ray 1963; Spier 1930). Although they shared the same basic language and many cultural traits, the Klamath and Modoc considered themselves as distinct but related people. They lived in geographically separate parts of the Klamath Basin. The Modoc territory centered on the Tule Lake/Clear Lake and Lower Klamath Lake basins and the Klamath homeland was to the north in the Klamath Marsh and Upper Klamath Lake basins (Stern 1966). In this discussion the term Klamath/Modoc is used when discussing traits both groups shared and the specific tribes name will be used for traits or locations specific to that group.

Some researchers believe that Klamath/Modoc culture may have been practiced, almost without interruption in the Klamath Basin, over at least the last 6,000 years (Cressman 1956; Sampson 1985). A long and continuous time depth for Klamath/Modoc culture is also suggested by the distinctive nature of the Klamath language. This lake/marsh based lifestyle may have once extended through the now less productive lake basins of the northern Great Basin (Oetting 1989, 1990; Aikens and Jenkins 1994). The inflow of substantial amounts of snow melt from the eastern slopes of the Cascades into the Klamath Basin probably saved it,

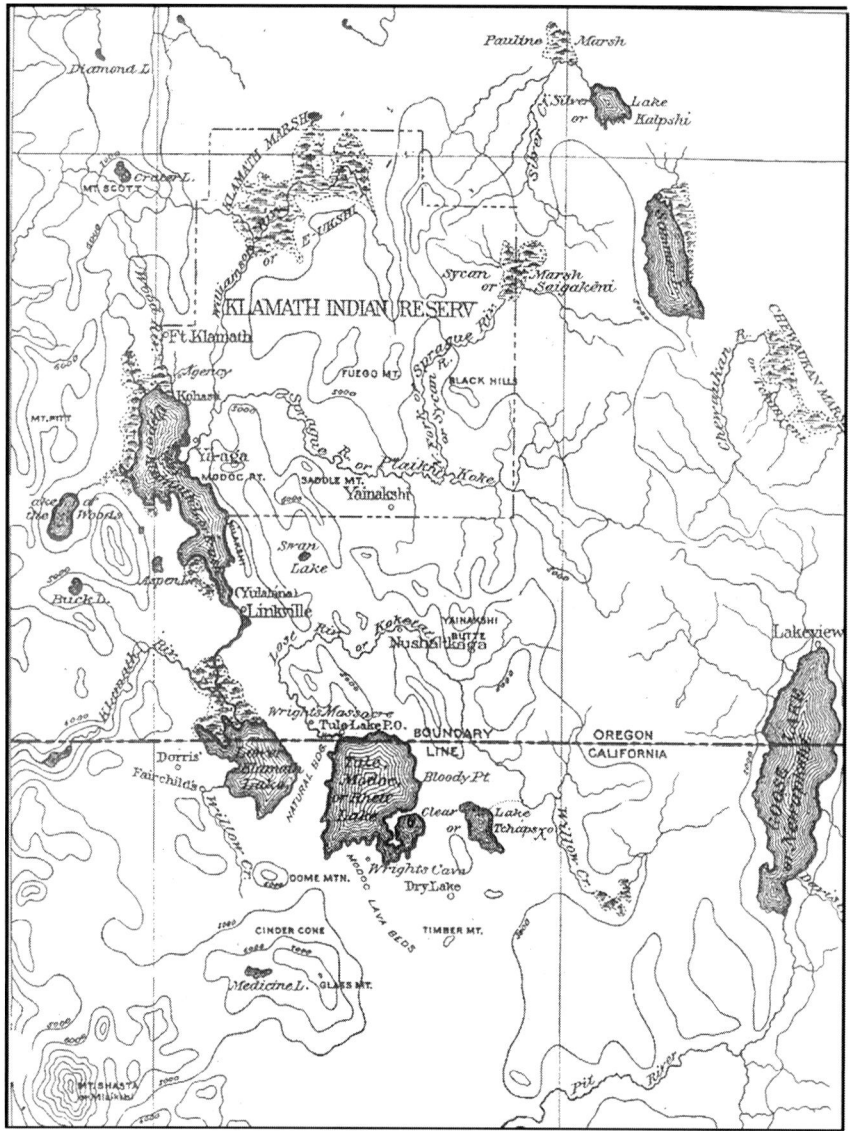

Figure 1. Map of Modoc and Klamath country from Gatschet 1890.

and its dependent cultures, from the fate of the dry and alkaline lakes of the Great Basin.

There has been considerable debate as to the proper position of Klamath/Modoc culture within the larger cultural divisions of the Pacific Northwest. Although most authors place them with the Columbia Plateau cultures (Aikens 1993; Spier 1930), they have also been grouped into the Interior Valleys, Great Basin, and Central California cultural areas (Baun and Lewis 1991; Stern 1966; Ray 1963). The Klamath/Modoc share some traits with all these groups, as is to be expected since the Klamath Basin abuts all of these areas. It is perhaps best to consider the Klamath Basin as a distinct cultural area considering the time depth of the lifeway and the unique reliance on wocus processing.

Klamath Basin Rock Art

There are over two hundred petroglyph and pictograph sites in the Klamath Basin ranging from a single glyph to several thousand images. Many, but certainly not all, of these sites have been recorded but most of these records are unpublished or published with limited distribution (e.g. Lee et al 1988; Loring and Loring 1983; Swartz 1978; Whitley et al 2004).[1] The lack of a comprehensive and readily available illustrated reference for Klamath Basin rock art has hampered the discussion of this significant corpus of Native American designs. Several distinctive techniques and styles of rock art can be found in the Klamath Basin (Swartz 1978). These include monochrome and polychrome pictographs and pecked, ground, scratched, incised, and drilled petroglyphs.[2] Of relevance to the upcoming discussion is the high percentage of circle and concentric circle motifs (Figure 2).

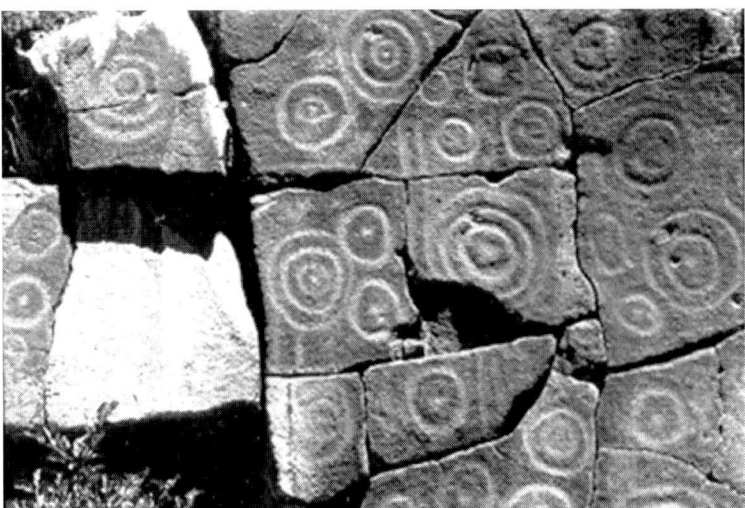

Figure 2. **Concentric circle motifs from the Paradise Creek site in the Klamath Basin.**

Ethnographic Research in the Klamath Basin

In the early 1880s Jeremiah and Alma Cartel Curtin were working as linguists and ethnographers for the Bureau of American Ethnology in Indian Territory (Oklahoma). They had a strong interest in

Indian religion, cosmology, and mythology inspired by Jeremiah's attempt to compose a model of the evolution of religion from "primitive" shamanic practices to "advanced" monotheism. Although clearly ethnocentric by modern standards, this attempt to apply the principles of Darwinism to the study of religion was innovative anthropology at the time. Curtin was a gifted linguist who studied the languages and mythology of several Indian tribes as well as cultures in many other parts of the world, including the Mongols while he was working for the U.S. mission to Russia in the 1860s. After they were married in 1872, Alma always accompanied Jeremiah in the field, often in hazardous and extremely uncomfortable conditions. Although not credited by either her husband or herself; it is clear that Alma Curtin played an important role in recording the material collected by the couple.

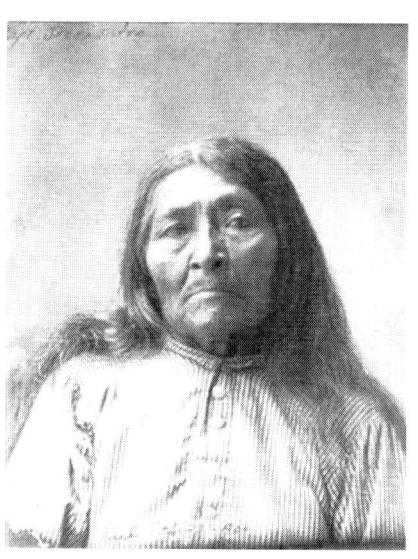

Figure 3. Ko-a-lak'-ak-a in exile in Oklahoma, 1903. Photo courtesy of the Klamath County Museum (Foster 1999).

While working with the Seneca Indians in Indian Territory (later the state of Oklahoma) in 1883, the Curtins chanced upon the survivors of the Modoc families who were exiled there after the Modoc War of 1873. The Modoc woman Ko-a-lak'-ak-a (Figure 3), assisted by her daughter, Jenny Clinton, provided extremely detailed information.[3] Ko-a-lak'-ak-a was described by Jeremiah Curtin as a truly incredible person:

"I had been on the reservation only a few days when I found. . .a most remarkable person; Ko-a-lak'-ak-a (Hard Working Woman), a woman who had in her mind all the lore her people possessed a hundred years ago. She was the daughter and granddaughter of a chief and when a child her grandfather taught her the wisdom of the Modocs. . . .She was willing to give me the myths and beliefs of her tribe. She had more stories in her head than I dreamed it possible for anyone to learn and keep without aid of books. Ko-a-lak'-ak-a and Norel-putis, a Wintu Indian, I consider the most remarkable persons I have ever met. Both possessed mental powers of the first quality. . . .Very little of the Modoc mythology would have been saved had I not met Ko-a-lak'-ak-a. Both were of the old-time Indians; neither one of them spoke English." (Curtin 1940:331).

In transcribing the material it appears that a complex four-way interaction was going on. Ko-a-lak'-ak-a would tell a story or mythic episode in the Modoc language, Jenny Clinton translated her mother's words into English, Mr. Curtin took linguistic notes and Modoc vocabulary, and Mrs. Curtin transcribed Jenny's English versions of the tales. Inspired by what they had learned in Oklahoma the Curtin's traveled to the Klamath Reservation in 1884 to gather additional Modoc and Klamath material. Although additional information was provided by several other sources, the bulk of the Modoc material collected by the Curtins was from Ko-a-lak'-ak-a.

Most of the material transcribed by the Curtins can only be found in their field notes at the Library of American Anthropology at the Smithsonian Institution. This material consists of over 1,200 legal sized pages, all written in longhand. Mrs. Curtin published 60 myths in 1912, after the death of her husband. Unfortunately, the myths presented in this book have been "sanitized" and edited to the point were their anthropological value is compromised. Additional material on Klamath and Modoc cosmology and mythology was transcribed by Albert S. Gatschet, also working for the Bureau of American Ethnology (Gatschet 1877-1892). Many of his unpublished field notes, as well as correspondence with Tribal members and employees of the Klamath Agency, are also housed at the Library of American Anthropology. More recently, Barker (1963a, 1963b, 1963c), Ray (1963), Stern (1966), and Marriott and Rachlin (1968) have provided additional material used in the present study.

In 1991 the authors, with the assistance of Mary Gentry of the Klamath Tribes and Anne Schneider, began the task of organizing and transcribing the unpublished Curtin and Gatschet material as part of a joint project between the Klamath Tribes, the Bureau of Land Management, and the U.S. Forest Service. The first phase of the project, which entailed organizing, indexing, and typing all the material on a computer format, was completed in 1994.

Klamath/Modoc Cosmology and Mythology

The ethnographic fieldwork that has taken place in the Klamath Basin provides an extensive collection of stories and legends dealing with mythological characters. Most of these characters are animals from the time when "animals talked like people," in the age before humans came into being. These types of tales include the Coyote stories told by many Indian tribes. Less familiar are a series of stories about the anthropomorphic cultural hero *Gmoḱam'č*, his son *A'isis*, and his brother *Wawńaˑk*.[4] These stories form a partly intact myth cycle where a series of interconnected stories were told over a period of many days (Barker 1963a:22).

The *Gmoḱam'č* myth cycle can be glossed, less the literary merit of the original tales, as follows (based on Curtin 1884, 1912; Gatschet 1890; Marriott and Rachlin 1968):[5]

Gmoḱam'č saw that the entire world was the water of Tule and Klamath Lakes. He reached to the bottom of the lakes and pulled up mud that he used to make the mountains, hills, and islands of the world. He used his fingernails to scratch out the courses of the rivers and streams.

Gmoḱam'č possessed a bright disk that made him immortal. No matter how mangled or scattered the parts of his body might be, he was returned to life by Morning Star:

"And nothing remained except the disk. And Morning Star (*Gmoḱam'č's* medicine) said to the disk 'why do you sleep so long? Get up old man!' And he got up as before, and he will last as long as the disk and the morning star." (Curtin 1884:book3/myth2)

Gmoḱam'č obtained the disk when he refused to bring its original owner, the "blue and beautiful" young man, Salmon, back to life. As he was adding wood to Salmon's cremation fire, Salmon's wife jumped into the flames with their baby on her back. *Gmoḱam'č* saw this just in time to grab the baby from his mother's back. He then searched through the ashes of the cremation fire for the disk. He found it and placed it on the small of his back:

"The minute he put it there it grew to his body, and right away he was beautiful and young and bright, the brightest person in the world. The disk had become a part of him, and he was the father of A'isis, for the disk was the father of A'isis." (Curtin 1912).

Gmoḱam'č hid the baby, A'isis, in his knee where it appeared as a boil. While traveling *Gmoḱam'č* stayed at the home of two old women. He complained of the pain caused by the boil in his knee and asked the women to press it. When they did the baby emerged from his knee. The people asked where he got the baby. *Gmoḱam'č* replied that the earth was kind to him and gave the baby to him.

Gmoḱam'č took A'isis to live on the south side of Tule Lake. There he fished and raised the baby to a young adult. They lived with *Gmoḱam'č's* younger brother *Wawńa·k*. *Gmoḱam'č* often taunted his brother and called him *Wnaga*, the Klamath word for son. Eventually *Wawńa·k.* became as wise and strong as *Gmoḱam'č* and took the name *Ẁas-Gmoḱam'č* (Coyote-

Gmoḱam'č).⁶ *Ẅas-Gmoḱam'č* became the leader of *Eine*, known in English as the Dancing Place, where the spirits of the dead arrive at the spirit world.⁷

Gmoḱam'č and *A'isis* moved to another house on a mountain and *Gmoḱam'č* taught *A'isis* how to gain spirit power through vision questing:

> "You must be wise, you must be great and powerful and strong. You must go to the top of *Laniswi* and swim in the pond of blue water that is there. When you get to the pond, you must stand and pile up stones and talk to the mountain. The mountain will hear you. Everything in the world will hear you and understand you. After you have talked to the mountain, you must dive in the pond. Dive five times to the bottom, and each time drink of the lowest water. When you come out of the pond, build a fire, warm yourself and then sleep. If you dream don't tell the dream to anyone. When you wake up, start for home. On the road don't talk to anyone, or drink any water. If you do as I tell you, you will be as great as I am and do the things that I do. You will live always. You will be the brightest object in the world. If you endure these things, you will be able to bear every suffering." (Curtin 1912).

A'isis visited all of the vision questing places and became a powerful man. He could have become a great leader but *Gmoḱam'č* didn't want that. They moved to a series of new homes together but eventually they had a falling out and moved apart.

Gmoḱam'č later had a daughter who he raised on his own. When it came time for her puberty ritual she dreamed that someone would die and *Gmoḱam'č* knew it would be her. When she died he followed her spirit on the path to *Eine*, a huge earth lodge where the spirits of the dead reside and dance. This is the path of the sun as it sets in the west. *Gmoḱam'č* knew this path well and was able to bring people back to life if he recovered their spirit on the path, before they reached *Eine*.

He went with his daughter to *Eine* were he visited with his brother *Ẅas-Gmoḱam'č*, the leader of that world. The spirits of the dead were offended by *Gmoḱam'č*'s presence because he was "raw" (still living). These spirits were bones in *Eine* at nighttime (day on earth) but looked like people during the day (night on earth). *Gmoḱam'č* collected a bag of these bones, including those of his daughter, and took them to the earth along the path of the sun, where they had first entered *Eine*. He scattered the bones and they became the various nations of people on earth today.

Gmoḱam'č and his daughter continued on the path of the sun to the middle of the sky at noon. Here he built the house in which he still lives with his daughter.

There are two main points from this condensed myth cycle that are relevant to the present discussion:

First, *Gmoḱam'č* is a solar deity who was clearly associated with shamanism and vision questing. This solar aspect is fairly obvious from the shape of the disk and the fact that it is Morning Star who revives *Gmoḱam'č*, just as the morning star is a prelude to the sunrise. His younger brother *Wawńa·k* is associated with the sun halo (Gatschet 1890:102). *Gmoḱam'č* first taught people how to gain spirit power through vision questing when he passed this knowledge to his son. Ray (1963:19) reports that *Gmoḱam'č* also provided human beings with instructions concerning shamanism. *Gmoḱam'č* knew and understood the path of the sun to *Eine* and had the power to revive people from the dead by retrieving their spirits from this path. His brother *Ẁas-Gmoḱam'č* provided an intimate connection to *Eine*. From the perspective of shamanic power, it is likely that the spirit of *Gmoḱam'č* would be about the most potent power a shaman could possess.

Second, the stories in this, and many other Klamath/Modoc myth cycles, are intimately related to objects in the landscape such as mountains, caves, and rock outcroppings. This "sacred geography" is evident in much of the contemporary nomenclature of the Klamath Basin. The Buttes of the Gods were the homes of Eagle and other characters from the time when animals talked like people. Yamsi Butte was home to the tricksters Mink and Weasel. *Gmoḱam'č's* sweat lodge and several of his homes are well known to the members of the Klamath Tribes.

The sacred geography could have served as a gigantic mnemonic device to aid in the remembering of the mythic cycles (Hann et al 2004). As the people traveled through the territory seeing the cliffs, mountains, and rock outcroppings would have triggered memories of the stories in which these are discussed. The order of the myths would also be recorded by the order in which the geographic features are encountered. It could also have functioned as a mental map of the Klamath/Modoc world. When returning from a trip to the east, for instance, travelers would know they were within a day's walk of Klamath Lake when they reached Eagle's village (Buttes of the Gods). They would know this, even if they had never made the trip before, since that is how long it took the Butterfly Sisters on their ill-fated walk to the wedding at Eagle's house (Curtin 1884:book12/myth44).

House of the Rising Sun

Near the shore of Tule Lake is Ufie Hill on which is located a small cave (Figure 4). The small cave (approximately three and a half meters wide by two meters deep) is formed in a red/orange volcanic tuff and faces southeast. Interior height ranges from one to two meters. The oval entrance measures less than two meters across. There is a small (less than 50 cm wide) "window" in the south wall. In general, the cave gives the appearance of being a giant bubble in the tuff. The interior and exterior of the cave, as well as an adjacent cliff face and boulder, are covered with deeply incised and ground petroglyphs. No other rock art has been found on Ufie Hill although there are ample locations where it could have been produced. Petroglyphs in and near the cave include curvilinear meanders, zigzags, V-shaped designs, circles, and concentric circles. These images are technically and stylistically similar to those

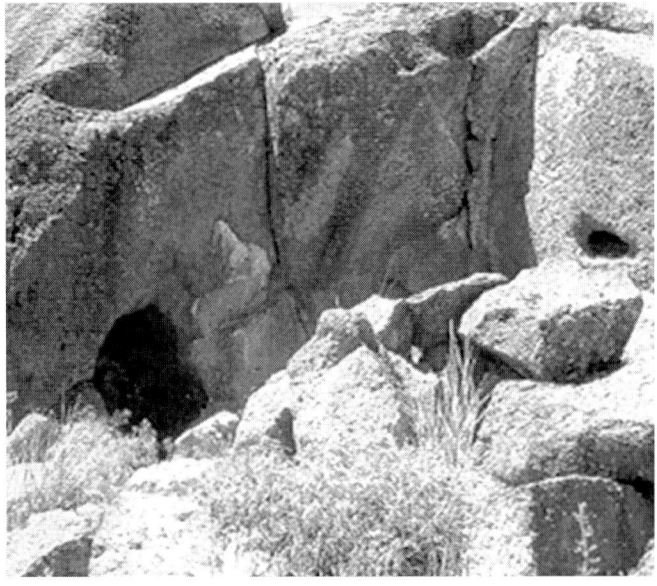

Figure 4. "House of the Rising Sun" cave atop Ufie Hill.

at the much larger Peninsula site in Lava Beds National Monument. The Peninsula is part of the Klamath/Modoc sacred geography associated with *A'isis* (Curtin 1884, 1912).

Ufie Hill is located at an important place in the physical Modoc landscape. Most Modoc winter villages were centered around Tule and Clear Lakes and along Lost River. These bodies of water are all connected, with Lost River beginning at Clear Lake and emptying into Tule Lake. What makes this unique is that Clear Lake was located only six miles east of Tule Lake (before Tule Lake was drained and Clear Lake was dammed) but, due to the ridge system which separates the lakes, Lost River meanders approximately seventy miles, first north, and then south, between the two lakes (Dicken and Dicken 1985). This nearly circular watercourse neatly defines the heartland of Modoc territory (Figure 1). Ufie Hill is located along the ridge that separates the lakes and is in effect at the center of the Modoc world. Its spiritual power may have been emphasized by the fortuitous combination of a female landscape attribute—the cave—atop a male attribute—the hill (Whitley 1998).

The location of Ufie Hill and the House of the Rising Sun rock art site in the sacred geography of the Klamath/Modoc was first pointed out to me by Arlene Benson in 1990 while I was assisting her in recording rock art on the Modoc National Forest. She noted that there was a small, red cave on the butte that corresponded with that described in one of the myths collected by Curtin.

"The passage, from Ko-a-lak'-ak-a, reads in part:
They went to the top of a high mountain and built a house among the rocks. The house was red and nice to look at. *Gmoḱam'č* thought that people around Tule Lake would see his house, but couldn't climb up to it. *Gmoḱam'č* had the north side, *A'isis* the south side of the house; the door opened towards the east. . . .The house in which *Gmoḱam'č* reared his son is seen half way up the mountain. One sees the crimson interior of the dwelling through the opening (windows) above the house." (Curtin 1912:7,10).

Evangeline Schonchin described the location where *Gmoḱam'č* made the world and where he now sleeps (Marriott and Rachlin 1968:44-46). The "hole in the rock, near its top, that was big enough to see through" corresponds well with the cave on Ufie Hill.[8]

"Then [*Gmoḱam'č*] was tired. He had done everything he could think of to do, and winter was about to begin. 'I will do what the bear does,' [*Gmoḱam'č*] thought. 'I will make myself a hole where I will be safe, and sleep the winter through.' [*Gmoḱam'č*] dug himself a hole under the bottom of Tule Lake, with the hill where he created the world to mark the spot. By now the hill had dried out and turned to solid rock, as it is today. Just at the last moment, as he was about to go underground, [*Gmoḱam'č*] thought, 'I might want to look out sometime and see what is going on, without bothering to move around.' So he scratched and scratched with his fingernail until he had made a hole in the rock, near its top, that was big enough to see through. It is still there, and people can climb the rock and look out through the hole."

The incised and scratched rock art in the cave (Figure 5) certainly gives the appearance that it could have been created through *Gmoḱam'č* scratching his hole to see the world. The softness of the rock of which the cave is formed, and the general size of the carvings, suggests the possibility that some of the petroglyphs may have been made with bare fingers. This was tested on a small cobble of tuff from the same flow, but from a different location. Deeply incised grooves can be made in the rock with fingernails, and with surprisingly little effort or discomfort. These closely resemble the many sharp-sided grooves that make up the tally marks, zigzags, and V-shaped designs at the House of

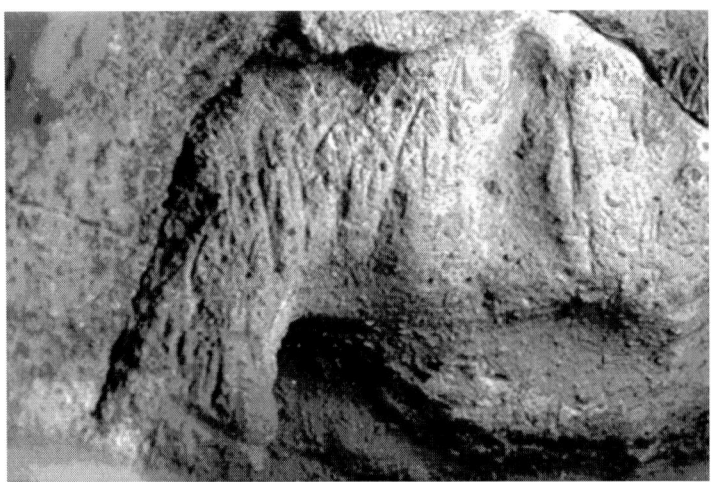

Figure 5. Incised and scratched rock art from House of the Rising Sun.

the Rising Sun site. The pad of the thumb can be used to abrade the wider ground designs, such as the circles and meanders at *Gmoḱam'č* cave, but the authors found it more efficient to start these designs with a stick or pebble. With more motivation, and thicker calluses, it is certainly conceivable that these designs could have been entirely made with the unprotected hand. A careful examination of the rock art at this and the Peninsula sites should reveal whether or not "finger carving" was the technique of choice.

Both stories treat the cave as a "door," or "window" for a larger "house" which is within the butte. Caves and hills were often considered the homes of mythological beings (Curtin 1884; Gatschet 1890:116)The use of caves and rock art sites by shamans as portals between the physical and spirit worlds is well documented (Benson and Sehgal 1987; Eliade 1964; Hann et al 2004; Whitely 1994a, 1994b). It seems apparent that at the House of the Rising Sun, the "window" between the world of the Modoc and the home of *Gmoḱam'č*, was a portal between the corporeal world and the spirit world. It was a place where *Gmoḱam'č* could check up on his charges in the physical world and it was a place where a shaman could "see the crimson interior of [*Gmoḱam'č* house]... through the opening" (Curtin 1912:7). This is consistent with the role of *Gmoḱam'č* as the teacher of shamanic knowledge (Ray 1963:19). The use of the cave by shamans is also strongly suggested by a map made by Jeff Riddle in an 1890 letter to Gatschet which identifies Ufie Hill as the location of a "ghost cave, medicine man's cave" (Riddle 1890).

Other evidence for shamanic use of the cave can be found in the myths and rock art itself. The bear/hibernation symbolism in the Evangeline Schonchin story is consistent with the association between bears and shamans in California and many other parts of the world (Eliade 1964; Whitley 1994a, 1994b). Besides its sheer physical power, which suggests its spiritual power, the bear is seen as a mediator between the physical and spiritual worlds since it hibernates underground, i.e. in the underworld. Hibernation is similar to the ritual death experienced by shamans during their ecstatic trances. Several of the deeply grooved elements of the rock art could be seen as representing the scratches of a bear.

Most of the imagery in and around the cave is consistent with that of the phosphenes observed during the altered states of consciousness produced during vision quest experiences (Benson and Sehgal 1987; Hedges 1987, 1992; Whitley 1994a, 1994b). This includes curvilinear meanders, zigzags, V-shaped designs, circles, and concentric circles. Of particular interest here are the circles and concentric circles which may represent the disk/spirit of *Gmoḱam'č*, the sun and sun halo of *Gmoḱam'č* and his brother *Wawṅa'k*, and the abodes of the dead in "shining settlements out in circles from the wide house" of *Ẁas-Gmoḱam'č* in *Eine* (Curtin 1884:book 3/myth 3, book 5/myth 4; Hann et al 2004). They may also represent a tunnel-like passage through which the shaman could travel to the spirit world (Benson and Sehgal 1987).

The eastern orientation of the cave entrance, which is specifically noted in the above Curtin myth, suggests that the site would have been a good location to view the sunrise. This would seem particularly relevant to a location for receiving spirit power from a solar deity. It also brings up the possibility that the site could have served as a viewing station for solstices or other solar events. The 1991 summer solstice sunrise was observed with negative results. The sun did not rise over any obvious marker on the horizon. The light and shadow patterns crossing the rock art in and around the cave did not appear to track the sun's movement in an obvious way. There was no specific indication in the ethnographic material that the solstice or equinox was a particularly significant event for the Klamath/Modoc.

Non-shamanic uses of vision questing at the cave at Ufie Hill are described in another myth provided by Ko-a-lak'-ak-a (Curtin 1884:book 8/myth 15). Here it is referred to as a "women's medicine cave" used during a young woman's critical puberty rites. It is also a good location to earn the spirit power of groundhog that allows one to be a great gambler.

> "There is a mountain between Tule and Klamath [Lakes] and the top is as smooth as a crown of one's head.[9] And there are swimming ponds there, and there is also a woman's medicine cave.[10] Now a young girl was sick and went to this mountain on the east side of it[11] Her mother told her she must have a string tied around her waist and when she started to come down (into the cave) 'tie it around some strong brush (so you can find the way back out of the cave.)'[12] There is a nice flat rock inside the cave and it has squirrel (*Moie*) teeth on the rock. If [you] hear the teeth making a noise on the rock you will know you will be a great gambler.[13] Pile up stones before you go into this cave.[14] Where they go down are stones just like steps and it is smooth inside like a wall.[15]
>
> After piling the rock she tied long string to brush then held the string in her hand. And while in the cave she dropped the string and hunted everywhere for it, feeling all around her, but couldn't find it, so she couldn't tell where she came in. It was very dark and she wandered way far in. She traveled five nights and five days way under the ground and it was all soft sand like duck feathers.[16] She felt lonesome and [had] nothing to eat and she cried all the time, [she] couldn't lie down. Her dancing (time) was over.[17] She stumbled over a rock and sat and cried with her loud voice. Her kinfolk were hunting day after day for her. As she sat there crying she slept, [she] thought somebody told her to look up and see the stars. Then she woke up and looked up and could see a bit of light overhead, as big as a pinhead. Then the ground like split open, the rocks above, and she got out.[18]
>
> After the earth opened and made a path for her, and she went quickly home. She named the place where she came out *Waltoka* (*Keakwasis*, she gave both names to it). She was nothing but skin and bones.[19] Her father tried to go inside the cave to search for her, but inside it stood up like a wall and wouldn't let him pass.[20] She heard the people mourning and found the people searching at the opening of the cave which was very far from where she came out. Took her home. Her mother made a sweathouse for her. This was in spring. They dressed her. (She went in at Ufie Mountain and came out on another mountain she called Waltoka). The mountain saved her." (Curtin 1884:book 8/myth 15)

Conclusions

At least a part of the significance and function of the House of the Rising Sun petroglyph site is documented in the ethnographic record for the Klamath Basin. Can any of this be extrapolated to other rock art sites in the area? It is tempting to speculate that the circle and concentric circle motif found so frequently at Klamath Basin rock art sites (Figure 6) might well represent the disc of *Gmok̓am'č* and, by extension, the sun (Hann et al 2004). Might these all be portals between the corporeal and spirit worlds? Places where spirits can turn into physical beings in order to enter this world, such as lizards darting from a crack in the rock, and where people can become spirits able to travel in the solid "ether" of the spirit world. This seems to be the case at least at some other Klamath Basin sites. In 1878 Dr. Denison, who worked at the Klamath Reservation, sent Gatschet a description of a rock art site near the agency:

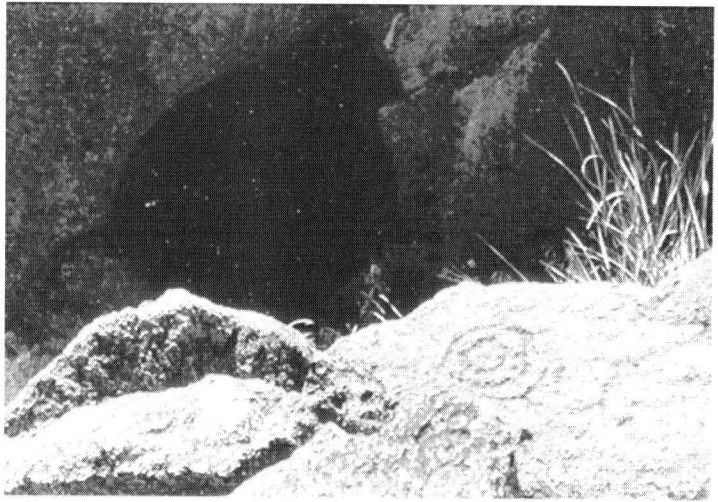

Figure 6. Concentric circle petroglyph at House of the Rising Sun.

"The only pictures painted on the rocks ... are circles painted with red and white paint. The circles are from four to six inches in diameter and about a inch or half inch in width [thickness of the painted line] and some have the center filled with red, then an inch or so of white, then another circle of red, and perhaps another layer of white [red and white concentric circles]. .... A few of the perpendicular rocks are covered with these. Minnie [a tribal informant] says they were made by doctors [shamans] and mean nothing but to inspire fear in the doctors' supernatural power." (Denison 1879).

There is compelling evidence that these concentric circle motifs do indeed represent portals through which shamans, and others, could travel between the physical and spirit worlds. And in the Klamath Basin at least they may also represent the disk of *Gmok̓am'č*, the original Klamath/Modoc shaman, and the spirit of the sun.

---

[1] Many of these are site records in various government agencies, including the Fremont, Winema and Modoc National Forests, Lakeview BLM, Lava Beds National Monument, US Fish and Wildlife Service, Klamath County Museum, and the Klamath Tribes culture and heritage department.

[2] Drilled petroglyphs are rarely discussed in the literature but are found in at least two locations in the Klamath Basin; House of the Rising Sun and the Peninsula. The matrix of these sites is a finely compacted welded tuff. There are numerous examples of drill holes in the cliff faces. They range up to 1 cm in diameter and up to 4 cm deep. They are sometimes found separately and sometimes grouped into patterns. In a replication experiment using a bow drill, similar tuff was easily drilled with an untipped wooden shaft.

[3] Ko-a-lak'-ak-a may have been Kientpoos' sister of that name, also called Queen Mary, who is known to have been exiled to Oklahoma. Kientpoos, commonly known as Captain Jack, led the Modoc rebellion of 1873. Jenny Clinton's Modoc name was Bap-pee Bin-pat-o-kit (Short Face) as per Curtin (1884). Kientpoos and three others were hung and most of the rest of the combatants and their families were exiled to Oklahoma. 39 men, 54 women and 60 children were exiled and many died during this time. In 1909 those who wished to were allowed to return to the Klamath Reservation. Sadly, Ko-a-lak'-ak-a died three years before she would have been allowed to go home. Jenny Clinton did return to the Klamath Basin in 1909 where she lived until her death in 1950. See the discussion following this paper for confirmation of the identity of Jenny Clinton and by extension, Ko-a-lak'-ak-a.

[4] *Gmok̓am'č* and *Wawńa·k* have counterparts from the time when "animals talked like people." These are *Sqel*, Old Marten, who is identified with *Gmok̓am'č*, and *Časga'y*, Weasel, identified with *Wawńa·k* (Barker 1963b:389; Gatschet 1890:108, 115).

[5] A number of factors make summarizing this corpus of mythic literature problematic and potentially misleading. First, there is its inherent complexity. There are multiple time periods including at least the mythic past and the supernatural present. The mythic past appears to have at least two components with the age of *Gmok̓am'č* and *Wawńa·k* being distinct from that of the time when animals talked like people (either in time or some form of supernatural space). Second, there are differences between Klamath and Modoc versions of the myths and there may have well been differences in versions between bands or even families within each tribe. These differences are particularly obvious when it comes to details of the sacred geography, people tended to place mythic events and places within their own territories. Third, there were differences in the completeness of the recollections by various people. This is made clear by their stated reluctance to tell myths they only had partial memories of. Much of

the importance placed by Curtin on the material told by Ko-a-lak'-ak-a was its apparent completeness. Fourth, There was likely some intentional variation between storytellers as each individual decided what was appropriate to share and how much detail was desired by the various ethnographers.

[6] The relationship between *Gmok̓am'č* and *Ẁas-Gmok̓am'č* in Klamath/Modoc mythology is complex and compelling. *Ẁas-Gmok̓am'č* appears to be *Gmok̓am'č* younger brother. In a number of myths *Gmok̓am'č* taunts him by calling him his son, *wnaga* in Klamath (Barker 1963b:452). *Wnaga* (son) is similar to *Wawña`k* (little red fox) and the words may be etymologically related (Barker 1963b:459). The Curtins used the phonetic spelling *Wanaga* and Gatschet used *Wanáka*. Gatschet translated *Wanáka* as silver fox but Barker demonstrates that red fox is more likely. The notes to the texts and the usage within the myths themselves suggests that both son and little red fox may be appropriate meanings. Gatschet (1890:102) notes that *Wanáka* was associated with the halo seen around the sun. This further ties *Wawña`k* (little red fox/sun halo) to *Gmok̓am'č* (sun disk). *Wnagal Wawña`k* is used as this character's proper name until he is as skilled and powerful as *Gmok̓am'č* and he takes the name *Ẁas-Gmok̓am'č*. *Ẁas* is the Klamath word for coyote (Barker 1963b:459). *Ẁas-Gmok̓am'č* "takes care of spirits and is in charge of that world [*Eine*]" (Curtin 1884:book 3/myth 3). *Ẁas-Gmok̓am'č* seems to have the same role in the spirit world as *Gmok̓am'č* has in the physical world. They appear to be functioning in two distinct non-physical realms, *Gmok̓am'č* in myth time (in the physical world but in the mythic past) and *Ẁas-Gmok̓am'č* in supernatural space (the present time in the supernatural world). Their ability to interact between realms is testament to their spiritual power.

[7] The concepts of the spirit world are more complex than this gloss indicates. The spirit world is very large but the spirits of the dead are restricted to certain parts (unlike the mythological spirit beings). They first arrive at *Eine*, a huge earth lodge ruled by *Ẁas-Gmok̓am'č*. If they fail to reach *Eine*, or break taboos while there, they would become *skoks*, the ghosts of the dead that roam the earth. If they are good people and follow the proper taboos after five years they will be allowed to live "in shining settlements out in circles from the wide house" (Curtin 1884:book 3/myth 3). In similar myths the good people move to a village in the sky and the bad go to *Skukshim Gheals*, the devil's place, located in a hole beneath *Eine*.

[8] This story was recorded in the mid-twentieth century and contains brief elements from several more complete myths in the *Gmok̓am'č* cycle. There appears to be some combining of places with the location of the creation spot being merged with the location where *Gmok̓am'č* sleeps today. The creation spot is described as being an island in Tule Lake that had "dried out and turned to solid rock." This is clearly the Peninsula site that was an island during periods of high water before Tule Lake was drained in the early twentieth century. No hole or "window" like formation as described by Schonchin has been located near the top of the Peninsula despite several efforts to do so. The cave and "window" at Ufie Hill match this description quite well. Interestingly, very similar petroglyphs are found in a soft volcanic tuff at both of these locations. These locations are closely linked in the sacred geography of the

Klamath/Modoc and it is likely they were intentionally or inadvertently combined in this simplified version of the *Gmoƙam'č* myth cycle.

[9] Ufie Hill is actually between Tule and Clear Lakes. There is no hill between Tule and Klamath Lakes, only a low ridge and marsh. Ufie Hill is distinctly round and smooth and stands out from the surrounding ridges and elongated hills.

[10] There are no ponds or other water sources on Ufie Hill. The ponds appear to be metaphors for spirit travel into the underworld. Going to ponds for vision quests and meeting spirit beings in the water are frequent adventures in the myths. The "cave" has been previously described and is more a shallow rock shelter than a true cave. The multi-day trek this young woman takes is clearly a spirit journey, not a physical journey.

[11] The beginning of puberty was described as a sickness. The cave is on the southeast side of Ufie Hill and faces east.

[12] The use of a string as a guide home is described in other Klamath/Modoc myths. It may have actually been used and may have served as a source of comfort for the initiates during their first vision quest experiences.

[13] There are numerous intentional small scratch marks in and around the cave that could give the impression of being made by rodent teeth. Rodents actually do gnaw on rocks, probably to file down their teeth which grow continuously. These gnawed rocks have caused considerable discussion during archaeological excavations when they are found.

[14] Piling rocks during visions questing was a common practice in the Klamath Basin. There are no obvious rock piles On Ufie Hill.

[15] The step-like path into the underworld is similar to that described on the path to *Eine* in other Klamath/Modoc myths.

[16] Five is a sacred number for the Klamath/Modoc and it is commonly giving as the proper number of days to fast and pray during a vision quest or purification sweat bath. Five years is the amount of time given for staying in *Eine* in those myths that describe it as the temporary home for the spirits of the dead. The ground being soft like duck feathers suggests the state of warmth and numbness that often accompanies an altered state of consciousness.

[17] The dancing time refers to the five days of ceremonial dancing during a woman's puberty ritual. During this time she fasted and danced. She was not allowed to sleep during this time because if she dreamed, it was likely that she would die. After this point she was allowed to sleep and recover from her vision trance.

[18] A metaphor for return of the spirit to the body and the regaining of normal consciousness.

[19] A common metaphor for the apparent death of the body that happens during a trance state. Shamans are said to have died when they travel to the spirit world.

[20] Only spirits can travel in the spirit world so the girl's father was unable to follow his daughter past the physical back of the cave.

Discussion

Linea Sundstrom: Don, is that mountain where the girl came out identified?

Don Hann: No. The myth gives two place names for the mountain where she exited but I have not been able to find these in either Modoc or Klamath geographies or dictionaries.

Linea Sundstrom: The story doesn't say what direction she was traveling from?

Don Hann: No.

Linea Sundstrom: Do you know her name?

Don Hann: No, that wasn't provided either.

David Whitley: The mountain may not be in either Klamath or Modoc territory. Remember the story of the old man who turned into a screw? He came out at Mt. Shasta as I recall. So we may need to look a little further away. In fact that's the first thing that occurs to me. Did she come out at Mt. Shasta? Which is out of Modoc territory.

Don Hann: That's a good thought. It is a very visible mountain from Modoc territory. It's a big snow-capped mountain.

James Keyser: Don, what, if any, relationship does your rock art have to do with the work that Dave and Jannie did down at the Lava Beds?

David Whitley: It doesn't fit [the model defined at Lava Beds].

Don Hann: Well, some stories don't fit. But if we just consider the women's puberty rite, that fits nicely with the landscape model that they've developed. Basically, theirs is a gender-based landscape model that hypothesizes the high points on the landscape would be male in the physical world, so they would be portals to female places in the underworld. Male shamans under that model should be attracted to springs and lower lying areas on the landscape. Much of the rock art *is* from lower lying areas on the landscape, but then we have the site I described up on top of a hill. So from this perspective it does make sense that it would be a female puberty location. But other ethnographic evidence suggests different uses for the House of the Rising Sun site. Jeff Riddle identifies the site on his map as being a shaman's cave and a ghost cave. And then there are the associations with *G'mok'amc* and his house. These aspects of the site do not seem to obviously fit the landscape model. One thing I've been thinking about may pull those things together. Perhaps it [The House of the Rising Sun site] had particular strength because it had both male and female aspects together on the landscape. It was a cave, which is female, on top of a mountain, which should be male.

David Whitley: That's a good point, and the issue that immediately jumps into my mind is: Are there many caves on high points in this area? Maybe this is extremely unusual.

Don Hann: I don't know of many. The Peninsula site is also a very unique site. It is a volcanic cone.

David Whitley: But that site is low—the lowest point in the basin because it was under water.

Don Hann: Right, good point. When you're on top of it now, it doesn't feel low, but it actually is.

David Whitley: The rock art is placed low on the formation.

Don Hann: Yes, but I've been on top of it, because there is good reason to believe that *G'mok'amc* created the world there.

David Whitley: Yes—it's cited as the origin place.

Don Hann: Yes. One of the stories I've read talks about *G'mok'amc* going to that point and then scratching a hole for himself. I've been all over the top of that formation trying to find something to fit the hole that *G'mok'amc* could look out of and I couldn't find it.

David Whitley: Yes, its not there. Let me just clarify that when we're talking about most of the sites being low, we're focusing on Lava Beds National Monument. It has the biggest concentration of lava tubes in the west and they are very low. The caves typically in the area are huge, low-lying lava tubes and the rock art is just inside them. But then there's this one cave that Don describes that's up high.

Don Hann: Yes, it's unique. Basically it's a rock shelter with a very small opening but then it opens up when you get inside. Its not *that* much bigger—I can't quite stand fully upright in it, but I can lie down. Its strange. Its like going into a closet with a window out one side. The door and the window—its very distinctive.

James Keyser: It is a unique form. I'm familiar with the Winema and Fremont national forests just to the north [in Oregon], and there's nothing else like it.

Don Hann: Nor on the Modoc National Forest [in northern California]—its unique.

Jannie Loubser: Don, what would you make out of the fact that most of the things in the lava tubes are of black pigment and that is red.

Don Hann: The "building" is red, but the images are petroglyphs.

Jannie Loubser: So there is no red pigment?

Don Hann: Not there. I think its interesting in general that in the Klamath Basin there's a lot more red outside of the Lava Beds. So the pictographs that are up to the north are red and white predominantly and then down at Lava Beds they're black. There's something going on there but I don't have a good idea of what it is.

Jannie Loubser: Klamath versus Modoc?

Don Hann: We'll have to look at that closer, but that's a good possibility.

James Keyser: That distinction is really notable. I knew a little bit about Klamath Basin rock art when I got a chance to help Jannie and Dave for a day or two at their Lava Beds project, and its almost all black pigment there, but the interesting thing is that there are red pigment sources within 25 miles of where the rock art is all black.

David Whitley: The ethnography says there is no red pigment in the area because to get it they'd have to get it from the Paiute and they didn't trade with them. But that's apparently not true—there are red pigment sources. Something else is going on.

One other point, Don, do you know that there are other putative *G'mok'amc* houses in the region?

Don Hann: Yes, that's true. I think there are different sets of these things between the Klamath and the Modoc—creation places as well as houses and other things. But I suspect it gets down almost to the level of families—actual areas that families are living in will have the nuances based on the geography they're most intimate with. In Gatschets's notes when more than one Indian was being interviewed, there seemed to be these little discussions going on to reach consensus about traditional geography. I think it isn't just loss of tradition, but in fact debate between traditionalists as to whose version is more authentic or correct.

David Whitley: Yes, and there's another thing that's interesting about this area—and it stands out from much of the rest of the far west. Anywhere else in California or the Great Basin the origin point is going to be the region's high mountain. Here it isn't. In fact, its the lowest place on the landscape. But that's probably somewhat a function of the fact that Klamath-Modoc territory is a large basin with lakes in the middle. Mt. Shasta is outside their territory and it's the high point for lots of groups, but the Klamath-Modoc don't have a central high mountain.

Linea Sundstrom: Don, do you find this concentric circle design in body painting or on altars? Is it showing up in other contexts?

Don Hann: Not very much. The body painting I can think of is all done with stripes; women had stripes on their chins, and basketry has nothing similar.

Linea Sundstrom: I'm thinking more of religious contexts.

Don Hann: Not that I know of. I have read that shamans had a plank they put outside their winter dwelling with pictographs on it—but they tended to be animal figures in red. Nothing with circles.

Linea Sundstrom: You may have said this—you certainly implied it. Part of what's going on with that [circle] motif is that it's a way of collapsing a multi-dimensional world into two dimensions. So you've got the above and the below with *G'mok'amc* and *Ẁas-G'mok'amc* and then you're bringing them all into contact at that point—and that may be what your little cave is all about too. Because at that site the story says they are going down and then they see the sky. Things sort of keep flipping around.

Don Hann: That a very interesting thought. What's going on between *G'mok'amc* and *Ẁas- G'mok'amc*—upper and lower—really intrigues me. I'm starting to make some sense out of that now that I know more about *Wenaka* and his role. I couldn't understand the relationship between *Wenaka* and *Ẁas-G'mok'amc* until I found a myth where *Wenaka* becomes *Ẁas- G'mok'amc*.

Jannie Loubser: This seems to be a kind of fusion—the axis mundi—where both parts come together.

Linea Sundstrom: And in some Indian religions there is almost the concept that the sky mirrors the earth and the earth mirrors the sky. We don't really have this because we think of the center of the earth as molten rock. But this is a different way of conceptualizing that. So it could be that sort of an idea where the wall comes up behind her and she's going down, but then she sees the stars—and then she doesn't.

Don Hann: I think there's a lot to that, actually. We have these wonderful descriptions of the path the soul or spirit takes from this world to the underworld. And nice descriptions of *Eine*, the dancing place, which is the Modoc underworld. It is an inversion of the world of the living. Night time down there is daytime up here. The living are rancid and decaying in the underworld. When *G'Mo'kamc* visits *Eine* he has to hide himself in the corner because he is offending the spirits of the dead.

David Whitley: Because he smells.

Don Hann: Because he is raw—he is uncooked—he offends people.

Linea Sundstrom: You don't have the original text in the native language?

Don Hann: Sadly, not this story.

Editors Note: Later in the session, the group returned to this discussion and provided a short addition.

James Keyser: Viola….would you share with us some of your knowledge about Klamath country?

Viola Kalama: I was very interested when Don showed Klamath and Modoc scenes—pictographs and petroglyphs. It seems like the Klamaths and Modocs were quite close to us. You know, they traveled through our country quite a bit to go over the mountains to the coast to trade and hunt. Their religion and customs were similar to ours. I had an older brother who worked for an old man in Chiloquin. He lived on the north side of the big lake and he worked for him as a driver for several years. They traveled—my brother drove—and all the while that old man would tell my brother a lot of stories.

Also, I wondered about this Jenny that was spoken about. My brother told us that they'd go to "Aunt Jenny's"—she lived just at the entrance of Wocus Bay. She was quite old at that time and she related how she watched Captain Jack and them [the other Modoc prisoners] take their last breath on the gallows. They were in the stockade. She was just a young girl—maybe 8 or 9—but she told my brother a lot of stories about the hills and what she knew. She was quite old at that time. He called her "Aunt Jenny" and I don't know if she's related to that Jenny Clinton you talked about.

David Whitley: Was Captain Jack her uncle?

Viola Kalama: He was her uncle. That's what she said—that Captain Jack was her uncle.

David Whitley: Because that increases the probability that she and Jenny Clinton were the same person.

Viola Kalama: Yes

Don Hann: Jenny Clinton actually was buried in 1950, so she lived that long.

Viola Kalama: That must have been her.

Don Hann: Yes, I think you're right. That's wonderful.

Viola Kalama: So he [Viola's brother] got a lot of information from her and this old man took him up to the hill there in Modoc country where they did their cremating—it was one of the places. He [the old man] told him [Viola's brother] that this was a regular place for their loved ones and all that was laying around was purple glass and bones, so he felt kind of bad when he went up there because he was one of those people that you folks are taking about today—he was a medicine man—and he sang up there. The petroglyphs and all that—they look familiar to me. It seems that the Klamath and Modoc were quite close with our reservation people. We had some on our reservation too—like they used to capture slaves from the Columbia—as the people came to visit, well they captured each other and so they captured a Klamath man, and after a while they got so acquainted with him and he learned their language and they learned each other's ways and he became a chief—*Pio-Nash* was his name. It was a Klamath name. Chief *Pio-Nash* and then he had all of his relatives that lived in Warm Springs. He married somebody from the Columbia River and there's a lot of them left over there.

What I heard from my brother was that their religion was like ours—the medicine singing and the winter signing—almost like us. When those pictures were shown I just felt like I was among my people—same customs, same habits, but different languages,

CHAPTER 10
The Blade Cuts Two Ways: Using Ethnographic Analogy to Interpret the Columbia Plateau Scratched Style
James D. Keyser and Michael W. Taylor

Introduction

The relevance of ethnography to rock art has long been a focal point of research in the Columbia Plateau region (Teit 1896, 1930; Malouf and White 1953; Coburn 1975; Keyser 1992; York et al 1993; Keyser and Whitley 2000; Hann et al 2004). Indeed, some of the earliest, most detailed ethnographic rock art references in North America are found in the region's literature (see Keyser and Whitley 2000), and references range from the identification of specific motifs (Teit 1930), sites (Malouf and White 1953), and practices (Cline 1938) to pigment sources and recipes (Barbeau 1960; Hann et al 2004). Direct ethnographic references are primarily centered on shamanic practices and the personal vision quest (Hines 1992, 1993; Keyser and Whitley 2000; Hann et al 2004). In addition to such direct evidence, researchers have also assembled and analyzed less direct, metaphoric references from various ethnographic sources that suggest the rock art also likely functioned in mortuary, mythic, and hunting magic rituals (Keyser 1990; Hann et al 2004).

Never-the-less, all of the Columbia Plateau ethnographic rock art research so far published can be viewed as occurring within a direct historical model (see Strong 1935; Wedel 1938) in which there are direct correlations between specific ethnographic references and the archaeological evidence—rock art images and sites. As Binford (1962:217, 1968:13-14) has pointed out, this is interesting because it increases our ability to *explicate* the past, but it does very little to actually increase our knowledge about and ability to *explain* the past. In essence, most of what has been done so far in Columbia Plateau rock art interpretation is to document that ethnographically known practices occurred in prehistory and place some of them on the landscape.

In contrast, Binford (1967) has illustrated how ethnographic analogy can be used to increase the explanatory power of archaeological data. His argument is that by correctly using analogy, archaeologists can formulate and test hypotheses about their data that can produce results that have the ability to actually increase our knowledge about, and understanding of, the past. In this paper we use ethnographic analogy in just this way to propose an explanation for a newly-identified Columbia Plateau rock art style.

The Area

The Columbia Plateau (Figure 1) is a large region of northwestern North America encompassing the watersheds of the Columbia and Fraser rivers.   Bounded by the Cascade Mountains on the

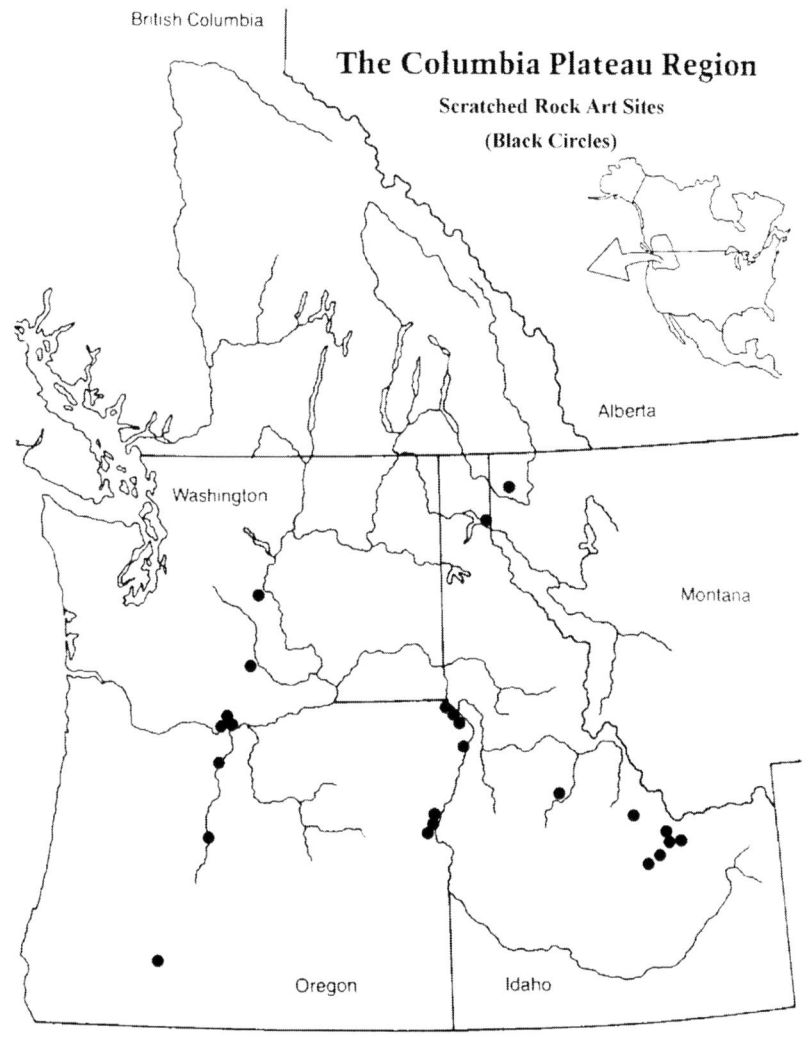

Figure 1.   The currently known distribution of scratched sites on the Columbia Plateau.

west, the Rocky Mountains on the east, and the Great Basin to the south (Keyser 1992), the region's climate is a dry, interior steppe with pine and fir forests covering the northern reaches of the plateau and the numerous mountain ranges scattered throughout the rest of the area. The central part of the region is an ancient basalt plateau, across which are scattered more than one thousand rock art sites, including both pictographs and petroglyphs of the Columbia Plateau tradition (Keyser 1992).

Although a few scratched petroglyphs have been noted as components of Columbia Plateau tradition rock art, they were first recognized as a distinct type during a survey of the Hells Canyon area (Leen 1988). While shown by later fieldwork to be widespread and culturally important, these scratched motifs were frequently overlooked in early studies and surveys, likely because they are often difficult to see,[1] and when noticed they appear less interesting than other images due largely to their typically abstract nature (Christensen 1992). In addition, in some cases these scratches can be mistaken for recent graffiti or vandalism especially when superimposed on painted images. Our research and that of other Columbia Plateau rock art scholars (Keyser et al 1998b; Klug 1999; Loubser 2002) has begun to recognize that these scratched images are found broadly across the Columbia Plateau region and to elucidate their specific relationship to other styles within the Columbia Plateau rock art tradition.

The Columbia Plateau Scratched Style

West of the Rocky Mountains one of the first works to describe scratched rock art and incorporate it into a broad regional synthesis was Heizer and Baumhoff's (1962:208) seminal study in which they define the Great Basin Scratched style. Following their lead some two decades later, Boreson (1980; Boreson and Peterson 1985) and Leen (1988, 1991) noted scratched motifs in Columbia Plateau rock art, but neither author defined a style nor made more than limited comparisons to scratched art in other areas of the Columbia Plateau or other regions. Keyser (1992:104, 111-113) and Boreson (1998:612) did the first comparisons of scratched petroglyphs between areas of the Columbia Plateau, but only recently have other studies in the region established the widespread presence of scratched motifs at numerous sites (See Figure 1)including newly recorded examples (Figure 2) at Miller Island (Werner et al 1995), Shearers Bridge (Bettis 1986), Owl Cave (Keyser et al 1998b), Horsethief Lake (Woodward 1982:80-82), Hells Canyon (Loubser 2002:59-61), and the Yakima area (Klug 1999). As of yet most of these scratched petroglyphs are not well documented, but we believe that as more examples are discovered their relationship to other Columbia Plateau styles will become better understood. Elsewhere, further work in the Great Basin and Southwest (Ritter 1993) has identified scratched art

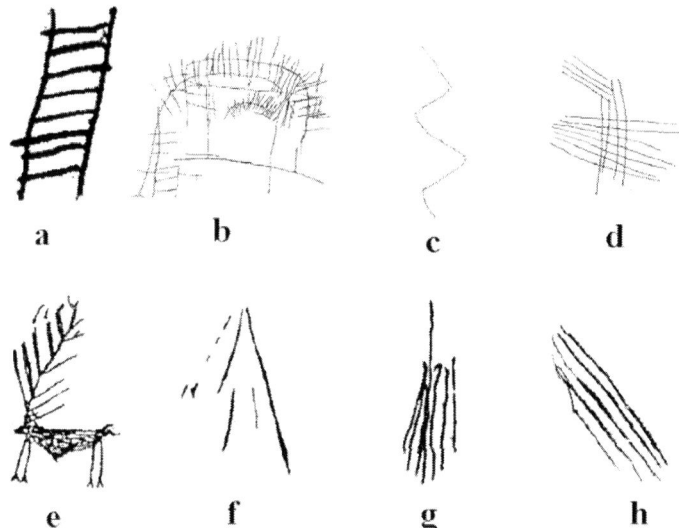

Figure 2. Motifs recorded as part of the Columbia Plateau Scratched style. A, ladder; b, concentric rayed arcs; c, zigzag; d, grid; e, Elk with scratched legs and antler; f, fan; g, phi; h, parallel lines.

styles as common components of several regional rock art traditions, and scholars have begun to attempt interpretation of these images.

In the Columbia Plateau scratched motifs are frequently found at a site in association with other petroglyphs and pictographs, often on the same panel. Some sites contain only a few scratched images while others show hundreds of scratches as the predominant rock art. The Hells Gate Landing Site, 45KL810 (Figure 3), is a good example of a predominantly scratched site where there are over 900 marks—some forming recognizable motifs, but most appearing as random marks widely spread over open basalt faces. Other sites on nearby Miller Island (45KL63, 45KL243, 45KL269) show a variety of scratched motifs scattered among pecked and painted examples of similar images.

Following Keyser (1992:16) the Columbia Plateau Scratched style has been defined (Taylor and Keyser 2002) as consisting of three classes of expression: scratches, modified cracks, and modified edges. Scratches include both ordered groups which form recognizable, recurring motifs (many of which also occur as painted and pecked examples in other styles), and other, apparently random, incisions that are usually widely dispersed across a rock face. Scratched motifs are primarily a wide variety of geometric designs, several of which are also common in pecked and painted examples in other Columbia Plateau rock art styles. Naturalistic representational motifs occur only rarely.

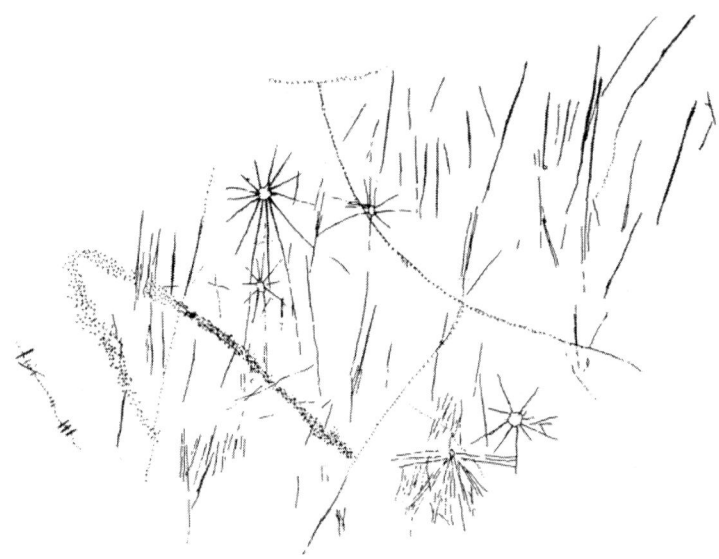

Figure 3. This large panel scratches at 45KL810 includes five starbursts incised around natural vugs in the basalt, a nicked edge at lower left, and numerous other scratches.

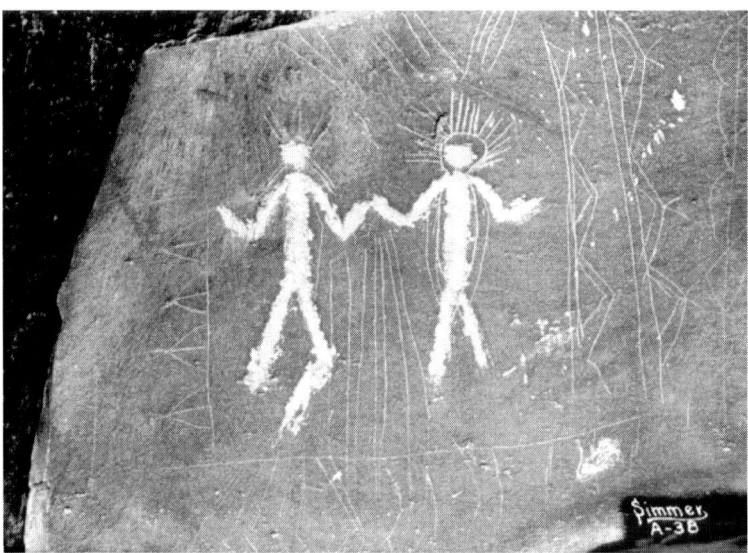

Figure 4. Scratches were used at the Rock Island site (45DO301 on the Columbia River near Wenatchee, Washington) both to augment previously pecked figures, and to add other independent imagery. Photograph courtesy of the Wenatchee Valley Museum & Cultural Center.

Scratched style motifs so far identified at Columbia Plateau sites include rayed arcs, rayed circles, zigzags, ladders, rectilinear grids, and starbursts, all of which also regularly occur as painted or pecked examples. Other motifs have so far been noted only as scratched designs. Animals and humans are rare, but they do occur in small numbers. Several elk and one human figure at three sites in the Dalles-Deschutes area have scratched digits, limbs and/or antlers and abraded or lightly scratched bodies (Figure 2e). The human figure also has scratches radiating from his body. These Dalles-Deschutes area examples are all closely associated with other scratched rock art. Further afield, several pecked figures at Rock Island Rapids (45DO301) near Wenatchee have been modified with scratches (Figure 4). One human has a body outline, hands, and a rayed arc added with scratches that are clearly related to other scratched motifs surrounding the image. Another has scratched rays coming from his head (Layman 1986:83), and a nearby elk has scratched antlers. These figures are closely associated with other panels of scratched designs including zigzags, diamond chains, crisscrosses, rectilinear grids, and random scratched lines (Layman 1986:83, Figure 6).[2] At 45KL243 one panel shows a small rudimentary scratched stick man associated with a similarly rudimentary stick animal (Figure 5). Finally, a series of scratched abstract anthropomorphic figures associated with probable stylized vulvaforms is

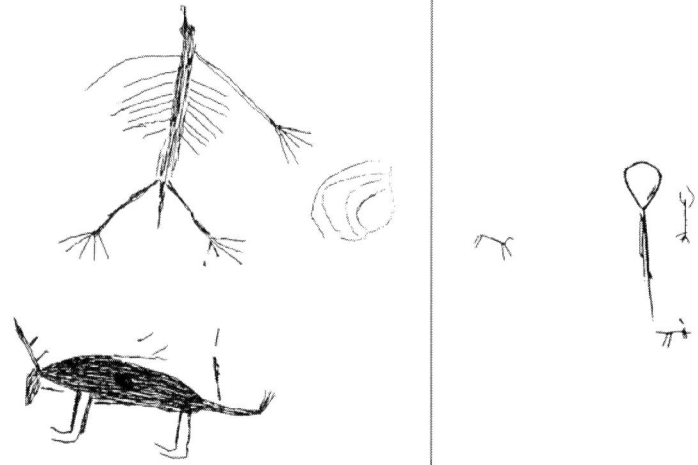

Figure 5. Scratched images are occasionally juxtaposed in typical Columbia Plateau vision quest compositions. The group on the left shows a human, an animal and a set of nested arcs. The lines extending outward from the man's body may represent blood flowing from cuts. The group on the right shows a stick animal and stick figure human juxtaposed with a large geometric design.

known at an incompletely documented Hells Canyon site (Leen 1991; Keyser 1992:112, Fig. 85f; Loubser 2002:59-61).

Although not common, scratched rayed circles and rayed arcs occur at two known sites. The most common scratched motifs are rectilinear grids, crosshatches, parallel lines, and the newly-named fan and phi motifs which have yet to be recognized in painted or pecked styles.

Scratches range from very lightly scratched lines—the result of a single stroke—to much wider, more deeply incised and sometimes polished lines which are clearly the result of repeated strokes. Experiments show that the polish is likely the result of using a liquid to form an abrasive slurry of the rock dust produced by the scratches at the contact between the incising tool and the rock face.

Modified cracks are the second class of rock art expression within the Columbia Plateau Scratched style. These are natural hairline cracks in the rock surface that have been widened and deepened by incising. Some were so extensively worked that they closely resemble the deeply incised and polished incisions described above. Sometimes the scratch or incision follows only a part of the crack, but for others the incisions extend beyond the length of the natural crack.

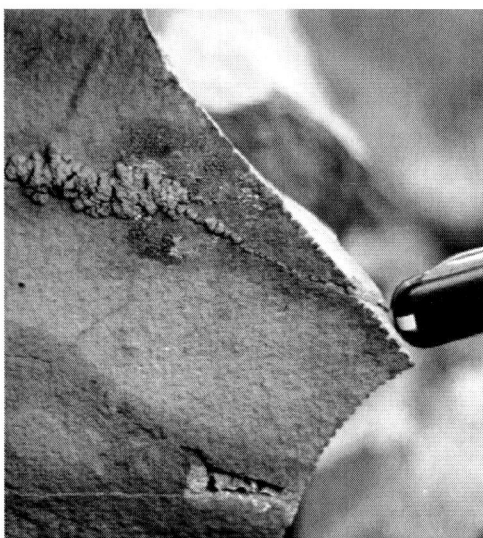
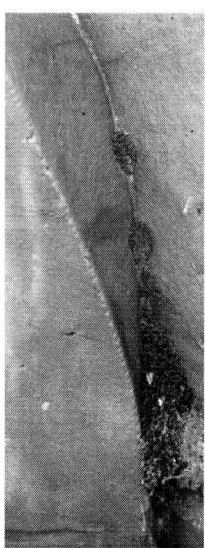

Figure 6. Nicked edges are the most common type of modified edge in the style. The tiny Swiss Army knife shows the nearly microscopic scale of these nicks along both edges of this angular rock face.

Figure 7. This modified edge shows dozens of tiny nicks along a projecting corner of a basalt formation at 45KL243.

Modified edges, like modified cracks, incorporate the natural features of the cliff into the art, albeit in a slightly different way. Such edges were previously recognized at several Columbia Plateau sites from Buffalo Eddy on the Snake River to Horsethief Lake at the Dalles (Keyser et al 1998b; Woodward 1982:55, 86; Boreson 1998:612) but it was only with the Miller Island project (Werner et al 1995:Vol. II:17-32; Keyser and Poetschat 2002) that their full nature and extent began to be identified. Modified edges occur when a ridge or wrinkle on a rock surface, the corner of a rock panel, or the edge of a distinct deep crack are crosscut with small incisions, or pecked or percussion flaked notches. Incisions are generally short, closely-spaced lines that cross the ridge or edge at an approximate right angle (Figures 6, 7). These range from minute "nicks" noticed only with close inspection of the surface, to deep grooves, but all such modification produces a distinctly "serrated edge" effect. Other both bifacial and unifacial percussion flaking are known, and some of the pecked scalloped edges appear to have been modified from initially flaked edges. Some of the most striking examples are wide deep cracks with both edges scalloped by consistently spaced, uniformly sized percussion flakes (Figure 8). Both modified edges and modified cracks are examples of the use of natural features as a part of the art itself. Such use of natural features has been recently recognized as a key element in Columbia Plateau rock art (Keyser and Poetschat 2004) and these utilized features further demonstrate that the rock canvas itself was much more than a static background for the art.

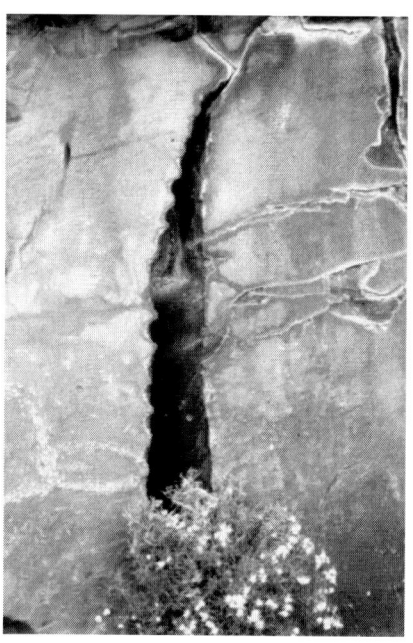

Figure 8. Scalloped edges are another type of modified edge found in the Columbia Plateau Scratched style. Here large percussion flakes (later regularized by light pecking) form scalloping along both edges of this large crack in the basalt cliff.

Relationship With Other Columbia Plateau Rock Art Styles

Columbia Plateau Scratched style petroglyphs are clearly part of the Columbia Plateau rock art tradition, but the distinctive nature of their expression warrants classification as a separate style. Scratched petroglyphs are found across the southern Columbia Plateau.[3] Known sites occur from Gold Creek on the Kootenai River in Northwest Montana and the Hells Canyon and Salmon River in central Idaho on the east, westward to The Dalles. Often they are found at the same sites and on the same panels as other Columbia Plateau styles.[4] More importantly, scratched petroglyphs include several characteristic Columbia Plateau motifs that are more common as painted or pecked examples in other styles (Figure 9). These are animals, rayed arcs, starbursts, rayed circles, and other more generic motifs such as chevrons and ladders. The occurrence of rayed arcs and starbursts and the prevalence of modified cracks and nicked edges separate Columbia Plateau Scratched rock art from a similar scratched style to the south in the Great Basin (Heizer and Baumhoff 1962; Ritter 1994). In addition, the modified edges and cracks reflect the strong focus of Columbia Plateau tradition rock art on incorporating the natural features of the rock surface. Furthermore, in a few cases the scratching has been incorporated as part of a typical painted or pecked Columbia Plateau tradition motif (Figure 4). Finally, ethnographic clues strongly suggest that the Columbia Plateau Scratched style functioned to obtain, acknowledge, and use spirit power—a strong link to other Plateau rock art styles.

Despite these strong connections to the Columbia Plateau rock art tradition, the Columbia Plateau Scratched style is distinct from other Columbia Plateau styles in that the overwhelming majority of the motifs (more than 99 percent of those so far identified) are abstract rather than representational. In the more familiar Columbia Plateau pecked and painted styles, representational images compose from ten to more than thirty percent of the total figures. It is clear that the focus on abstract images is deliberate. We know that the artists could, and did, create representational images using the incised techniques but all but one known site (in Hells Canyon showing primarily abstract but identifiable anthropomorphs) the overwhelming choice for scratched images was abstract.

Another disparity with other Columbia Plateau styles is the linear form of most scratched images. Curved lines and circles play an important role in most Columbia Plateau styles, and while they also occur in the Columbia Plateau scratched style the great majority of individual scratches are straight, and most motifs are strongly rectilinear in form.

A final, but important, difference between the Columbia Plateau Scratched style and other Columbia Plateau styles is the major focus on incorporating the natural features of rock surfaces as integral parts of motifs. While use of these natural features occurs in all other Columbia Plateau styles, only in the Columbia Plateau scratched style are they used

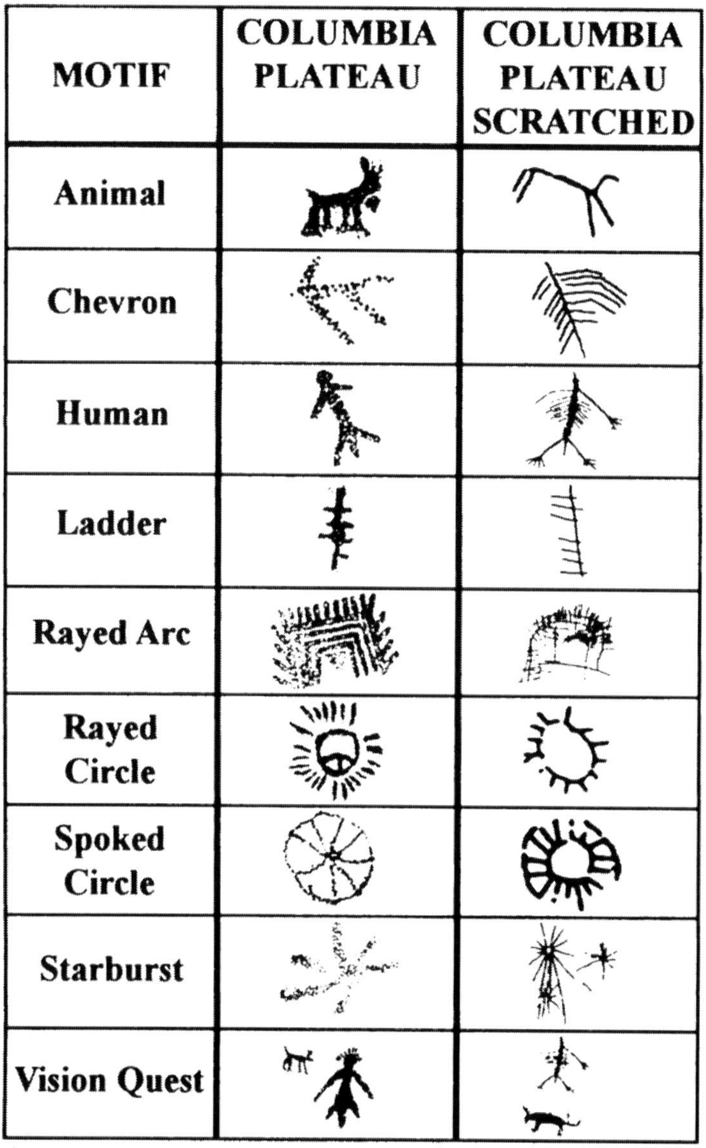

MOTIF	COLUMBIA PLATEAU	COLUMBIA PLATEAU SCRATCHED
Animal		
Chevron		
Human		
Ladder		
Rayed Arc		
Rayed Circle		
Spoked Circle		
Starburst		
Vision Quest		

Figure 9. The occurrence of typical Columbia Plateau tradition images carved as Columbia Plateau scratched motifs is a major reason that we classify the style as part of the broader tradition.

so overwhelmingly. In the lower Columbia River area examples abound of modified edges, worked cracks, and vugs used as parts of motifs. In fact, it is rare to find a panel of scratches in this area where some conscious use of a natural feature does not occur. Recent research at Hells Canyon sites suggests that modified edges also occur at scratched sites in that area (Loubser 2002:60) further work there and at nearby Salmon River sites will document the extent to which this preference for using natural features extends to scratched sites in the eastern Columbia Plateau.

How Were The Scratches Created?

Because technique is a key defining element for this style we conducted experiments to determine the likely methods and tools used to create these scratched images (Taylor and Keyser 2004).

Using a variety of stone and metal tools, we discovered that flakes of the local basalt were best suited for scratching and incising marks similar to those composing Columbia Plateau Scratched petroglyphs. This is consistent with the basalt incising tool (Figure 10) we recovered below one scratched panel at 45KL273 (Keyser and Taylor 2002).

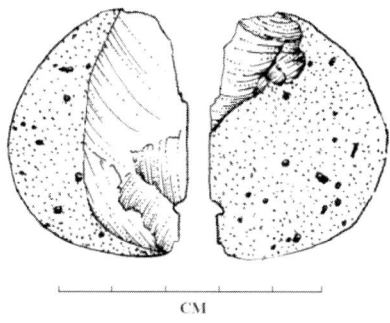

Figure 10. This worked basalt pebble, carefully cached on a small ledge below scratched panels at 45KL273, suggests that it was made as a petroglyph manufacturing tool. Scale bar is 10 cm.

In addition to experimental scratches, we also replicated the relatively deeper grooves, which often co-occur with scratches at our sites. Although we could produce these grooves by directing multiple cuts to the same scratch on a dry surface, we noted that on a vertical surface the highly abrasive rock powder produced by this repeated cutting would simply fall or blow away. To retain the abrasive powder we wet the basalt surface with saliva and found that it significantly enhanced the cutting action of the flaked tool and polished the resulting groove. The liquid unites the rock powder ground from the groove (and also particles from the tool) into a highly abrasive slurry that works in concert with the tool edge to cut and polish the basalt. This wet technique produced deep smooth grooves that appear identical to the deeply incised grooves found at numerous sites. Adding liquid also permits the retention of significant rock dust since it can be easily collected (initially in the form of the muddy slurry but quickly turning to dust as it dries). Clearly if the rock artist wanted rock powder from these incisions for ritual purposes—as is ethnographically known to be the case for some cupules (Whitley 2000b)—using the wet technique would be by far the most efficacious way to collect it from these vertical faces.

Interpretation

Although scratched rock art has often been overlooked and thus poorly studied, the distribution of this art style, coupled with ethnographic and ethnohistoric information, indicates that the Columbia Plateau Scratched style is as culturally significant as the better known pecked and painted Columbia Plateau tradition rock art forms. Initially, the amount and distribution of this scratched art across the Columbia Plateau shows that scratched petroglyphs were made at the same sites as other rock art and in similar quantities to painted and pecked images found there. Clearly, for groups in some areas, these scratched images shared equal billing with the pictographs and petroglyphs whose ritual importance has been identified as a central theme of Columbia Plateau religion by ethnographic sources spanning more than a century (Keyser and Whitley 2000). Given this co-occurrence and the formal similarities between these styles it is tempting simply to attribute these scratched petroglyphs to vision questing and shamanism like their pecked and painted counterparts. But the occurrence of several sites where scratches are the only (or greatly predominant) expression, coupled with the dominance of abstract imagery for all scratched sites, begs for some additional interpretation.

Our initial effort was to scour the detailed Columbia Plateau ethnographic record trying to find references to scratched abstract petroglyphs that had escaped others' attention up to this point (possibly because the rock art had not been widely recognized). This proved to be unsuccessful, so we queried Phillip Cash Cash (a participant in our recording project for four field seasons) who has numerous contacts with traditional tribal elders and is himself quite knowledgeable about Columbia Plateau oral history related to rock art. Like the ethnography, Cash Cash could provide no direct references to scratched rock art, but in discussions with him about ritual gashing that we had encountered in one reference (Teit 1909:590), he directed our attention to this act among other Columbia Plateau groups where it was associated with a particularly impressive form of shamanism. In examining numerous ethnographic sources (including those suggested by Cash Cash) we regularly encountered references to such ritual cutting. Among these numerous references the factors cited that could lead a person to self-mutilate are personal rituals, religious rites, contact with spirits, the acquisition and use of various types of supernatural power, and other shamanic practices (Townsend 1839:359; Kuykendall 1889:83; Coues 1893:618-619; Teit 1906:266-267, 1930:169-170; Voegelin 1959:99; Boyd 1996:133; Cash Cash 1997). Both men and women, and shamans and laypersons were documented as doing such ritual gashing.

Among the first non-Indians to settle in The Dalles area—a major population and cosmopolitan culture center in the Columbia Plateau even before the coming of Europeans—were missionaries who brought Christianity to the Indians of the region. From 1834 to 1844, three of those Dalles area missionaries, Henry Brewer, Henry Perkins, and Daniel Lee, kept detailed diaries of their experiences with the local Indian people (Boyd 1996). In these diaries the missionaries captured many descriptions of native beliefs and ceremonies, and all three mention the gashing of the body as a component of native ritual behavior. One major religious ritual of the Dalles area was the Winter Ceremony. According to Brewer, who observed the ceremony in 1846, one of the main participants in the Winter Ceremony was a man from "tother [sic] world" who appeared naked or near-naked with "his arms and breast gashed in different places and the blood streaming down" (Boyd 1996:130).

Another ceremony in the same area, the Chinook Wind Dance, is reported by Kuykendall (1889:83) to have also involved ritual gashing:

"While the drumming and dancing went on, the shamans grew excited, and gyrated about frantically. Finally the more bold bared their arms, and with a butcher knife cut deep gashes across the fleshy parts of the arm. Sometimes several cut about half an inch or more apart. Blood flowed profusely; and the demoniac [sic] conjuror sucked it out and drank it."

Elsewhere on the Columbia Plateau, the noted ethnographer, James Teit, also described ritual gashing behavior linked to the gaining or use of supernatural power. Among the Shuswap, youths on their spirit quest cut themselves to gain specific types of power:

"The novice ran until quite hot, and then cut the points of his eight fingers with a sharp arrow-stone, after which he sweat-bathed. Others usually cut four half-circles or four straight lines, not very deep, on the outside of each leg, between the ankle and the knee, with a stone knife or dagger, afterwards piercing the inside of each leg in four places between the ankle and the knee with the point of a dagger, or, instead, cutting four dot-like cuts or four crosses. He made these cuts in very cold, clear water, and afterwards sweat-bathed. Meanwhile he prayed that he might be enabled to withstand pain stoically and without fear, and that, if wounded, his wounds might heal quickly. The cutting of the finger-tips was supposed to let out all bad blood. Besides the above, lads training to be warriors slashed their sides and breast—generally four cuts on each side, and from four to eight on the breast. Those training to be gamblers also cut the point of their tongue, and some of them swallowed the blood. This was supposed to make them lucky." (Teit 1909:590).

In a study of cutmarks on human skeletons, Cash Cash (1997) noted that on the evening of October 9, 1805 Lewis and Clark observed firsthand another example of ritual gashing.

"The Indians came about our camp at night, and were very gay and good humored with the men. Among other exhibitions was that of a squaw who appeared to be crazy. She sang in a wild, incoherent manner, and offered to the spectators all the little articles she possessed, scarifying herself in a horrid manner if anyone refused her present. She seemed to be an object of pity among the Indians, who suffered her to do as she pleased without interruption." (Coues 1893:618-619)

Sergeant John Ordway, a member of the expedition, also observed this same incident, and his recollection adds significantly more useful information about the action of the Indian woman:

"She began Singing Indian and to giving all around hir Some commass [camas] roots, and brasslets which hung about hir one of our party refused to take them from hir. She then appeared angry threw them in the fire. Took a Sharp flint from hir husband and cut both hir arms in Sundry places So that the blood gushed out. She Scraped the blood in hir hand and eat it, and So continued in this way about half an hour then fainted or went in to a fit" (DeVoto 1981:245)

The expedition had just penetrated the eastern Columbia Plateau in the heart of what is now traditional Nez Perce territory. Although their terminology is understandably ethnocentric, and their spelling creative, the Nez Perce woman whom they describe was, in fact, an example of the Plateau's most widely feared and specialized type of shaman known as *isxiipin*. Later ethnographers (Stern 1998:411) more fully describe such shamans as "the most feared of shamans were the *isxiipin*, whose powers were derived from the tutelary of a dead shaman or, among the Umatilla, from the ghost itself."

For the person desiring to become such a shaman, the acquisition of such a spirit is extremely dangerous

"having sought out the spirit, [the quester] sought to 'domesticate' it to himself, but for some three months or more. . .was in danger of being driven to slash his upper arms and thus kill himself. A vigil had to be mounted over him (or her) to prevent this from happening. Once acquired, the spirit gave powers of clairvoyance but continued to be dangerous to others" (Stern in Boyd 1996:135-136).

As these references demonstrate, the *isxiipin* were prone to gashing themselves with a sharp instrument, and could easily carry this to the point of producing fatal results if not closely monitored. In Lewis and Clark's experience, the Nez Perce woman *isxiipin* likely entered a shamanic trance simply based upon the display of new and mysterious possessions by the expedition (Cash Cash 1997).

In summary, then, archaeological fieldwork has identified a previously little known and even less well understood Columbia Plateau Scratched rock art style, and ethnographic research has identified an important ritual gashing behavior, but there is no known direct historical link between these two phenomena. With this in mind, our only avenue for further interpretive possibility lies with Binford's model of using analogy to formulate testable hypotheses that might enable us to link the scratched rock art with the ritual gashing.

Following Binford (1967), we have demonstrated that Columbia Plateau scratched rock art and ritual gashing behavior co-occur spatially in the region and are likely temporally linked, since most scratched rock art appears to be of Late Prehistoric period origin just pre-dating the historic references to ritual self mutilation. Likewise, the form of the scratched petroglyphs is primarily abstract rather than representational. This closely mimics ritual gashing which is reported to have involved only the simplest of "motifs" such as crosses or half circles in far fewer number than the seemingly random blood-letting slashes. In addition, one Columbia Plateau Scratched style human figure has his body formed by numerous vertical slashes with other cuts radiating outward and slightly downward like gashes or flowing blood. Another pre-existing pecked stick figure human has been similarly "gashed" with scratches alongside the body, and has had a rayed arc power aura added with scratches.

Together these bits of evidence form a reasonably strong positive analogy between ritual gashing and scratched rock art. Based on this we postulate that the scratched rock art style was the product of the same sorts of behaviors as the ritual gashing recorded in Columbia Plateau ethnography. Several testable hypotheses lend further credence to this conclusion:

(1) If scratched rock art is a functional analog to ritual gashing, it should occur primarily in locations where supernatural power was thought to exist, and where persons seeking to acquire or manipulate it are known to have gone.

Almost all of the known Columbia Plateau scratched petroglyphs were made at places where rock art already existed, and throughout the Columbia Plateau such sites were routinely identified as places of supernatural power where shamans and vision supplicants regularly went to acquire power and to maintain their relationships with the supernatural world (Keyser and Whitley 2000; Hann et al 2004). Even the Hells Gate Landing site (45KL810), which had very few if any pre-existing pictographs, is in an area of extremely high rock art site density and has at least two other major sites directly visible from the incised panel. Its location is clearly within a highly charged power place. In the Hells Canyon variant of this style the scratches often superimpose painted images as if the artist was intentionally focusing the scratching directly on pre-existing supernatural images. Similar superimpositioning and the use of scratches as a basis for later painted figures occur in the Dalles-Deschutes study area (Loubser 2002).

In contrast, there is little segregation of scratched imagery from other ritual rock art motifs—as one might expect if its function was not associated in some way with supernatural power. Currently only a few scratched sites are documented at locales not otherwise rich in other rock art (Klug 2002: Leen 1991; Loubser 2002).

(2) If scratched rock art was made as part of rituals like those reported ethnographically to have been undertaken to obtain, control, or manipulate supernatural power it should express formal similarities to other rock art identified as having been produced in those rituals.

Several key motifs in the Columbia Plateau Scratched style exactly mimic other rock art images (done both as pictographs and pecked petroglyphs) found at Columbia Plateau sites and identified as functioning in vision quest and shamanic rituals. Probably the most significant of these are the rayed arc and rayed circle motifs that are the key identifiers of the entire western Columbia Plateau style zone and four Columbia Plateau styles[5] found within it (McClure 1980; Keyser 1992:57, 61-62, 71, 92, 121-125). Other motifs such as tally marks, elk, rectilinear grids, ladders, and zigzags also occur regularly in both scratched and other rock art. In addition to sharing specific motifs, the Columbia Plateau Scratched style also has a few compositions similar to those in regional pecked and painted styles. Compositions showing a human juxtaposed with an animal, a rayed arc, or a geometric design are characteristic vision quest compositions in painted and pecked Columbia Plateau rock art (Keyser 1992). Although not common in the scratched style, we have found a few examples that are nearly identical to those painted and carved in other Columbia Plateau styles. One of these is the previously mentioned scratched human with scratches angling from his body that is juxtaposed with an animal (Figure 5). Others are the pecked human figures modified with scratched rayed arc and rayed head at Rock Island Rapids (Figure 4).

Clearly the scratched style shares both motifs and compositions with the more common pecked and painted styles, but these are proportionally less important (compared to random scratches) than they are in the pecked and painted styles (compared to analogous lines and blobs).[6]

(3) If scratched rock art was made as part of rituals like those reported ethnographically where ritual gashing was done it should express formal similarities to the cutting done in those rituals.

One of the key distinctions between the Columbia Plateau Scratched style and other rock art is the preponderance of apparently random incisions and the numerous "motifs" which are in fact simply compilations of scratches done in various combinations. The categories crisscross, phi, fan, deeply incised line, line cluster, and nicked and scalloped edges all are without close parallels in Columbia Plateau painted and pecked styles. Each of these documents a different (but obviously related) focus or emphasis on repeatedly cutting one specific area of the rock surface. As has been suggested for the actual physical act of pecking a pecked petroglyph (Hann 2002), some of this cutting may have been actually done during trance. Cutting or sawing on the rock like this is repetitive in terms of both motion and aural stimulation—just like many other of the factors used to create the hallucinatory vision in Columbia Plateau religion (Hann et al 2004). Even if it was not done during an altered state of consciousness, the randomness of so many of the scratches closely parallels the semi-controlled "slashing" described in several of the references to ritual gashing among Lower Columbia River tribes. Likewise, the preponderance of simple scratches and lines in this style fits very well with the ethnographic reports of ritual gashing, where only the simplest of "motifs"—parallel lines, dots, crosses, and half circles—were cut by the practitioners.

(4) If scratched rock art is an analog to ritual gashing with respect to the latter's demonstrable link to power through the supplicant's consumption of the resultant blood, and bits of their own flesh (Evans 1889:83), then it should be possible to show instances where parts of the rock art site (rock powder, flakes) were being taken away for ritual use analogous to the use of the blood and flesh.

There is strong evidence that the blood resulting from ritual gashing was seen as food for a powerful individual's spirit helper.[7] In addition to Evans (1889:83) and Ordway (DeVoto 1981:245), ethnography gathered by Jacobs (Voegelin 1959) among the Clackamas Chinook demonstrates this very directly:

> 1. "Some person would sing, man or woman. They would listen to what he said (in the words of his spirit-power song). Some person (whose name Mrs.Howard could not recall) sang. He said, he would say (in his spirit power song) that he wanted the blood of something. They (the people at the dance) then said, 'Seek it' (a bird whose blood he asked for in his song). They would kill something (some bird), and they would give its blood to him (during his singing and dancing of his spirit power). 2. He would

drink it. He did not do like that just for nothing. Whatever was his spirit power, blood was its food, (and so) he did that (too). Sometimes (during a spirit-power dance) some woman or man would cut his (own) arm. Blood would flow out from there, they would give that blood (his blood from the cut on his arm) to him (to drink)" (Voegelin 1959:99)

This reference, and others, indicates that Columbia Plateau people thought of the body as a container for spiritual power, which could be released, in the form of blood, by gashing. The body's power could then be nourished by consuming the blood.

Although the Columbia Plateau has no direct ethnography detailing the removal and retention of parts of rock art sites for later use in ritual activity, northern California has detailed ethnographic accounts of using rock powder for ritual purposes. Whitley (2000b:98-101) reports ethnographic evidence that rock powder produced by scratching and pecking petroglyphs was ingested, painted on the body, or inserted into the vagina to enhance fertility and induce pregnancy. In fact, two of his photographs of California sites ethnographically documented as sources of ritually used rock powder, show scratches and incisions that would not be out of place at any of the Columbia Plateau Scratched style sites we have recorded (Whitley 2000b:Figures 34, 91). Other reports document the removal of small rock chips from a site for later grinding into powder that was similarly used.[8]

The deep incisions, heavily scalloped edges, and some of the more robust nicked edges (where the nicks are actually deep cuts that produce a markedly serrated edge) suggest the production of powder and flakes from the site that could be removed for ritual use. Our experiments (Taylor and Keyser 2002) show that the deep, highly polished incisions (and the deep cuts on the more robust nicked edges) were almost certainly done by adding liquid to form an abrasive slurry which provides a readily capturable "sludge" that flows from the incision. While there is no direct evidence that this was collected and used, it would have been relatively easy to do so. The scalloped edges almost certainly were produced by people removing flakes of basalt to take away, although what these rock flakes were later used for is not known.[9]

The fairly significant evidence that scratched rock art produced a usable by-product suggests the possibility that the powder and rock flakes were used for the same "power nourishing" purpose as is documented for the blood and bits of flesh produced from ritual gashing. That the powder originally forms as a sludge that appears to flow from the rock scratch—almost like blood—seems to us to enhance the analogy. We suggest that the rock powder and rock chips from rock art sites were regarded as "blood" and "flesh" from the supernatural world and their use mimicked the drinking of blood from ritual gashing that was thought to feed one's spirit helper and strengthen its power.

(5) Because ritual gashing is reported to be closely affiliated with shamanistic practices in the southern Columbia Plateau, we might expect scratched rock art linked to the practice to commonly show entoptic imagery.

Evidence for shamans producing images in several western North American rock art traditions has been broadly linked to the entoptic imagery of the neuropsychological model first proposed by Lewis-Williams (Whitley 1994a, 1994b, 2000b; Sundstrom 1990; Keyser and Klassen 2001:139-150). Pecked and painted styles of the Columbia Plateau tradition have some motifs whose origin is likely entoptic (e.g. arcs, grids, and various curvilinear and rectilinear abstracts), but—other than the rayed arc—these are neither as prevalent nor as central to the compositions as entoptics are in other rock art traditions (e.g. Whitley 1994b, 2000b; Sundstrom 1990).[10] Instead, shamans' rock art on the Columbia Plateau has been identified more by repeatedly detailed depictions of identifiable supernatural beings, transformer imagery, public visibility of the art, integration of natural features into compositions, and the care and craftsmanship of the individual images (Keyser 1992; Keyser and Poetschat 2004; Keyser et al 1998a; Hann et al 2004; Loubser 2002).

In contrast, the Columbia Plateau Scratched style contains numerous, albeit simple entoptic images. At least three types of grids (rectilinear grids, crisscrosses, and ladders), three types of parallel or nearly parallel lines (phi, parallel lines, and fans), nested curves, zigzags, and starbursts are repeated at site after site in this style. In fact, such simple entoptic imagery predominates at several of the most impressive sites.[11] This is exactly what one might expect in a very simple artistic expression associated with shamanism where most of the images record the first component of the neuropsychological model (Whitley 1994a:10-11, 2000b:107). In this sense the art seems well suited for the frenetic behaviors described for the *isxiipin* shamans in this part of the Columbia Plateau.

Summary

Despite its overall formal simplicity, Columbia Plateau Scratched style rock art is emphatically not "doodling" or some other type of accidental marking of these sites. Given the special nature of rock art sites in general to Columbia Plateau people, the number and placement of these scratched petroglyphs indicates that they are undoubtedly associated with some sort of ritual. The region's ethnography is replete with references to the special powers of rock art sites,[12] and even today traditional Indian people consider rock art sites highly powerful, and not to be places where casual activities are undertaken (Craig 2000:3). In our own research fieldwork on the Lower Columbia River we have been instructed by traditionalists as to our behavior at these sites and told of their own ritual preparation for visiting and working at them. Each year of our project Phillip Cash Cash has offered a supplication and song in his native language to request favor for our recording efforts. Throughout the Columbia Plateau it is common to find modern offerings (coins, jewelry, bits of colored cloth) left by Indian people who still use the sites to access power. Given the plethora of evidence from ethnographic informants spanning more than a century that such sites were venerated, and the fact that modern Indian people still respect rock art sites, it is inconceivable that this much scratched rock art would have been done at them without a strong religious or ritual reason.

As per Binford's (1967) model, we have demonstrated a positive analogy between the Columbia Plateau Scratched style and ritual gashing behavior in the region. Using that analogy we have formulated and tested five hypotheses that support the conclusion that Columbia Plateau scratched style rock art was produced at places of power, using symbols that have been identified in other Columbia Plateau rock art styles as relating to supernatural contact. The overall structure of the art differs slightly from the shamanic and vision quest rock art characteristic of other Columbia Plateau styles and seems more focused on "first stage" entoptic imagery than most of them.

There seems to be a strong likelihood that scratched rock art was focused in part on producing rock powder and rock flakes that could be taken away from the sites for ritual reuse. This may be linked to the drinking of blood to "feed" and strengthen a spirit helper.

The ethnography is very clear that Columbia Plateau people viewed the body as a "container" for spirit power, which could be released in the form of blood flowing from self-inflicted gashes. This blood could then be consumed to nourish the body's power. If we extend this logic to the rock art site, the rock itself could also be described as containing spiritual power, and this power could be released by scratching. The resultant rock powder could then be used to nourish a person's spirit power—just like blood.

Finally the formal characteristics of the scratched art seem to parallel the semi-controlled gashing that characterizes descriptions of ritual gashing by Columbia Plateau shamans.

Although our research has no direct ethnographic demonstration that these scratched petroglyphs are the rock art expression of ritual gashing behavior, such a conclusion appears likely based on the support for our identified hypotheses. Among the tribes of the Lower Columbia River region such ritual gashing was the behavior associated with a special class of *isxiipin* shaman, who gashed themselves to acquire certain types of power, to demonstrate it, and to "domesticate" it for their own use. Non-shamans also did ritual gashing to acquire specific spirit helpers. The power was so dangerous that supplicants had to be watched closely lest they gash themselves so severely that they died. We propose that these shamans and non-shaman vision supplicants, in their quest to obtain and use this power, produced the Columbia Plateau Scratched style rock art so prevalent in the lower Columbia River region.

Acknowledgements

We thank Phillip Cash Cash, whose interest in this project, and insights into the ethnographic and ethnohistoric literature, have helped us make a significantly more compelling analysis and conclusion. The Wenatchee Valley Museum & Cultural Center, Wenatchee, Washington, provided a photograph of the scratched style motifs at the Rock Island Rapids site. Keo Boreson, Linda Klug, Carolynne Merrell, and Robert Betts provided data used in this research. Several of the sites described herein were recorded as part of The Dalles–Deschutes Rock Art Research Project, sponsored by the USDA-Forest Service and the Oregon Archaeological Society. Volunteers from the Oregon Archaeological Society and the Archaeological Society of Central Oregon assisted with various parts of the project. We especially appreciate the help of project supervisor, George Poetschat.

---

[1] Our own discovery of the Hells Gate Landing site (45KL810) is a typical example. Although we parked within fifty meters of the site for two one-week field projects and had had knowledgeable fieldworkers check the rock face, it was not until we had begun recording scratches at another pictograph site that the hundreds of scratches at 45KL810 were recognized.

[2] The few historic photographs from this site that have been published (Layman 1986; and one in this volume) show a variety of scratched petroglyphs that rivals both in number and types of images those at any site in the Dalles-Deschutes region. Additional study of this site—if other historic photographs are available—would be an opportunity for future research designed to further test some of our hypotheses.

[3] These scratches may also be equally common in the northern Columbia Plateau but just not yet recognized, as was the case for many years in the southern part of the region.

[4] So far the Columbia Plateau Scratched style is known to be directly associated with the Western Montana, Eastern Columbia Plateau, Central Columbia Plateau, and Yakima Polychrome styles.

⁵ These are the Western British Columbia, Central Columbia Plateau, Long Narrows, and Yakima Polychrome styles

⁶ A review of 28 study area sites shows that formal motifs compose only 29 percent of the scratched style but 46 percent of the painted and pecked styles.

⁷ In some cases these individuals were clearly shamans, but for other examples it is not clear if the supplicant who drank his blood and/or ate his own flesh was a shaman. However, the way most of these references are structured, it is clear that the individual being described had considerable power.

⁸ Archaeological evidence from Foothills Abstract tradition pictograph sites on the Northern Plains indicates that paint was extensively scratched off of some motifs there for what is interpreted as ritual reuse (Scott et al 2000). Other scratches at these sites were apparently not for pigment removal, but they do indicate ritual reuse of the pictograph images. Many of these are similar to the scratches recorded in the Hells Canyon (Leen 1988; Keyser 1992) and they may provide a clue as to the function of the extensive scratching in the Hells Canyon variant of the Columbia Plateau Scratched style.

⁹ We are aware of no such flakes being discovered archaeologically, although there have been no organized efforts to recover them from archaeological deposits at the sites where flaked edges occur. Identifying flakes of this sort in lithic collections from nearby village sites would be very difficult given the production of chopping tools from basalt cobbles. Never-the-less, several possible alternative uses suggest themselves for these flakes. They could have been used to self-mutilate the person who struck them from the rock edge; or they could have been used to carve scratched petroglyphs elsewhere on the rock at that site (as our experiments have demonstrated to be possible). Or they could have been taken away to be used as amulets, or ground into powder that was used like the rock dust reported by Whitley in California. Unfortunately, in the absence of specimens we cannot test any of these hypotheses.

¹⁰ Among Columbia Plateau rock art styles only the Yakima Polychrome style has a marked preponderance of entoptic imagery focusing on concentric circles, concentric arc "rainbows," and zigzags (Keyser 1992; Keyser et al 1998a) and this art style has been more closely linked to shamanic practices—curing and mortuary rituals—than any other style (Hann et al 2004).

¹¹ Loubser (2002:60-61) also notes the prevalence of entoptic imagery in Hells Canyon scratched petroglyphs and relates it to the neuropsychological model.

¹² Only single ethnographic sources in both the Columbia Plateau and the adjacent Northwest Coast refer to rock art as "doodling" and attribute it to casual activity (Boreson 1975:49, Appendix A:6, 8). In light of the preponderance of contrary references (see Keyser and Whitely 2000 and sources therein) it seems quite possible that these statements were intentional misrepresentations by people who either were not privy to special knowledge or were trying to avoid breaking a taboo.

Discussion

Jannie Loubser: Mike, at Miller Island, where we examined the superimpositioning, it seemed for the majority of cases that scratching was done first and then red was put over it. What do you make of that?

Mike Taylor: That the scratching was older than the red? We found that in the rock shelter, and we may have found it at one other place.

James Keyser: We looked at 45KL281 and it's also that way. There is a case where the scratches come over the red at 45KL62. But I don't think the temporal relationship between the two types of art is as important as the fact that it is located at a power place. Maybe it was the start of the power place and then the paint was put there because it had been so identified, but it doesn't change the hypothesis of the association of this art style with places of power.

Mike Taylor: And there are plenty of examples, not on the Miller Island, but in other places, where scratching is consciously done over pictographs—maybe to collect some of the red pigment.

Jannie Loubser: That definitely occurs in Hell's Canyon.

Mike Taylor: Yes, in Hell's Canyon they seem to deface the pictographs—maybe to collect powerful pigment powder by removing it from the pictograph. But, in the Columbia Gorge we don't find them "defacing" pictographs to remove pigment. You don't see that very much. That seems to be a Hell's Canyon phenomenon.

Jannie Loubser: So stylistically the types of art are similar; because, as you said, the rayed arcs look the same, the circles, and some vision quest figures. But the technique is different, so it's the same tradition but something slightly different is going on. And in different areas, it seems that the sequence is different—because in Hell's Canyon its just the other way around—they scratch on the mountain sheep.

Jean Auel: Is there a correlation between the red and the blood.

Mike Taylor: Historically, there's plenty of ethnography that shows that red is related to blood. Its related to life and vitality—that kind of thing.

David Whitley: One thing I'd suggest is to look more at the symbolism of the rock to get at the question of the use of the powder. Off the top of my head, I don't know any Columbia Plateau ethnography that might be pertinent, but I suspect that its there. The other point that I was going to make concerns blood. Again, the sources that immediately come to mind are northeastern California and the Klamath Basin—the Pitt River and Modoc-Klamath tribes. In those groups there was a very big concern with nasal bleeding during trance, and unless there was copious bleeding from the nose, the trance wasn't considered particularly effective. So, this just provides another reference to the importance of blood.

James Keyser: We had a really interesting reference—not to nasal bleeding, but to a certain kind of shaman. Phillip Cash Cash pointed it out to us in a paper he did, using a Lewis and Clark reference. When Lewis and Clark came into Nez Perce country, there was a woman shaman who slashed herself and gave small things away in the use of power in that situation. Phillip was really instrumental in helping us find many of the references to this sort of shaman.

Linea Sundstrom: I don't want to keep pushing Plains ethnography but I think it's really interesting that your starbursts are all around natural entrances into the rock. And the modified cracks focus on "opening" the cracks and some of the scalloped edges are at cracks. In my part of the country that would tend to be saying you're trying to get in the rock. We're making a window into the rock, a pathway into the rock.

Mike Taylor: I think the idea of cracks and little holes being ways to move through the rock face barrier is a legitimate idea.

Jannie Loubser: Also in the ethnography there seems to be purification involved with cutting—you get rid of bad things.

Mike Taylor: In some cases that's true.

James Keyser: Do you think that could relate to cutting the rock in any manner—that you want to release bad things?

Mike Taylor: Well, they claim that during some puberty ceremonies, they prick the tips of their fingers and let out bad blood or bad power. So there is a relationship to letting out power. The parallel there is that you're also doing that same kind of scratching on the rock—

trying to get the power out. But I don't have any sense of whether it's good or bad. It's the idea of letting it out.

David Whitley: Let me just read you a quick statement from Maurice Zigmond (1981) on Kawaiisu ethnography, which is in my paper and seems to relate here. "Younger people, to procure dreams, walk through a growth of nettles pressing them against the bare chest causing severe lacerations." So the idea of cutting is even there in south-central California.

Mike Taylor: Also, there is ethnography on people who are going to become gamblers who cut the tips of their tongues to get good luck power. They would then swallow that blood that resulted from the cutting of the tongue. Whether it's good or bad power, the important part seems to be cutting and interacting with the power; releasing it, doing something with it.

CHAPTER 11
Rock Art, Physical Setting, and Ethnographic Context: A Comparative Perspective
Johannes H. N. Loubser

Introduction

Conventional rock art studies tend to focus on rock art motifs, their classification, chronology, and regional similarities and differences. Geographic regions are typically compared and contrasted solely in terms of stylistic similarities and differences; little, if any explicit attention is paid to the rock art landscape, site, and motif setting. I suggest that only when these settings are considered in an analysis, can we glean otherwise overlooked information concerning intra-regional and inter-regional differences. It is furthermore important that appropriate ethnographic parallels are the basis for decisions as to what might constitute relevant physical settings. Prior to the work of rock art researchers such as Hedges (1993), Lewis-Williams and Dowson (1988), and Whitley (1998), considerations of physical and ethnographic settings have for the most part been incidental in rock art studies. This chapter intends to show that the ethnographically based, "altered states of consciousness model" for the interpretation of rock art is not monolithic, but instead accounts for variations in the appearance and placement of images. Moreover, I propose that certain recurrent relationships that can be shown to exist between physical and social aspects of rock art might allow researchers to interpret very ancient rock art without an ethnographic context.

The acquisition of imagery, the manufacture of paint, and the making and use of rock paintings appear to differ from one society to the next (see Lewis-Williams 1995 on the four stages in the production and consumption of rock art). Although ethnographic evidence on these social conditions of rock art production and consumption is not always available, archaeological context often allows informed interpretations of likely social contexts. The paucity of primary ethnographic information specific to most areas with rock art leads some to suggest that reliable interpretation is not possible, but fortunately, ethnographies have been collected for most colonized regions of the world. In almost all of these there are a few documents that explicitly refer to rock art, and other documents that enable an understanding of the systems in which rock art must have functioned. I suggest that, when placed within regional ethnographic contexts, the rock art patterns within broad regions become meaningful. Additionally, I argue that a worldwide comparative perspective helps us further understand certain trends in rock art and associated social formations, especially similar rock art traditions that are geographically separated. For instance, the separate appearance of large mural paintings in Baja California, Utah, and Texas during the Late Archaic period (Hyland 1997, Turpin 2001) is most likely indicative of social aggregation and stratification as evidenced in the archaeological record.

Given that more recent rock art traditions have lasted until historic times in many colonized areas and considering the conservative nature of world-views (Bloch 1974, Schiffman 1994) that structure the art, it is safe to interpret recent prehistoric and protohistoric traditions in terms of the historic period ethnographic record. Furthermore, I suggest that physical evidence, such as the placement and execution of the rock art images and their archaeological setting, allow us to assess their social context.

Comparative ethnographic information shows that hunter-gatherers and some agriculturalists view rock art sites as places of concentrated supernatural potency, or interfaces with the spirit world. These are the locales visited by shamans to portray their visions (dreams) and to obtain supernatural assistance. Among certain groups, initiates or the lay population in general also paint or engrave rocks to fix their visions and/or obtain supernatural assistance. Taçon (1983) has drawn a distinction between "shamanic" and "shamanistic" traditions, partly to distinguish rock art made by shamans from that made by non-shamans. My research indicates that the contrasting roles that shamans and non-shamans play within societies condition the ways in which their associated rock arts are placed and executed. Furthermore within shamanic art it is sometimes possible to identify sorcerer art.

My research considers rock art from two regions in order to illustrate the proposed differences and similarities between shamanic and shamanistic rock art. The regions are sub-Equatorial Africa (central Tanzania and central South Africa) and the Columbia Plateau of North America (northern California, Oregon, Washington, and British Columbia. Although physical evidence is presented prior to social evidence, this does not imply that the two are separate; the distinction is primarily made to facilitate a systematic presentation of information.

Physical information pertaining to rock art not only includes the types of motifs but also their relevant settings (Table 1). Lewis-Williams (2001) has arranged social information concerning the production and consumption of rock art in a clear sequence (Table 2). Considering the inconsistent fieldwork strategies of rock art site recording and the fragmentary nature of the ethnographic record, there will almost always be some gaps in the physical and social information base. Thus,

Table 1

The rock art landscape—macrocosm to microcosm

Landscape Setting

    Are there nearby features, such as trails, rivers, rockshelters, camps?

    What is necessary to journey to the rock art site?

Setting of the Rock Art Site

    What is the morphology of rock art site?

    What is the approach to the rock art site?

Setting of the Rock Art Motifs

    What integration is there between rock art and rock surface features?

    What body movements are necessary within the site to approach or view the motifs?

Table 2

Social Conditions of Rock Art Production

Acquisition of imagery

    Who are the people who acquire the imagery?

    What is the context and place for acquiring ideas?

Acquisition of raw material for rock art production

    Who prepares the pigment and tools?

    What is the context and place for acquiring material for rock art production?

Production of rock art

    Who makes the rock art?

    What is the context and place for making rock art?

Use of rock paintings

    Who uses the rock art?

    What is the context and place for using rock art?

interpretations must be formulated with care using the broadest amount of appropriate information. In this way, trends and processes detected in one region might help scholars interpret observations in other regions with related rock art and rock art settings.

Hunter-Gatherer and Agriculturist Rock Art in Sub-Equatorial Africa
Rock Paintings of the San and Sandawe Hunter-Gatherers
Physical Setting

San rock paintings date from approximately 27,000 years ago (Wendt 1976) to the early twentieth century (Lewis-Williams 1986). The earliest paintings so far known are on loose slabs recovered from stratified deposits within habitation shelters (Thackeray 1983). Radiocarbon dates on charcoal associated with painted flakes that derive from wall paintings at the back of rock shelters in southwestern Zimbabwe (Walker 1987) show that fixed art is at least 10,000 years old. Some rock paintings on the back walls of rock shelters formerly occupied by Sandawe hunter-gatherers in central Tanzania must be older than 2,000 years, because they occur underneath the cattle paintings of pastoral immigrants who arrived in the area roughly two millennia ago (Leakey 1983).

All the rock shelters mentioned above show evidence of long-term human habitation, so it is probably justifiable to infer that during the terminal Pleistocene and Holocene, most of the hunter-gatherer rock paintings in sub-Equatorial Africa occurred within rock shelters that were inhabited. Regional rock art surveys tend to support this interpretation. For example, the survey of San rock paintings in the Caledon River valley showed that almost all painted sites contain occupation debris, with a few exceptions of nineteenth century historic paintings that occur in obscure crevices at a time when San society fought for its survival (Loubser and Laurens 1994).

For the most part then, San rock paintings occur in or near shelters that have been occupied. This implies that the journey the painter had to make to execute the paintings was limited. Although some painted shelters in the Drakensberg and Brandberg are isolated and difficult to reach in relation to modern settlements and access routes, the rock art sites were part of the hunter-gatherer landscape and not necessarily more inaccessible than other sites, places, or resources. From a preservation point of view it is possible to see why paintings have survived within well-protected overhangs, yet it is still not clear why so many overhangs with good integrity have no paintings. Nothing from excavated deposits suggests specialized use of sites with paintings. In terms of size, contents, complexity, and location within a valley scholars have not yet been able to identify or group special-purpose rock art sites. It appears that rock paintings in the region were an integral part of domestic life; an inference supported by ethnographic evidence.

Most rock paintings of San and Sandawe hunter-gatherers occur within well-lit rock shelters, or shallow caves, with clearly defined driplines. The painted shelters are usually visible from a distance, and (with few exceptions) access does not take too much physical exertion or involve extraordinary danger. Even those few sites that have steeply sloping floors strewn with fallen boulders have at least some traces of occupation.

The paintings typically occur against the rock shelter's back wall or lower ceiling, mostly at eye level but sometimes higher and only occasionally close to the ground. Individual motifs tend to fall within bedding planes and seldom overlap joints, cracks, or other rock surface discontinuities. Some motifs are meticulously painted against cracks, red iron veins, or stains of white mineral salts. This technique gives the appearance of motifs emerging from cracks or incorporating iron or mineral stains as part of the overall design (Figure 1). To best view the majority of paintings one merely stands upright on the shelter floor. To notice finer details within many paintings it is necessary to get very close to the rock face. In a very few instances motifs are hidden from view when standing in the shelter, and it might be necessary to kneel down or climb the rock face in order to see them better. As mentioned below, unusual locations tend to contain unusual motifs.

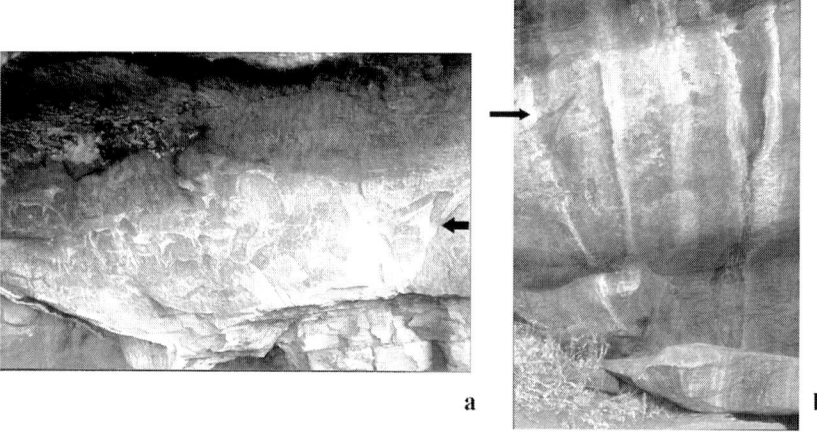

Figure 1. San and Sandawe rock art shows images that incorporate natural cracks or mineral stains: a, serpent-like creature (indicated by arrow) painted against a crack in this South African rockshelter; b, partially painted giraffe (indicated by arrow) located against a white mineral stain in this site from central Tanzania.

Most hunter-gatherer paintings in sub-Equatorial Africa consist of red ocher mixed with water and a binding medium. This mixture was meticulously applied with a brush to the rock surface, as evidenced by the clean edges of individual motifs. Close examination of thickly applied pigment, particularly white clay, shows fine brush-strokes. Very fine lines (e.g. figures' digits or hair) are less than one millimeter wide and were probably painted with a single hair. With the exception of historic period paintings that include bright red grainy pigment, the dark red ocher of earlier paintings appears to have better binding properties. In interior South Africa, outcrops of red hematite typically occur in basalt flows that are far from the majority of painted sites. From a visual examination of the paintings alone it appears that hunter-gatherer artists in the region took effort in the acquisition and preparation of raw materials and care in the execution of the paintings.

According to Garlake (2001:639) the meticulously executed hunter-gatherer rock art of sub-Equatorial Africa consists of "images that were immediately and readily legible and identifiable to any observer." Paintings are mostly of humans followed by depictions of clearly recognizable animals, which, depending on the geographical area, include eland, kudu, gemsbok, giraffes, felines, and elephants. Plants and certain animal species, notably the wildebeest, that feature so prominently in the dietary records of these hunter-gatherers, are only infrequently depicted in the rock art of the region (Loubser and Zietsman 1994, Loubser and Brink 1992). Interestingly, in those few instances that wildebeest or plants are depicted, they are painted comparatively small and/or placed in obscure locations. Whereas geometric forms are virtually absent in San rock paintings, concentric circles and nested U-shapes are closely associated with representational Sandawe rock paintings.

Historic period San of South Africa added depictions of domestic cattle, sheep, horses, and people dressed in European clothes to their traditional repertoire of motifs. Traditional motifs, particularly the eland, continue to be depicted along with historic period motifs. Considering the selection of subject matter and the conflation of human and animal forms throughout the sequence of San rock art, including the historic period, this tradition cannot be construed as depictions of the everyday world. In the Kondoa area of central Tanzania, later polychrome Sandawe rock paintings appear to be bigger and more hastily executed than the earlier red paintings (Leakey 1983, Loubser 2001). Nevertheless, animals and geometric forms seem to continue in this tradition, perhaps with a decline in the depictions of people.

In spite of regional and chronological variations in shape, color, complexity, and subject matter, the rock paintings of sub-Equatorial

Africa display certain striking similarities (Garlake 2001). In addition to the shared location and placement preferences outlined above, these similarities include squatting figures with distended abdomens, elephants surrounded by agitated non-hunter human figures, figures in forward bending postures, nasal blood, and the conflation of human and animal forms.

Social Context

The general similarity of rock paintings over such a wide region is perhaps not surprising considering that both the San of South Africa and Sandawe of Tanzania spoke click languages (Greenberg 1963), shared certain physical characteristics, such as steatopygia and light skin pigmentation (Ten Raa 1969), and had similar girls' puberty rituals (Lewis-Williams 1987). Both San and Sandawe shamans danced in public to achieve altered states of consciousness and access to the supernatural powers that enabled them to transform into animals, travel out of body, visit distant people and places, and ensure hunting success (Lewis-Williams 1987).

More published ethnography concerning the production and consumption of rock art exists for the San than the Sandawe, so the following discussion focuses on the San. Approximately half of San men and a third of San women become shamans in their lifetime (Katz 1982). These ritual specialists entered an altered state of consciousness and acquired insights into the spirit world during the trance dance, during special curing rituals that did not entail a full dance, while viewing rock art, and in dreams (Lewis-Williams 2001).

Trance dancing is a group, or public, activity where male and female shamans follow each other in a circular fashion in front of the rest of the camp (Marshall 1969, Orpen 1874). Lewis-Williams (2001:26) writes that after the trance dance: "Everyone, not just shamans, listens avidly to the shaman's reports from the spirit world, and such circumstances contribute to the construction and reinforcement of the community's concepts of supernatural entities." Spirit world encounters helped the shaman perform various tasks in this world that benefited the community, such as curing, influencing movement of game animals, making rain, and ensuring the success of raids. Moreover, trance and its visions of the spirit world were frightening experiences, so shamans took time and great care to instruct other shamans and novices in what to expect while hallucinating (Katz 1982). Even though the community's concepts about the spirit world were open to manipulation and change, significant variation would have made no sense within the conservative world-view of small scale San society.

Shamans' curing rituals were more private than ordinary trance dances but other individuals besides the shaman and patient were nevertheless present (Marshall 1969). The shaman often went to great lengths to explain to those present about supernatural events visible to the shaman only, such as the arrows of sickness that the shaman extracted from the patient's body. Certain successful shamans became widely known for their healing abilities and their supernatural encounters became public knowledge (Lewis-Williams 2001). Rock art was one way of making these invisible experiences in the supernatural world visible for everyone to see, such as detailed depictions of shamans expelling their patient's sickness through the back of their necks (Lewis-Williams and Dowson 1999). For example, Lewis-Williams (1995) suggests that viewing depictions of healing in the rock art might have instructed novice shamans and non-shamans about this activity. Other activities depicted in the rock art, such as rain-making or control of eland, might likewise have influenced the ideas of the community living within the painted shelter or visiting nearby rock paintings. Paintings of kudu among the Sandawe seem to have played the same role (Lewis-Williams 1987, Ten Raa 1971)

Shamans and non-shamans among the San have reported that they dream about out-of-body journeys. For example, shamans among the southern San, or /Xam, believed that they could make rain while dreaming (Lewis-Williams 2001). A non-shaman woman among the !Kung was given a giraffe song in a dream (Biesele 1993). Importantly, this song only became accepted and popular among other San shamans once her shaman husband heard and accepted the significance of her dream in terms of his own visions. This example shows that it is the ideas and approval of shamans, instead of experiences of non-shamans, that ultimately informed and legitimized San ideology and by extension their rock art.

The /Xam referred to their shamans as people who are "filled" with supernatural potency and shamans among the !Kung were seen as "owners" of potency (Lewis-Williams 2001). The /Xam believed the potency within their shamans largely came from the eland, the largest African antelope. A "Master of the Game," or trickster-deity, known as /Kaggen, created and placed eland potency within shamans. When activated in the trance dance, this potency helped shamans enter and safely journey through the spirit world. The San not only believed that eland contained more supernatural potency than any other animal (Lewis-Williams and Biesele 1978), but that their "fatness" is beneficial to the community as a whole (Lewis-Williams 1981, Vinnicombe 1976). Animals that were painted most frequently and in the most conspicuous locations within South African rock shelters are socially beneficial "red meat" antelope (see Biesele 1993), particularly eland.

/Xam shamans were believed to "possess" or "own" one or more specific animals. For example, a shaman that possessed springbok power became known as the "medicine man of springbok," whereas another medicine man had possession of locusts and rain animals (Bleek 1933). !Kung shamans referred to themselves as possessing powerful songs of animals instead of the actual animals. When speaking of a shaman's song, however, the !Kung might say that the shaman has eland medicine powers or giraffe medicine powers (Marshall 1969). According to ethnographic information it is probably safe to say that San shamans were privileged to possess specific power animals.

Whereas the socially beneficial powers and activities of San shamans were most frequently displayed and conducted in the public arena, some shamans were known to privately use supernatural powers for anti-social purposes, such as personal gain or at the request of a client. Malevolent shamanic activities included shooting invisible arrows of sickness at enemies or adopting a feline form (Lewis-Williams 1987). Malevolent shamans are generally labeled as sorcerers in the social anthropological literature (Beattie 1964). Among the Sandawe of Tanzania, "lion dancers" adopted a feline form to fight off the evil feline spirits sent by sorcerers (Lewis-Williams 1987). /Xam stories suggest that wildebeest might have been a power animal of sorcerers. One story relates how a wildebeest deliberately crushed a hunter (Bleek 1924), and !Kung San viewed wildebeest as displaying "angry" behavior (Lewis-Williams and Dowson 1999). "Black meat" animals, such as wildebeest, were considered to have a different kind of potency than "red meat" animals, such as eland (Biesele 1993). The placement of wildebeest paintings in inconspicuous locations, such as behind a boulder and close to the ground within a dark rock shelter in Lesotho (Loubser and Brink 1992), might be indicative of sorcery art. This hidden and private art, painted with black pigment, contrasts with the public art that depicts eland and other "red meat" animals in shades of red on the highly visible back walls of rock shelters.

The acquisition and processing of red pigment for painting among the San was a co-operative undertaking accompanied by ritualized procedures (Lewis-Williams 2001). According to an early twentieth century informant in the central mountains of South Africa, highly prized and scarce hematite could only be obtained from the high lying basalt flows in the region (How 1962). Once brought down from the high mountains a specially appointed old woman had to grind and heat the special pigment at full moon. The blood of a freshly killed eland was then mixed with the specially prepared hematite. Significantly, the need for fresh blood implies that painting occurred soon after an eland kill (Vinnicombe 1976). Such large kills were normally communal occasions, sometimes accompanied by a public trance dance (Marshall 1969). According to How's informant, blood was only mixed with special hematite to paint eland; other pigments were mixed with different media (see also Jolly 1986). I suggest that the co-operative and socially sanctioned efforts behind the painting of benevolent eland in generally highly visible locations reflect the socially supported nature of shamanic activities among the San.

The inference that shamans were the painters among the San is supported by a number of independently collected statements. A /Xam identified rock paintings as shaman's things (Stow 1930). Dornan (1917) was told of a great rain shaman who was also a painter. An old woman of partial San descent told Jolly (1986) that her father was a shaman-artist. Generally speaking, San painters appear to come from prominent communities, such as the Makhomokholo San from western Lesotho (Norton 1910) and the Ngqabayi San from the opposite side of Lesotho (Stanford 1910). Lewis-Williams (2001) suggests that the delicate lines so characteristic of South African rock art make it unlikely that all shamans painted; only some probably had the special skills. He goes on to argue that very much like there were specialist shamans of the eland, rain, curing, and so on among the /Xam, there were probably shamans of the paint in the interior mountains of South Africa.

Considerable effort was sometimes taken to include the rock face within the paintings. Examples of eland and snake paintings entering or leaving cracks or other inequalities in the rock surface are probably related to the San belief that shamans visit the spirit world through gaps in the ground or rock (Bleek 1935, Lewis-Williams and Dowson 1990). By going to great lengths to portray these supernatural visits in rock paintings and by painting these portrayals in readily observable locations within rock shelters, shamans were probably able to instruct and display their spiritual prowess to other shamans and non-shamans. The fact that at least some Sandawe rock paintings seem to appear from mineral accretions in the rock suggests that similar principles operated there in connection with the shamanic lion-dance (Loubser 2001).

Sandawe informants told Ten Raa (1971) that shamans like to conduct trance dances within shelters that have rock paintings. Jolly's informant (1986) told him that San people also danced in front of rock paintings to intensify their potency. The same informant said that if a person placed a hand on an eland painting, the potency in the painting would flow into the person. In the far southern coastal area of South Africa patches of paint that have been rubbed smooth might be indicative of similar behavior (Yates and Manhire 1991). The Bantu-speaking agriculturist neighbors of the San and Sandawe told me that scraping off the red pigment from hunter-gatherer paintings and ingesting the ground-up powder gives a person special powers to ward off sorcery and lightning. They added that not any person can do this, only specialized diviners are qualified to interfere with the rock paintings without running the risk of being harmed by the spiritual powers inside the pigment and the rock.

Rock Paintings of Irangi Agriculturists
Physical Setting

Like most other Bantu-speaking groups in sub-Equatorial Africa, the Irangi people of the Kondoa area in central Tanzania traditionally produced iron tools, practiced animal husbandry, and planted summer-rainfall crops. Judging by charcoal dates obtained from sites in coastal Tanzania and along Lake Nyasa (Chami et al. 2001), the earliest archaeological traces of iron producing people in central Tanzania probably date to at least the first half of the first millennium AD. Archaeological excavations of deposits within certain painted shelters in the Kondoa area yielded the remains of iron smelting (Leakey 1983). Iron smelting in sub-Equatorial Africa normally occurs in isolation from main settlements and its presence within painted rock shelters suggests that the shelters were separate from the main areas of habitation, very much like the abandoned rock shelters are today in the Kondoa area.

Wherever they overlap, the characteristically thickly applied white rock paintings of the Irangi occur atop the red rock paintings of the earlier Sandawe inhabitants (Leakey 1983, Loubser 2001). Exactly when the Irangi replaced the Sandawe in the area is not clear, but there is no trace of Sandawe communities in the immediate area today. The painted rock shelters in the area occur in relatively resistant granite rim rock, mostly along lines of low cliffs, although a few occur at the bottoms of boulders. Irangi villages are located on the fertile plains below the granite-lined Masai Escarpment. Unlike earlier Sandawe hunter-gatherers who inhabited the actual rock shelters, Irangi agriculturists only visit the shelters above and behind their villages on specific occasions, such as for the storing and threshing of millet, for ancestor veneration ceremonies, and for boys' puberty ceremonies. The journey from the nearby villages to the majority of rock shelters is not too arduous, although a few rock shelters and boulders are in fairly obscure locations along higher elevations of the escarpment.

Although Sandawe and Irangi rock art frequently occur within the same shelters, certain obvious differences separate the two traditions. Whereas Sandawe rock art appears to be limited to the bigger rock overhangs in the area, Irangi rock art occurs in big rock shelters and within obscure crevices. Access to Sandawe rock art is fairly straightforward, whereas access to a few of the smaller crevices with Irangi rock art involves scrambling over cliffs and rock climbing.

Sandawe motifs are carefully painted between joints and other inequalities in the rock surface, but some motifs appear to emanate from salt flows on the rock surface. Irangi paintings are roughly applied to the rock irrespective of inequalities; and there is no evidence that they incorporated cracks or mineral stains into their paintings. Sandawe art is easy to view from a standing position, including those that occur higher up the rear walls of shelters. Although some Irangi art is easy to view from a standing position on the shelter floor, only by kneeling, crawling, or even twisting can one see Irangi paintings tucked away underneath low ceilings. A number of Irangi paintings occur high up against the back walls and ceilings of rock shelters.

In contrast to the finely textured red pigment of Sandawe paintings, the primarily white and less frequent pale red pigments used in Irangi paintings are powdery. Transparent surface mineral accretions cover many Sandawe paintings, whereas Irangi paintings occur on top of these natural layers. This stratigraphic separation suggests a substantial chronological gap between the two painting traditions. Whatever the time differences, broad-lined Irangi motifs differ quite drastically from the underlying fine-lined Sandawe depictions. Boldly painted concentric rings, grids, dots, the occasional depiction of cattle and giraffes, and a few handprints characterize Irangi paintings (Figure 2). Most Irangi. paintings were applied with a finger or a stick.

Social Context

There are no published ethnographic or detailed oral accounts concerning the ideas that might have structured Irangi imagery. However, various Tanzanian informants told me in the field that groups of boys painted the images during puberty ceremonies. As elsewhere in sub-Equatorial Africa, these ceremonies were done in secluded conditions, away from main settlements. It is not certain how similar Irangi puberty ceremonies were to those among Bantu-speaking groups in South Africa (e.g., Hammond-Tooke 1981), but archaeological and other lines of evidence suggest that differences were probably minimal. In South Africa the rites for boys traditionally took place in secluded spots far from villages and were designed to effect the change from boyhood to manhood. The main aim of initiation schools was to create camaraderie among males of the same age in order that they might become cooperative adults.

The scale of puberty initiation schools varied, ranging from the village level among the Xhosa to the chiefdom level among the Pedi. Regardless of scale, much of the initiates' time was spent in making things. North Sotho Bantu-speaking initiates stacked large stone cairns and made grass costumes (Mönnig 1967). According to information I gleaned from Venda-speaking informants, initiates among the western

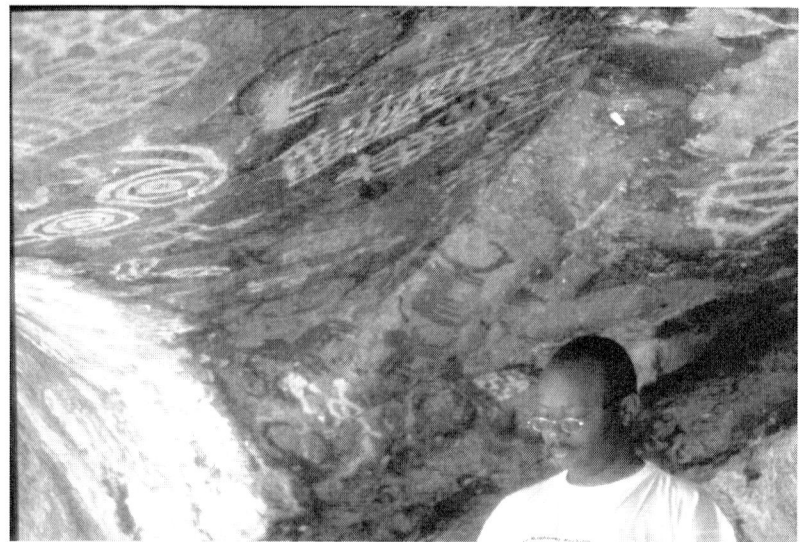

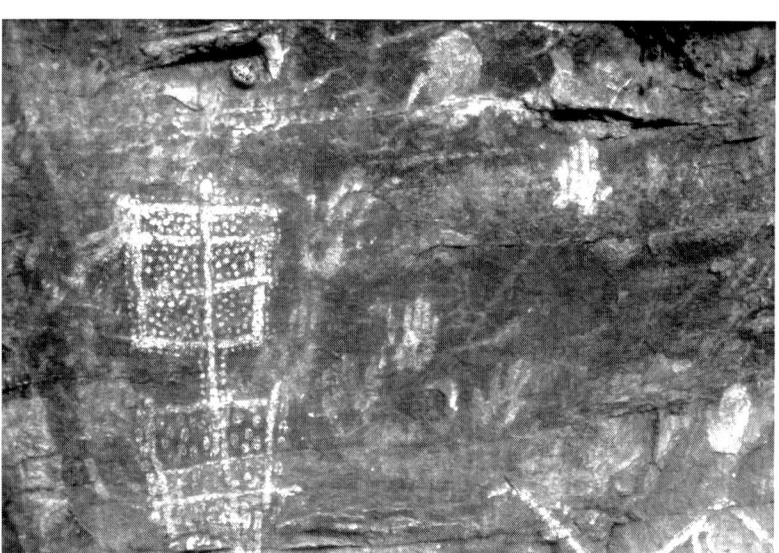

Figure 2. Irangi rock art from central Tanzania shows abstract motifs, cattle, and handprints. a, paintings on low ceiling of rockshelter; b, paintings on back wall of second rockshelter.

Venda and the northwestern Sotho made rock art as part of their tasks. In addition to these chores, initiates hunted small animals, underwent trials of endurance, and danced (Van Der Vliet 1974). Specially appointed diviners normally oversaw the proceedings. These diviners prepared medicines and instructed initiates about the secrets of the spirit world and proper conduct toward ancestor spirits. At night the young adults were taught songs with the emphasis on memorization.

Another common theme during puberty rites of passage was that initiates were deprived of food and sleep. They were frequently whipped and immersed in the cold water of specifically selected river pools, often thought to be the abode of ancestor spirits. Venda from the Soutpansberg and Southern Sotho in the Caledon River valley told me that being subjected to these harsh conditions caused them to have strange dreams and visions (see also Van Warmelo 1932). The application of white paint to the bodies and dancing sticks of initiates was common among many southern Bantu groups. The exact meaning of the color white varied from one group to the next, although generally speaking the white paint signified their transient condition and feeling of discomfort. The initiates normally collected the white clay from the closest available sources, typically from within the mountainous terrain in which they were secluded

It is not inconceivable that the puberty initiation among the Bantu-speaking Irangi agriculturists generally followed the same general strictures as the various southern Bantu agriculturists described above, bearing in mind that these groups share so many things, including common prehistoric roots (Huffman 1989). From the above evidence it is suggested that tales and visions of the spirit world inspired Irangi initiates to conduct the paintings in isolated locations. Whereas the bigger Irangi painted panels in the large shelters appear to be a group effort, those hidden in narrow and secluded locations were almost certainly individually executed. To do the higher paintings, an initiate was most likely supported on the shoulders of a fellow initiate, an activity that promotes camaraderie.

The preparation of the pigment used in Irangi paintings appears minimal. Based on the South African evidence, however, additional research might reveal that Irangi initiates added blood as a binder to the white clay. This blood might be obtained from circumcised wounds or from a sacrificial animal. Multiple springs and creek beds along the escarpment where the paintings occur are likely sources of the white clay. Today the area is a known source of good quality clay for the manufacture of ceramics and house bricks. In any case, visual examination of the powdery white pigment suggests that its preparation was not a specialized task. The pigment also seems to have been applied in a rush, as evidenced, for example, by splash marks and disregard of rock surface discontinuities. The overall appearance of Irangi rock art and its frequent position in places that are hard to find and see strongly suggests that the art was intended for private rather than public viewing.

At least some of the bigger rock shelters with Sandawe art in the Kondoa area have ongoing spiritual significance for the Irangi people. This significance appears to be related to Sandawe paintings instead of puberty rock art. As part of recent healing and rainmaking rituals, Irangi participants used castor oil leaves to spatter millet beer onto Sandawe paintings at Mungumi wa Kolo, a prominent rock shelter visible from afar on the skyline of the escarpment. Interestingly, this ritual is reminiscent of lion-dance trance rituals among the Sandawe, where "a woman takes a méraa [castor oil] twig, dips it in beer and sprinkles the dancers with it" (Van de Kimmenade 1936:413). Some of the millet spatter against the rock wall at Mungumi wa Kolo is pink in color and resembles pigment. Considered together, the beer spatters, castor oil leaves, and the removal of red pigment from Sandawe paintings within the site indicate continued ritual use of Mungumi wa Kolo.

The ritual importance of Mungumi wa Kolo probably has some antiquity bearing in mind that Louis Leakey wrote in 1951 that: "five local elders. . .told us that before we could start work we would have to provide a goat for a sacrifice to propitiate the spirits of the painted site, which are regarded as very powerful." (M. Leakey 1983:17). Sacrificing goats to the ancestor spirits as part of curing and healing ceremonies is an ongoing practice at Mungumi wa Kolo. Moreover, powerful Irangi diviners are known to acquire supernatural assistance by staying in a cavernous hollow immediately below Mungumi wa Kolo for two weeks. If successful in communicating with the spirit world by means of dreams and visions, the diviner emerges from the hollow with physical objects, such as python dung on his head and/or ancient iron points in his hands. On his return to the villages on the plain he uses these objects as evidence of his visit to the world of ancestral spirits.

It is important to note that Irangi diviners do not paint pictures on rock, but instead use physical objects to publicly display their privileged access to the spirit world. Unlike the hunter-gatherer shamans in sub-Equatorial Africa, diviners among Bantu-speaking agriculturists carefully guard their knowledge of the spirit world and would only share with the rest of the community those aspects that might increase their personal prestige. The absence of diviner rock art is most likely one result of the secret and private nature of their communication with the spirit world.

Overview of Hunter-Gatherer and Agriculturist Rock Art in Sub-Equatorial Africa

It appears from the evidence cited above that hunter-gatherer rock art from sub-Equatorial Africa shared the following characteristics: 1) the public trance and dream experiences and duties of semi-specialist shamans informed the art, 2) the acquisition, preparation, and transport of the pigment involved ritualized and co-operative efforts of various individuals, 3) shamans painted the images in or near living areas, 4) great care and skill were involved in painting the images in easily visible areas, and 5) people interacted with the art after its completion.

The rock paintings of subsequent agriculturists in the same region exhibit somewhat different features. These are: 1) the private trance and dream experiences of initiates possibly informed the art, 2) initiates gathered pigment from nearby sources without too much preparation, 3) initiates painted the images away from living areas, 4) the images were ostensibly painted fairly quickly and frequently in obscure locations, and 5) no interaction with the art is evident after its completion. It is proposed here that in terms of Taçon's (1983) shamanic versus shamanistic dichotomy then, sub-Equatorial hunter-gatherer rock art best fits the shamanic category whereas the rock art of non-shaman agriculturists initiates share certain characteristics of the shamanistic category.

Hunter-Gatherer Rock Art of the Columbia Plateau
Physical Setting

The Columbia Plateau cultural area roughly coincides with the geographical boundaries of the Columbia River watershed east of the Cascade Mountains, but also includes the Klamath Basin on the state line between southern Oregon and northern California. The oldest reliable dates for rock art on the Plateau are a 6,700 year old abstract carving partially covered with Mount Mazama volcanic ash in south-central Oregon (Cannon and Ricks 1986) and roughly contemporary red painted rock fragments from Bernard Creek rock shelter in western Idaho (Randolph and Dahlstrom 1977). Directly dated AMS pigment from three overlapping motifs in Fern Cave in the Lava Beds of northern California range from 1,000 years ago to the present (Armitage et al. 1997). Historic period paintings include depictions of horses and depictions of faces that resemble dated portable art from cremation burials (Keyser 1992).

A great variety of rock art sites are scattered throughout this region. Rock paintings predominate in most areas, except along the mid and lower Columbia and lower Snake rivers. The vast majority of rock art sites are small panels scattered along a particular slope, line of cliffs, or boulder field. Larger sites are primarily located along the central and lower Columbia River, parts of the Klamath Basin, and near the bigger rapids along the Snake River.

The primary Plateau rock art motifs are abstract designs, such as rayed arcs, tally marks, concentric circles, and zigzags that are associated with stick figure humans and block body animal figures. The selection, ratio, and intricacy of these motifs vary from one area to the next, a phenomenon that might be due to ethnic divisions. However, variations within a small area might be due to different kinds of painters, as suggested below.

Judging from the rock art of the Modoc Plateau in northern California and the Hells Canyon between Oregon and Idaho, not all rock art sites are at habitations (Loubser and Whitley 1999, Loubser 2002). In fact, most rock art sites in these areas appear to be located away from major settlements. For those sites (e.g., Fern Cave, Rattlesnake Shelter, Steiwer Ranch) that have rock art at a major occupation, the chronological relationships between occupation layers and rock art are not yet clear. With few exceptions, such as Fern Cave and Owl Cave (Keyser et al 1998b), rock art panels do not occur within dark zones.

In Hells Canyon, sites with the most layers of rock art motifs occur above large rapids in the narrowest portion of the canyon (Loubser 2002). Miller Island has the most complicated rock art stratigraphy on the lower Columbia River. These multiple layers suggest repeated journeys to these locations. The stratigraphically complicated rock art sites in Hells Canyon and Miller Island are located in areas that are dangerous to reach by water compared to other sites in the area. The Snake River is the main access route to the sites within Hells Canyon, considering the steep and rugged nature of the canyon walls. Rock art sites within the canyon often occur closely together as groups, or complexes. Within each complex, the rock art site closest to the Snake River typically has the most carefully executed paintings (Loubser 2002). Leen (1988) has found that side canyons have virtually no rock art, even though some of the bigger ones contain fairly accessible rock shelters. Rock art also tends to cluster at the entrances of lava tubes on the Modoc Plateau (Loubser and Whitley 1999). Particularly dense concentrations of rock art sites in this area seem to be associated with cinder cones and hills. Overall then, Columbia Plateau rock art is placed at the entrances of canyons, lava tubes, or boulder fields. In some instances, these are associated with mountains or river rapids. A dramatic example of this association is the lower Columbia painting concentration near Celilo Falls and Mount Hood.

Whereas accessibility to sites is as a rule not difficult, some paintings occur high up on cliff faces that can only be reached by experienced rock climbers. Site morphology is highly variable and it is often hard to guess from a distance which locations are high probability. As a rule motifs are applied to the rock surface without much regard for cracks or other irregularities. Sites where motifs do abut natural features or mineral stains typically occur at the canyon entrances, lava tubes, or

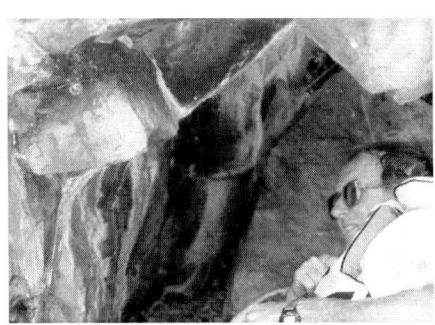 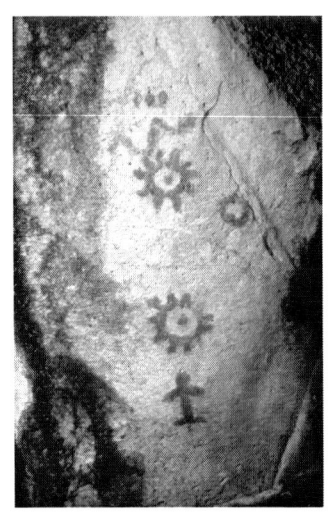

Figure 3. Columbia Plateau rock art. a, red pictographs from Hells Canyon in Eastern Oregon; b, black pictographs from the Klamath Basin of northern California.

boulder fields. Paintings often occur high against the back walls and ceilings of shelters or underneath very low and inconspicuous boulders. To see some rock art painted within cramped spaces it is necessary to contort one's body by twisting, squatting, and crawling. The artists clearly had to do the same.

Paintings are mostly red (Figure 3a), but along the lower Columbia River there are significant numbers of red and white polychromes. Black and white paintings are predominant in the southern Klamath Basin (Figure 3b). Occasional scratched rock art, charcoal drawings, and green paintings are found throughout the region. Materials to make the art, particularly red ocher, are readily available in the predominantly volcanic rocks of the Columbia Plateau. Charred sticks are also easy to obtain. In Hells Canyon, shelters with green clay outcropping in veins have green paintings (Loubser 2002). Evidence from the Plateau then suggests that materials to make the rock art were by-and-large locally available and easily obtainable.

Studies of rock art stratigraphy in the region show no overall sequence of motifs or techniques (Loubser and Whitley 1999; Loubser 2002; Keyser et al 2004) and the latest images resemble those done in other techniques. This continuity suggests a fairly conservative rock art tradition.

When occurring at sites without any other rock art, scratched motifs are surprisingly detailed depictions of grids, U-shapes, and even human-like figures. These elaborately scratched motifs typically occur in locations hidden from direct view, such as on steep and narrow terraces.

Approximately 90 percent of Columbia Plateau pigment is applied in a liquid form to the rock face with a finger or a thick brush (Keyser 1992). In a number of instances pigment is also applied directly to the rock with charred sticks or ocher crayons. Pecking and engraving are often interspersed with painted motifs. Generally speaking, it appears as if pigment was applied in a hurry and that no great care was taken to obtain a smooth outline or to depict details. Exceptions to this tendency are a few highly visible panels that normally overlook rivers, access routes, or entrances to lava tubes and boulder fields. Another exception is the rare but detailed scratched panels occurring in hidden locations.

In spite of sub-regional variations in topography and rock art placement, certain suggestive trends become apparent in the overview of the physical setting of Columbia Plateau rock art. Sites tend to occur in concentrations, sometimes near dramatic landforms, such as mountains or river rapids. The most elaborate and carefully executed sites tend to occur at entrances to rock art complexes. Rock art concentrations typically include multiple small panels within canyons, lava tubes, or boulder fields. With the exception of a few detailed panels that are visible from access routes, rock art tends to be simple and inconspicuous. Considered together then, Columbia Plateau rock art sites are located along access routes that link settlements with isolated areas; their placement on the landscape reflects their liminal nature.

Social Context

Ethnographic evidence throughout the Columbia Plateau unambiguously states that the majority of the rock art was painted by Indian adolescents to record their experiences while in a secluded location on a vision quest (see Keyser and Whitley 2000). These experiences included striking visions and dreams, objects obtained from personal guardian spirit helpers, and real animals or things actually seen during seclusion. By painting these visions, the supplicant believed they could better remember their spirit helpers and make their powers permanent. Moreover, children were required to make rock art as physical evidence that they indeed visited the requisite location to obtain their visions. These powerful places were often difficult to reach and sometimes required the assistance of an adult proctor, usually a parent who camped nearby (Cline 1938). Across the region both boys and girls were expected to seek spirit helpers so that they could become effective and responsible people within society. Among some groups adults gained additional power through subsequent visions that helped them maintain or achieve success in hunting, raiding, or gambling. The number of guardian spirits seen was indicated by short red lines (tally marks) beside the paintings of the relevant spirit (Cline 1938).

Shamans, both men and women, distinguished themselves from other adults by having sequential vision quests, often over many years, to obtain additional, or more powerful, spirit helpers (Ray 1963, Teit 1906). The supernatural powers they obtained enabled shamans to cure sickness, control the weather, locate game, and lead ceremonial winter dances. Very powerful shamans were said to fall into trance at will and could predict the future (Teit 1906). Shamans painted too, often to advertise their special powers. Among the Okanogan, for instance, shamans painted conspicuous rock surfaces, preferably in the company of another shaman who spread the word to the rest of the community (Cline 1938). Klamath shamans painted their spirit helpers on medicine boards prior to communal winter ceremonies for everybody to see (Curtin 1884). At these communal winter dances shamans and non-shamans accentuated their individual bonds with their particular spirit helper(s) through song and dance. During these events shamans also helped non-shamans enter trance to permanently 'fix' the spirit helpers that they acquired in childhood (Spier and Sapir 1930).

Ethnographic information on the type of visions acquired by Columbia Plateau Indians is some of the most complete in the world. Spirit helpers were principally animals but could also be unusual natural objects, artifacts, mythological figures, or heavenly bodies (Cline 1938). Spirit helpers that appeared in visions to children sometimes approached "with a great roaring sound, accompanied by flashes of fire" (Spier and Sapir 1930:240). Similarly, informants told Ray (1942) that they saw their spirit helpers as a "spark." Spier and Sapir (1930:240) write that the lonely and exhausted child on a vision quest eventually "fell into a trance ('a kind of sleep') in which he seemed to dream the words spoken by this animal. He dreamt that the power spoke like a human." Other accounts indicate that spirit helpers would first appear in human guise prior to turning into animals (Cline 1938, Teit 1918, Turney-High 1941).

When portrayed graphically in rock art, these visions may range from geometric patterns ('flashes' or 'sparks') to human figures or animals or combinations of humans, animals, and geometric patterns (Keyser 1992; Whitley et al. 2004). This kind of imagery is indeed common on the Plateau, and it is often difficult to identify precisely what the motifs were intended to portray. I suggest that the abstract nature of the depictions reflects the private nature of an individual's spirit helper; non-shamans only announce their spirit helpers in song and dance during the public annual winter dance. Shamans, on the other hand, displayed the powers of their spirit helpers by wearing masks or painting or scratching designs on their faces (Teit 1906). Although some of these designs were representational, most of them appear abstract.

As a rule, both shamans and non-shamans acquired visions in lonely, secluded locations. These places, believed to contain an abnormal concentration of supernatural power (Coburn 1975, Teit 1918), were normally close to running water or natural gaps in the rock. To obtain power, individuals undertook a tiring regime of exercise, purification, praying, and fasting. Physical tasks included construction of stone cairns and/or vision quest blinds (Ray 1963). The blinds probably facilitated sensory deprivation for hallucinations and dreams. Artificial depressions in front of many rock art panels in Hells Canyon and on Miller Island might have served a similar purpose as a vision quest blind (Loubser 2002). Teit (1906) mentions Lillooet vision seekers who dug holes in the ground.

The raw materials to produce rock art were readily available across the Columbia Plateau. Teit (1918) observed that the ocher was generally mixed with animal fat and applied with the point of the index finger. Spinden (1908) mentions that the Nez Percé used greasy ocher pencils for some of their rock drawings. Interestingly, the Kutenai referred to pigment, rock art, and spirit helpers by similar terms, all of which translate as "power" (Hann et al. 2004). This underscores the powerful nature of rock paintings.

In spite of the power of these images, for the most part painting remained a private and lay activity on the Plateau. Shamans and non-shamans made their own rock art; it was not the domain of specialized or privileged individuals within the community. In a literature survey of Columbia Plateau ethnography, Keyser and Whitley (2000) found that explicit mention is made of shamans and rock art production among five groups and that non-shamans made rock art in least fifteen groups. Whitley has proposed that the difference between shaman and non-shaman vision questing and rock art on the Columbia Plateau is one of degree, not kind (Loubser and Whitley 1999). Whereas the general ethnographic literature tends to support Whitley's contention (see Hann et al. 2004), the degree of separation varied from one group to the next (cf, Park 1938 and Ray 1963). Okanagon shamans did rock art to advertise their power and provide a place where friends could petition it for help (Miller 1998). Among the Klamath only shamans reputedly painted the circle motifs representing their powerful spirit helper, the sun disk (Hann et al. 2004). Interestingly, the recording of eight rock art sites in the Modoc Plateau near the Klamath people showed that circular motifs tend to occur at the entrances of lava tubes (Loubser and Whitley 1999). Compared to other motifs deeper inside the tubes, the circular paintings are carefully executed and placed in prominent locations. This supports the interpretation that shamans' rock art tended to be more public and carefully executed than that of non-shamans.

Although there is no direct ethnographic reference to sorcery art in the Columbia Plateau, malevolent sorcerers are known to steal other peoples' spirit helpers or talk to spirits dwelling within rock art sites in order to get their assistance in harming other people (Hines 1993). Teit (1918) mentions that paintings were also made to ward of misfortune or serve as protection against sorcerers. Shamans scarified people to purify their patients or extract invisible spells sent by sorcerers, but shamans and non-shamans were also known to cut themselves during dances when others recited their songs (Spier and Sapir 1930). Current ethnographic research (Taylor and Keyser 2003, see also this volume) relates some scratched rock art to the body cutting done by a special type of shaman.

These clues suggest that the scratches on mountain sheep motifs in Hells Canyon are attempts of sorcerers to obtain the spirit helper powers of other individuals. The rare and detailed scratched motifs in unusual locations within the same canyon might also be the work of sorcerers, or at least the work of a special category of shaman.

Overview of Columbia Plateau Hunter-Gatherer Rock Art

From the above information the following characteristics seem to be present in Columbia Plateau hunter-gatherer rock art: 1) private trance and dream experiences of initiates structured the majority of art even though shamans also made rock art to represent their visions, 2) people individually gathered pigment from nearby sources without too much preparation, 3) people painted the images away from living areas, 4) the images were ostensibly painted fairly quickly and predominantly in obscure locations, and 5) only infrequent interaction with the art is evident after its completion, perhaps by sorcerers and other individuals wishing to obtain power. I propose that in terms of Taçon's (1983) shamanic versus shamanistic dichotomy then, Columbia Plateau rock art incorporates elements of both. However, since most Columbia Plateau rock art is ultimately the result of young initiates' visions, it should be considered shamanistic.

Some Implications

The proposed shamanistic art traditions of the Irangi of Tanzania and Indians of the Columbia Plateau are primarily the result of encounters with the spirit world during a critical liminal period—the transition to adulthood—in these people's lives. Individual adults on the Plateau who wanted to reverse personal misfortune also conducted vision quests and did some rock art. Such liminal periods are considered very dangerous to the community as a whole and must be accompanied by the physical separation and seclusion of initiates or adult vision seekers. The physical separation of the rock art is accordingly an apt spatial metaphor of the social isolation during this period of transition and uncertainty. In terms of public avoidance and fears of pollution, initiates feed themselves and prepare their own pigment. Private visions and dreams are the basis of rock art conducted in isolation; the art chiefly functions as a private mnemonic device instead of a tool of public instruction. I propose that partly for this reason rock art motifs in these regions are by-and-large not diagnostic of particular things. Also, the level of trance experienced by initiates or adults seems to be less intense than those experienced by shamans or sorcerers. Perhaps for this reason shamanistic rock art primarily depicts geometric entoptics instead of iconic imagery (cf. Lewis-Williams and Dowson 1988 on the stages of hallucination). The fact that children and young adults made most of the shamanistic art perhaps also explains the lack of detail and relatively careless execution. I suggest that images made by shamans within the Plateau tradition demonstrate more detail and care than initiate's art, and are placed in more publicly conspicuous places. Rock art made by sorcerers also displays care but is placed in less conspicuous locations.

The proposed shamanic rock paintings of the San and Sandawe seem to have been done primarily in public places. San and Sandawe shamans performed their trance dances in public and experienced altered states of consciousness in a public setting. The position of shamans within San and Sandawe societies was not liminal like that of initiates or adults who seek to reverse their personal fortunes. The placement of their rock paintings within highly conspicuous public places is an apt spatial metaphor; the rock face is but a thin veil that separates the spirit world from the rest of the community. By juxtaposing the spirit world in this fashion, shamans could perform their pro-social activities, such as curing and rainmaking. People other than shamans were involved in the acquisition and preparation of pigment; the community probably cooperated in this fashion to reciprocate shamans for their curing and other public services. Being more adept at trance experience, shamans probably entered deeper states of trance than did novices and so were able to recall clearer visions of people and animals instead of only entoptics. Moreover, as semi-specialists, shamans probably had more time to practice the craft of painting than initiates. Shamans also wished to share their visions of the spirit world with the rest of the community; the art was a tool of public instruction instead of a private mnemonic device. The few examples of San sorcery art tend to occur in more secluded locales or to be smaller.

The distinction between shamanic and shamanistic rock art is not a rigid one, but might nevertheless give some clues as how to interpret rock art traditions that have less definite ethnographic contexts, such as the Paleolithic dark zone cave art in southern France.

Acknowledgements

I thank sponsors Ray and Jean Auel and Donna Tallman, and all of the co-sponsors for making the symposium possible. I thank Jim Keyser for inviting me to participate, and Keyser, Dave Whitley, Carl Davis, and Sara Scott for affording me numerous opportunities to study rock art in the American West. I am indebted to David Lewis-Williams for introducing me to South African rock paintings in 1979 and for showing me elegant ways to study rock art. Webber Ndoro gave me the opportunity to visit the Kondoa rock art sites in Tanzania. George Poetschat, Mike Taylor, and Cathy Poetschat are commended for organizing the symposium and hosting my visit to Portland. Finally, Karen McNamee, Kellee Taylor, and Nola Queahpama went to extraordinary effort to provide us with good food.

Discussion

Bob Layton: I very much like the idea of relating the style of the art to the cultural context its produced in. What is the ethnographic evidence—actual statements from native South Africa people—about the rock wall as a veil between this world and the next?

Jannie Loubser: Well, a Transkei informant, the Xhosa-speaking woman from the Northeast Cape—that Lewis-Williams called "M," was the daughter of a shaman. She was part San and part Bantu-speaking agriculturalist. She said that these spirits are behind the rock and that people must be qualified to put their hand against the rock. But there's not a lot of direct ethnographic evidence to say that because the Eland abuts the crack (that means that it is coming out of the rock). That is more inference that one makes from the rock art itself.

Linea Sundstrom: I thought it was interesting what you said about the children's art—it just shows the entoptics and maybe they just got that far into trance and couldn't formulate what they experienced into more of a representational type of image. My impression from things that I've read about visions is that oftentimes the vision starts with a voice or a sound—then you see an image of the sound or voice that you're hearing—and it occurred to me that maybe that overlaps with experiencing the entoptics. Maybe they got that far and then panicked or otherwise lost the vision and so they have only that entoptic image to represent.

My other question is whether those images themselves help to induce the trance state. Has anyone done any cognitive work on that?

Dave Whitley: In essence, yes. Context is always important and it influences the form of your vision. If you're staring at something, that will influence the mental image that you will generate.

Linea Sundstrom: But that's not really what I'm asking. What I'm asking is do the images themselves help bring about trance—is staring at images a way of inducing it? Has anyone studied that?

Jean Clottes: There are some references in neuropsychological literature to that kind of thing. I have in mind a book by a French psychologist, Catherine Lemaire (1993), which was published about ten years ago. She's been experimenting on that. She said that at the beginning it is quite difficult to get into trance—you've got to use all sorts of help. She never used drugs but she said she had to use strong concentration. Eventually she progressed and got used to it. And then she said that she could get into trance just by focusing on an image that was generally linked with her first experiences.

Linea Sundstrom: So maybe it could induce it, but more specific to an individual.

Jean Clottes: Yes, absolutely. It works both ways. It is the specific individual, but it may become a cultural trait and it can be taught also.

There is also something else. It is the location where it may happen. For example, I'm persuaded that in the deep caves of Europe, the images might have played a role, but the location *definitely* played a role. Personally, working in deep caves, I have had—not a vision, but an auditory hallucination. At the time it was so vivid I didn't' think I was experiencing it—I thought it was real.

Jim Keyser: Can you describe it.

Jean Clottes: Well, in 1981 I had been working for a couple of hours right at the bottom of Niaux—a cave about a mile long—and there is a lake you had to wade across, and the other members of the team were in quite a different part of the cave—more than half a mile away—so there was no way we could hear each other. I was alone, tracing some images, and then I heard people talking and I thought a couple of them were coming to me for some reason. I heard voices but I couldn't tell what they were saying. But I heard people talking—coming near, then they sort of faded away. Then I thought maybe not. This lasted for a couple of minutes and then I went on working. When I came out of the cave, I said [to the other team members] "You came so close, why didn't you come to where I was?" And they said "We never went there."

That was when I realized I had had an auditory hallucination. I could not make anything out, I was not expecting it and it was extremely vivid. Somebody said [in a previous discussion] that it is not like having jet lag—it is not something fuzzy—it is very vivid. Lemaire also said the same thing, and many neuropsychologists note how vivid it is when you have visions—more vivid because all the senses are enhanced. Visions can also have pathological causes. Since I have been working on the book with Lewis-Williams (Clottes and Lewis-Williams 1996) I have had many testimonies to such visions. In particular, one of my colleagues (whose name I'm not at liberty to say) told me of an accident he had—he was in his attic and he raised his head quickly and there was a nail sticking out that he drove into his skull. He had an operation and afterward they told him "You're lucky because you could have had it much worse." He told me "Yes, I was cured and everything is fine, except that occasionally I have visions that come on suddenly. For example if I am down with the flu or very tired and I'm sitting working on the computer, suddenly I feel myself leaving my body and I see myself sitting there while I'm floating around. If I think of the next village, immediately I'm in that village and I see people talking and its all extremely vivid. Of course, I know it's an hallucination—a vision—but I can't believe it. Intellectually, rationally, I know it, but it is so vivid, its incredible."

And he even confessed something quite strange—he said "You know, this is not rational, but one time this happened, I flew (he called it flying) to a village (he gave me the name of the village which I know very well) and I saw miles away where I could see clouds forming. I thought there was a storm brewing, and then I came back and woke up. A couple of hours later there was a big storm." Of course, he could have subconsciously felt the storm because of the salt breeze or a slight change in pressure, but he told me he was of two minds. Intellectually he knew it was an hallucination derived from the accident, but when he was experiencing it, it was so vivid because all his senses were heightened.

Linea Sundstrom: This is interesting. In terms of what you're saying about being in caves, I have heard people describe that experience. They talk about a water drop falling from the cave ceiling and they characterize the sound as reverberating like a gong.

Jean Clottes: Yes, it can be like that. It depends on your state of mind.

Dave Whitley: In part it's a function of sensory deprivation.

Linea Sundstrom: But the other thing in my area [the Plains]—and I think this is true in the rocky Mountains as well—is the idea of the little people being in the rock. An American Indian woman told me that her son went all the way back in Ludlow Cave—its about 400 feet back—and she said sort of offhandedly that he could hear the little people talking. He stayed there a while and then he came out.

Jean Clottes: Being inside a cave is a striking experience, especially if you are alone, you see. If you are with people and you just are quiet and listen and you turn off the light. Some people cannot bear it; others, on the contrary, they revel in it. You hear just a drop [of water] or two, you know, and you *hear* the silence, which is something you never do in ordinary life.

Don Hann: To get back to the original point of inducing trance, Lewis-Williams and others break trance into a series of stages. I think that possibly may be the connection. There is something to induction of the earlier stage—being quiet, being in a small spot when you start to see these things [entoptic phenomena]. Then, if you focus on those things, that may be what leads to the induction of further stages and ultimately the clarity of the vision. I think that requires more training, more expertise, to be able to easily get into that stage. So maybe children just have not had that degree of training and they are focusing on that initial thing. Once they do that multiple times they will jump to the next stage, but initially they are recording their initial stage.

Linea Sundstrom: One of the reasons I asked that question is that in the Black Hills there is a style of rock art that only has phosphenes or entoptics. It does not combine those with human or animal images—it's just abstract images. I interpret those as places where people would go to try to induce trance—to carry it to the next step. That's why I was curious if there were any studies about that.

Phillip Cash Cash: What Don was saying is correct, at least from the Nez Perce perspective. What they call a trance is *Tuyakeen* and they say that the young medicine people, when they first come out with their songs, they revisit that experience they had when they were a child and the *Tuyakeen* is the trance they go into. It is the same experience repeated over, only now they are a mature individual adult and they tell them that the trance will better themselves in the days ahead, each time they experience that, it becomes more and more meaningful. So when they are children what they experience at that time does not mean anything. Only later in life—in adulthood—does it become meaningful.

Dave Whitley: So, they understand it as they get older? They get a greater understanding?

Phillip Cash Cash: Yes.

Linea Sundstrom: There are studies that indicate that when children are falling asleep at night they see entoptic images.

Dave Whitley: We do—we all do!

Linea Sundstrom: But in that sense it is something cognitively familiar to them, although they are in this really strange, limbic state—between awake and asleep. Maybe that is a way into trance.

Dave Whitley: It's a hypnogogic or hypnopompic state, we hallucinate them all the time. If you are driving late at night and you're tired, you have micro-hallucinations on your peripheral vision. You just ignore them.
    Culturally we pay no attention to these things. The only cultural perception we have of them is the cartoonist who—when the safe falls out of the sky and lands on Roger Rabbit's head—uses those images. But they are there.

Editors Note: Later in the session, the group returned to this discussion and provided a short addition.

Willie Selam: I want to reflect back a little bit on part of [this] discussion. About how we were relating the ways that the old people used to travel back into their state of power. Even my father [James Selam] made mention of a little part (of this topic) when we were discussing that word [tahmanawis—see Keyser et al., chapter 8, this volume] and the lineage back, where a person of power would place his mark in a certain place and that would take care and hold his power and then he could call upon that. And this is part of what you were wondering about—going into the trance or going into what we would call dreaming.

Jean Auel: What would a mark look like?

Willie Selam: It's a personal thing and its not generally discussed in public or in a public manner. So this is all inside our belief structure, our traditions—these markings of power, places of power, and the way to travel—to find or search for a means to cure (if it's a person who is ill). And if its a person that's injured, it [means] prevailing upon that power to help you heal them—whether it be an actual physical injury or a sickness. So its just a small mention in reference to the discussion that was going on.

CHAPTER 12
Nymphs, Waterfowl, and Saints: The Role of Ethnography in the Interpretation of the Rupestrian Tradition of Valcamonica, Italy
Angelo Fossati

Introduction

As an archaeologist, I have always believed that interpretation of rock art requires knowledge of both the chronological and cultural contexts in which it was formed. But I have also been attracted by the possibility of finding the meaning of the rock art by using ethnographic data. One possibility would be "paleoethnography[1]" which uses sources written not intentionally as ethnography but rather to describe the customs of unfamiliar peoples. In Europe such information can often be gleaned from Roman historians who wrote about the customs of populations contemporary with the Roman Empire (one of the best examples is the important work of Tacitus on the *Germania*). Unfortunately we have no such writings for the Camunni (the prehistoric inhabitants of the Valcamonica) or any other alpine population of northern Italy during the end of the Iron Age.

When I began researching Alpine rock art, I thought there might be recent ethnography that could help my research. But at the beginning of the eighties, when I first approached the rock art of Valcamonica, I realized that no one had ever researched (or at least, published) ethnographic references to this area's rock art.[2] A connection between the rock art tradition and recent folklore was completely lacking. Using the bibliography of "I Camuni" (Anati 1982), the major work of Emmanuel Anati, one of most important scholars of Camunnian rock art in the third quarter of the twentieth century, one finds an interest in ethnography only by Raffaello Battaglia, who compared general European folklore with Camunnian rock engravings.[3] Other authors of the 1930s (e.g. Marro 1930; Altheim and Trautmann 1937; Jacobsthal 1938) report nothing of interest in terms of ethnography. Their only useful aspect for my study is documentation of the original rock art site names in the valley[4]—but none of these different authors did additional research to find the meaning of these names. I demonstrate the importance of this point with the case of Naquane (below).

In his book, Anati (1982:343) notes that during the 1950s, at the beginning of his research when he was visiting various rock art sites, he asked what local people thought about the engravings. He reports that they used to attribute some engravings to a local strange and very solitary man. Anati also once met a woodcutter who said that the engravings were "secret marks that can transmit occult magic powers." This hint is very important because the petroglyphs are attributed to the sphere of the initiation, the interpretive key of my own research on Iron Age rock art (Fossati 1991).

In this paper I discuss legends and toponomies that help to find elements that relate rock art to local traditions. Concluding my paper I expose the recent creation of a new (but completely invented) ethnography whose intention is to put the presence of Valcamonica rock art in a more "mythical" context.

Before I start, however, it is necessary to summarize the rock art of Valcamonica for those readers unfamiliar with the archaeology of Northern Italy. In particular I concentrate on the valley's Iron Age and Copper Age rock art.

The Valcamonica Rock Art Tradition

The rupestrian tradition of Valcamonica consists of about three hundred thousand engraved figures. However, at the beginning of the twentieth century, only the Cemmo boulders (*Massi di Cemmo*) were known in Valcamonica. These were first noted by Gualtiero Laeng (1914), a geographer who published a general description of the two boulders that local people called "the rocks of the puppets" (*le prede dei pitoti* in local dialect). In fact, most discoveries in Valcamonica were made during the 1930s thanks to the archaeologist Raffaello Battaglia (1934) and the anthropologist Giovanni Marro (1930). A more scientific understanding of the different phases appeared during the 1960s and 1970s, with the works of Emmanuel Anati (1976) and other scholars, among them especially Raffaele De Marinis (1988, 1995). With the discovery of rock art on the east side of Lake Garda in 1964 (Pasotti 1965) and in Valtellina, a border valley north of Valcamonica, in 1966 (Pace 1968), we know today that this zone of the central-eastern Alps, from Valtellina to Lake Garda, can be considered a single petroglyph area, with common stylistic, thematic and chronological characteristics. The principal area remains Valcamonica, which constitutes an archaeological, artistic, ethnographic, and historical patrimony of inestimable value (since 1979 the valley has been listed as a UNESCO World Heritage Site), not only for its antiquity but, above all, for its thematic and iconographic wealth (Anati 1982; De Marinis 1988; Arcà et al 1995). In the present paper I focus on the original Valcamonica area, but use some other alpine sites as comparative data.

Geologically the north Italian alpine valleys were excavated and polished by the glaciers during the last hundred thousand years of the Pleistocene, and the art is mainly located in the open air on horizontally-lying bedrock outcrops. From Pisogne on Lake Iseo, in southern

Valcamonica, to the sites of Sellero and Grevo in the middle valley, the bedrock is primarily sandstone, while in the upper part of the valley (and the entire Valtellina) the bedrock is schist. Around Lake Garda is limestone bedrock. Everywhere these sandstones, schists, and limestones are very polished and sculpted by glacial action. In these areas the rock art is primarily engravings; only 6 paintings have been discovered to date (Fossati 2001b). The artists used hammering (pecking) and scratching techniques, with hammering being the most common and important. To peck petroglyphs they used quartz hammer stones—examples of which are frequently found where they have been abandoned near the rocks (Fossati 1993a).

In this area, at present, the rock art is distributed across four major periods from the Neolithic to the arrival of the Romans in the valleys (Figure 1, see also Anati 1976; De Marinis 1988; Fossati 1991, 1993b). Analysis shows slight differences in the predominant motifs and other attributes in every period, indicating that the art's meaning was not static throughout its 4000 year history.

In the first phase, from the terminal Neolithic through the beginning of the Copper Age (fourth Millennium BC; Camunnian rock art styles 1A, 2A and the beginning of 3 A, see Figure 1), topographical figures are found—the first representations of territory, whose execution on cliffs is perhaps tied to a real division of agricultural lands sanctioned by the ritual practice of rock art (Fossati 1993a, 2002b). Other figures attributed to this phase are spirals and necklaces.

It is more or less accepted that this first phase is preceded by a more ancient period, perhaps going back to the end of the Paleolithic (Anati 1974). The figures of this ancient period are very few and all represent animals, especially elk and deer. This phase, called Proto Camunnian (Figure 1) for its great antiquity and content, is in some way tied to the style and chronology of Ice Age Art, which has recently been found outside caves, on cliffs and flat rocks in the open air in Spain and Portugal (Abreu et al 1995).

The second phase of Camunnian rock art corresponds to the full Copper Age (third and fourth Millennia BC, Camunnian style 3 A, see Figure 1), and is characterized by the production of stelae and menhirs—boulders that represent the alpine peoples' first anthropomorphic divinities (Casini and Fossati 1994). The most important depiction is the sun, sometimes represented as a man crowned by a solar circle with rays, and often associated with weapons. Two other personages are also represented: one feminine, adorned with numerous jewels (double spiral pendants, necklaces, combs), and another male divinity, symbolized by a fringed cloak. The iconographic repertoire of the boulders is very rich, including animals (e.g. deer, dogs, foxes, wolves, chamois, ibexes, boars, and bovines) and weapons (e.g. axes, halberds and daggers).

Style	Themes	Chronology
Protocamunnian	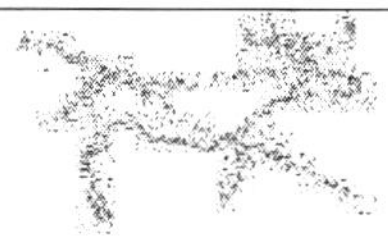	13th-6th Mill. BC
1st-2nd		5th-4th Mill. BC
3rd A	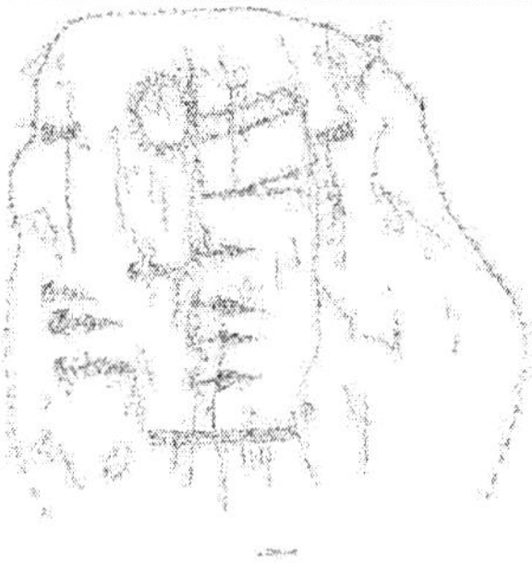	4th-3rd Mill. BC
3rd B-C-D	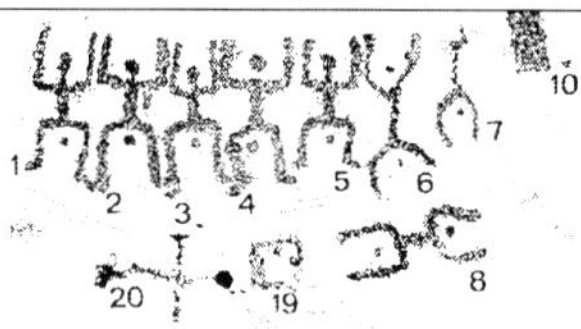	2nd Mill. BC
4th	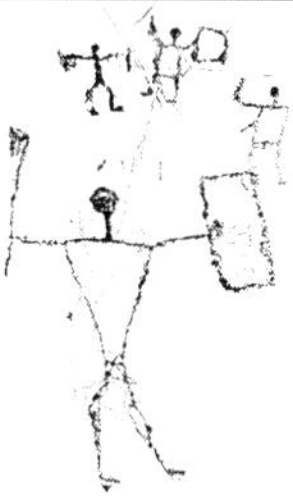	1st Mill. BC
Postcamunnian	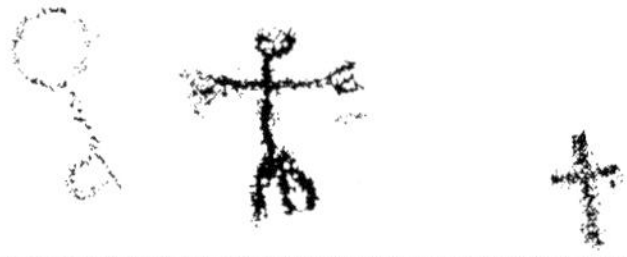	Roman - Mediaeval – Recent

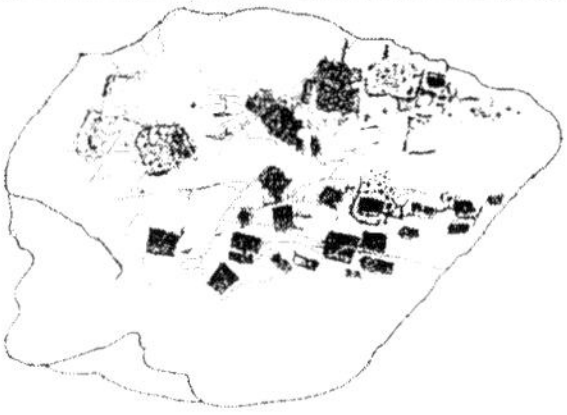

Figure 1. Themes and Chronology in the Valcamonica Rock Art Tradition.

The third phase of Valcamonica (and Valtellina) rock art (Camunnian styles 3B, C, and D, see Figure 1) is generally dated to the second Millennium BC and corresponds to the Bronze Age (De Marinis

1995). The iconographic repertoire is more reduced in comparison with Copper Age figures, but no less important. Images include numerous weapons (in this case no longer associated with divinities), ploughing scenes, ritual scenes formed by praying anthropomorphs, and symbols (solar signs and shovels).

In the Final Bronze Age (1200 to 800 BC) the first warrior figures appear, a prelude to the immense repertoire of Iron Age art that is dated to the first Millennium BC (Fossati 1992). This last phase of prehistoric Valcamonica and Valtellina rock art (Camunnian style 4, see Figure 1) is the most interesting and richest from a thematic viewpoint (Fossati 1991). It is tied to the initiation rites of young people of the local warrior aristocracy. Among these figures are recognizable hunting scenes, ritual duels, races and armed dances, constructions, wagons, weapons, musical instruments, agricultural scenes, figures with a strong symbolic value (such as footprints, cup marks, swastikas, stars, shovels), divinities, and topographical representations. In this period engraved figures took on greater realism, to the point where one can speak of descriptive naturalism, inasmuch as it appears the prehistoric artist wished to recount real life scenes. In these scenes warriors appear as images of great strength, but actual combat is relatively rare. More often than not these heavily armed warriors are shown with weapons raised in sign of exultation. Similarly, in the numerous dueling scenes, contenders face each other lightly armed, as if for a sporting event—their armament being no more than a stick and a small leather bag strapped to the protecting arm, which acts as a shield. In these scenes duelists and onlookers are placed side by side, with the former much smaller in size, leading one to assume they are boys. The engravings representing footprints, or footwear with laces, also appear to belong to boys, since they are smaller than adult feet.

In fact, this constant reference to boys has led scholars to interpret Iron Age rock art in the area as votive images engraved on the occasion of initiation rites through which young men of the local aristocracy gained access to adult society. Social differences are also shown by some rock engravings where riders are escorted by their attendants.

Some images relate to the trials the young men underwent— dueling, horse riding, balancing feats, racing and dancing fully armed, and deer hunting. Others (e.g. cup marks grouped in eight and the "Camunnian Rose"—a symbol originating from the swastika, which was originally a solar symbol [Fossati 1991, Farina 2000]) probably symbolize the initiation itself. The repeated occurrence of these indicates that, although specific meaning is lost today, in the Bronze Age their meanings apparently must have been very clear to the initiate. Regarding the Camunnian Rose, Paola Farina (2000) adds a bit of ethnographic information: local shepherds used to touch a figure of this type engraved along the path to the site of Coren di Sellero, because they said that it "brings fortune." In fact her study demonstrates that, in prehistory, this figure developed through time a significance of prosperity and good luck.

The latest rock art is obviously the product of the *Camunni*, a population often associated with the *Euganea gens*, especially by Roman historians (Cato cited by Plinius III, 1998:133-135). More recent research testifies to the cultural homogeneity of the region that extends from Valtellina to the Giudicarie. At least from the fifth century BC, this region shares pottery types with similar features (Breno, Dos dell'Arca and Lovere type vessels), the development of an autonomous writing tradition that utilizes the north-Etruscan alphabet (the "Camunnian alphabet") and, last but not least, the strong appearance of the figurative "language" that we now call "rock art." This wide area, even though strongly connected to the "Retic" world of the Adige Valley, would have been united by cultural links that we would today explain as a common *ethnos*—that of the Euganei (De Marinis 1988).

In Valtellina the prehistoric rock art tradition ended earlier than in Valcamonica—probably during the sixth century BC—for reasons that remain unknown (Fossati 1995). In Valcamonica the rupestrian tradition continued until the arrival of the Romans, who reached there in 16 BC. A legion (about 6,000 soldiers), under the direction of the consul Publio Silio Nerva, conquered the *Triumplini*, *Camunni* and *Vennonetes* (the inhabitants of Valtrompia, Valcamonica, and Valtellina respectively) in a single fast military campaign. This is documented by the registration of these three names on the *Tropaeum Alpium*, a monument constructed by Emperor Augustus in 6-7 AD at La Turbie, France (Rossi 1987). The resulting interruption of the Valcamonica rock art tradition was probably due to a combination of three factors: the enculturation process of local populations into Roman culture during the second part of the first century AD (the Flavian Age); diminution of authority of the Camunnian social classes that held power prior to the Roman invasion; and the increasing economic, cultural and religious attraction caused by the Roman settlements, particularly the new colony of *Civitas Camunnorum*[5] (today Cividate Camuno). These factors reduced and finally destroyed the power of the social aristocracy whose traditional themes had constituted, until then, the iconographic patrimony of the rock engravings (Fossati 1991).

With the arrival of Christianity, artists returned to the rocky areas and engraved new themes taken from Christian symbols: crosses, keys, shears, Solomon's knots (a cabalistic design of a knot without ends), warriors, castles, and dates and inscriptions. This art has nothing to do functionally with the prehistoric art tradition. At the moment it is not possible to date this phase (called Post Camunnian, see Figure 1) more precisely, since sufficiently detailed studies have yet to be undertaken (Sansoni 1993).

Ethnography of Valcamonica Rock Art

With this background in Valcamonica rock art, I can now show examples where ethnography aids us in interpreting various sites and evaluating claims made for the reasons behind the creation of these petroglyphs.

Contrada Aquane and the Lady with Goat's Feet

In 1989 a cadastral map (Figure 2) of the *Contrada Aquane* was brought to my attention.[6] Contrada Aquane was the original toponym of today's site of Naquane (corresponding to the central area of today's National Petroglyph Park) as the linguist Alinei had already proposed (Fossati 1991; Alinei 1984). Alinei was not aware of the map but had linked the toponym Naquane to the *Aquane*—semi-divine beings widely known by diverse names and attributes in the folklore of the central-eastern Alps, especially in the Dolomites where the dominant culture

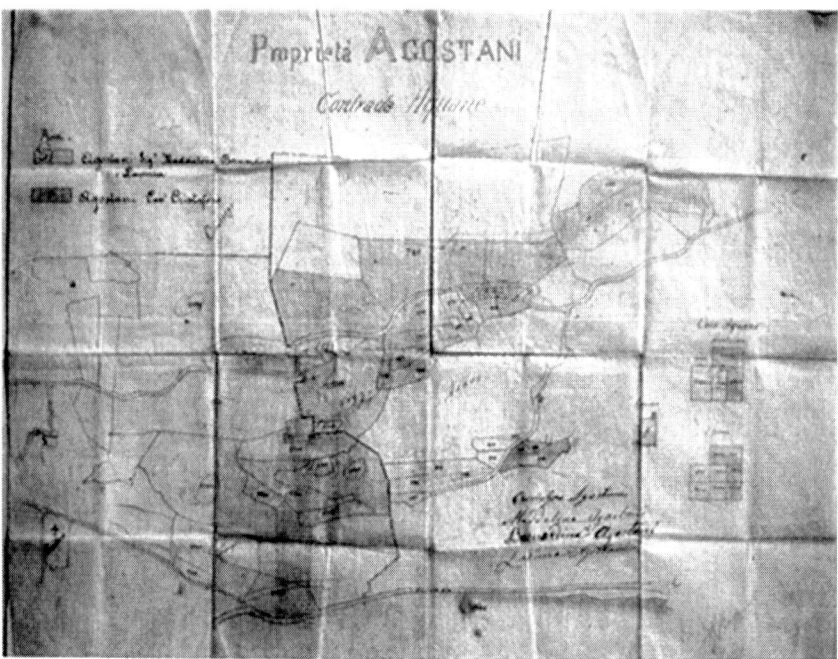

Figure 2. Map of the Contrada Aquane.

was that of the Ladins (Wolff 1987). A few of the known names include: Aquane, Anquane, Enguane, Eguane, Gane, Guane, Sagane, Sguane, Aivane and Vivane. They are also referred to in the classical world. Remember Aganippe, the nymph and the homonymous well on the Elicona in Beozia; the witch by the name of Sagana mentioned by Horace; and the Latin *saga*, from *sagus*, meaning sorceress, or prophetess.

For Alinei, Naquane represented the westernmost such toponym in the central-eastern alpine area. Our recent research has discovered other examples—there is a Roman age inscription from Cantù, not far from Como, dedicated to Aquane (*Corpus inscriptionum latinarum* V, 5671), and at Soncino (province of Cremona) the toponym of Aguane is found in close proximity to a spring. This southern locale testifies to the presence of the cult of Aquane in the Po River plain. According to Raffaele De Marinis, also the name of the Euganei, from the ethnic group to which the Iron Age inhabitants of Valcamonica belong, would not be too far removed from the form Eguane or Enguane (Fossati 1991).

But who were the Aquane? Descriptions collected by Alinei show that in folklore the Aquane are remembered as anthropozoomorphic beings. The oldest legends describe them as women who can change into otters, or beautiful sirens with hair of water and feet turned backwards. They inhabit lakes, caves and springs. In more recent legends they have acquired the attributes of the Faun, with the legs and feet of a goat.

In general Aquane have the ability to know the past and the future, but the present is lost to them. Furthermore they have powers over all types of water on earth and over the rain itself. Although they are often described as fearful of humans, sometimes they have been said to marry humans. In these cases, after a certain time they disappear, never to be seen again. They can sing mysterious dirges or laments and often come to give advice to young men. According to several accounts, it is better to not know the personal names of the Aquane, for fear of being spirited away forever. In some legends the Aquane are accompanied by waterfowl and weave on the loom. Here it is very interesting to note that on the rock 1 of the National Park of Naquane there are seven petroglyphs of looms!

Alinei also describes sites that would appear to be evidence connecting the Aquane with rock art. In Friuli, near Clauzetto, one hears of the Clap des Aganes (rocks of the Aquane) that bear engraved "footprints" (most likely cup marks), which are related to the legend of the Aquane. Naquane is therefore not the only prehistoric rock art site connected to the Aquane. Finally, at Lagole de Calalzo, in Cadore, the local inhabitants spoke of the Laganes (Aquane) who lived around the sulfur springs, where there was a Paleo-Veneto sanctuary, as indicated by numerous *ex voto* offerings found therein.

Just beyond the borders of Naquane Park in Valcamonica is a small church dedicated to Saints Faustina and Liberata. These two women lived as hermits in small caves in the Medieval period, and are said to have saved Capo di Ponte from an avalanche by blocking the falling boulders with their own hands. In the church crypt one can, in fact, still see a large rock with the deeply engraved prehistoric handprints and cup-marks, which legend would connect with these two Saints. This site is also connected to the Christian celebration (the Ascension) that takes place in May and precludes a long nocturnal vigil with extravagant use of candles. It is quite probable that this ceremony has transplanted an earlier pagan rite of spring (called "May") closely related to fertility rites. This nighttime festival (which was abolished after the visit of San Carlo Borromeo to the valley because he deemed it immoral) was also the occasion for participants to conclude their commercial affairs. Items bought and sold included not only domestic animals, as still happens today, but also iron instruments forged in the local blacksmith workshops which were among the most important Medieval period manufacturing sites in the Valley (Bontempi 1989). Here one discerns a clear tie between the rite, the fertility theme, and the iron that was made into weapons. According to those living near the church of the Saints, until the 1950s, pilgrims came from all parts of the valley to place their hands in the prints carved in the boulder and ask for protection and grace.

To me it appears valid to connect these Saints with the Aquane, not only due to the church's proximity to the site of Naquane, but also because the church and engraved stones lie near the stream Serio, which flows only a few meters away. Furthermore, legend describes the Saints just as the Aquane are—they live in caves and act as helpers, another role that folklore often attributes to the Aquane. It is also interesting to note that on the Great Rock of Naquane, there is an Iron Age male anthropomorph (identifiable by his phallus) who holds his own spread-apart legs in his hands. This is an extremely rare rock art scene but a close parallel is found in the nearby Church of the Monastery of San Salvatore (dating to the eleventh century), where one of the Romanesque capitals has a siren motif (an Aquane) who holds her own legs spread apart around the corners of the capital.

This connection between aquatic divinities and the occurrence of rock engravings also has a precedent in the Copper Age rock art locality of *Valzel de Undine* at Borno (the valley and stream of the *Ondine*). These Ondine are aquatic nymphs, always present in the legends of the Ladin, who bear all the same attributes as the Aquane.

Returning to Naquane a very important point of discussion is the well-known fact that there is no water at this site.[7] So why is the water theme so important in both rock art (boats and waterfowl) and toponomy? The glacial morphology of the site itself offers some clues. Two points seem paramount. The first is the rocks' morphology, glacially polished and sculpted in a way that sometimes shaped true waves into the horizontal bedrock surfaces (Figure 3). The second point is that the glaciers have sometimes created hollows and small pools where rain water remains for significant time after a storm. I suggest that the prehistoric imagination created some questions about the origins of these phenomena: Who created the waves? Is this petrified water? Is someone living in these petrified waves? Are these small pools the places where the Aquane can emerge from the petrified waters? Answers to these hypothetical questions all appear in the rock art imagery.

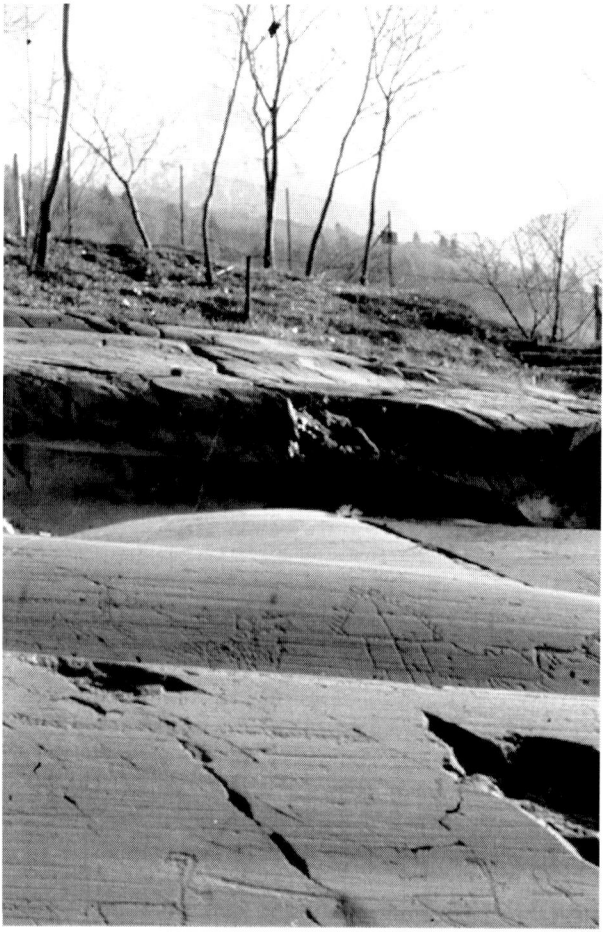

Figure 3. "Petrified waves" on rock 35 in the National Park of Naquane, Capo di Ponte. The peak Pizzo Badile is in the background.

For me this was only an interesting hypothesis until I found that local tradition contained a belief of spirit beings living in engraved rocks. This happened in 1997 during an archaeological project conducted with a school class at Esine, in Valcamonica. The archeological cooperative, Le Orme Dell'Uomo, manages classes where we teach students to draw and record the engravings. With such classes we usually go to local rock art sites of less tourist importance, hence we were working at a petroglyph site called Librinì at Esine, in the township of Plemo. As usual, I asked the students to ask their parents and grandparents if they knew of any legends about the area's rock art. The next day a student indicated a huge rock with a single cup mark—which had not attracted our attention before—and said, "According to my grandparents, and other people in Plemo, this rock has an interesting tradition." I was surprised and asked her to continue. "They say that in this area lived a lady called *sciurina dei pé de cavra* (in Camunian dialect 'the young lady with the goat's feet') who, putting her hoof into a cup mark, opened the rock where she used to eat her prey. The legend says that the lady enjoyed scaring people, above all hunters and visitors to the woods. When they were passing, she jumped out of the rock to kidnap them. Behind her house, says the legend, there was a well where she threw the skulls of the victims. The legend further relates that a group of men captured and chained her to a mountain but she was able to escape and during the full-moon nights one can still hear the sound of the chains that she is carrying to revenge her capture."[8]

This legend was very important for me because it proves that the idea of spirit beings living in the rocks really existed, and it also gives one interpretation for the cup marks.[9] However, most important was the fact that the spirit living in the rock is described as are the more recent Aquane, a woman with goat's feet. In this later guise, she lost the mermaid attributes but kept the more evil characteristics. The skulls referenced in the legend also imply some sort of votive ritual (human sacrifice?) related to the rock art.

The Images at Naquane and Their Religious Iconography

Currently this is the only local legend known that describes beings living in engraved rocks. However, the art contains other figures best interpreted as "living" in the rocks. The "busts of praying people" are anthropomorphs engraved to show only their upper body, head, or head and shoulders (Figure 4). Some of these hold weapons as if to indicate males. Gaudenzio Ragazzi (1995) hypothesizes that these engravings are functionally similar to figures painted on Greek and Etruscan vases that represent ground-dwelling spirits appearing in front of the warriors. This evidence suggests that the Aquane are not the only beings living in this "other world" inside the rocks.

Angelo Fossati 265

Figure 4. One warrior and a "bust" of another on rock 1 in the National Park of Naquane, Capo di Ponte.

Sometimes these "praying bust" rock art figures are engraved near deer. The association with deer is best understood in the context of initiatory and cultural interpretation that appear to have influenced Cammunian rock art of the first millennium B.C. Deer are represented in different contexts: Sometimes hunted, sometimes ridden like a horse, and sometimes drawn in all male herds.

Although deer riding seems strange at first glance, it could have been imitative of some divinity. In the Irish saga of Cu Chulainn, the Celtic hero tames a deer and ties it to his chariot, then later in the story hero does the same with two swans. This union of deer and bird is by no means coincidental and has a very precise religious meaning.

Camunnian rock art shows what is considered the most ancient European version of the God Cernunnos, a divinity that is a cross between deer and bird. The God, engraved on Naquane's rock 70 (Figure 5), is shown standing wearing a long tunic. He has deer antlers on his head, clasps a knife in his right hand, and wears an armlet on the same arm. A swan's neck and head emerges from his upper body. A worshipping figure stands beside him. The other images we know of Cernunnos are mostly from the Celtic world. He appears on an altar in Paris (where his name is also written), on the famous Gundestrup Cauldron from Denmark, on an embossed silver sheet from Waldalgesheim, Germany, and on a number of Irish stelae. In all these representations (spanning the period from the fourth century BC to medieval times) the divinity, appears with his head crowned by deer's antlers, sitting cross-legged, and clasping a torque (a metal bracelet) or a knife. He is often associated with snakes and wild and domesticated animals, including oxen and bulls, wolves, and deer (Fossati 1991).

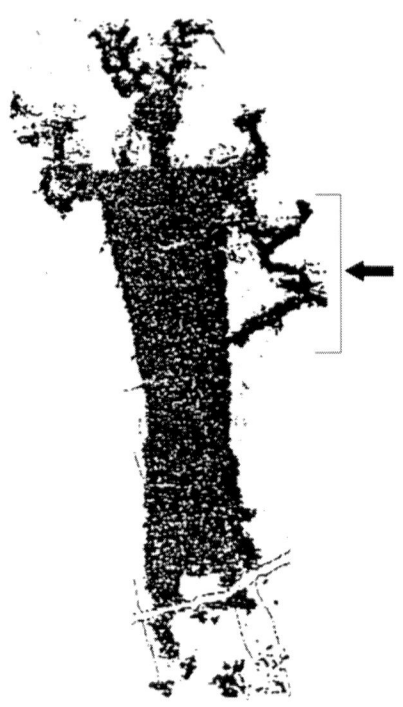

Figure 5. Cernunnos, engraved on rock 70 in the National Park of Naquane, Capo di Ponte. The arrow at right indicates the ornithomorphic protoma coming out of the god's body (see also Figure 6).

The ornithomorphic protoma motif (bird's head and neck) appears elsewhere in Valcamonica and Valtellina rock art (Figure 6). In Camunnian rock art the boat is not associated with the sun, even though such imagery is common as decoration on weapons and bronze laminae in central Europe starting from the thirteenth century BC. Shields, breastplates and greaves (lower leg armor), some of which were found in northern Italy not far from Valcamonica, illustrate this ancient myth of the sun being transported by flying swans. The idea of swans carrying the sun evidently arose from the observation that swans can both fly and swim, hence they can carry the sun through the sky and underwater where it disappears at night.

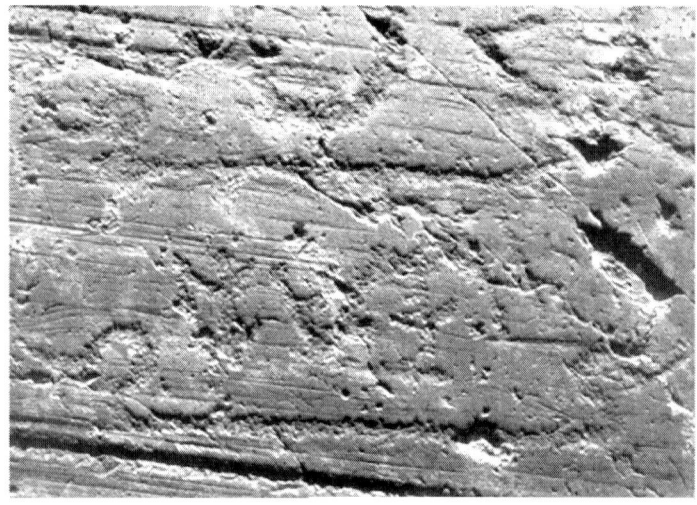

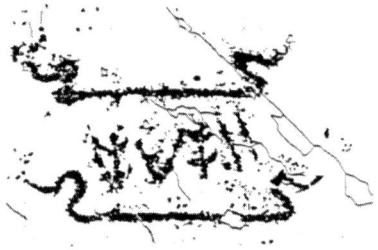

Figure 6. Ornithomorphic boats on rock 50 in the National Park of Naquane, Capo di Ponte. Inset at lower right shows tracing of figures in photograph.

At the end of first Iron age the sun boat progressively loses its symbolic meaning in favor of an iconography where horse motifs occur ever more frequently. After the fifth century BC the sun boat virtually disappears from the figurative language of manufactured articles. The ornithomorphic boat and waterfowl, as well as transporting the sun, also transport the souls of dead warriors to the world beyond. The boat—with ornithomorphic protomae—is thus the sun's "vehicle" in the cosmology of the prehistoric peoples. It is thus probable that the Camunnian Cernunnos, prior to the 5th century BC was considered to be a sun God for these reasons. The Celts adopted the cult of Cernunnos following their contact with the alpine peoples, and with him came the association of deer, important not only in economic terms but also from a religious viewpoint (De Marinis 1988; Fossati 1991).

Cernunnos does not exclusively have a solar meaning. The court of animals that surrounds him on the Gundestrup cauldron suggests he had the role of "lord of the fairs." In the Welsh Gaelic account of the Mabinogion, in the story of The Lady of the Fountain, a black character appears with one eye, one foot and a great iron club in his hand. He is described as guardian of the forest. Asked by the story's protagonist what power he had on the forest animals, the black man

> "took the club in his hand and with it struck a stag a mighty blow till it gave out a mighty belling, and in answer to its belling, wild animals came till they were as numerous as stars in the firmament, so that there was scant room for me to stand in the clearing with them and all those serpents and lions and vipers and all kinds of animals. And he looked on them and bade them go graze. And then they bowed their head and did him obeisance, even as humble subjects would do to their lord" (Ross 1967:183).

Cernunnos is not the only horned divinity worshipped by the Celts, nor is he the only one to be associated with deer. Ross (1967) has amply discussed the presence of horned divinities in the Celtic religious world of Great Britain. Among these are Esus and Vosegus who also frequently have a deer as a companion in their iconography. Vosegus is particularly interesting in that he is also associated with a bird, recalling the Camunnian Cernunnos.

One also sees a connection between Cernunnos and water. The birds that accompany these divinities are usually waterfowl. Given the role of these water birds in soul transport (discussed above) we can infer that the associated deer may have had a similar psychopompous role in this context.

Naquane: A Change in Site Structure Through Time

Returning conceptually to the site of Naquane, the presence of the Aquane—female spirits—seemed out of place in a masculine site dominated by Iron Age warriors. This caused me to rethink the general view of the site's structure that I had developed. The principle question was why were there female figures in a male site? Only after I had phrased the question in this way did it occur to me to ignore the Iron Age figures engraved at Naquane and focus exclusively on the earlier images. It was then that I discovered that almost all of the remaining figures belonged to the Bronze Age and the majority were female anthropomorphs or objects that could be interpreted as female symbols (e.g. shovels and looms). Imagining the site with only Bronze Age figures, it is possible to understand the relationship between rock 50 of Naquane, where numerous schematic praying figures are present, and rock 35 where a group of six engraved shovels is placed apparently to act as public art to interdict entry to the site by occasional visitors.[10]

Another interesting scene is engraved on rock 32 where a group of female figures stands just above a small glacial channel observing

Figure 7. A group of female figures on rock 32 in the National Park of Naquane, Capo di Ponte.

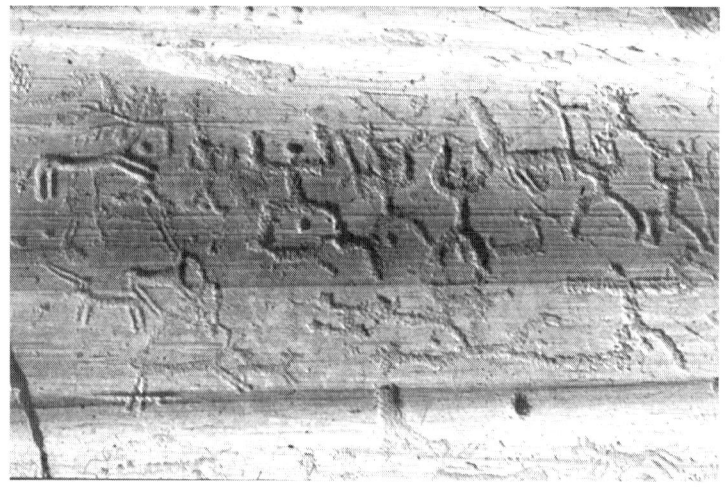

Figure 8. A group of female figures on rock 1 in the National Park of Naquane, Capo di Ponte.

another reclining female figure carved in the channel bottom (Figure 7). Previous interpretations[11] described these figures as a scene in which the prostrate woman was variously identified as dead, in childbirth, or as a ritual initiate. This scene is considered to be a ritual gathering because it appears in the same form not only on rock 32 of Naquane, but also on rocks 1 (Figure 8) and 44 in the same site, on rock 4 of the site *In Valle* and on rock 51 of *Vite* at Paspardo.[12] However, if one considers the placement of the reclining woman in this glacially carved channel, there is reason to associate this scene with a water theme. The surface on which this scene is carved is mostly dry (the area where the group of women stands), but sometimes the area where the one woman lies is wet. Visiting the site one day after a rainstorm I noticed that the soil above the petroglyph was still water saturated and, like a sponge, it released a slow trickle down this glacial channel. As the water flowed down the channel it suggested the idea of a stream in which the reclining woman became a swimmer.[13]

Thus, Naquane originally appears to have been thought of as a female site. It became a male site later, during the Iron Age, when female figures were replaced by images of a warrior world. However, this Iron age masculine world did not cancel the idea that the site was a female space in ancient times, because despite the fact that the area's Iron age rock art is interpreted as votive images engraved on the occasion of young men's initiation rites, we must remember that these warrior images were probably dedicated to the Aquane, who (as noted in legends) helped the young warriors to pass their tests.

This was my first success in finding legends and ethnographic information that could be used for interpretating Valcamonica rock art. But other information soon came to light.

The Three Brother Saints and the Copper Age Menhir

In 1993 I was working on the theme of "deer in rock art" for a major exhibition held in New Delhi in collaboration with the Indira Gandhi National Centre for the Arts (Fossati 1993b). A local legend attracted my attention due to its apparent relationship with Copper Age rock art.

Alpine Copper age rock art is linked by a series of common features. Rather than using the smooth, horizontally-lying, glacially sculpted bedrock, Copper Age artists preferred to carve and erect 'menhirs,' large tombstone-shaped boulders set vertically into the ground, or 'statue-stelae,' rough-hewn boulders carved to represent anthropomorphic forms.

Copper Age menhir rock art in the alpine area can be subdivided into four main geographic groups: two to the west (the Aosta-Sion and Lunigiana groups); and two in the east (the Valcamonica-Valtellina and Trent-South Tyrol groups). This distinction is not merely geographical, but also morphological: In the two western groups the illustrated monuments form true and proper statue-stelae, while engraved menhirs and stelae-menhirs are mostly to be found in the Valcamonica-Valtellina group. The Trent-South Tyrol group contains both stelae-menhirs as well as statue-stelae. Furthermore the Valcamonica-Valtellina group has its own peculiarities inasmuch as the anthropomorphic elements are virtually always suggested by symbolic imagery (Casini and Fossati 1994).

These Valcamonica-Valtellina monuments, associated as they are with analogous objects present elsewhere in Europe during the Copper age, are recognized as the first representation of anthropomorphic divinities in the alpine region. Male and female elements are equally present and marked by an entire series of recurring attributes. The male stelae are nearly always armed, the dagger being most frequent, while the female figures are characterized by breasts or by double spiral pendant symbols that mimic breasts. Some stelae bear armed figures that also wear this double spiral pendant. Perhaps these relate to mixed (androgynous) deities, or a female warrior similar to Minerva or the alpine goddess, Reitia. Stelae of small people are also present, perhaps depicting adolescents or children.

On the monuments of the two central-eastern groups, especially those of Valcamonica-Valtellina, tame and wild animals are represented in addition to the symbolic objects that also recur in the stelae of the western groupings (e. g. the eye pendants, daggers and axes). The peculiarity of the Valcamonica-Valtellina group lies in the presence of deer among these animals. The antlers of this animal are sometimes straight but others are crescent-shaped with undoubted allusions to the shape of the sun. This is best illustrated in the Ossimo 7 stela where a stag with crescent-shaped antlers has been engraved in the upper center, placed in a prominent position in relation to the other animal figures. Here sun and deer seem to share the same symbolic meaning. In this context the deer seems to play an important role from a symbolic point of view, acting as an intermediary between the cosmic world and the earth.

Anthropomorphic figures on some stelae, representing a personage called the "Sun god," are symbolically united with the deer. In fact sometimes the solar crown that hovers above the head of the sun god engraved in the Camunnian menhir is very similar to a crescent-shaped deer's antlers. Some authors (especially De Marinis 1994) have studied the three recurring anthropomorphic figures (as in Ossimo 9, see Figure 9) and the three apparently related deer. The Ossimo 9 stela shows we are dealing with two male characters, one of whom carries the solar emblem, and a third female character. The solar characters are also associated with two axes, thus taking on a warlike connotation.

Having categorized the Valcamonica-Valtellina menhirs in this way, I was reminded of an ancient Christian legend particularly alive in Valcamonica, especially in the Borno-Ossimo Plateau—the area where several of these engraved boulders have been found. The legend, often called "Glisente and his siblings" or "The three solitaries (hermits) of the mountain" is set at the time of Charlemagne, in the Carolingian period (eighth and ninth centuries AD). It tells of two warrior brothers and their sister, who decided, after various trials, to give up their warlike

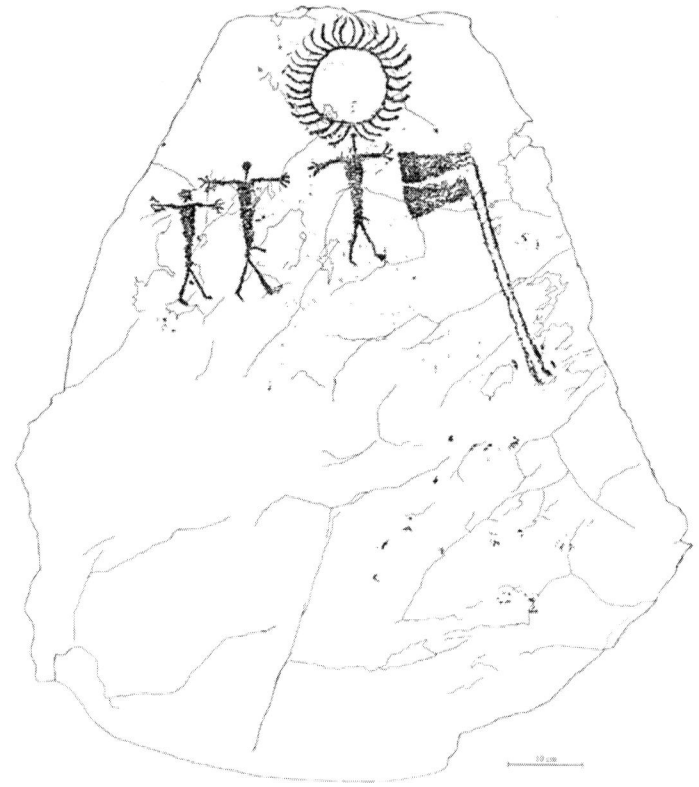

Figure 9. Three anthropomorphs with the Sun symbol on the Ossimo 9 menhir. Note that the anthropomorph at left is a woman, as indicated by the dot between her legs, while the other two males have erect phalluses.

activities and retire to the mountain as hermits. Every morning, at the rising of the sun, Glisente, the elder brother was visited by a white stag (or a white doe in some legends) who came from the East, bringing him a mysterious branch with golden fruit. In the evening a wolf brings him a burden of firewood. Every night after that the three hermit siblings sent luminous signals to each other by lighting fires because

"then we will pray together. The fire of the night will be the only bond of our existences, the sole remembrance of the world and of the blood" (Morandini 1927)

The connections between the characters of this legend and the three figures usually engraved on the menhirs seem evident. Furthermore Glisente seems to have the solar association that the engraved boulders show for one of the characters of the triad. But the most interesting part of the legend is when it refers to the Borno-Ossimo Plateau and to menhirs thereon:

"Left at the beginning of the evening, from Breno, they went all over the top of that mountain chain that, elongating in the middle of the valley, divided it into two different parts and they stopped in that esplanade that the descendants called *of the hermits* and where up to this time it is possible to see three boulders that remember their rest…" (Morandini 1927; Ertani ND; Gaioni 1990).

The data that emerge from recent studies at the site of Asinino close to Ossimo (Fedele 1995) correspond with what we know of this legend. Around the stelae at this site, rituals were carried out that included the use of fire, as evidenced by some burned objects, among which a seed and a bone have been recognized. Additionally, the stelae faced eastward in the direction of the rising sun.

Furthermore, fire, light and deer appear related by comparative linguistics. In some Indo-European languages, the word 'deer' derives from the root *bhren*, from which come the Greek *brendos* and the Grecomessapic *bréntion*. The Messapi lived in ancient Puglia, and their capital city *Brindisi* takes its name from the same root word because its port, according to Strabone, was shaped like a deer's head. The connection with fire is evident not only in the German *brennen* and English *burn*, but also in plant names like *brendolo* (from the Pugliese dialect), a pyrophitic plant that grows in the forest after a fire, where it is especially sought after by deer. Finally the Greek *bronté* means thunder and lightning.

Here one might ask what kind of association could exist between deer and the sun to make them symbolically similar? This similarity is so strong, in fact, that prehistoric artists created formal parallels of shape between antlers and the sun, and made these relationships part of their linguistic structure.

The deer can be thought of as emblematic of nature due to its well-known annual shedding and regrowth of antlers. This annual cycle mimics the growth of plant leaves (that emerge, grow, fall, and then sprout again to renew the cycle) and even the rising and setting of the sun. The associations with fertility and fecundity are strong and striking. It is not known, however, whether this is a true possible zoomorphization of the sun, or instead if the deer merely represents the sun's vehicle, like the swans of the Iron age and the horse at a later date (Fossati 1993b). In either case, the deer then could stand for the link between the sky and the earth and thus explain why they are frequently the principal animals in the compositions.

Sliding on the Devil Rocks: A Cautionary Note

I have always been attracted by site names, but only a few are obviously (or metaphorically) able to provide some explanation of their rock art. Names of some famous sites indicate biological or geological characteristics (e.g. *Bedolina* is linked to the presence of the birch-tree in the area, while *Seradina* is the place where the valley narrows). Such names provide no clue about the rock art. Other names are more interesting, in that they give a general idea that the site was thought to be inhabited by spirits. *Vite-Deria,* one of the major sites near Paspardo, has a special locality called *La 'al di spiriti* (The valley of the Spirits), where there is a rock engraved with more than 700 figures! Another similar name is *Coren de le Strie* (the Rock of the Witches[14]) at Sonico, in northern Valcamonica, where the rocks show engraved shovels (a typical female object [Fossati 1998]). In the south of Valcamonica, at Rogno, we have *Coren Pagà* (the Rock of the Pagans), where the use of the word pagan is from the ancient Christians who labeled as pagan anything that was not related to Catholicism. Another southern site, at Piancamuno, is *Coren di Marte* (the Rock of Mars), a rock where more than 150 cupules may be related to the Roman cult of Mars.

References to the devil occur at two sites in southern Valcamonica. At Pisogne *Coren del Diaol* (the Rock of the Devil) is a site with cupules, and near Paspardo is the *Bröscaröla del Diaol* (the Slide of the Devil). This rock has Iron Age warrior figures several of which have been almost "erased" by its use as a slide by the youth of Paspardo.[15] Sliding was done by gliding directly on the rock surface or using a wooden tablet or flat stone as a "sled." In Valcamonica we have several archaeological examples of these rock slides at rock art sites. Slides are found on rocks 1 and 50 in the National Park of *Naquane* at Capo di Ponte (Figure 10); at *Foppe di Nadro* (rocks 1, 2, and 3),

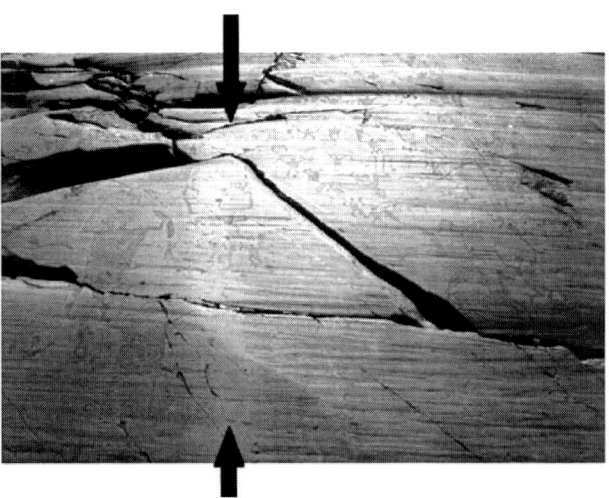

Figure 10. A slide, the light-colored abraded area indicated by the arrows, is superimposed on Iron Age figures on rock 50 in the National Park of Naquane, Capo di Ponte.

Bröscaröla del Diaol at Paspardo, and *Campanine* at Cimbergo in the Regional Park of Ceto, Cimbergo, Paspardo; at the site of Bedolina at Capo di Ponte, at *Dos Mirichi* near Pescarzo, and at *Coren de le Fate* at Sonico. Elsewhere in the Italian alps we find similar slides in the National Engravings Park of *Grosio* in Valtellina, in the petroglyph area of *Bard* in Val d'Aosta, at *Malesco* (Figure 11) in Val Vigezzo, and in the Natural Park of *La Bessa* near Biella. Outside Italy there is a well known slide in the Archaeological Park of *Le Lozes* near Aussois in the Haute Maurienne, France.

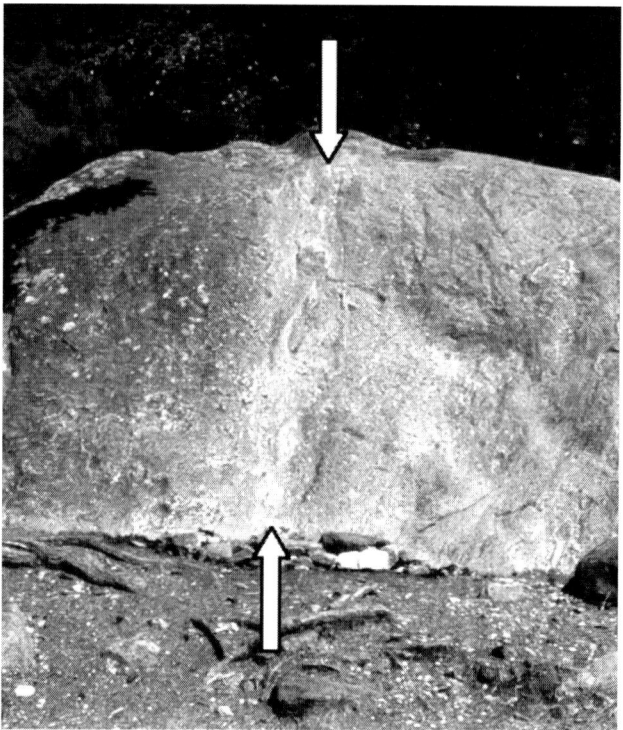

Figure 11. This slide, indicated by the arrows, is called "Sasso Scivolone" (the rock of the Big Slide). It is at Malesco in Val Vigezzo, Piemonte, Italy.

Today sliding on the rocks is done for fun rather than ritual, but there are special European sites where ritual sliding was done. In Brittany (France) women slid on particular rock surfaces in the belief that it enhanced conception or childbirth (Sébillot 1990). In other cases women did not slide but simply sat on stones and rubbed their belly.

Why might such gestures and touching behavior occur? In many religions, touching an object with magic or religious meaning (as modern Christians kiss relics or touch parts of statues like the feet of St. Peter in the Vatican) puts the believer in direct contact with the power of the object. This power mysteriously transfers to the person making the gesture. Sometimes it is believed that objects can be "infected" by such power, and thus today pilgrims rub handkerchiefs on a particular sacred site, like a tomb of a saint or the place of an apparition.

Based on ethnographic analogy it is widely accepted that, since Paleolithic times, prehistoric humans believed that some rocks had particular magic capacity or power and sometimes were a medium to communicate between different dimensions of existence. Moreover there was the belief (which still exists as relic folklore as shown by this paper) that rocks were inhabited by spirits. So in the case of sliding it could have been believed that fertility or easy delivery would have been a power in the rock that could pass to needy women. The problem in Valcamonica is to apply these ethnographically known rituals and beliefs to the rock slides found here and elsewhere in the Alps.

To evaluate this we must consider two facts. First, the rocks are today still used by youth as non-religious play, but not by women looking for easy conception or delivery. There are no indications of fertility rituals using the rocks at these sites in the recent ethnography. Furthermore, the activity of sliding, especially in those places where the slide is made on top of an engraved rock, usually has canceled the prehistoric engravings. On rock 50 at Naquane some warrior figures belonging to the first century AD have been almost erased. Additionally, there is no instance yet known where pre-Roman petroglyphs are superimposed on any slide. This combination of factors demonstrates that this sliding activity is not prehistoric but must be of more recent age. Thus until better direct information can be provided, I think it is misleading to talk about the sliding on the rocks as "a surviving unconscious belief of a pre-Christian and archaic faith" (Sansoni et al. 2001:226).

Invented Ethnography: The Case of the Spirit of the Mountain
To conclude my paper I describe a case that is well known in Valcamonica and constitutes a point of interest for my discussion. This is the so-called "Spirit of the Mountain" (Figure 12). What is this Spirit of the Mountain and what is the history that has popularized it so much, that if you go to the Capo di Ponte Municipality Internet page (www.voli.bs.it), you will discover that it is listed as one of three primary reasons for the presence of rock art in the area?[16]

The name Spirit of the Mountain refers to an atmospheric phenomenon that takes place during spring and autumn equinoxes. Anati (1962) describes this strange phenomenon in the book "Capo di Ponte," one of the first dedicated to the rock art of Valcamonica, where he presents a photograph with this caption:

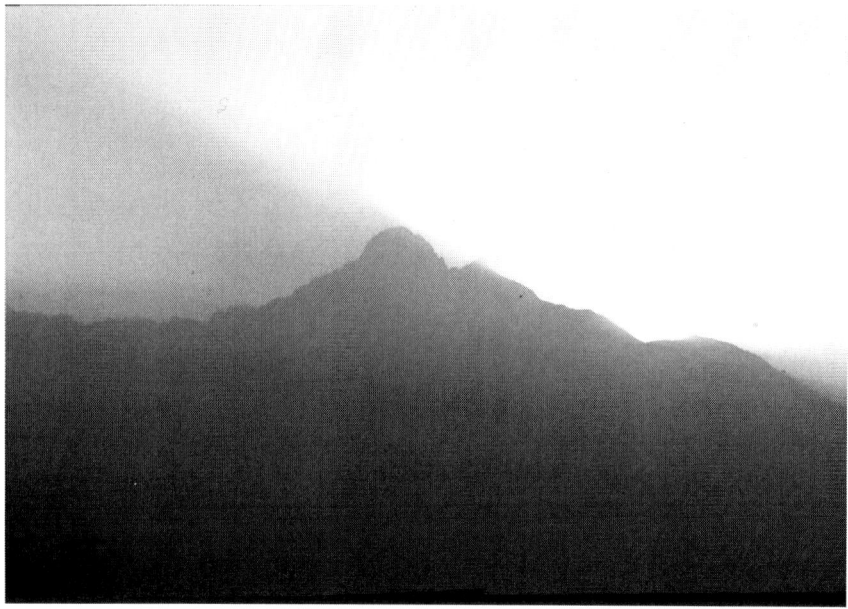

Figure 12. The "Spirit of the Mountain" is a shadow projected in the Sky from the sun rising behind the top of the major peak, Pizzo Badile.

"In springtime and in autumn the sun rises behind Pizzo Badile. The shadow of the top is projected towards the sky sometimes forming suggestive shapes which the popular legend call[s] 'the spirit of the mountain.' The Naquane area is located at the foot of Pizzo Badile."

It must be noted that in following volumes dedicated to Camunnian rock art Anati never returned to this point, nor again attributed the presence of the rock art in the valley to this atmospheric phenomenon. I have tried to find the origin of this popular legend without success. To the best of my knowledge there are no ethnographic sources for it.

So why is this phenomenon now so important in the local explanation of the rock art imagery? So important, in fact, that local tourist guides who conduct school groups to the rock art sites (especially *Naquane*) describe it as the major causal factor for the presence of rock art in Valcamonica. I believe that this is the fruit of an organized advertising campaign by a local rock art scholar, A. Priuli.[17] In his books, especially those addressed to the general public, he always mentions the Spirit of the Mountain. He suggests that, due to this phenomenon, Pizzo Badile was considered sacred even during prehistory and this is the reason why "maybe the engravings of Valcamonica are concentrated along the sides of the mountain and on the rocks of the opposite side of the valley" (Priuli 1983).

He also considers Concarena, the mountain on the opposite side of the valley, sacred because at sunset at the same time of the year there is a similar phenomenon.

I have always been fascinated by this interpretation, since first seeing the image in Anati's book, but having lived in Valcamonica since 1986 I can say that in recent years this phenomenon has assumed an importance with which I cannot agree.

Several factors are contrary to this explanation, which links the presence of important rock engravings to the Spirit of the Mountain. Specifically, there is rock art all along the valley, exactly where there are rocks suitable for engravings (because they were polished by the glaciers), sometimes in places where Pizzo Badile is not visible (e.g. the already cited *Coren de le Fate*). Moreover this phenomenon of projecting sunrise and sunset shadows across the sky is well known for many other mountain peaks in this same chain and others elsewhere in the Alps. Many of the areas associated with these other peaks have no rock art.

Given the conflict between the popularized interpretation and the archaeological evidence, I decided to interview some elders in the Capo di Ponte area.[18] From my interviews there was no one who could remember their grandparents or anyone else of that generation referring to the "Spirit of the Mountain." For them this is a well known and beautiful phenomenon, but nobody has ever associated it with mountain spirits or rock art.

Conclusions

In conclusion, Valcamonica rock art has only recently been studied in light of ethnography, but my research has uncovered evidence from site names, local legends and folktales, and various artifacts that can be used to help explain several aspects of the region's petroglyphs. These interpretations can then be integrated to help explain the structure of sites, which then leads to further avenues of study. Obviously, more research of this sort must be conducted, but these first successes show that there is no need to resort to invented "ethnography" to explain the rock art of the European Alps.

Author's Note: All figures courtesy of "Le Orme dell'Uomo."

[1] Usually called Ethnohistory in North America.
[2] My interest in the ethnography of Valcamonica dates to the period when I started documenting traditional dances, tales, songs, and legends of Lombardy
[3] In his major writings regarding Valcamonica rock Battaglia (1934) shows his wide knowledge of the European ethnography. He routinely compares some themes of Camunnian rock art with European ethnographical knowledge. The best examples of this are his description of dwellings (often correctly defined as granaries or haylofts, anticipating today's interpretation of these architectural figures) and of some ornamental elements of anthropomorphic figures such as helmets or hats.
[4] Some original names are still used, such as Redondo, Naquane, Foppe di Nadro, Campanine, and Seradina.
[5] *Civitas Camunnorum* was a city of great importance during the roman times, not less important than Brescia, Bergamo or Verona. In the city archaeologists have found a stadium, a theatre, a spa, and numerous private and public buildings of major size, including a temple of Minerva, from which a statue of the goddess has been recovered.
[6] The Map of the Contrada Aquane was brought to my attention by the former owner of the area, Battista Ruggeri, at that time guardian of the National Park. I was explaining to him that Alinei thought that the original name of Naquane could come from Aquane. Although I agreed with Alinei, I indicated that he had no proof of this because "...there is no map indicating this." "But I have this map and I will show it to you!" said Ruggeri. Dated to the beginning of the nineteenth century, the map is not the only document that testifies to this name. Later I discovered that also the cadastral maps of the area of Foppe di Nadro show the original name of the road that connects Naquane to Nadro as the *Strada delle Aquane* (Road of the Aquane).
[7] The two modern fountains available in Naquane take their water from a pool situated quite distant.
[8] The legend has been collected by Anna Erculiani, I C Scuola Media Statale "Don A. Sina" Esine.
[9] This particular cup mark can be interpreted as a technique to create a contact between two different realities, that of the real world with the world of the spirits.
[10] Ritual interdictions to special sites (sometimes with rock art) are known in many other parts of the world. One of the most famous is in Australia, where the site called Bulajang is linked to the God Bula (Gunn 1992).
[11] Including my own that I wrote a few years ago and which is still found on the interpretive panel at rock 32 in the National Park. Now, after a better understanding of the relationship of this site to the Aquane, I would add also this new hypothesis.
[12] But the scene on rock 32 is the only case where the woman lies in a glacial channel.
[13] I originally discussed this idea with G. Camuri who interprets the association of this female figure and the water in a slightly different way (Camuri 1995:282).

[14] This is the original toponomy. Today this rock is known as *Rock of the Fairies*.

[15] This rock was shown to me in 1988 by the late Giovanni Dassa, a guardian of the National Park of Naquane, who told me that when he was a child, he used to play on this rock, sliding with his friends.

[16] The other primary reasons are the "favorable climate" and the "richness of flat promontories." The presence of the beautiful sculpted and polished sandstone is not even mentioned!

[17] Priuli is considered a descendant of the Brescian school of rock art studies. In fact, he developed his chronological and interpretative ideas following the studies of E. Süss and M. Roberti. His works are very interesting for documentation and iconography but I completely disagree with him regarding chronology and interpretation of Camunnian rock art.

[18] Among them was Lucia Bottanelli, a well educated and very knowledgeable scholar of the traditional folklore of Pescarzo di Capo di Ponte, probably the most traditional place in the entire middle Valcamonica.

Discussion

Jean Auel: I just have one comment. When you were talking about the swans and the weaving looms, I thought of a fairy tale that I remember from growing up about seven brothers who were made into swans. In the daytime they had to be swans but at night they were brothers. And their sister had to weave jackets for them. Is there a correlation with that?

Angelo Fossati: Maybe that is related.

Jannie Loubser: When you showed the pictures of the slides [the evidence of sliding found on the rocks], I recalled Jasper Chalcroft who did some studying of them with Anati. If I recall correctly he said that sometimes infertile young women would slide deliberately across the (petroglyphs) so they can maybe gain fertility.

Angelo Fossati: Yes, this is something that occurred in Britany. We have ethnographical sources in the north of France where we have Sebillot who was an ethnographer at the end of the nineteenth century who wrote this. And there are also some popular reports of people sliding to obtain fertility on some particular places (in Britany).

Robert Layton: Also, in Sweden, as well.

Angelo Fossati: Yes, in the north we have this, but in the Alps we don't have any ethnographic information to support it. What we are told is that this is only a recent thing done for fun by young people.

James Keyser: I think it's important to remember that if those slides were, in fact, prehistoric we would probably find some petroglyphs superimposed on them. But you don't find that?

Angelo Fossati: Right, you don't find that. It's the opposite.

James Keyser: Yes, so, it seems that the sliding is a very much later phenomenon than the rock art.

Angelo Fossati: Yes.

CHAPTER 13
Fertility and Sexuality in Rock Art of the Southwestern United States: Rock Art Research and Cultural Affiliation
Kelley Hays-Gilpin

Introduction

Not much unites the diverse indigenous peoples of the American Southwest, apart from pervasive concern with rain and other aspects of the hydrological cycle. Most (but not all) groups grew corn, beans, and squash, and depended on scarce and unpredictable water sources. Their crops came from Mesoamerica, and for millennia, northern Mexican groups provided bridges for trade, migration, and cultural exchange between Mesoamerican civilizations and the Southwest. Many Southwestern peoples have linguistic relatives in California, the Great Basin, and the Plains as well as in Mesoamerica. It should come as no surprise, then, that rock art here reflects cultural connections in many directions. Rock art probably played active roles in negotiating boundaries, facilitating trade and migration connections, and promoting over-arching ideologies.

Almost every culture in the Southwest has traditions about rock art—who made it, why, and what it means to living people today. Members of at least a few native cultures, including some Hopi, Zuni, Yavapai, and Navajo people, still made rock art well into the 20th century, and perhaps continue today.

Ethnography and Contemporary Thought About Rock Art

Rock engravings and paintings had many contexts and many functions, even within a single cultural group. The historic and recent ethnographic record of rock art production, use, and meanings in the Southwest includes religious and non-religious, shamanistic and non-shamanistic contexts. Rock art imagery refers to individuals, kin groups, ethnic/tribal identities, ritual sodalities, territory, fertility, agriculture, rain, hunting, warfare, farming, and animal husbandry.

In the last couple of decades, culture resource management has expanded to include consultation with Native communities. Many Southwestern tribes have constituted their own cultural and historic preservation departments. Legislation such as NAGPRA and Section 106 of the National Historic Preservation Act put Native people in the position of having to seek scientific validation for their claims of cultural affiliation, site significance, and even land and water rights. Rock art is important in this process because it is tangible and located in particular places. Much of the time it can be dated, at least in a relative sequence. Many tribal representatives see rock art as providing validation for oral traditions, yet some interesting differences appear among tribes.

Hopi

Hopi consultants almost always identify rock art as the "footprints" of migrating clans, put on the rocks to mark the passage of particular social groups through a landscape. In this way, rock art is comparable to potsherds and remains of stone buildings. These were made by individuals, but each indicates what social group the maker represented. Thus, material culture that remains "in place" marks a locality as *socially* significant, in contrast to, for example, Yavapai and other Yuman interpretations, which often emphasize *spiritual* significance. Ethnography suggests a wide range of purposes and contexts for Hopi rock art, but the social element is always prominent.

As recently as the early 20th century, Hopi men made petroglyphs at Tutuveni, near the Willow Springs shrine, to record the clan identity of pilgrims on the Salt Trail. Of one such journey, Don Talayesva said,

> "we arrived at the shrine where Hopi salt gatherers carve their clan emblems on the rocks. Our ancestors had gathered salt for many generations, and there were hundreds of clan emblems cut into the rocky base of the shrine. Every traveler, on each successive trip, had carved another symbol to the left of his original one. My father had carved eleven sand dunes in the course of his life, and Talasvuyauoma had carved ten coyote heads. I selected a smooth surface nearby and carved my Sun symbol, also tracing my initials on the emblem; but I kept this secret, fearing that my companions would object to it as something modern. When I had finished, I placed the breath line of a prayer feather at the mouth of my Sun symbol, pounded it with a stone until it stuck, sprinkled corn meal upon the face of the emblem, and prayed" (Simmons 1942:234).

Further along the same trail, "upon the stone were tracings of chickens carved by the War Twins, a rooster daubed with red ocher, and drawings of hens and baby chicks." The War Chief leading the expedition said, "Here is a Chicken shrine. If you wish to have success with chickens, make an offering and pray for good luck" (Simmons 1942:139).

The Hopi are not descended from a single ethnic group, but from a variety of clans who migrated from different localities to join together between the AD 1100s and 1700s. Many petroglyphs depict items or kinds of knowledge owned by particular matrilineal clans or members of sodalities, which are owned by clans but whose membership cross-cuts kin groups. For example, images of the sun and petroglyphs that function as solar markers belong to the sun watchers, a priesthood owned by the Sun Clan and related clans. Members of other clans usually do not talk about such figures or sites. Different clans have different histories, different origins, and different ritual responsibilities, some secret.

Not all clan people spoke the Hopi language when they arrived to settle at Hopi, and some still do not. Many of the inhabitants of First Mesa still speak Tewa, not Hopi. Some petroglyphs were attributed to the Tewa, some to inhabitants of now abandoned villages founded by migrating clans. Water serpent petroglyphs near some Hopi villages are identical to those found in Eastern Pueblos (Stephen 1936:1011, Figure 496). Alexander Stephen lived on First Mesa in the late 1800s. He recorded Hopi identifications of many petroglyphs by subject matter, ethnic attribution, and function. His consultants identified shield figures on First Mesa as representing encounters with Ute and Apache warriors. One includes a tally of Apache men and women slain (Stephen 1936: Figures 83-84). Young men who found themselves in an "amorous" mood tossed stones at a particular shield figure, which is now thoroughly pockmarked (Stephen 1936: Figure 495). Stephen noted that somebody periodically repainted the pecked and rubbed figure of a maiden (Stephen 1936:1012, Figure 497), but he did not record a function or meaning for the image (Figure 1).

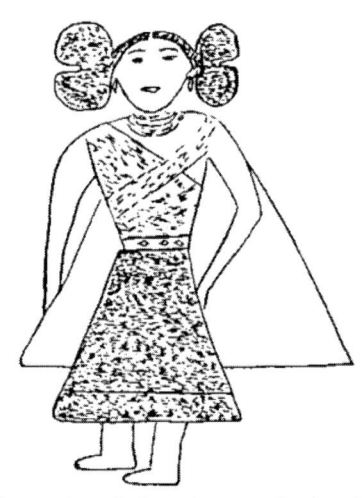

Figure 1. Painted petroglyph of a Hopi maiden with butterfly hair whorls, two feet high, sketched by Alexander Stephen in 1886 (Stephen 1936:Figure 497).

Zuni

Zuni pueblo lies about 100 miles southeast of Hopi. Although their languages differ (distantly Penutian vs. clearly Uto-Aztecan), traditional, historical and archaeological sources all point to frequent interaction between Hopi and Zuni people. Many clans and some ceremonies are shared. Jane Young studied rock art with Zuni consultants in the 1970s and 80s. Young is most interested in what rock art means to Zuni people today, not in how ethnography can help us understand past meanings and functions of rock art. Most Zuni consultants felt they had little to say about it. They thought older people might know more, and that Hopi people were likely to know more about "those designs on the rock" (Young 1988:xvii). Nonetheless, in visiting sites with Zuni people, Young found that they viewed rock art as important aspects of the landscape, integrated with springs, plants, birds, and so on. They associated some rock art with events from myths and legends. She noted that rock art continues to be produced by some tribal members today (Young 1988:6), but in deference to privacy, does not provide details. The early 20th century paintings of masks made by archaeological laborers at the Village of the Great Kivas are a well-known example

Young suggests that reasons for making rock art in the past probably differed from those of today, and that imagery has changed over time as well. Even where imagery is similar, meanings may have changed (Young 1988:7). For Zuni people today, rock art is visible evidence of the involvement of ancestors in daily life, of continuity with the ancestors, reminders of traditional Zuni stories, myths, and cosmological relationships, and how the landscape encodes past events and evokes the past in the present. Rock art links the power of images with the power of particular places (Young 1988:173)—not only with beings who did great deeds in the past, but with places where one finds water, game animals, particular plants, and other important resources. As at Hopi, some rock art near Zuni represents clans, the places where certain groups received their clan names, and the places where they stopped in their migrations to the Center Place. At least two sites near Zuni function as shrines for parents who wish to ensure the sex of a future child and one of these seemed to function as a fertility shrine for women who have been childless (Stevenson 1887, 1904; Young 1988:177).

Young noted that some sites seemed to be sacred because rock art was there, while in other cases, the rock art was thought to be there because the place was sacred. The question of cause and effect did not apparently interest the Zuni as it did the ethnographer. In at least one case, Young noted that Zuni consultants attributed spiritual potency to painted images, but not to the carved images at the same site. She suggests that the efficacy is in the paint itself (Young 1988:178), a concept consistent with other Pueblo and Mesoamerican ethnographic data about the equation of painting with "making sacred" and "finishing" an item (Odegaard and Hays-Gilpin 2002).

Rock Art Research

Despite a rich ethnographic record about rock art, in most cases ethnography about rock art itself does not help us very much with specific images and sites. We have to take some concepts from the rock art ethnography in combination with oral traditions, linguistic data, and cross-media comparisons. Sometimes, by looking for consistent patterns of association among images, or between landscape features and contexts and imagery, we can link images on the rocks with specific stories that are still told. By consulting with Native people about our interpretations, we can challenge, enhance, and expand them. That is, we can all learn something new or think about old things in new ways, as opposed to simply confirming our own Western preconceptions on the one hand, or accepting often anecdotal and unsystematically obtained fragments of traditional knowledge about rock art on the other.

Case Study: Maidens and Fluteplayers

As a case study in the indirect use of ethnography to understand Southwestern rock art, I will focus on certain sexed anthropomorphic images and Puebloan ideas about fertility, sexuality, and the social and spiritual roles of masculine and feminine personages and principles. Some of the images are sexually explicit. Traditional Pueblo people find such images both humorous and sacred, and not offensive, at least not in their original contexts. I do not intend to offend. I chose these images because we all know what they are: We understand their *iconicity*—what they represent (an icon is a signifier which resembles that which it signifies--in other words, something which carries meaning by virtue of resemblance, and iconicity refers to resemblance). Not all rock art images have this quality of iconicity—at meetings of rock art enthusiasts, discussions inevitably arise about whether a particular wavy line represents a map of a river, a snake, or the Milky Way, or whether a circle represents the sun, the moon, a shield, or a portal to a separate reality. Answers are few. In contrast, images of human bodies and sexual activities can be recognized by people of all cultures, at least most of the time. What we cannot say without contextual analysis and ethnography is why people drew these pictures when and where they did, and what they meant—that is, *iconology* (the study of subject matter and symbolism in the visual arts). Southwestern rock art imagery includes a very large number and variety of figures that are clearly identifiable as male or female, although the majority of human forms have no sex indicated. I will focus on two familiar figures: the maiden with butterfly hair whorls, and the phallic fluteplayer.

We can interpret figures with butterfly hair whorls as female for several reasons: first, some of them include explicit depictions of female genitals, and almost none can be interpreted as male. A few are ambiguous—does a simple line between the legs represent a penis or menstrual flow? Second, Hopi mothers still dress their daughters' hair this way as part of their puberty rite (Figure 2). Other pueblos have similar practices and similar hair styles.

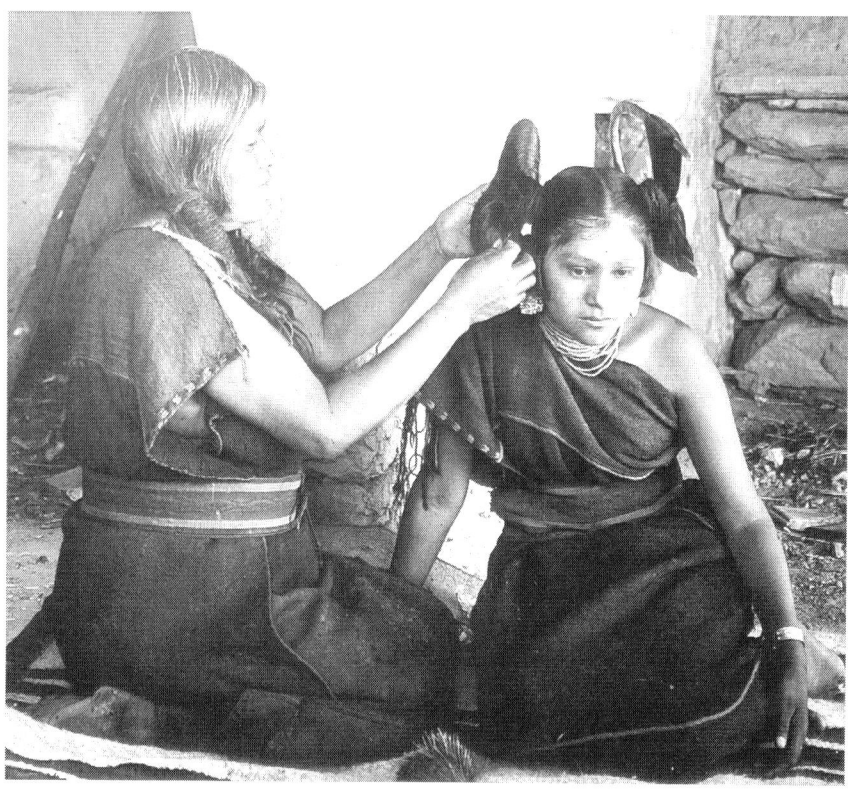

Figure 2. Hopi mother dressing her daughter's hair in butterfly whorls. (Photographed by Henry Peabody, ca. 1900. National Archives and Record Administration catalog number 79-HPS-6-3274.)

We can identify the fluteplayers as male for a similar set of reasons: many, though not all, have obvious penises. All oral traditions about a variety of flute-playing characters refer to them as males. The flute is one of several "tools" that are gendered masculine in the pueblos, together with digging sticks, bows, arrows, spears, and so forth (Loftin 1991). Flutes are the instrument of choice in courtship. Flutes found in burials are found with adult males only.

Euroamericans have long interpreted images of Pueblo maidens and fluteplayers as referring to "fertility." The litany usually goes like this: all people in all places and time are concerned with human procreation, "primitive" people are especially interested in procreation, "primitive" people are especially uninhibited when it comes to sex, and Indian cultures revered women because of their ability to procreate, etc. etc. One rock art enthusiast, a psychoanalyst from Germany (Hunger 1983) even insisted that depictions of sexual intercourse in rock art were depictions of real ceremonies, Indian versions of the ancient European "heiros gamos" or sacred wedding, in which 19th century scholars like James Frazer alleged that perfect strangers had sex in the fields to make the crops grow. This appeal to human universals is undoubtedly rooted in European Primitivism (Kehoe 1996), and in a fascination with sex stemming from Victorian mores that both repressed sexuality and promoted an obsession with it. This attitude is now firmly entrenched in American culture. The ethnographic reality is very different.

Consultation with Hopi elders suggested instead that for Hopi people, the girls' puberty ceremony is more about getting ready to fulfill social and ritual roles in Hopi society than it is about "fertility" (Hays-Gilpin 2002). "Maidens" are about social and ritual roles within the family and community. These roles include providing certain kinds of food for ritual practitioners, contributing to the family's reputation for hard work and generosity, and taking care of clan-owned ritual paraphernalia and knowledge. Images of "maidens" refer to fertility, yes, but not just of marriageable women. They are a metaphor for all kinds of potentiality, primarily of the growing corn plants, but also growth and the promise of future abundance, the continuation of families, and continuation of the whole ritual system they support.

In rock art, as in pottery and murals, images of maidens are not all the same thing, and they clearly do not all refer to the ability to have babies. Sometimes paintings of maidens are associated with granary structures, as in Canyon de Chelly, or with depictions of corn plants (Figure 3). Sometimes they are clearly vegetal/human combinations—corn maidens or squash maidens. Sometimes they appear with game animals. They often appear together in groups, often holding hands, sometimes alternating with other figures, possibly males, as in some contemporary social dances.

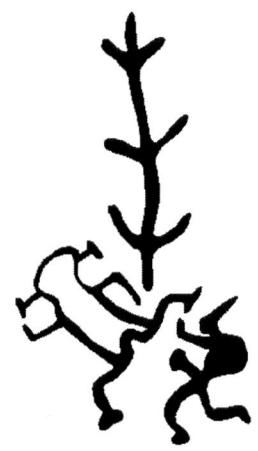

Figure 3. Fluteplayer, maiden, and corn plant, Velarde, New Mexico. (Slifer 2000:Figure 57t, courtesy of Dennis Slifer and the Museum of New Mexico Press).

Sometimes maidens are paired with male fluteplayers (Figure 4). Fluteplayer-maiden pairs, and other depictions of sexual activity, are much more common in the northern Rio Grande region than in the Western Pueblo (Hopi and Zuni) areas, suggesting they are more central to Tanoan and Eastern

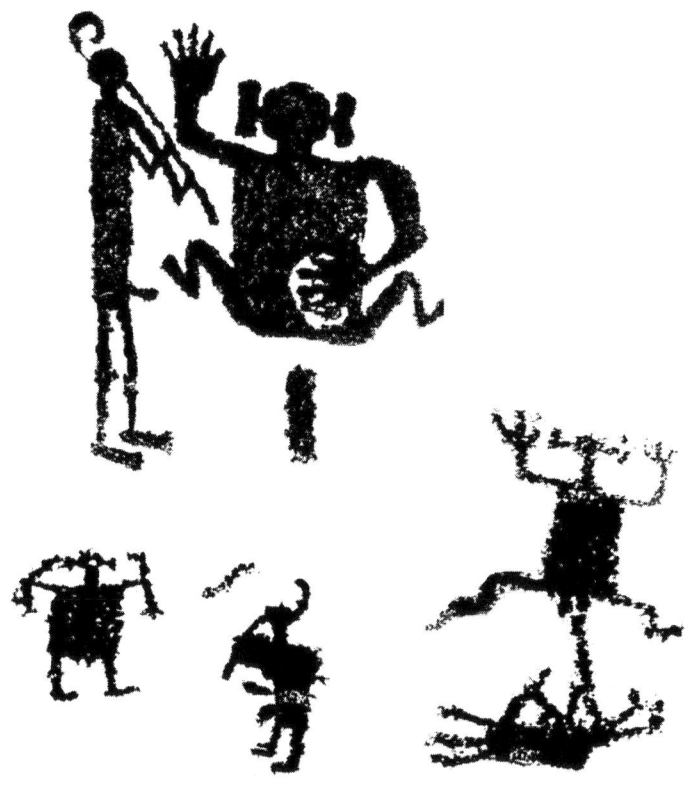

Figure 4. Fluteplayer-maiden pairs: upper, Catron County, New Mexico, courtesy of J. Louis Argend-Farlow; lower, La Cieneguilla, New Mexico, photo drawings by K. Hays-Gilpin.

Keresan traditions. Many pueblos share stories, ritual sodalities, and kin relationships, even across language groups, and western pueblo traditions include stories that could account for fluteplayer-maiden pairs, such as the Zuni story about how Paiyatamu, a young male solar deity, lures home the Corn Maidens, who fled mistreatment in the village. At Hopi, Stephen and Fewkes were told that a pair of men's and women's sodalities descended from *Taawa*, the sun, "who met a maid in the underworld and lured her to him by inhalation through a flute." He gave the mysteries of *Wuwtsim* to their son, and of *Mamzrau* to their daughter (Fewkes 1895:447). These remain the most important men's and women's sodalities at Hopi today.

Phallic fluteplayers are clearly not all the same thing, even though most may refer to fertility in a broad sense. Ironically, few, or perhaps none, of them are "Kokopellis" except in the popular imagination and the misidentifications of a few early scholars (Hawley

1937; see Malotki 2000). In the popular literature, several Hopi characters have been conflated, and attributed to rock art undoubtedly made in a number of cultural traditions from Mexico to Canada. *Kookopölö* is the Hopi robber fly/trickster figure, which does not carry a flute but often does have a prominent penis. *Lenhoya,* Flute Boy, is a totem of the Hopi Flute clans, several groups of affiliated families in several different Hopi villages. *Maahu* is a cicada whose "fluting" brings warmth. Neither *Maahu* nor *Lenhoya* necessarily has an erect phallus. *Maahu* traveled with the Flute Clan on their migrations, but also with a number of other clans as well, including the Sun clan, which also has something to do with bringing warmth necessary for germinating crops. The humped back of many of these figures may refer to the actual shape of certain insects, such as the robber fly and cicada, or to a backpack filled with seeds of all kinds, or perhaps both. *Kookopölö* is a seducer of young women, but notably used to appear with a female counterpart, *Kookopölmana,* his sister or wife, who "captured" and feigned intercourse with young men (Titiev 1939). The Zuni *Paiyatamu* and his eastern Pueblo counterparts also have to do with the sun and germination, as well as courtship and seduction. Nonetheless, Jane Young's Zuni consultants identified petroglyphs of humpbacked fluteplayers on the Zuni reservation as "*Hopi* rain priests." They also identified figures of maidens as *Hopi* maidens (Young 1988:208), even though Zuni girls in the past also had their hair put up in a somewhat similar style of butterfly whorls.

It is possible that many of the flute-playing figures in Southwestern rock art have no direct ethnographic referent, but refer to bygone practices and characters. Ann Phillips (2002) recently connected the curving headgear of many fluteplayer images with mountain sheep horns, rather than insect antennae, and points to several images of flute-playing mountain sheep along the San Juan River (Figure 5). She posits a transition from earlier rain-making practices associated with mountain sheep spirit helpers, probably shared by Hopi ancestors and other Uto-Aztecan speaking groups of the Southwest, Great Basin, and California, to flute-playing rainmakers. The earliest maize-bearing Uto-Aztecan migrants from Mesoamerica undoubtedly displaced local Archaic hunter-gatherers in some areas and merged with them in others, and migration, fission, and fusion continued unabated for millennia. The specific incorporation of referents to sun, warmth, courtship, insects, and germination as well as rain may have different histories. These ideas ended up in the same rich mix of oral traditions and iconographies seen in the Pueblos later on.

By the early 1300s, deliberate fusing of analogous symbolic traditions was probably an effective strategy that allowed Hopi clans, and those of other pueblos, to coalesce into villages with an integrated ritual

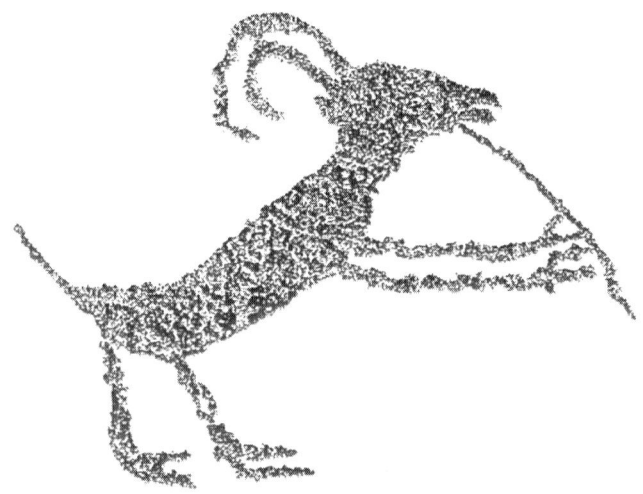

Figure 5. Fluteplaying mountain sheep, southeastern Utah (courtesy of Ann Phillips).

calendar that preserved a diversity of ceremonial responsibilities. Today, Hopi people recognize two major divisions of clans: Katsina clans who mostly came from the north, including Kayenta, Mesa Verde, and the Fremont area, and Palatkwapi clans, who mostly came from the south, but by various routes, including ancestors archaeologists would identify as Classic Hohokam, Chaco, Mimbres, northern Mexican, and so on. The two groups are complementary and their ritual roles are often viewed as mutually supportive and reciprocal. Eastern Pueblo dual divisions such as Turquoise/Squash and Summer/Winter "moieties" (actually sodalities because they are not exogamous) are even more overtly complementary.

I submit that the whole notion of reciprocity, rather than "fertility," best helps outsiders understand Pueblos in general, and the sexed rock art figures in particular. Within each clan and each family, men and women have complementary and interdependent relationships (Schlegel 1977). In Hopi cosmology, earth and sky, feminine and masculine personages respectively, exist in a dynamic inter-promoting relationship in which lightning fertilizes earth, the sun warms earth to promote germination, and the earth gives back crops, wild plants, and game animals. Water that comes from underground and water that comes from the sky move in a cycle, but they will not move without the efforts of living creatures. Humans, due to our moral shortcomings, have to work harder in our prayers and offerings than creatures like butterflies, birds, insects, snakes and flowers. Prayers are productive work, just as much as planting and weeding crops. Smoking, singing, making prayer sticks with "breath feathers" and paint blown from the mouth are part of the work it takes to move water in the form of clouds and breath from the earth to the sky (this not "sympathetic magic" or "bribing the gods" as previous anthropological traditions seem to indicate). Humans can enlist the help of other creatures, from frogs to spirit beings called the *Katsinam*. Making images of them, as well as of maidens, fluteplayers, warriors, and hunters, *may* also be viewed as a form of productive work that "gives back" for blessings requested or already received, though this notion bears further discussion.

It is within the context of reciprocity that we should understand the pueblo concept of "fertility" as well as sexuality. Although there *is* a "big picture," and probably common historical roots with many other cultures including those of the Great Basin and Mesoamerica, the details and differences are what will help us use rock art to establish migration routes, clan histories, and cultural affiliation. Rock art imagery also provides clues to the longevity of certain cultural practices. For example, Hopi women were interested to learn from Northern Arizona University archaeologists that the tradition of pubescent girls' wearing butterfly hair whorls goes back at least 1800 years, according to rock art evidence (Hays-Gilpin 2002). They suggested that knowing the practice is that old makes it even more urgent to preserve the girls' puberty ritual today. Perhaps, they suggested, if they know how long it has worked for their ancestors, girls might have more respect for their family traditions, and more pride in their own growing and changing bodies.

In all cases I know about, indigenous consultants indicate that they and the people they represent are interested in rock art. Rock art is an important part of the landscape. Its setting is just as important as the imagery, so recording alone is not a sufficient substitute for *in situ* preservation. Rock art is viewed as an important clue to cultural affiliation, who was where when, and what they were doing.

Acknowledgements

I extend my thanks to the symposium organizers and sponsors for a successful and productive gathering. Thanks to my Hopi language teacher, Emory Sekaquaptewa, and to the Hopi Cultural Preservation Office for their instruction, to Dennis Slifer for illustrations, and to the Museum of Northern Arizona, Harvard University, Hopi Tribe, and the Getty Foundation for co-sponsorship of the Southwest Mural Project. Any errors, misconstruals, or unjustified leaps of imagination are my own.

Discussion

Linea Sundstrom: This pairing. Does it appear in other media?

Kelley Hays-Gilpin: No, the alternating ones appear on pottery, but paired….. I don't think so.

Linea Sundstrom: Then it's only in rock art?

Kelley Hays-Gilpin: I think it's only in rock art.

Jean Auel: Is it on just open rock faces?

Kelley Hays-Gilpin: Usually, yes, especially in the Rio Grande where you have the basalt cliffs like you do here [on the Columbia River]. That's where most of those paired figures are—actually over on the Rio Grande. Then that one very stylized Mesoamerican-looking one with the Mother Earth/Father Sky pair is just an isolated boulder at the bottom of a canyon looking quite out of place, and it has to have broken off from somewhere else, but I can't figure out where it fell off from.

James Keyser: So, you think the petroglyph was incised and then the boulder broke off?

Kelley Hays-Gilpin: Yes, probably from the edge of the mesa.

Robert Layton: Can you expand a bit more about the ritual interdependence of females?

Kelley Hays-Gilpin: It's always been lost in the ethnographies. It's been reported as though the women prepare the food and nothing more. You know, the women prepare the food and the only time they're allowed down in the kivas is when they're bringing food to the men and then they have to leave. But that's absolutely not true. And you can read it in the early journals and accounts that women were in the kivas a lot. They were masculine gender places, so they called them men's places, but that didn't structure all the activities. Women were down there a lot; and it often didn't have to do with food. But at Hopi they also had their own women's societies and the two most important ones were paired with a men's society. The ceremonies are done at different times of the year, so they are seen as alternating. The men who are part of the *Wuwtsim* Society will help the women with the *Maraw* Society and vice versa. So there's a complementarity, but it's dynamic, it's in motion.

They're always passing the ball back and forth as it were. Another thing that's pretty interesting is about the act of spurting the paint from the mouth towards something and then painting it. That's finishing it—making it sacred—and Emory Sekaquaptewa (author of the Hopi Dictionary) thinks that's analogous to when women chew a little bit of food, especially corn, and spit in the pot—that's said to make it sweet. There may be something chemical to that.

David Whitley: Yes, it breaks down the carbohydrates, that's how you make beer.

Jean Auel: I read somewhere, that when they just first started making wine, that was one of the ways to make wine at home. One of the ways to get it to be right—to be wine instead of vinegar—was to chew some of it and spit it in.

Kelley Hays-Gilpin: Yes, and only the women did that, spitting the food. So Emory thinks that's the primary activity. And the men spitting the paint may be a metaphor for that, or a referent to that women's activity.

Don Hann: These complementary groups, do they share the same kiva at different times then, or do they have different ritual places. I assume they have some separate rituals.

Kelley Hays-Gilpin: Yes, they are doing some things separately, but there's almost never a woman's ceremony where there isn't some old man present to do certain things—mostly involving tobacco that only the men do. Although women will smoke it to make the clouds; but they don't prepare it. So they share a kiva and in some villages there might be a women's society kiva that's actually used most of the year by men. But then, that [kiva] is the focal point for the women's society in October, when it's their turn to focus on that. Women will come and go all day long, because they're also feeding their families and taking care of their kids. And the older they are, the more time a woman will spend in the kiva. Often the continuity is provided by an older man. He's the one who's there all the time, because he's the only one who's got time to do it. Women have to juggle all these other things, as well as their ritual responsibilities, and they don't even have menstrual seclusion. A Hopi woman is busy all the time.

CHAPTER 14
Rock Art and Rites of Passage in Far Western North America
David S. Whitley

That rock art was sometimes made during puberty initiations is well known, as demonstrated by over 100 years of ethnographic accounts in far western North America. But despite wide acknowledgment of this fact by ethnologists and archaeologists, this type of rock art has been somewhat ignored or at least understudied in favor of shamanic art [1]. Why this has occurred is uncertain; perhaps because the puberty art is aesthetically less spectacular; perhaps because its common mention in the ethnographic record makes it seem somewhat mundane. Regardless of cause, it is clear that it is deserving of study in its own right, not least because of recent confusions about this puberty art that some of those using the secondary and tertiary sources have introduced into the literature (e.g., Kehoe 2000:74-75). Indeed, it might be inferred that the ethnographic interpretation of rock art itself is now under attack (e.g., Quinlan 2000; Hedges 2001) and thus that an airing of the sources and evidence is warranted.

A review of the ethnographic record from far western North America—by which I mean California, the Great Basin and the Columbia Plateau—suggests that there were at least four general traditions of puberty rock art. These are: (1) the Takic tradition of SW California; (2) the Yuman tradition of the Colorado River and Desert region; (3) the cupule tradition of south-central California and the western Great Basin; and (4) the vision questing tradition of the Plateau. I discuss each of these, in turn, below. As this shows, puberty rock art was quite common although its manifestation varied, in some cases substantially, from tradition to tradition and region to region.

Takic Rock Art of Southwestern California

One ethnographically well documented rock art tradition was created by speakers of the Takic family of the Uto-Aztecan stock (called by Kroeber [1925], using an earlier linguistic classification, the "Shoshonean wedge" in southern California). These groups resided from the Los Angeles Basin and Transverse Ranges south to San Diego County, and from the Pacific Ocean eastward to about Palm Springs. They include the Gabrielino (Fernandeño/Tongva), Luiseño-Juaneño, Cupeño, Cahuilla and Serrano. The Diegueño (Ipai-Tipai/Kumeyaay), Yuman-speaking southern neighbors of the Luiseño who resided in San

Diego County and northern Baja California, also adopted aspects of the Takic tradition, including puberty initiate rock art (Kroeber 1925). As we shall see, however, this appears to have been grafted onto an existing Yuman puberty art tradition, further demonstrating the widespread nature of the general practice in the far west.

Ethnographic information about the Takic puberty initiation and, in certain accounts, the rock art that resulted, has been provided by DuBois (1908), Kroeber (1906, 1908a, 1908b, 1925), Sparkman (1908), Hooper (1920), Strong (1929), Harrington (1934,1978, n.d.a), Driver (1941), Drucker (1937), White (1963), Hill and Nolasquez (1973), Boscana (1978), Hill (1992) and Henshaw (n.d.). These have been synthesized by Steward (1929), True (1954), Hedges (1970), Minor (1975), Oxendine (1980), Cohen (1987) and Whitley (1992, 1996, 2000b, 2003), with Oxendine (1980) providing a useful comparative summary specifically of Luiseño sources. As a number of these last authors have noted (e.g., True 1954; Minor 1975), while the ethnographic accounts differ in minor detail, the general patterns are similar and hence can be readily synthesized into a regional pattern (see also Strong 1929; Driver 1941). And as I have shown in a recent summary of these syntheses (Whitley 2003), there is substantial concurrence among these secondary sources concerning the nature, origin and meaning of this art.

As is commonly the case, the primary sources are not all complete, with some emphasizing certain aspects of the ritual meanwhile omitting other details although, in aggregate, a detailed description results. Likewise more information is available from certain groups than others, due to differential historical disruption and intensity of ethnological study. In general terms, too, the accounts are quite limited for boys' puberty art in contrast to the information on the girls' initiation (see below). In this last case this may be the result of an earlier (probably mid-19th century) termination of the boys' ritual, whereas the girls' ceremony was conducted into the 1890s [2].

In general terms, the Takic initiations were boy or girl group rituals that involved: (a) isolation; (b) instruction, usually by shamans, in religious esoterica and general moral precepts; (c) sometimes the creation of one or more sand paintings (which commonly were cosmological maps), by the shamans, as part of the instruction; (d) fasting, the ingestion of hallucinogens, and/or extreme physical ordeals; and (e) at the culmination of the initiation, a ritual race to a rock art site where the initiates made paintings. Kroeber summarized the salient aspects of the girls' ritual, and its relationship to the boys' rite, as follows:

"[T]he Luiseño, having more nearly equated the [girls'] ceremony with that for the boys, make of it almost an initiation cult, with sermons over the sand painting, an ordeal of retaining swallowed tobacco, foot racing, and painting of rocks by the candidate." (Kroeber 1925:716)

As is clear from a series of recent statements (Quinlan 2000; Hedges 2001; Kehoe 2000), confusion has been introduced into the literature concerning a number of issues related to this puberty art. These confusions include: (a) which groups made the art; (b) whether boys or just girls were responsible; (c) whether visionary experiences occurred during these initiations; (d) whether spirit helpers were obtained by the initiates; and (e) what was depicted by the initiates.

The first issue—which groups made puberty rock art?—can be addressed in two fashions. The first results from the fact that the known girls' art is stylistically distinct (True 1954; Hedges 1973; Minor 1975). It consists of motifs that are predominately red zigzags, diamond chains and hand prints (Figure 1). Based on the distribution of sites characterized by these conventions, the girls' puberty art tradition can be inferred to have extended from the Los Angeles Basin and Transverse Ranges south to San Diego County, and inland from the coast to the Palm Springs area (e.g., see Minor 1975:32, Oxendine 1980:48 and Cohen 1987:23). Hedges emphasizes this point with respect to the connection between this style and the non-Takic speaking Diegueño:

"[The 'Luiseño Rectilinear Abstract style,' corresponding to puberty art] is a characteristic element of Luiseño culture, and for it we have substantial ethnographic documentation. Pictographs in this style were painted by Luiseño girls, and occasionally by the boys, as part of their puberty ceremonies. . .Where this style appears in Diegueño territory, its purpose must have been very similar to Luiseño practice." (Hedges 1970:143-144)

The second approach to the question of participation in the puberty art tradition is the examination of the ethnographic record. There is positive documentation for the making of girls' puberty art among the Luiseño and Cupeño (e.g., DuBois 1908:96; Sparkman 1908:225; Kroeber 1908b:174-176, 1925:675; Strong 1929:227, 257, 299; Hill and Nolasquez 1973:35; Harrington n.d.a). Strong (1929:118, 173) and, following him, Minor (1975:31) infer that the Cahuilla also made girls' puberty art, whereas Driver (1941: Table 14) records it as a known ritual trait among this group. True (1954:69) suggested that the Serrano may have made puberty art. A statement in Harrington's linguistic notes supports this supposition: "At *anít:tsapa't* are rock paintings of [informant's] dead sisters and mother" (Hill 1992:1). Diegueño puberty art is documented by Waterman (1910:293).

If we compare the distribution of the puberty style rock art with the ethnographic evidence, only one Takic group listed above is missing [3]. This is the Gabrielino (Fernandeño/Tongva) of the Los Angeles

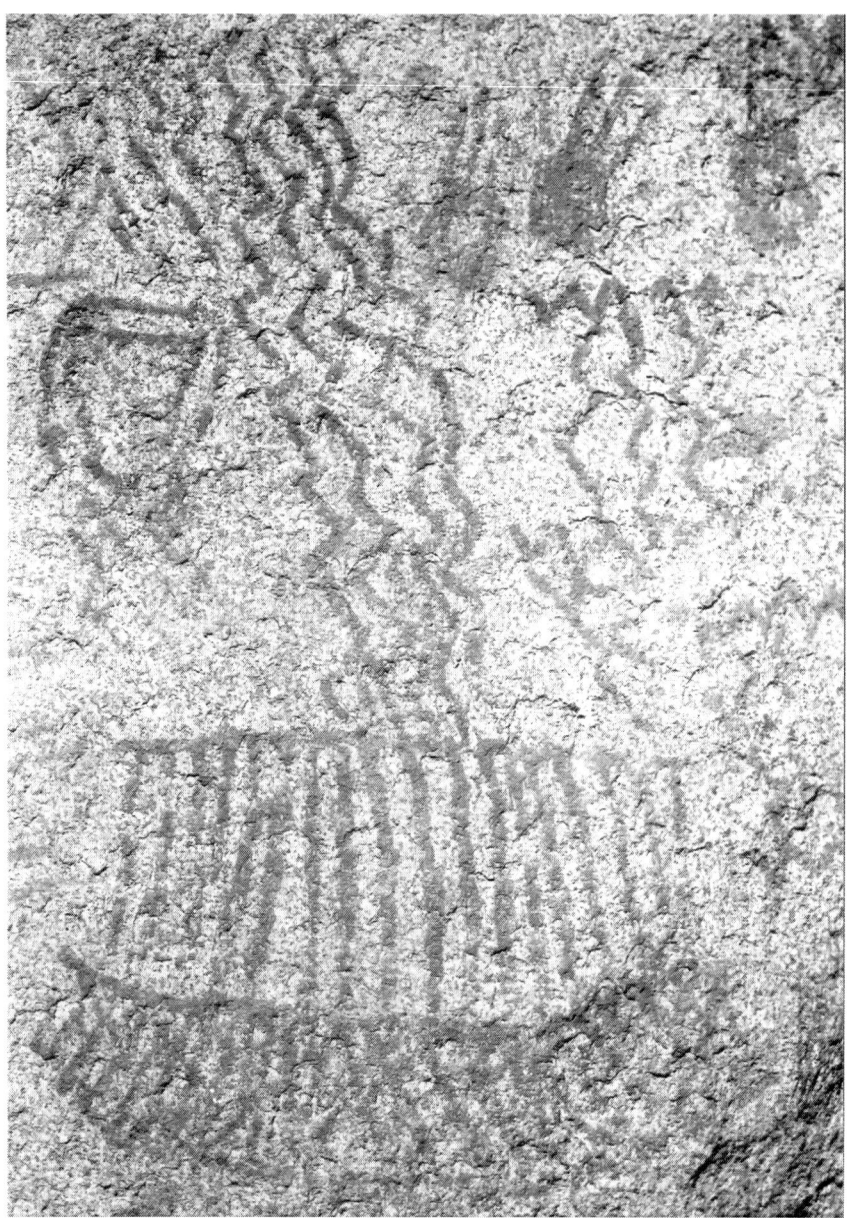

Figure 1. Red painted pictographs from the Puberty Rock site (CA-RIV-114), outside of Perris in southwestern California. Sets of zigzags, diamond chains and handprints are characteristic motifs from sites such as this, made by young girls at the conclusion of their puberty initiations. (photo: D.S. Whitley)

Basin, a group that effectively suffered cultural extirpation due to the early growth of Los Angeles and is therefore poorly known ethnologically. It seems likely that they too made puberty rock art. Puberty rock art, regardless, was then a widespread practice in southwestern California, as the ethnographic and archaeological evidence demonstrate [4].

The second point of confusion concerning Takic puberty art involves the sex of its authors. Kehoe (2000:75) has stated, for example, that:

"[B]oys did not paint vision creatures on rock; the art associated with boys' initiations, as with the adults who taught the girls, was sand paintings."

As noted above, while the evidence concerning boys' puberty art is limited, it nonetheless makes clear that boys in this region made rock art as part of their initiations (Hedges 1970:143-144; Minor 1975:32; Oxendine 1980; Cohen 1987). Positive mentions of boys' puberty art are provided by Harrington (n.d.a), who illustrates black pictographs painted by Luiseño boys (Figure 2), and DuBois, also in reference to the Luiseño. She states that, following the ant ordeal during the boys' initiation,

"A race was then made by the candidates. . .and the winner of the race painted the rock in the designated place, with red and black paint." (DuBois 1908:92)

Waterman (1910:293) similarly states that:

"Rock-paintings exist in the Diegueño country, but are said to have been made by the boys in connection with [the boys' *toloache* initiation]."

That is, Waterman's point is that Diegueño pictographs were made by boys rather than by girls. There is simply no question, in other words, that boys did make puberty art, at least in portions of this region.

Question has also developed in the literature concerning visionary experiences during these puberty initiations, with both Kehoe (2000) and Quinlan (2000) essentially arguing that these were restricted to the boys' ingestion of *toloache* (jimsonweed). Because, by their logic, the *toloache* initiation did not involve rock art, they correspondingly imply that there is no connection between visions and puberty art (ignoring the fact that the ant and stinging nettles ordeals, after which the art was made, were integral components of the initiations).

The ethnographic record is actually quite clear on the fact that boys and girls both were involved in multiple types of activities conducive to achieving altered states of consciousness (ASC) and that they in fact did hallucinate. These activities included periods of fasting, isolation and sensory deprivation, extreme physical pain in the form of whipping by stinging nettles, and/or the ingestion of tobacco, red

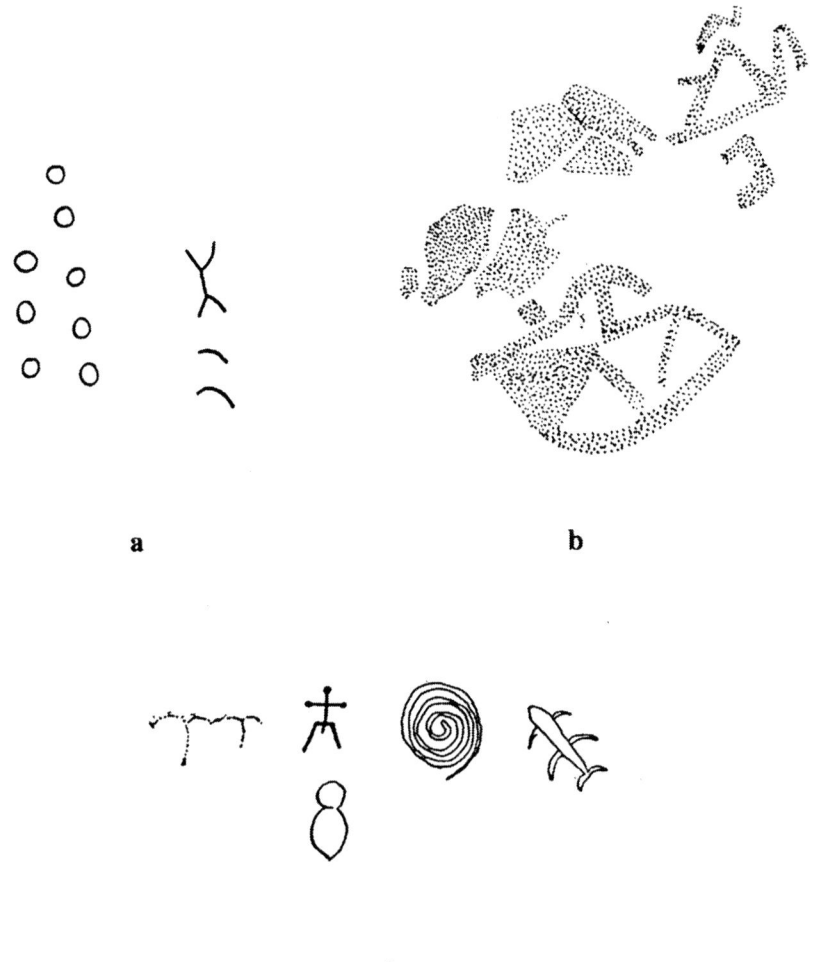

Figure 2. Limited ethnographic information exists on rock art made during boys' puberty ceremonies in southern California, although drawings of three sites have been published. a, John Peabody Harrington's drawing of Luiseno boys' black pictograph (after Oxendine 1980:48); b, Cucupa boys' red pictographs (after Alvarez de Williams 1973:44); c, petroglyphs at the Mojave boys' nasal piercing ceremony site (after Bourke 1889:175).

harvester ants and/or *toloache*. Any of these circumstances or agents typically will result in hallucinations; when combined they can be almost guaranteed to yield ASCs.

The hallucinatory effects of *toloache* need no comment. That visionary experiences resulted from tobacco ingestion and that these visions were a central part of the puberty initiations was established in our earliest detailed ethnological account from California. This was written, about 1822, by Fray Geronimo Boscana, and it concerned the Juaneño (i.e., Luiseño) residing around Mission San Juan Capistrano (Whitley 2003). In describing the boys' and girls' initiations, Boscana stated that:

"At the age of six or seven years, the children were given a god as protector. This was an animal in which they were told to place entire confidence, and which, it was believed, would defend them from all dangers. . .They were not, however, to consider this animal as the real god [i.e., the culture hero Chinigchinich] . . .That they might know the class of animal which the god, Chinigchinich, had selected for their particular veneration, a kind of drink was administered to them made from a plant called *pibat* [tobacco], which was reduced to a powder and mixed with other intoxicating ingredients. Soon after taking this preparation, they became insensible, and for three days were deprived of any sustenance whatever.

During this period they were attended by some old men or women, who were continually exhorting them to be on the alert and not sleep, for fear the coyote, the bear, the crow, or the rattlesnake might come; to observe if it were furious or gentle, and to inquire of the first that should come what were its desires. The poor Indian thus intoxicated, without food or drink, suffering from delirium, beheld all kinds of visions; and when he made known that he had seen any particular being, who explained the observance required of him, then they gave him to eat and drink, and made a grand feast; at the same time advising him to be particular in obeying the commands of the mysterious apparition." (Boscana 1978:45-46)

Boscana's reference to elderly male and female attendants makes clear the fact that his description is of boys and girls both, as old men were invariably boys' guardians during these initiations whereas old women were the girls' watchers.

Confirmation of the occurrence of visionary experiences during the use of tobacco in the girls' puberty initiations is provided in other accounts. DuBois, for example, writes that:

"The chief. . .[placed] the ball of tobacco in the girl's mouth. Warm water was then administered in a basket. . .If she should vomit, it was taken as a sign that she had not been virtuous; but if she were good she would not vomit. This was a severe test.

The tobacco induced drowsiness, and in this state the girl was placed in a large hole that had been previously dug in the ground. . . .

The girl is placed there for three days. Only her mother or the wife of the chief can see her and attend her. A basket. . .is put over her face...she can drink only warm water." (DuBois 1908:94)

Here DuBois appears to have confused 'drowsiness' with what might more accurately be described as 'wooziness.' William Duncan Strong (1929:297-8) states this directly by referring to the vertigo that the tobacco induced:

"[The ritual official] gives each girl a drink of tobacco and water from a clay vessel...The girls then became dizzy and were laid in the pit which had been heated with hot rocks."

That ASCs result in vertigo is well known.

Additional ethnographic data from Native California confirm the intoxicating effect of native tobacco, even when smoked. Zigmond (1980:9), for example, notes that it is so potent that only about three puffs of the tobacco are "enough" for one night's dosage. Harrington (n.d.b) states that:

"A good gulp of the [native tobacco] smoke was so strong it made [his informant] for a moment like drunk."

Moreover, recent pharmacological, clinical and ethnological data demonstrate, conclusively, that the ingestion of native tobacco (which has 8 times the nicotine content of modern commercial tobaccos) has strong hallucinogenic effects (see Wilbert 1987).

Similarly, the hallucinogenic effects of red harvester ants (usually wrapped in eagle down feather balls and ingested) are also well known (see Blackburn 1976). For example, Harrington records that:

"Once... Francisca took [red ants] as a medicine...While she was taking red ants thus, about 4 or 5 o'clock one bright afternoon, she looked up at the sky and saw all the stars, just as one sees them at night." (Harrington n.d.b)

In a similar fashion, Zigmond (1977:77) notes that "After swallowing the ants, you fall into a deep sleep at once like being drunk."

The cause of the hallucinations is the formic acid injected into the stomach lining. In the case of the boys' initiation the ants were not ingested, but were poured on their bodies and allowed to sting them until, "after a time" (DuBois 1908:91), they were brushed off with stinging nettles. The application of stinging nettles likewise was a well known medicinal treatment in Native California and, as with many such treatments, was believed effective because of the plant's connection to supernatural power – manifest in visions and dreams. Zigmond (1981:68) thus reports that:

"Younger people, to procure dreams, walked through a growth of nettles pressing them against the bared chest causing severe lacerations."

Although the potency of the ant stings—meaning their ability to generate hallucinations—was certainly greater for the stomach lining than the body as a whole, the difference in the quantity of poison injected was almost certainly substantially greater during the ant ordeal and, when capped with lashings by stinging nettles, can be assumed to have generated hallucinations.

That sensory deprivation results in hallucinations is also well established (e.g., see LaBarre 1980:39-40). When combined with the weakened physical state resulting from prolonged fasting, there simply can be no question that the initiates, whether girl or boy and regardless of whether administered *toloache* or tobacco, had visions.

The related question concerns whether the initiates received spirit helpers while in ASCs. Such a conclusion is straightforward given Boscana's quote above. John Peabody Harrington, who annotated Boscana's manuscript, confirmed this fact, specifically identifying the observed object or animal as the individual's *pet*, the standard Native California gloss for 'spirit helper' (Kroeber 1925:513; Gayton 1930:368; Applegate 1978:27):

> "The object or animal which the pummal, initiate, sees after drinking the toluache [sic], is heeded, its commands, if any, are obeyed, and it can be spoken of as *pu'áac*, his pet." (Harrington 1978:161)

Note that Harrington here assumed that Boscana meant that the children had ingested *toloache* (jimsonweed) due to the resulting hallucinations, because Harrington himself (like many other ethnologists) assumed that tobacco would not have such effects; hence Harrington took Boscana's reference to *pibat* as a minor error. In fact, Boscana appears to have specifically meant the use of tobacco in this instance but, regardless, it is clear from his statement that the initiates hallucinated and received spirit helpers.

This conclusion was also reached by DuBois, partly based on her reading of Boscana and in part due to her own Luiseño and Diegueño research. She states:

> "[Her Luiseño consultant] knows nothing about personal "totem animals" or guardian spirits with which this part of the ceremony was probably connected. Boscana's account of the connection of the guardian spirit animal with the toloache ceremony is so clear to the modern reader of his work as to be undoubtedly founded on fact; and at Mesa Grande it was possible to extract enough from some of the old men to be sure that the personal totem had long ago existed among the Diegueño Indians." (DuBois 1908:80)

Strong concurred. He notes that:

> "Boscana makes a positive and clear statement concerning the acquisition of personal guardian spirits at this time, and it is very probable that the above-mentioned [Cahuilla] antics are a reflection of this widespread belief." (Strong 1929:312)

Although specifically concerned with the boys' initiation, the evidence led Driver to conclude that:

> "In southern California [puberty initiations]. . .the central theme was the obtaining of contact with the supernatural through the medium of a narcotic plant. . .The hallucinations consisted principally of visions of animals. . .Such animals became the lifelong spirit helpers of the boys." (Driver 1969:350)

The centrality of the acquisition of spirit helpers to the puberty initiations is then obvious.

The final question about Takic rock art concerns the nature of the pictographs: that is, their origin and symbolic meaning. Unfortunately, with the exception of Harrington's (n.d.a) quick sketch, we have no graphic information about the boys' art, including the identification of sites created during the boys' initiation from which archaeological information about the sites might be gained. Hedges nonetheless concludes that:

> "[T]he rock art of [the Luiseño and Diegueño]. . .provides prime examples of parallels between the aboriginal art and known characteristics of hallucinatory imagery. Precise ethnographic data have not come to light, however, although the evidence for associating this rock art with datura use is very persuasive." (Hedges 1992:81)

By this statement Hedges apparently means that the boys' art portrays hallucinatory imagery. Inasmuch as visionary imagery was taken as the appearance of spirit helpers which, as Driver (1969) contends, was the purpose of the ritual, it follows that the boys' art portrays the animal helpers they received during their ASC experiences.

More information is available concerning the girls' art, and on various levels. First, there are a series sites historically identified as the product of girls' ceremonies, providing a reasonable amount of archaeological information about the sites. Second, as noted above, this art is stylistically distinct inasmuch as it is invariably red, and is heavily predominated by zigzags, diamond chains and hand prints. Third, from the perspective of *depiction (*as opposed to symbolic meaning), zigzag and diamond chain motifs in Native California were universally interpreted as rattlesnake designs, regardless of whether this pertained to imagery on basketry, tattoos, face painting, or pictographs. For example, Strong (1929:299) notes that "informants said such [pictograph] designs were always diamond-shaped and represented the rattlesnake."

Similarly, Steward records that:

> "After further ceremonies in which a ground painting was used the girls had a race to a certain rock. Here relatives of the girls stood to give them red paint when they arrived, and they painted

diamond-shaped designs, representing the rattlesnake, on the rock." (Steward 1929:227)

Given the facts that diamond-chain and zigzag were consistently and widely said to represent rattlesnake, the confirmation of this fact with respect to the rock art motifs [5], and the heavy preponderance of such motifs at the girls' sites, it is clear that rattlesnake was the most commonly depicted motif resulting from the girls' puberty initiations (cf. Steward 1929:227; Hedges 1970:161; Oxendine 1980:48; Cohen 1987:24).

What rattlesnake symbolized is of course a slightly different question. Given the nature and purpose of the initiation, the obvious hypothesis is that the depictions are symbolic representations of the girls' spirit helpers. Again, different kinds of evidence support this inference. The first of these is analogical and involves the general nature of rock art in the far west. Substantial evidence demonstrates that a major purpose of far western rock art was the depiction of spirit helpers specifically and visionary experiences more generally (see sources cited in Whitley 2000b). That is, interpretation of the girls' art as also depicting visionary experiences fits rather than runs counter to a larger, well-supported general interpretation of this region's rock art. Second, this ethnographic interpretation is further supported by neuropsychological information on the nature of visionary imagery: the so-called Neuropsychological (NP) Model (Lewis-Williams and Dowson 1988). As outlined elsewhere (Whitley 1994b), the expectations of the NP Model are satisfied by much Native California rock art. The girls' puberty art likewise fits the expectations of the model – not in the sense of illustrating all aspects of it but instead due to this art's heavy emphasis on just a few basic entoptic forms and principles of perception identified by the model.

Third, and most importantly, there is ethnographic support for such a conclusion. For example, Hill and Nolasquez recorded the following concerning the termination of the Cupeño girls' ceremony, the period during which they painted pictographs:

"And then they eat [something bland, not meat or salt], *she comes to know some way or other that her painting is coming.* And they say that those who are patient [i.e., maintain the meat and salt fast] finish their paintings, they would repeat again, but those who were not patient would eat something in the middle. Those who have finished, their mothers sympathize with them, then make them eat meat or something with salt in it [i.e., break their fast], and then they would vomit. And it is said that long ago the ones who were initiated would get married, but I never saw that, this is the end of what I know." (Hill and Nolasquez 1973:35; emphasis added)

The implication is that the girls acquire their paintings through some undescribed cognitive process, of which a visionary experience is obviously a candidate. This is clearly implied by Parker (cited in True and Baumhoff 1981:261):

> "It is now well established that after the girls' roasting ceremony, and *while they were still groggy* they were given paint made from tree pitch and mineral pigments and told to draw on the rocks." (Parker 1966:31; emphasis in True and Baumhoff 1981:261) [6]

White then infers that the images are the girls' spirit helpers. He notes that:

> "The meaning of the symbol painted on a large boulder at the terminus of the race was in each instance known only by the individual girl, but possibly was representative of some form of bird, animal or other *ayelkwi* object with which she identified." (White 1963:141)

Ayelkwi is sacred knowledge-power (White 1963), which is to say supernatural potency that, throughout Native California, was acquired from and manifest in a spirit helper (Bean 1976; Applegate 1978).

Fourth, Boscana's description, quoted above, indicates that rattlesnake was one of the four spirit animals that the puberty initiates might receive. The rock art at the girls' sites, as emphasized many times above, is heavily predominated by rattlesnake motifs. It therefore follows that these snake motifs were the spirit helpers that the girls received during their visionary experiences.

Indeed, the importance of supernatural snake spirits to the girls' initiation is symbolically codified in a Cahuilla myth, the Fiesta for Growing Girls (Patencio 1943:40-41). This recounts the fact that Day Star Snake was exclusively singled out as an important attendee at the initiation, and great efforts were made to ensure its presence. But when, due to unfortunate circumstances, the snake left the ceremony early, flying away "like lightning" (i.e., in a zigzag), the girls turned to stone and the initiation was a failure. The symbolic implications are clear: the presence of a supernatural snake spirit who moved in a zigzag – which is to say a supernatural rattlesnake – was required for a successful girls' initiation [7].

Takic puberty rock art then was minimally created by four ethnolinguistic groups, the Luiseño-Juaneño, Cupeño, Cahuilla and Diegueño (who in fact were not Takic). It is highly likely that it was also made by the Gabrielino and Serrano and thus that it was made from the Transverse Ranges and LA Basin south to below the Mexican border, and from the coast to the Palm Springs area. It was made by both boys and girls during puberty initiations which included the ingestion of hallucinogens and visionary experiences, and whose primary purpose was the acquisition of a spirit helper. The girls' art is predominated by rattlesnake motifs and the existing evidence supports the conclusion that these were the spirit helpers of the girls.

The Yuman Puberty Art Tradition

Yuman-speaking tribes occupied the lower Colorado River Valley and delta, and portions of the Colorado Desert and northern Baja California. They included the Mojave, Quechan (formerly 'Yuma'), Kamia, Cocopa (Cucapá) and Kiliwa [8]. These are interesting to the rock art researcher because they created two kinds of rock art, both in a variety of different contexts. Shamans, first, made rock art portraying their re-experiencing of the mythic creation of the world, during which they obtained supernatural power from their culture hero Mastamho; alternatively, they made rock art for purposes of sorcery. Pictographs and/or petroglyphs were also made by boys during their puberty initiation. Second, geoglyphs or earth figures were created to mark and commemorate mythic events, and were used in ritual pilgrimages and other group ceremonies, but they were also made by shamans for sorcery (see Whitley 1998, 2000b) [9].

Despite this diversity, the Yuman-speaking tribes are frustrating for the rock art researcher because, while their ethnographic record establishes the above general origins for their rock art, it tells us almost nothing more about it.

The production of puberty art, nonetheless, is known to have occurred during the boys' nasal septum piercing ritual. Depending upon tribal group, this ritual varied in length, intensity and formality (see Forde 1931:150-151; Gifford 1931:37, 54-55, 1933:291; Meigs 1939:47-48; Devereux 1949; Kelly 1977:98-99). In general terms it involved fasting and isolation, the piercing of the septum for a nose ornament, tattooing in some cases and, always, a ritual "run." According to Devereux (1949), the run was more than 60 miles in length across the desert; other ethnologists record shorter runs, but all appear to concur that it was undertaken during the summer. The tattoo and/or nose ornament obtained during the ceremony were required to enter the land of the dead upon death (Gifford 1933:291; Stewart 1977:17). According to Forde (1931:151), the initiation was associated with acquiring warrior power, a circumstance which is understandable in terms of the state of endemic warfare that existed in this region during the protohistoric and historical periods.

Alvarez de Williams provides our most complete account of the place of rock art in the initiation (see Figure 2):

"Onesimo Gonzalez Saiz, a contemporary [1973] leader of the Cucapá people...told me that this [site], on the eastern side of the Sierra Cucapá, was once used by his people in connection with the nose piercing ceremony for their young men. He said that they chose this and one other place, (which has no painting), because they were special, noted for large natural holes [*tinajas*] in the rock...The red painting is on one 'wall' of a short natural tunnel in a granite outcropping atop a small hill. The painting is for the most part very faded, some of it obliterated, but solid and linear geometrical forms may be distinguished, among them four triangles...When I mentioned to Onesimo the faded condition of some of the painting, he told me that when someone died, it was the custom to rub out the old painting, and paint anew. He didn't seem to know any details beyond this, but when I asked him whether the place was used by all the Cucapá, or just one family, he told me, 'nada mas una familia' (just one family). By this he probably meant one *shamul*, or 'clan.'" (Alvarez de Williams 1973:44)

Alvarez de Williams' interpretation of Saiz' reference to *una familia* conflicts with Gifford's earlier and more complete account of the Cocopa boys' ceremony (which unfortunately does not mention rock art). Gifford (1933:291) notes instead that "[The initiation] Took place when number of boys, regardless of gens ['clans'], attained to about 15 (14-17) years age."

The Cocopa creation of rock art nonetheless is confirmed for the Quechan by Densmore, who writes:

"[W]hen a man reached a certain age he 'put his mark on a rock for future generations.' All the men in a family were said to have the same 'animal mark.' It was also said that a 'kind of record' was kept on rocks, some of which remain near Laguna." (Densmore 1932:8-9)

Creation of boys' puberty art during the nasal septum piercing ceremony is also suggested for the Mojave in Bourke's (1889:175) early account, which identifies the mythic location of the first such ceremony, and illustrates an adjacent rock art panel at this location (Figure 2).

No information exists on this puberty art beyond these short accounts. Alvarez de Williams and Densmore's statements might be taken to suggest that the resulting rock art represents a kind of totemic clan symbol. Although not speaking directly to puberty art, a statement by Kroeber argues against such a possibility:

"The clans do not enter into religious activities, so far as is known. In fact, the ceremonial scheme of these tribes is such that it is difficult to see how the natives could have found serious points of contact between their clan organization and cult practices if they had been so inclined. The impress which this gentile scheme makes is that it rests lightly on society and not at all on cults." (Kroeber 1925:741)

Kroeber's contention appears to be supported by the rock art itself. Although there are only two sites that are known or can be inferred to have resulted from the ceremony (the Alvarez de Williams and Bourke localities respectively), there is little evidence that I know of in the regional corpus suggestive of repeated possible "clan" symbols at sites (as, for example, can be immediately recognized at Willow Springs, Arizona, which was made by Hopi clans during their Salt Pilgrimage; see Michaelis 1981). Moreover, there is a general paucity of iconic imagery in the regional corpus, Bourke's illustration notwithstanding. (Like many casual observers, Bourke apparently drew the few recognizable iconic images at the site, almost certainly ignoring the majority of the others which should be geometric in form.)

Densmore's characterization of the puberty art as 'animal marks' is then suggestive of the possibility that the initiates portrayed spirit helpers which were taken to be animal in nature but not necessarily animal in visionary form [10]. This interpretation is supported ethnographically on a number of points. Forde (1931:182), first, records the fact that spirit helpers are animals but that they do not necessarily appear in animal form. Given his contention that one purpose of the initiation was the acquisition of warfare power, second, he further records that war powers were received from one of the animal spirits in a dream, but in a "different language and set form" (Forde 1931:181). He also notes, third, that:

"Men when they are old become weak and lose their vision, their power goes from them and they give it up to younger people." (Forde 1931:139)

That is, power is passed down from the old to the young, perhaps reflected in the statement that all the men in a family had the same animal mark.

The related question of the place of visionary experiences in the boys' initiations, and thus hallucinations, is unclear in the ethnographic record, however. Most ethnologist denied that dreaming was an important element in the ceremony or they stated that any concern with dreaming was 'no more than usual,' though it must be recalled, as Devereux has noted, that the "major interest" of the Yuman speakers was "the acquisition of power through subjective dream experiences" (Devereux 1949:19; see also Devereux 1957; Kroeber 1925, 1957). And it is hard to imagine that an initiation would *not* result in hallucinations when, as described by Forde (1931:150-151), it involved nasal piercing without anesthesia and a 10-15 miles run across the Colorado Desert during the summer, followed by four days without sleep, with sustenance limited to a single bowl of watery gruel.

The interpretation of Yuman puberty art, as in all circumstances, must be based on our existing evidence even though, in this case, our data are quite limited. Still, a variety of lines of evidence suggest that the art may portray the initiates' spirit helpers. First, the rock art (particularly along the river and in the Colorado Desert) heavily emphasizes geometric forms and these appear to correspond to common entoptics and the principles of perception experienced during ASCs. Second, the initiation itself involved extreme physical stress and exertion along with bodily mutilation – precisely those physical conditions used to promote visionary experiences among many Plains groups, where vision questing is well documented (e.g., see Irwin 1994). Third, one purpose of the rite was the acquisition of warfare power and this was said to come from animal spirit helpers who appeared to the supplicant in a non-animal form. Finally, the art itself is described in one case as an individual's 'animal mark' and this seems only understandable in terms of a spirit helper.

The Cupule Tradition

While the direct ethnographic record on Yuman puberty rock art is quite limited, even less exists concerning the creation of cupule rocks which are commonly associated with protohistoric and historical villages in south-central California and the western Great Basin. The existing ethnography on this kind of rock art can be augmented, however, by analogical evidence from north-central and northern California. The combination of the two sources suggests that cupule rock art reflected concerns with fertility and was made, by young girls, during puberty initiations (Whitley 2000b).

The ethnographic record on the so-called Pit and Groove rocks of north-central and northern California is well known (e.g., see Goddard 1903, 1904; Dixon 1907:449; Barrett 1908:175, 1952:386-387; Loeb 1926:247-248; Spier 1930:21; Driver 1939:364, 421; Parkman 1986, 1993), with a summary provided by Heizer (1953). Heizer identified two origins and functions for this art: motifs created by shamans for weather control, which have been termed "rain rocks," and those made by individuals to enhance fertility, commonly called "baby rocks." The so-called rain rocks, which were restricted to northern California, functioned to help control the availability of anadromous salmon by influencing river flow through rain or snow (Parkman 1993:100; Whitley 2000b). The creation of cupule rock art in this context, then, served as a kind of increase ritual related to the First Salmon ceremony and was consistent with the function of the more dominant priestly cults in this region, which likewise emphasized renewal and increase [11].

In north-central California, in contrast, "pit and groove rocks" were created to ensure conception and childbirth. Barrett provides a detailed Pomo explanation:

> "The sterile pair went to one of these rocks and there first a prayer for fertility was made. Then, by means of a pecking stone, some small fragments were chipped from the sides of one of the grooves or cuppings on its surface. These were then ground into a very fine powder which was wrapped in some green leaves and taken to

some secluded spot. Here this powder was made into a paste and with it the woman's abdomen was painted with two lines, one running from the top of the sternum to the pubes, the other transversely across the middle of the abdomen. Some of this paste was also inserted in the female. Intercourse at this time positively assured fertility, due to the magic properties of this rock." (Barrett 1952:386-387)

Although other descriptions vary in minor detail, it is clear that the rock itself was believed to hold supernatural potency and that, by acquiring this potency in its material form and anointing the body with it, fertility could be ensured.

The limited ethnographic data in south-central California and the western Great Basin suggest similar symbolic beliefs about rocks generally and cupule rocks specifically. Rather than created by an ostensibly sterile individual or couple, however, the evidence points to more generalized girls' puberty initiations. The first such evidence was published by Smith and Lerch (1984:7) who, citing a Kawaiisu consultant, note that cupules were said to be associated with young girls' fertility. Smith and Lee (2002:209), second, cite a 1904 manuscript by J.W. Hudson who "observed cupule production being part of fertility rites" among the Owens Valley Paiute [12].

These two very brief suggestions are augmented by a third more detailed description of girls' puberty initiations that was recounted to me on 5 November 1997 at the Rocky Hill, Exeter, site, by a contemporary Yokuts consultant. Notably, this consultant had previously demonstrated his traditional knowledge about rock art by providing explanations that, on the general points, confirmed my analysis of the ethnographic record (which he had not seen) and, more importantly, corrected one minor error in the published documents (see Whitley 1994b; 2000b:134-135).

Rocky Hill is a major historical Wukchumni Yokuts village that is unusual because it contains numerous different pictograph panels which are found in small individual caves on a steep but very rocky grano-diorite slope. Typically villages have one or just a few associated painted rockshelters or caves; the dozens at Rocky Hill may reflect the fact that it is considered the second oldest place in the Wukchumni universe (after the creation place at Bell Bluff, which has been destroyed), and thus is thought particularly sacred. Regardless of cause for this concentration of pictographs, however, it is clear that the site experienced a level of ritual activity that is essentially unmatched elsewhere in the Yokuts realm.

The cupule rock, which is called "Moon Turn," is located at the foot of the rocky slope, within or immediately adjacent to the village midden deposit (Figure 3). It is close to a "pounding rock" (bedrock mortar), a fact that was considered important because the pounding rocks

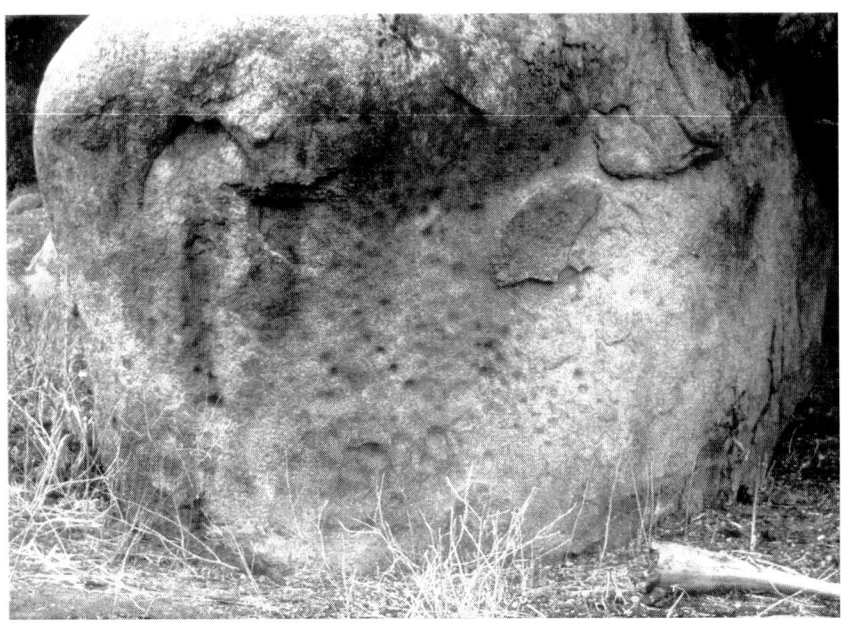

Figure 3. Cupules at the Yokuts site of Rocky Hill, south-central California. A contemporary ethnological account indicates that these were made by girls during their puberty initiations. (photo: D.S. Whitley)

were used by women and the symbolism of the cupules reflected this central female activity. The initiates were first isolated in a small rockshelter for a few days with family members (probably mothers or aunts) and perhaps a shaman. This shelter is about 20 meters north of the cupule rock and bears traces of pigment on its wall, suggesting that it may have once had pictographs and that these may have played some role in the girls' initiation. After this period of isolation, the girls came to the cupule rock and, using a small ritual pestle (which is retained by the consultant and which was showed to me), proceeded to briefly grind within each of the existing cups. This is said to not only symbolically duplicate the plant grinding that is the central woman's task, but also to connect each young girl to all the previous women in the tribe who have conducted the initiation.

The existing ethnographic record includes very little information on the puberty initiations for young Yokuts girls, but what does exist provides general agreement with this account. For example, it was said that "girls followed the moon" (Gayton 1948:104), referring to the way in which they gauged their menstrual cycle. This appears to be reflected in the name given to the cupule rock. Likewise a period of ritual isolation was widespread in Native California, and is documented for the Yokuts (Gayton 1948; Driver 1937:97). (While in many regions this was said to occur in a warmed pit, duplicating post-partum practices, for the Yokuts it was commonly recorded as isolation in the girl's house with her mother.) But with the exception of a few additional minor details about taboo activities (e.g., eating meat, scratching with one's fingers), the Yokuts ethnographic record is devoid of additional information on girls' initiations.

The limited ethnographic information from south-central California and the western Great Basin may also be augmented by information from southwestern California; that is, from the area of the Takic pictograph puberty tradition. According to information collected from a Luiseño consultant about 1953 by Parker:

> "In a nearby wash on the undersurface of a boulder was a cluster of round peckings in the boulder about the size of a silver dollar. I was told by the Indians who lived here that these were a kind of score card with each peck representing an initiate of the ceremony. They neglected to state whether the round markers were for the boys or the girls." (Parker 1966:31-32, cited in Minor 1975:16)

Minor (1975:16) further notes DuBois' (1908:92, 95, 115) mention of ringing stones as accompaniment for a song during the boys' and girls' initiations, suggesting that these ringing stones may also be cupules and thus that they were created by pounding (see contrasting view by True and Baumhoff 1981), an idea elaborated by Parkman (1993). Although this last author's primary concern is the possible association of cupules with rain-making, following Baumhoff (1981) he suggests that cupules may represent a kind of archaic substrate of Hokan culture, given that Hokan speakers are believed to have once inhabited all or much of California.

The ethnographic information on this cupule making tradition is, thus, scant and, in some senses, confusing. First, even though quite cursory, there are a few consistent suggestions linking cupules with girls' puberty initiations. Second, on a symbolic level these are also consistent with the symbolism of cupule making in adjacent parts of north-central California, although the specific functions and rituals varied. Third, the distribution of cupules in California extends into the Takic region, where there is also an ethnographic reference associating them with puberty rites. While this supports the origin of cupules in girls' puberty initiations in general terms, it is hard to know how to reconcile it with the much better documented Takic pictograph tradition (e.g., see discussion in True and Baumhoff 1981).

With reference to the last issue, True and Baumhoff (1981) favor the idea that cupules in Takic country predate the movement of this language branch into southwestern California. While this may be true for some or many of the cupules, Minor's (1975) contention for an archaeological association with protohistoric if not historical villages for at least some of the cupules is, to me, convincing evidence that certain of them are quite late dating. Equally to the point, there is increasing archaeological evidence that the Takic moved into southwestern California much earlier than the AD 500 datum that Kroeber (and following him Baumhoff) originally hypothesized, probably as early as 1500 BC, making it much harder to attribute all of the cupules to an earlier and historically extinct ethnolinguistic group in this region.

These issues aside, a series of other questions about cupules also remain. For example, at least one Yokuts site has painted cupules (red with white borders), suggesting that some rock painting may also have occurred during the girls' initiations in south-central California (Figure 4). One region, in Tataviam territory along the Santa Clara River Valley in northern Los Angeles County, has village sites with massive concentrations of cupules (Figure 5). These imply either an intensity of ritual activity and/or a function that differs from what is archaeological visible elsewhere.

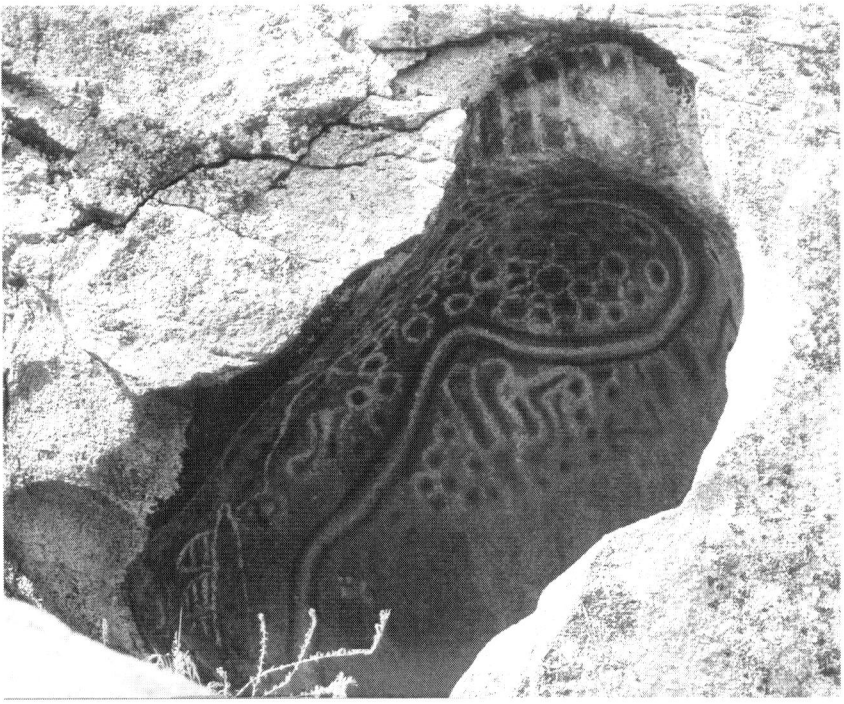

Figure 4. Painted cupules (red center with white outline) in a natural rock alcove at Round Valley, south-central California. The alcove and the painted-engraved line in its center at this Yokuts site are both reminiscent of the form of a quail topknot feather. (photo: D.S. Whitley)

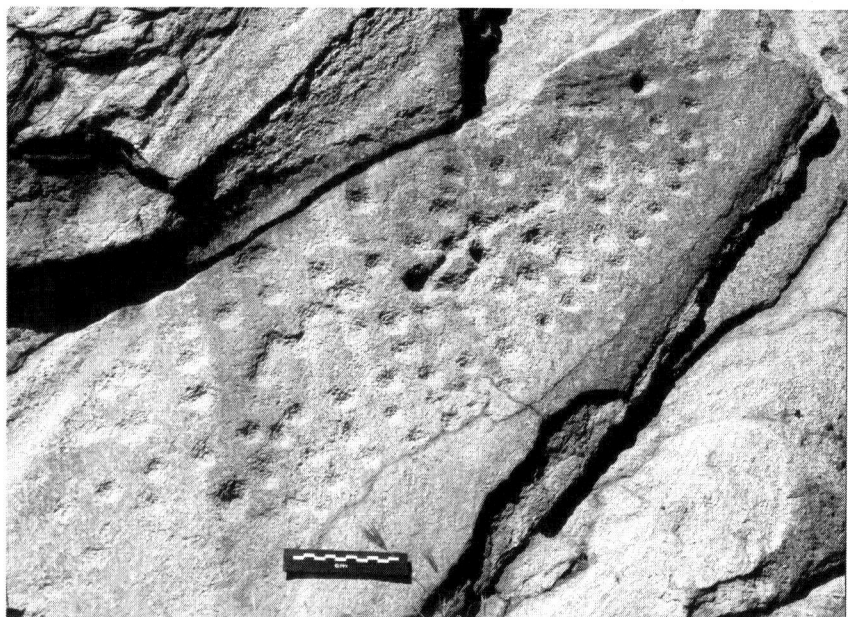

Figure 5. Cupules (and petroglyphs) on a schist outcrop on the Lannan Ranch near Agua Dulce in the upper Santa Clarita Valley (northern Los Angeles County), southern California. This region, part of the ethnographic territory of the Takic-speaking Tataviam, contains a large but poorly documented series of major cupule sites. (photo: D.S. Whitley)

Despite the paucity of information and uncertainty that results, our best interpretation at this point is the creation in south-central California and the western Great Basin (if not the Basin more generally) of these cupped rocks in girls' initiatory rites. This practice may have also extended into the Takic area of southwestern California and served as a minor (and hence rarely mentioned) aspect of their puberty initiations. (Alternatively, some of the cupules in this last region may have been made by lithic drumming.)

The Takic case, however, points to a conclusion suggested earlier, also in reference to their puberty art. This is that far western North American religions were fundamentally open and syncretic, thereby adopting and blending traits and beliefs. On one hand this enhances our abilities to argue analogically from one ethnic group to another. On the other hand this also means that hard and fast boundaries between cultures, cults and kinds of rock art are unlikely to have existed.

Puberty Vision Questing on the Columbia Plateau

No rock art tradition is better documented, anywhere in the world, than the puberty art created by Columbia Plateau boys and girls during their vision questing initiations. Ethnographic accounts of this tradition have been synthesized in detail by Keyser (1992), Hann et al. (2004.), Keyser and Whitley (2000), Whitley (2000b), Whitley and Loubser (n.d.), and Hays-Gilpin (2004), eliminating any need to do so again here. Instead, I duplicate a previously published table (Keyser and Whitley 2000), which summarizes the evidence for the puberty art in this region (Table 1), emphasizing only a few points at this time.

The first point worth emphasizing again is that there is over 100 years of internally consistent primary ethnographic documentation on Plateau puberty art. (Note that, given the use of elderly informants 100 years ago [e.g., Teit 1896:227], this actually suggests continuity extending back for roughly 140-150 years.) This record demonstrates widespread similarities in the tradition across the region, as well as temporal continuity during the recent past. In general terms the puberty art was created by boys and girls during individual rather than group vision quests, at remote and isolated spots, under the direction of a family member. The youths fasted, conducted various vigorous activities (like swimming, creating rock piles and pulling down trees), and were sent to spots imbued with power where they received a spirit helper, which might appear as a spark or as a human before revealing its "true" form.

In light of recent debate about the relationship of puberty art to visionary experiences (e.g., Kehoe 2000; Hedges 2001), it is important to note that the puberty rock art that resulted on the Plateau is widely acknowledged to have portrayed the children's dreams, meaning their visionary experiences: throughout far western North American, visionary experiences were glossed as 'dreams.' In part this is because no distinction was made between an REM dream and a waking hallucination (a circumstance, not incidentally, which can be supported neurochemically and neurophysiologically; see Hobson 1994). But on the Plateau the link was in fact drawn even more explicitly. Hill-Tout, for example, notes the following about the spirit helper:

> "This guide, protector, influence, charm – for it partakes of the character of all these – the Chilliwack call by the name *sulia* or *solia*. This is an abstract or nominal form of the verb *ulia*, 'to dream.' It is thus because these potencies come to and communicate with them in dreams and visions." (Hill-Tout 1978:49).

Other depictions have also been identified in the puberty art, including red fir branches in particular (e.g., Teit 1896). Although this might seem to indicate that mundane natural objects were painted, in fact it does not. The importance to the girls' puberty initiation of "mystic red-fir," as it was sometimes called, is partly explained by Hill-Tout:

"During the whole period of seclusion the girl busied herself in various ways – by spinning yarn or picking off needles from fir branches, by frequent bathes and scrubbings and by walks in the forest where she was supposed to hold converse with the spirits of the trees, in particular that of red-fir, whose branches were a sovereign remedy against sickness and bad medicines of all kinds." (Hill-Tout 1978:112)

Red fir, in other words, was the girls' preferred spirit helper. Other accounts demonstrate that red fir branches were a central component in many shamanic rituals.

There is one final point about Plateau puberty initiations that warrants mention, because of its potential implications for rock art in other parts of the far west. This concerns the creation of rock cairns, walls and other structures. It is well documented ethnographically that the construction of rock structures occurred during Plateau vision quests (by shamans, adults during life crises and puberty initiates), with numerous archaeological examples identified (e.g., Spier and Sapir 1930:239; Ray 1932:183, 1942:236, 1963:79; Caldwell and Carlson 1954; Chartkoff 1983; Buckley 1986; Jett 1986; Winthrop et al. 1995). For example, Curtis (writing in 1911) notes that, among the Spokan, girls went into the hills at night and, at various points, piled rocks:

"This was intended, by supernatural means, to give her strength of body, and to afford the spirit creatures the opportunity to speak to her and grant her their protection." (Curtis 1970:75)

Among the Kalispel, Curtis (1970) states further that "At intervals she would build cairns, usually on mountain peaks." A number of other ethnographers also record this practice, with Turney-High (1937:27) stating that, among the Flathead, the supplicant would build a low wall (a "vision quest structure") around himself and then wait for his vision.

What is not immediately apparent in these discussions is an important fact: rock art and rock structures were both created during vision questing (puberty or otherwise), but not always in the same location. That is, with the exception of the vision quest structures, *per se*, cairns and rock piles were apparently constructed at different places than the pictographs or petroglyphs. The result is a kind of ritual movement across the landscape during the vision quest, most likely from relatively high spots (mountain tops), where the rock features concentrate, to lower ground where rock art was made (Whitley, et al. 2004). Hence, as Winthrop et al. (1995) have shown, rock structures of various kinds are very common on Mt. Hood, one of the highest and most sacred places on the Plateau, but there are no rock art sites at this location to my knowledge.

The relevance of this well-documented Plateau pattern concerns the fact that creating rock cairns and structures was apparently common throughout the far west, even though only minimal ethnographic documentation of this activity exists (Whitley et al. 1999). For example, rock cairns were created by shamans during their vision quests in south-central California (Gayton and Newman 1940:43; Applegate 1978:34) and northeastern California (Dixon 1908:24), whereas they were built in the Colorado Desert by non-shamans seeking supernatural aid (Patencio 1943:73; Bean et al 1991:96). The important point here then is the widespread association of rock structures with ritual activities (regardless of whether made by shamans, puberty initiates, or non-shamans), and not exclusively (nor even primarily) for mundane purposes (such as game drives or hunting blinds), as archaeologists commonly have assumed.

It is then worth noting that the Coso Range, eastern California, has the largest concentration of petroglyphs in the far west, and it probably is no coincidence that the largest concentration of rock cairns and alignments in the Great Basin is located in the Panamint Valley immediately adjacent to the Cosos. No ethnographic information on the Numic construction of rock structures was recorded, to my knowledge. But, based on an analogy with the Plateau evidence, it can be inferred that these alignments and cairns were constructed as part of the vision questing that created the Coso engravings, despite the distance between the sites. This analogical inference, moreover, is supported by some preliminary archaeological research that I have conducted with Russ Kaldenberg on the Panamint sites, where we have found concentrations of shattered quartz around and a quartz crystal offering under a rock cairn (Figure 6). As noted elsewhere (Whitley et al. 1999), quartz was associated with Numic vision questing and petroglyphs, thus providing an independent line of evidence to support the analogical interpretation of these features.

As the above brief discussion of Plateau puberty rock art implies, this specific topic has been well covered by ethnologists and archaeologists and, for this reason, I have little (if anything at all) new to add to our understanding of this type of art, in this region. But another consideration of the topic is helpful because of its implications for understanding some of the larger issues in far western North American rock art.

Rites of Passage in the Far West

Perhaps the most surprising aspect of this descriptive review of puberty rock art in the far west is the simple fact that no far western North American-wide summary had, heretofore, been attempted. As stated at the outset, many of us have certainly acknowledged the existence of puberty art and studied some of the sites and motifs that it produced within our regions of interest. But it still seems to me that this

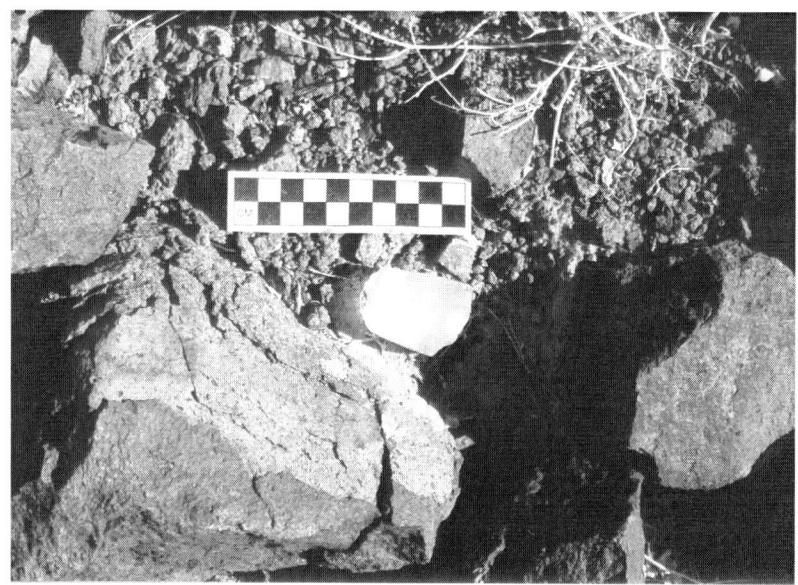

Figure 6. Quartz crystal associated with a rock cairn, Panamint Valley, eastern California. The Panamint Valley region, immediately east of the concentration of petroglyphs in the Coso Range, contains an unusual number of rock cairns, geoglyphs and other rock structures. Some of these, like this example, are associated with quartz crystals or shattered quartz cobbles, both of which were used during vision quests. This suggests that, following the well-documented Columbia Plateau pattern, the geoglyphs and other rock structures were created as part of the vision questing ritual which also produced the petroglyphs. (photo: D.S. Whitley)

type of rock art has been somewhat understudied and underemphasized; this is a first attempt at correcting this imbalance.

Based on this descriptive review, a few general conclusions for the far west can be offered. The first, and most important, is that the creation of rock art of some kind during puberty initiations is almost as typical as the initiations themselves. That is, while we know that rock art was *not* created in all puberty initiations (e.g., there is no evidence of the creation of rock art of any kind during the boys' jimsonweed initiation in south-central California [13]), puberty art was nonetheless fairly common, and probably more common than Driver's (1941) summary of puberty rite traits might imply. With the exception of north-central and northwestern California – a region somewhat depauperate in rock art generally – some type of puberty art in fact appears to have been present throughout Native California, the Plateau and at least into the western Great Basin, if not extending further east in Numic territory. That is, as long as we include cupules in our definition of rock art.

Second, there simply can be no debate that some of the puberty art portrays visionary imagery (e.g., on the Plateau), while the evidence is quite good that such was the case in another area (the Takic region), and with such a connection likely despite minimal evidence in still another tradition (the Yuman). That said, some of the puberty art – the cupule tradition – is clearly not shamanistic in any direct sense, although aspects of the underlying symbolism of the rite (e.g., the rock as supernaturally potent) are consistent with the wider system of shamanistic beliefs that suffused far western Native American cultures (see Whitley 2000b). This results because symbolic systems are necessarily coherent systems.

Perhaps more to the point, not all of the motifs even within a shamanistic tradition necessarily portray visionary imagery. Specifically here I refer to the hand prints that are found at many sites in the far west, but that are particularly common at the Takic girls' sites (and, in fact, are relatively common, worldwide, including in other shamanic and shamanistic rock art traditions). As noted elsewhere (Whitley 1996), hand prints result partly from our inherently tactile nature and impulses. In the far west they probably reflect the fact that the rock face was believed a permeable barrier between the natural and supernatural and that, by touching this face, it was possible to physically interact with the supernatural realm – a perception also reflected in the symbolic logic of the cupules. But they are not depictions of visionary imagery and, in a sense, they are not "depictions" at all. They recall instead Sahlins (1985) contention that symbolism is highly empirical. Nothing could be more empirical than this material trace of touching the sacred.

Perhaps most importantly, this review points again to the diversity in rock art traditions in the far west.

End Notes

[1] Following Taçon (1983), I use shamanic to indicate rock art made by a shaman, *per se*, and shamanistic for art made by non-shamans but within the context of shamanistic beliefs and practices.

[2] An alternative explanation can be suggested for the relative paucity of information on the "Takic" boys' art, which is limited to comments by Waterman (1910) for the Diegueño, and DuBois (1908) and Harrington (n.d.a) for the Luiseño. As is discussed subsequently, there is evidence for a widespread boys' puberty art tradition among the neighboring Yuman speaking groups. It is acknowledged that aspects of the Takic initiation were adopted by the Diegueño (Kroeber 1925; Hedges 1970), and it appears that this initiation was grafted onto their existing Yuman traditions. Given the adjacency of the Takic speaking Luiseño and the

Yuman speaking Diegueño, the clear cultural diffusion of religious ideas between them, and the absence of any reference to boys' puberty art in the other Takic speaking groups, it is possible to hypothesize that the Takic boys' art was an adoption of the Yuman tradition, exclusively by the Luiseño boys. That is, that Takic puberty art, *per se*, was originally restricted to girls but that, with the Diegueño grafting of the Takic toloache initiation for boys onto their Yuman tradition, the Luiseño also adopted the Yuman boys' art-making tradition, whereas other Takic groups did not. Note that, while this hypothesis is plausible and somewhat appealing, it still must be emphasized that our Luiseño ethnographic record is, by far, the most complete with respect to Takic rituals. The apparent restriction of Takic boys' art to the Luiseño, in other words, may likewise be a simple function of the existing evidence.

[3] Additional Takic speakers lived in the Transverse Ranges, Tehachapi Mountains and Antelope Valley but do not appear to have participated in this rock art tradition. These include the Kitanemuk/Haminat, Tataviam, and Vanyume. As discussed below, these groups appear have participated instead in the cupule tradition along with other groups from south-central California.

[4] Cultural practices do not necessarily correspond precisely to ethnolinguistic boundaries, of course, nor are these boundaries necessarily as fixed as we might like, with "transitional cultural areas" therefore potentially existing. One possible example of such is suggested by archaeological evidence near the eastern edge of Chumash territory, near their boundary with the Gabrielino. This concerns pictograph site CA-VEN-119 which consists of a small rock shelter with a ceiling covered with children's red handprints. Although there is no ethnographic evidence supporting the creation of pictographs during Chumash puberty initiations (and no real evidence for Chumash puberty initiations of any kind, in fact – as discussed below), it is easy to infer on archaeological and analogical grounds that this site was the result of such an initiation.

[5] Hedges (2001) has contested my interpretation of zigzags as rattlesnake motifs, claiming that there is no ethnographic support for this. In fact there is substantial support for such an interpretation. First, as noted above, there was essentially universal agreement that zigzags were graphic images for rattlesnakes, throughout Native California and regardless of medium. Second, this was confirmed for the girls' puberty initiations with respect to their face paintings by Strong (1929:298) who notes that "wavy, red, horizontal lines were put on. This was called 'the rattlesnake' design." Third, the relevance of face painting designs to the rock art motifs is direct, as DuBois (1908:96) states "The face of the girl is painted each month in a different design and corresponding marks are made upon the rocks." This is confirmed by Sparkman (1908:225) "her

face was painted, and a similar painting was also made on a rock." That is, both the facial design and pictograph were rattlesnake motifs. (Note that, while the DuBois comments may be interpreted as if different kinds of motifs were painted each month, the rock art demonstrates otherwise. That is, the same design was clearly repeated, hence DuBois' comment most likely should have been phrased to indicate that *another* [rather than *different*] design was painted on the girls' face, and rock, each month.)

[6] True and Baumhoff (1981:261-262) attempt to use this statement to demonstrate that Parker, a local historian, was an unreliable ethnographic source. Their contention was that he had confused the girls' ceremony with the boys' use of jimsonweed, due to this reference to "grogginess." In fact, they overlooked the earlier statements of DuBois (1908) and Strong (1929) that confirm Parker's assertion about as well as the literature on the effects of tobacco (e.g., Wilbert 1987).

[7] The Takic association between rattlesnake spirits and females is a specific example of much wider Uto-Aztecan symbolic associations. This is most dramatically seen in the Mexica (Aztec) goddess Coatlicue, 'serpent skirt,' with the implication being that rattlesnake guards the vaginas of women.

Note further the important fact that a significant portion of the girls' puberty motifs are clearly *not* depictions of spirit helpers. Here I refer to the hand prints that are common at certain sites. The anthropometrics of these have been studied by Freers (2001) from a number of perspectives, including the possibility that some may be adolescent male or adult rather than adolescent female—possibilities that are interesting in light of the general paucity of information on the boys' art, and statements in DuBois (1908) and Kroeber (1925) that the "chief's wife" made pictographs at the conclusion of the race. Unfortunately, given the inherent subjectivity in Freers' measurements (which he acknowledges), as well as the difficulties in distinguishing adolescent male from female based on size and inferred height when age cannot be controlled, his only results are that "the data does [sic] tend to ratify the notion that a neoadolescent female indoctrination ceremony may have at least produced some of the hand print imagery" (Freers 2001:330), which of course is already well established by the ethnographic record.

[8] Other Yuman-speaking groups, classified linguistically as the Upland Yumans or the Pai speakers (Walapai, Havasupai, etc.), occupied the upper Colorado River, while additional Yuman speakers (e.g., Maricopa) resided in portions of central Arizona. None of these groups are considered here inasmuch as they fall outside the limits of the hunting-gathering-fishing far west.

[9] For example, Harrington (n.d.c) records that:

"A fresh picture or image of a person was held to be doctor business, capable of causing grief or even death. But a pictograph or an outline effigy of a person made by placing stones on the ground was held to have the intention of being everlasting and was considered as good as [i.e., for] a man [as] having an ancestral name as his name or as one of his names." The use of Yuman-speakers rock art (petroglyphs, pictographs and earth figures) for sorcery is confirmed in a number of additional sources, including the following early account by Trippel (1889:582) "[T]he bewitcher generally goes off to a quiet place to make his spell. He draws an image of his victim and with a sharpened stick pierces the image where the heart is."

[10] In a parallel fashion I have argued elsewhere (Whitley 2000b) that, while the shamans' art portrayed the mythic creation of the world, it is almost entirely entoptic in form because it was intended to depict the essence or pattern of the creation, not the narrative sequence of events (which everyone already knew), as occurred in the 'shaman's song' which recounts the creation but by use of nonsense syllables.

[11] In my recent synthesis of California rock art (Whitley 2000b), I identified the geographical distinction between the so-called rain rocks of northern California and the baby rocks of the north-central region, and argued that the cupules in other parts of the state were produced during girls' puberty initiations. In rereading Breck Parkman's (1993) article on rain-making rituals for this paper, I discovered that he had made these same distinctions and inferences in his footnotes, which I had previously overlooked, and credit for these interpretations should go to him. I am encouraged, however, by the fact that we both came to the same conclusions about the ethnographic evidence.

[12] An intriguing bit of potentially important information on girls' puberty art is provided by Stoffle et al. (2001) who report the identification of a First Menses site in southern Nevada by contemporary Numic consultants. This is close to but not at a petroglyph site, but it is not clear whether it has cupules. Regardless, it confirms at least a general relationship between the Numic girls' initiations and rock art.

[13] Gayton (1948:118) does describe the fact that Wukchumni Yokuts male initiates were taken on a ritual run past the Bell Bluff pictograph site (CA-TUL-2), which I have inferred was painted by the shaman Haichacha or Jim Hangton, a Pohot family member (Whitley 1992:93). This occurred before the boys were administered jimsonweed. Note however that Bell Bluff was also the Wukchumni creation spot, hence the ritual importance of this run is not entirely clear. It nonetheless suggests that rock art may have been used, during male initiations, to give the boys an idea of the appearance of the supernatural that they themselves were about to visit under the influence of *toloache*.

Table 1
References to Plateau Puberty Rock Art

1896 Thompson River Indians – boys and girls reaching maturity go to the hills for a long ceremony of purification and make offerings to secure good luck. At the end of this period they record their offerings, ceremonies and dreams on a boulder. (Teit 1896:227-230)

1906 Among the Lillooet, "Paintings were made on rocks and trees by adolescent boys and girls as a record of their [puberty] observances, but also by men as a record of their dreams." (Teit 1906:282)

1908 Nez Percé girls made rock paintings during their vision quest to portray objects seen during their dreams or connected with the ceremonies (Spinden 1908:231-232).

1909 For the Shuswap, "All pubescent lads and some girls made pictures with paint on rocks during...their training period. Most. . .[paintings] were representations of objects seen in their dreams, and the painting of them was. . .to hasten the attainment of a person's manitou [power]." (Teit 1909:590)

1916 For Lower Columbia River tribes (Wasco, Warm Springs, Yakama), "in his early teens [each] Indian youth had to visit [a petroglyph boulder] at night by himself, cut his sign upon it and remain there all night alone. . .with the job finished. . .his was a charmed life." (Oregonian 1916)

1918 For Interior Salish Tribes and Kutenai, "[rock] paintings are found in places. . .where Indians were in the habit of holding vigil and undergoing training during the period of their puberty ceremonials when they generally acquired their manitous [power]. . .At the expiration of the training (or sometime during it. . .) the novice painted pictures on cliffs or boulders near by...The paintings were records of the most important of the novices experiences. . .things seen in striking visions, things obtained as guardians" (Teit 1918:1-2)

1926 Kutenai people go to pictographs for visions. There they talk to the spirits about the future. The spirits told them how they would live and what they would do. Red paint was a medicine; it had supernatural power. They painted pictures to make things happen. (Barbeau 1960:207-211)

Table 1 (Continued)
References to Plateau Puberty Rock Art

1930 For the Coeur d'Alene, "Rock paintings were. . .records of dreams, objects seen in dreams, guardian spirits. . .they were supposed to transmit power from the object depicted to the person making the pictures. . .young men during their puberty ceremonials made rock paintings. . .older men also painted dreams on cliffs." (Teit 1930:194)

1930 For the Okanagan, "In connection with the training period, adolescents of both sexes made records of remarkable dreams, pictures of what they desired or what they had seen." Rock paintings were also made by adults as records of notable dreams. (Teit 1930:283)

1938 Among the Okanagan, to announce his power, a man would "paint symbols of [his guardian spirits] on a large rock in the hills." A man might "send his child to rock paintings he had made many years before [to obtain a guardian spirit]. . .for each [spirit] he scored a short red line on the rock surface beside the paintings." (Cline 1938:136-138)

1953 A Kutenai informant said "[the spirits] held a big meeting at Painted Rocks. . .and one said 'I'm going to give this power to them [human vision questors]. If they seek me for it I will give it to them.' Finally all the [guardian spirits] put their names [signs] on the rock." (Malouf and White 1953:30-31)

1954 Okanagan informants reported: "When a person has a power he paints a picture [pictograph] of it." Pictographs were made by children on their spirit quest, a painting represents their power. (Lerman 1954:99, 142, 191)

1959 Pictograph panels were used by the Flathead and Pend d'Oreille to receive their spirits during vision quests (Dusenberry 1959).

1975 Elderly Spokan informants knew of paintings painted by one's grandfather, and they identified a pictograph site as a place for a vision quest where one got power. (Coburn 1975:39)

1991 The Elmo pictograph site, Montana, is used by the Kutenai and Flathead for vision quests. "There are hundreds of such sites in Western Wyoming and neighboring Idaho and Wyoming" (Walker 1991:110).

Table 1 (Continued)
References to Plateau Puberty Rock Art

1993 Among the Thompson Indians "Old people train the young in the mountains. . .They teach them about the red paint and how to put it on the rocks. From the writings on the rocks they teach young people how to live. You use [your] drawing in later life. . .that's your strength. . .any. . .animal you dream that's going to be your power." (York et al 1993:6)

1998 For the Lillooet, "during puberty training, some boys and girls made a record of some parts of the ceremonial. These pictographs were painted on rock bluffs, stones or trees" (Kennedy and Bouchard 1998a:184).

1998 Among the Northern Okanagan, "In connection with puberty training, some adolescents painted pictographs of their visions on boulders or rock faces" (Kennedy and Bouchard 1998b:249).

Discussion

Angelo Fossati: Only a comment about leaving quartz on the rocks. We are very, very far away in Valcamonica, but we have just this same attitude of leaving quartz tools on the site. Probably they were also used to peck the petroglyphs.

David Whitley: Yes, interesting. Quartz tools do work very well as pecking stones, but you can use any kind of rock—experiments show that you can use basalt on basalt and it will work perfectly well. Maybe there was a selection for quartz because of its properties in your area as well.

Robert Layton: Doesn't Teit refer to cupules on the Fraser River as a boys' puberty ritual—they made themselves strong as they were working away.

David Whitley: Yes, he does (see Teit 1900:320). Although I wasn't looking at cupules on the Columbia Plateau, it may have a more widespread relationship with puberty initiation.

PART 4
EPILOGUE

Editors' Introduction to Spilyay Tymoo Articles

As part of the 2002 symposium, *Spilyay Tymoo*, tribal newspaper for the Confederated Tribes of the Warm Springs Reservation of Oregon, published a pair of articles describing the participation of Indian people in both the field trip and the presentation of papers. The articles were brought to our attention by Brigette Whipple, who participated in all the sessions, and with her help we obtained permission from the author, Shannon Keaveny, and the newspaper's editor, Dave McMechan, to reprint them here. In addition to providing strong support for many of the things discussed at the meeting, they show one more way that traditions are kept alive and communicated in the modern world of Indian people. We take this opportunity to thank once again, all of the Indian people who assisted us in any way with this session.

qe'ciyew'yew'
(thank you)

Spilyay Tymoo Articles

New theories shed light on tribal rock art
By Shannon Keaveny, Spilyay Tymoo
Warm Springs, Oregon, September 14, 2002

New discoveries and theories regarding the significance of rock art were presented during a recent public forum, *The Shamans of Prehistory: New Perspectives on World Rock Art*.

Speakers at the event, held Sept. 6 at Portland State University (PSU), included rock art specialists from around the world. During the previous days, the same rock art scholars met with various tribal members of the Columbia River Basin.

Among those from Warm Springs invited to the forum were Brigette Whipple, Viola Kalama and Larry Dick. The scholars sought insight from river tribes in this area to help solve the mystery surrounding petroglyphs and pictographs in the Columbia Gorge.

Western scholars once thought of rock art as primitive and rudimentary depictions of hunting scenes.

The idea now widely accepted among world-renowned archaeologists is that rock art was the practice of shamans and highly spiritual people.

With a renewed academic zeal archaeologists are reviewing the documented reports from tribal members between the years of 1890 to 1940.

They are also talking to tribal members who have knowledge that has been passed down for generations.

Among the participants at the public presentation at PSU were Jean Clottes, scientific advisor for the French Ministry of Culture, famous for his study of the 32,000-year-old paintings in Chauvet Cave in France; David Whitley, an archaeologist and author of *"Art of the Shaman: Rock Art of California"*; and James Keyser, a regional archaeologist with the U.S. Forest Service and a Columbia River Basin rock art specialist.

Shamanistic Rock Art
Tribal Elders from the Columbia River Basin share their knowledge with world scholars.
By Shannon Keaveny, Spilyay Tymoo
Warm Springs, Oregon, September 14, 2002

"It is my perspective that rock art is associated with specific places of vision quests, rights of passage, and first kill ceremonies."
Brigette Whipple
Cultural Resources

On an early September morning near The Dalles area, lower Columbia Plateau elders, who grew up on the river with their families, boarded a small, motorized boat.

The wind blew slightly, the sun shone, and the water was placid with a swift subtle current, the most notable contrast to their childhood, when Celilo Falls still fell and water rushed and swirled dangerously below the cliffs.

In that time, at this stunning geographical place, paintings above the rushing rapids could be seen.

Jean Clottes, world rock art specialist, concludes from his global studies, "Where ever there are natural geological marvels, you can be sure to find stories about them."

What was perhaps, at one time someone's story drawn on the cliffs, became folk tales for the following generations of people living on or near the Columbia River.

Dams along this stretch of the Columbia River inundated more that half of the known rock art sites. Water monsters over whirlpools, protecting the fisherman, are now sites for only the fish. Other pictographs at higher altitudes still can be seen, and their significance continues to intrigue modern generations.

Among the elders on the boat were Viola Kalama of Warm Springs and James Selam of the Yakama Indian Reservation.

Accompanying them were their direct descendants and a group of world-renowned rock art specialists.

Some of the rock art specialists included Dr. Jean Clottes, the previous Director of Research for the 32,000 year old Chauvet Cave and co-author of "Shamans of Prehistory," Dr. David Lewis-Williams, Director of the Rock Art Research Institute in Johannesburg, South Africa and also co-author of "Shamans of Prehistory," Dr. David Whitley, national rock art specialist and author of "The art of the Shaman: Rock Art of California;" and Dr. James Keyser, a Pacific Northwest Archaeologist and lead organizer of their exposition called "The Ethnography of World Rock Art".

The elders were invited to share their knowledge of the past. The group headed toward Miller Island, east of the mouth of the Deschutes River.

There, the specialists listened and learned from what the elders had to say.

The pictographs viewed included stick figures with arced rays over their heads. Elk, deer, and bighorn sheep were painted with arrows surrounding them. Zig-zags and other geometrical figures were portrayed.

Brigette Whipple, granddaughter of Viola Kalama and also invited on the excursion, explained the significance of the Columbia River Basin tribes presence, "We were invited for the purpose of giving a historical tribal perspective on Columbia rock art."

Her grandmother, Viola Kalama, who is 80, Whipple noted, was raised on the river in a traditional way. She is fluent in Wasco and Sahaptin and as a child she heard stories about the paintings. She is known for her rich sense of heritage and culture.

Kalama used this opportunity to share her version of what the rock art means/meant to the Wasco people with willing Western archaeologists.

To the Natives of the Columbia area, rock depictions were always seen as scenes of cultural and spiritual importance.

Now, views like Whipple's, instilled in her from the teachings of her grandma, have gained international recognition.

Whipple relates, "It is my perspective that rock art is associated with specific places of vision quests, rights of passage, and first kill ceremonies. I think the pictographs in this area were written/drawn by medicine people, holy people or people performing rites of passage into manhood or womanhood."

"For instance, if I became a woman, I would learn to harvest my berries, collect my roots, then, I may go out into the wild by myself and write my story. Those paintings on the walls could be my story."

But, she reiterates, "nobody really knows."

In fact, among the scholars visiting on that day, all believed the same. Combining the world knowledge of rock art, they now assert rock art was the practice of shamans.

In Portland at the public presentation "Shamans of Prehistory: New Perspective on World Rock Art," Whitley took the time to explain, "Shamans are people who speak with the gods which is commonly associated with hunter-gatherer peoples but has been documented in most religions of the world."

He explained that in a trance-like state, hyperventilation is often symptomatic. When hyperventilating, vomiting and bleeding from the nose can occur, as many animals in rock art throughout the world are displayed.

The animals, themselves, may be the artist's spirit helper, he said, explaining why many depictions have both human and animalistic qualities.

Whipple loosely defines her impression of spirit helpers. "A spirit helper may be the animal that person most closely relates to. Maybe a hunter's spirit helper would be the deer."

Petroglyphs and pictographs in the Columbia Plateau commonly contain geometric symbols. World specialists theorize that these designs are common neuropsychological symptoms experienced by all *Homo sapiens* in altered states.

Whitley explained seven common visual patterns, including zig-zags, grids, and dots, and provided examples in rock art from around the world.

Whipple thinks geometric symbols on the Columbia plateau aren't necessarily common neuropsychological symbols everyone sees in altered states.

In contrast, she thinks, "They could come from visions. A zig-zag could be water, a snake, or lightning. Maybe they were spirits. Maybe a woman saw a mountain place to harvest in her rite of passage for berry picking," referring to the triangular zig-zag at the site on Miller Island, which she said immediately made her think of the Three Sisters mountain range.

She hypothesizes about the Columbia plateau's rock art origin, "I think they were either seeking something for themselves or seeking something for someone else."

Whipple is pleased that today's archaeologists are eager to listen to elders like her grandma.

"They seemed really receptive to our theories," she said, "We both made great accomplishments. We (the tribes) now have a better understanding of rock art globally and we also know there is a respectful intention to know more from the other side."

Mystery shrouds the petroglyphs and pictographs found throughout the Columbia River Plateau.

Much of the rich oral mythology associated with the petroglyphs and pictographs was lost in European epidemics that swept through the area. In The Dalles area approximately 90 percent of the population was wiped out due to disease by 1840.

More that 160 sites have been identified in the lower Columbia area, an area defined as the watershed between Priest Rapids and The Dalles, excluding the Snake River.

About 90 of the sites can be found between The Dalles and Pasco with other large concentrations found along the middle and lower Deschutes River.

Many were flooded when they dammed the Columbia below Celilo Falls and other areas.

Some pictographs have suffered vandalism by chalk, paint, and scratched initials.

A few sites are fading from natural weathering.

A unique natural preservation occurrence, keeps those still with us around. Pictographs, defined as rock paints, are most often red, but white, black, yellow, and even blue-green pigments were also used. The red pigment was made from various different minerals.

Crushed iron oxides (hematite and limonite) produced the commonly seen red and yellow colors. Clays bore white and copper oxides, green.

Both charcoal and manganese oxide produced black. These mineral pigments were crushed with binding agents, like blood, egg, fat, plant juice, or urine, to produce paint.

The paintings are estimated to be between 200 and 12,000 years old. Their current presentation state is a stroke of luck.

Mineral deposits that seep over cliffs, after a rain, act as a fixative for paintings.

When the rainwater evaporates, it leaves a thin film of mineral that is transparent in ideal situations. Heavy mineral build up will cloud images.

Between the pictographs unique preservation, Viola Kalama's memories of childhood stories, and dedicated scholars, the story once told, may someday be told again.

Some factual information for this article was taken from the book "Indian Rock Art of the Columbia Plateau" by James D. Keyser.

REFERENCES CITED

Abreu, M. S. De, A. Arcà, and A. Fossati
1995 As Gravuras nao Saben Nadar! Le Incisioni non Sanno Nuotare. *Archeologia Viva*, 53(XIV):28-36, Firenze, Italia.

Aikens, C. M.
1993 *Archaeology of Oregon*. USDI Bureau of Land Management, Oregon State Office, Portland.

Aikens, C. M. and D. L. Jenkins
1994 *Archaeological Researches in the Northern Great Basin: Fort Rock Archaeology Since Cressman*. University of Oregon Anthropological Papers 50, Eugene.

Alinei, M.
1984 Naquane nella Valcamonica nei suoi Rapporti con le Aquane, Esseri Mitologici delle Alpi Centro Orientali. *Quaderni di Semantica* 1:3-16.

Altheim, F. and E. Trautmann
1937 Nordische und Italische Felsbildkunst. *Die Welt als Geschichte* III:83-113, Berlin, Deutschland.

Alvarez de Williams, A.
1973 Five Rock Art Sites in Baja California South of the 29th Parallel. *Pacific Coast Archaeological Society Quarterly* 9(4):37-46.

Ames, K. M. and H. D. G. Maschner
1999 *People of the Northwest Coast: Their Archeology and Prehistory*. Thames and Hudson, London, UK.

Anati, E.
1962 *Capo di Ponte Centro dell'arte Rupestre Camuna*. Edizioni del Centro, Capo di Ponte, Italia.
1974 Lo Stile Sub-naturalistico Camuno e l'origine dell'arte Rupestre Alpina. *Bolletino del Centro Camuno di Studi Preistorici* 11:59-84.
1976 *Evolution and Style in Camunian Rock Art*. Archivi 6, Capo di Ponte, Italia.
1982 *I Camuni. Alle Radici della Civiltà Europea*. Milano, Italia.

Anonymous
1955 Prehistoric Stone Carving. *Screenings: Newsletter of the Oregon Archaeological Society* 4(11):2.
1956a Untitled. *Screenings: Newsletter of the Oregon Archaeological Society* 5(4):1-2.
1956b Untitled. *Screenings: Newsletter of the Oregon Archaeological Society* 5(8):2.
1979 Site Survey Form for 45CL258. On file Washington State Office of Archaeology and Historic Preservation, Olympia.

Applegate, R. B.
1978 *?Atishwin: The Dream-Helper in South-Central California*. Ballena Press, Socorro, NM.

Arcà A., A. Fossati, E. Marchi, and E. Tognoni (editors)
1995 *Rupe Magna. La Roccia Incisa più Grande delle Alpi.* Quaderni del Parco, 1, Sondrio, Italia.

Armitage, R. A., M. Hyman, J. Southin, C. Barat, and M. W. Rowe
1997 Rock-Art Image in Fern Cave, Lava Beds National Monument, California: Not the AD 1054 (Crab Nebula) Supernova. *Antiquity* 71:715-719.

Arndt, W.
1962 The Interpretation of the Delemere Lightning Painting and Rock Engravings. *Oceania* 32(3):163-177.

Atkinson, J. M.
1992 Shamanisms Today. *Annual Review of Anthropology* 21:307-330.

Bahn, P. G.
1995 Cave Art Without the Caves. *Antiquities* 69:231-237.
1997 Membrane and Numb Brain: A Close Look at a Recent Claim for Shamanism in Paleolithic Art. *Rock Art Research* 14(1):62-68.
1998 *The Cambridge Illustrated History of Prehistoric Art.* Cambridge University Press, Cambridge, UK.

Bahn, P. G. and J. Vertut
1988 *Images of the Ice Age.* Windward, London, UK.
1997 *Journey through the Ice Age.* Weidenfeld & Nicolson, London, UK.

Barbeau, M.
1960 *Indian Days on the Western Prairies.* National Museum of Canada Bulletin 163 [reprinted 1965].

Barker, M. A. R.
1963a Klamath Texts. *University of California Publications in Linguistics* Vol. 30. University of California Press, Berkeley.
1963b Klamath Dictionary. *University of California Publications in Linguistics* Vol. 31. University of California Press, Berkeley.
1963c Klamath Grammar. *University of California Publications in Linguistics* Vol. 32. University of California Press, Berkeley.

Barrett, S. A.
1908 The Ethnogeography of the Pomo and Neighboring Indians. *University of California Publications in American Archaeology and Ethnology* 6(1). Berkeley.
1952 Material Aspects of Pomo Culture, Part One. *Bulletin of the Public Museum of the City of Milwaukee* 20(1).

Barrow, F. J.
1942 Petroglyphs and Pictographs on the British Columbia Coast. *Canadian Geographic Journal* 24:94-101.

Bass, A.
1966 *The Arapaho Way: A Memoir of an Indian Boyhood.* Clarkson N. Potter, New York.

Battaglia, R.
1934 Ricerche Etnografiche sui Petroglifi della Cerchia Alpina. *Studi Etruschi* 8:11-48.

Baumhoff, M.
1981 The Evolution of Pomo Society. *Journal of California and Great Basin Anthropology* 2:175-185.

Baun, C. M. and R. Lewis
1991 *The First Oregonians*. Oregon Council for the Humanities, Portland.

Bean, L. J.
1976 Power and Its Application in Native California. In *Native Californians: A Theoretical Retrospective*. L. J. Bean and T. C. Blackburn, editors, pp. 407-420. Ballena Press, Socorro, NM.

Bean, L.J., S.B. Vane, and J. Young
1991 *The Cahuilla Landscape: The Santa Rosa and San Jacinto Mountains*. Ballena Press Anthropological Papers 75, Menlo Park, CA.

Beattie, J.
1964 *Other Cultures: Aims, Methods and Achievements in Social Anthropology*. Routledge, London, UK.

Beaune, S. de
1997 Compte-rendu. *L'Homme* 144:153-236.
1998 Chamanisme et Préhistoire. Un Feuilleton à Épisodes. *L'Homme* 147:203-219.

Beckwith, M. W.
1938 *Mandan-Hidatsa Myths and Ceremonies*, Memoirs of the American Folklore Society, Vol. 32. [Reprinted 1969 by Kraus Reprint, New York.]

Bednarik, R.
1994 Miscellanea, an Editorial Digest of World Archaeology. *The Artefact* 17:67-80.

Bégouen, H.
1924 La Magie aux Temps Préhistoriques. *Mémoires de l'Académie des Sciences, Inscriptions et Belles-Lettres* 1890, II:417-432.
1939 Les Bases Magiques de l'art Préhistorique. *Scientia*, Series 4, Year 33, pp. 202-216.

Bégouen, H. and H. Breuil
1958 *Les Cavernes du Volp: Trois-Frères - Tuc d'Audoubert*. Arts et Métiers Graphiques, Paris, France.

Benson, A. and L. Sehgal
1987 The Light at the End of the Tunnel. *San Diego Museum Rock Art Papers*. 5:1-16.

Bettis, G. M.
1986 *Indian Rock Art of the Lower Deschutes River*. Rock Art Research Education, Portland, OR.

Biesele, M.
1993 *'Women Like Meat': The Folklore and Foraging Ideology of the Kalahari Ju/'hoan*. Witwatersrand University Press, Johannesburg, South Africa.

Binford, L. R.
1962 Archaeology as Anthropology. *American Antiquity* 28:217-225
1967 Smudge Pits and Hide Smoking: The Use of Analogy in Archaeological Reasoning. *American Antiquity* 32:1-12

1968   Archaeological Perspectives. In *New Perspectives in Archaeology*. S. R. Binford and L. R. Binford, editors, pp. 5-32. Aldine, Chicago, IL.

Blackburn, T. C.
1976   A Query Regarding the Possible Hallucinogenic Effects of Ant Ingestion in South-Central California. *Journal of California Anthropology* 3:78-81.

Bleek, D. F.
1924   *The Mantis and His Friends: Bushman Folklore*. Blackwell, Oxford, UK.
1933   Beliefs and Customs of the /Xam Bushmen. Part V: The Rain. Part VI: Rain-Making. *Bantu Studies* 7:297-312, 375-392.
1935   Beliefs and Customs of the /Xam Bushmen. Part VII: Sorcerers. *Bantu Studies* 9:1-47.

Bleek, W. H. I. and L. C. Lloyd
1911   *Specimens of Bushman Folklore*. George Allen, London. Reprint: 1968. Struik, Cape Town, South Africa.

Bloch, M.
1974   Symbols, Song, Dance and Features of Articulation: Is Religion an Extreme Form of Traditional Authority? *Archives European Journal of Sociology* 15:55-81.

Blundell, G.
1998   On Neuropsychology in Southern African Rock Art Research. *The Anthropology of Consciousness* 9(1):3-12.
2004   *Ngabayo's Nomansland: San Rock Art and the Somatic Past.* In Press. Uppsala University Press, Uppsala, Sweden.

Boller, H. A.
1972   *Among the Indians: Four Years on the Upper Missouri, 1858-1862*. M. M. Quaife, editor. University of Nebraska Press, Lincoln [reprint of 1867 publication].

Bontempi, F.
1989   *Economia del Ferro. Miniere, Forni e Fucine in Valcamonica dal XV al XIX Secolo*. Edizioni del Circolo Culturale Ghislandi, Milano, Italia.

Borden, C. E.
1983   Prehistoric Art of the Lower Fraser Region. In *Indian Art Traditions of the Northwest Coast*. R. L. Carlson, editor, pp. 131-165. Archaeology Press, Department of Archaeology, Simon Fraser University, Burnaby, British Columbia.

Boreson, K.
1980   Serrated Edges on Petroglyph Boulders. Paper presented at the 33rd Annual Northwest Anthropological Conference, Bellingham, Washington.
1998   Rock Art. In *Handbook of North American Indians: Volume 12, Plateau*. D. E. Walker, Jr., editor, pp. 611-619. Smithsonian Institution, Washington, D.C.

Boreson, K. and W. R. Peterson
1985   The Petroglyphs at Lake Pend Oreille, Bonner County, Northern Idaho. *Eastern Washington University Reports in Archaeology and His*tory, pp.100-49.

Boscana, G.
1978 *Chinigchinich: An Historical Account of the Indians of the Mission of San Juan Capistrano Called the Acagchemem Tribe.* Translated by A. Robinson, annotated by J.P. Harrington. Malki Museum, Banning, CA.

Bostwick, T. W.
2001 North American Indian Agriculturalists. In *Handbook of Rock Art Research*, D. S. Whitley, editor, pp.414-458. AltaMira Press, Walnut Creek, CA.

Bourdieu, P.
1977 *Outline of a Theory of Practic.* Translated by A. Morton. Cambridge University Press, Cambridge, UK.

Bourguignon, E.
1973 Introduction: a Framework for the Comparative Study of Altered States of Consciousness. In *Religion, Altered States of Consciousness, and Social Change*, E. Bourguignon, editor. Ohio State University Press, Columbus.
1977 Altered States of Consciousness. In *Myths and Rituals: Drugs, Rituals, and Altered States of Consciousness*, pp. 7-24. Balkema, Rotterdam, Netherlands.

Bourke, J. G.
1889 Notes on the Cosmogony and Theogony of the Mojave Indians of the Rio Colorado, Arizona. *Journal of American Folk Lore* 2(4):169-189.

Bowers, A. W.
1950 *Mandan Social and Ceremonial Organization.* University of Chicago Press, Chicago, IL. [Reprinted 1991 by the University of Idaho Press, Moscow.]
1963 *Hidatsa Social and Ceremonial Organization.* Bureau of American Ethnology, Smithsonian Institution, Bulletin 194. [Reprinted 1992 by the University of Nebraska Press, Lincoln.]

Boyd, C. E.
1998 Pictographic Evidence of Peyotism in the Lower Pecos, Texas Archaic. In *The Archaeology of Rock Art.* C. Chippendale and P. S. C. Taçon, editors, pp. 229-246. Cambridge University Press, Cambridge, UK.
2003 *Rock Art of the Lower Pecos.* Texas A&M University Press, College Station.

Boyd, R.
1996 *People of the Dalles: The Indians of Wascopam Mission.* University of Nebraska Press, Lincoln.

Bradley, J. H., Lieutenant
1961 *The March of the Montana Column: A Prelude to the Custer Disaster.* E. I. Stewart, editor. University of Oklahoma Press, Norman.

Bradley, R., C. Chippindale, and K. Helskog
2001 Post-Paleolithic Europe. In *Handbook of Rock Art Research*, D. S. Whitley, editor, pp.482-529. AltaMira Press, Walnut Creek, CA.

Bray, E. C. and M. C. Bray (editors)
1976 *Joseph N. Nicollet on the Plains and Prairies.* Minnesota Historical Society, St. Paul.

Brown, J. E.
1953 *The Sacred Pipe: Black Elk's Account of the Seven Rites of the Oglala Sioux.* University of Nebraska Press, Lincoln.

Brugge, D. M.
2001 A History of Navajo Rock Art Research. *American Indian Rock Art* 27:5-16.

Buckley, T.
1986 Lexical Transcription and Archaeological Interpretation: "A Rock Feature Complex from Northwestern California". *American Antiquity* 51, 617-618.

Caldwell, W.W. and R.L. Carlson
1954 Further Documentation of "Stone Piling" During the Plateau Vision Quest. *American Anthropologist* 56, 441-442.

Camuri, G.
1995 In Contrada Aquane: il Linguaggio dell'acqua nelle Figure di Cervo della Roccia 14 del Parco Nazionale delle Incisioni Rupestri. *Notizie Archeologiche Bergomensi* 2:281-287, Bergamo, Italia.

Cannon, W. and M. Ricks
1986 The Lake County, Oregon, Rock Art Inventory: Implications for Prehistoric Settlement and Land Use Patterns. *Contributions to the Archaeology of Oregon, No. 3.* Association of Oregon Archaeologists, Portland.

Carlson, R. L.
1983 Changes and Continuity in Northwest Coast Art. In *Indian Art Traditions of the Northwest Coast*, R. L. Carlson, editor, pp. 197-205. Archaeology Press, Department of Archaeology, Simon Fraser University, Burnaby, British Columbia.

Carroll, J. M. and L. A. Frost (editors)
1976 *Private Theodore Ewert's Diary of the Black Hills Expedition of 1874.* CRI (Consultant Resources International) Books, Piscataway, NJ.

Cash Cash, P.
1997 Ritual Cutting: An Example from the Columbia Plateau. Paper presented at the 96th Annual American Anthropological Association Conference. Washington, D.C.

2004 *To Witness Creation: A Southern Columbia Plateau Rock-Art Ethnography.* Report to USDA Forest Service, Pacific Northwest Regional Office, Recreation. Portland, OR.

Casini, S. and A. Fossati
1994 Le Stele e i Massi Incisi della Valcamonica e della Valtellina nell'ambito dell'arcoAlpino. In *Le Pietre degli Dei. Menhir e Stele dell'età del Rame in Valcamonica e Valtellina.* S. Casini, editor, pp. 59-68, Bergamo, Italia.

Catlin, G.
1973 *Letters and Notes on the Manners, Customs, and Condition of the North American Indians.* Dover Publications, New York. [Reprint of 1844 edition, London, UK.]

Chakravarty, K. K. and R. G. Bednarik
1997   *Indian Rock Art in its Global Context.* Motilal Banarsidass Publishers Private Ltd., Delhi, India.

Chaloupka, G.
1982   *Burrungguy: Noulangie Rock.* Northart, Darwin, Australia.
1993   *Journey in Time. The World's Longest Continuing Art Tradition.* Reed/Heinemann, Chatswood, Australia.

Chami, F., G. Pwiti, and C. Radimilahy (editors)
2001   *People, Contact and the Environment in the African Past.* Dar Es Salaam University Press, Dar Es Salaam, Tanzania.

Chartkoff, J.L.
1983   A Rock Feature Complex from Northwestern California. *American Antiquity* 48:745-760.

Chaumeil, J. P.
1999   Les Visions des Chamanes d'Amazonie. *Sciences Humaines* 97:42-45.

Chen, Z. F.
2001   Asia. In *Handbook of Rock Art Research*, D. S. Whitley, editor, pp.760-785. AltaMira Press, Walnut Creek, CA.

Chippindale, C.
2001   Studying Ancient Pictures as Pictures. In *Handbook of Rock Art Research*, D. S. Whitley, editor, pp.247-272. AltaMira Press, Walnut Creek, CA.

Christensen, D.
1992   Scratched Glyphs in Arizona: A Reevaluation. *San Diego Museum Rock Art Papers* 9 (28): 101-110.

Clark, W. P.
1885   *The Indian Sign Language.* Hammersly and Co., Philadelphia. [Reprinted 1982 by University of Nebraska Press, Lincoln].

Cline, W.
1938   Religion and World View. In *The Sinkaietk or Southern Okanagan of Washington.* L. Spier, editor, pp. 133-182. General Series in Anthropology 6, Menasha, WI.

Clottes, J.
1998   Twenty Thousand Years of Paleolithic Cave Art in Southern France. *Proceedings of the British Academy* 99:161-175.
2001   Le Thème Mythique du Faon à l'oiseau dans le Magdalénien Pyrénéen. *Bulletin de la Société Préhistorique de l'Ariège* LVI:53-62.
n.d.   Discrete Composite Creatures. To be published in the David Lewis-Williams Festshrift. (In Press)

Clottes, J., M. Garner, and J. Courtin
1994   Magdalenian Bison in the Caves of the Ariège. *Rock Art Research* 11/1:58-70.

Clottes, J. and J. D. Lewis-Williams
1996   *Les Chamanes de la Préhistoire: Transe et Magie dans les Grottes Ornées.* Editions du Seuil, Paris, France.
1997a   Préhistoire. Les Chamanes des Cavernes. *Archéologia* 1997/336:30-41.

1997b   Transe ou Pas Transe: Réponse à Roberte Hamayon. *Nouvelles de l'Archéologie* 69:45-47.
2000   Chamanisme et Art Pariétal Paléolithique: Résponse à Yvette Taborin. *Archaeologia* 368:6-7.
2001   *Les Chamanes de la Préhistoire. Texte Intégral, Polémiques et Réponses.* Le Seuil, Paris, France.

Coburn, L. W.
1975   *A Theoretical Framework for Investigating the Relationship of Pictographs to Mythology in the Northern Plateau.* M.A. Thesis, Washington State University, Pullman.

Cohen, C.
1999   *L'Homme des Origines. Savoirs et Fictions en Préhistoire.* Le Seuil, Paris, France.

Cohen, W.
1987   Indian Sandpaintings of Southern California. *Journal of California and Great Basin Anthropology* 9:4-34.

Coles, J.
1995   Rock Art as a Picture Show. In *Perceiving Rock Art: Social and Political Perspectives.* K. Helskog and B. Olsen, editors, pp. 181-199. Novus forlag, Oslo, Norway.

Conner, S. W. and B. L. Conner
1971   *Rock Art of the Montana High Plains.* The Art Galleries, University of California, Santa Barbara.

Conway, T.
1993   *Painted Dreams: Native American Rock Art.* NorthWord Press, Minocqua, WI.

Conway, T. and J. Conway
1990   *Spirits on Stone: The Agawa Pictographs.* Heritage Discoveries, San Luis Obispo, CA.

Corner, J.
1968   *Pictographs in the Interior of British Columbia.* Wayside Press, Vernon, British Columbia.

Coues, E.
1893   *History of the Expedition Under the Command of Lewis and Clark.* F. P. Harper, New York.

Craig, C.
2000   Diggers and Thieves Busy Along River. *Yakama Nation Review* (Newspaper), March 3, pp.1, 3. Toppenish, WA.

Cressman, L. S.
1956   *Klamath Prehistory.* Transactions of the American Philosophical Society 46(4). Philadelphia, PA.

Curtin, J.
1884   Miscellaneous papers and notes collected by Jeremiah and Alma Curtin from the Klamath and Modoc Tribes in 1883 and 1884. Bureau of American Ethnology documents 1299, 1762, 2569, 3538, and 3799, Washington, D.C.
1912   *Myths of the Modocs.* Little, Brown and Company, New York.

1940   *Memoirs of Jeremiah Curtin.* State Historical Society of Wisconsin Biography Series, Vol. 2.

Curtis, E.
1970   *The North American Indian, Vol. 7, Columbia Plateau.* Johnson Reprint Company, New York.

Custer, E. B.
1885   *Boots and Saddles, or Life in Dakota with General Custer.* Harper and Brothers, New York.

Custer, G. A
1874   Brevet Major General, U.S.A, letter to Assistant Adjutant General, Department of Dakota, July 15, 1874 Custer's Black Hills Order and Dispatch Book, unpublished manuscript, Coe Collection, Yale University, New Haven, CT.

Darwin, C.
1893   *The Variation of Animals and Plants Under Domestification* [2nd edition]. John Murray, London, UK.

David, R.
2004   Testing and Refining Landscape Symbolism models in the Klamath Basin. Paper presented at the 57th Annual Northwest Anthropological Conference, Eugene, OR.

Davidson, D.S.
1935   Archaeological Problems of Northern Australia. *Journal of the Royal Anthropological Institute LXV:145-183.*

DeMallie, R. J. (editor)
1984   *The Sixth Grandfather: Black Elk's Teachings Given to John G. Neihardt.* University of Nebraska Press, Lincoln.

De Marinis, R. C.
1988   Le Popolazioni Alpine di Stirpe Retica. In *Italia omnium terrarum alumna.* G. Pugliese Carratelli, editor, pp. 101-155, Milano, Italia.
1994   La Datazione dello Stile IIIA. In *Le Pietre degli Dei. Menhir e Stele dell'età del Rame in Valcamonica e Valtellina.* S. Casini, editor, pp. 69-87, Bergamo, Italia.
1995   Problèmes de Chronologie de l'art Rupestre du Valcamonica. *Notizie Archeologiche Bergomensi* 2:99-120, Bergamo, Italia.

Demoule, J. P.
1997   Images Préhistoriques, Rêves de Préhistoriens. *Critique* 606:853-870.

Dempsey, H. A.
1994   *The Amazing Death of Calf Shirt and Other Blackfoot Stories.* University of Oklahoma Press, Norman.

Denison, J. S.
1879   Unpublished letters to Albert Gatschet. Bureau of American Ethnology document 315, Washington, D.C.

Densmore, F.
1918   *Teton Sioux Music,* Bureau of American Ethnology Bulletin 61. [Reprinted 1992 by University of Nebraska Press, Lincoln.]
1932   Yuman and Yaqui Music. *Bureau of American Ethnology, Bulletin* 110. Smithsonian Institution, Washington, D.C.

Devereux, G.
1949 The Mohave Male Puberty Rite. *Samiksa, Journal of the Indian Psycho-Analytic Society* 3(1):11-25.
1957 Dream Learning and Individual Ritual Differences in Mohave Shamanism. *American Anthropologist* 59:1036-1045.

Devlet, E.
2001 Rock Art and the Material Culture of Siberian and Central Asian Shamanism. In *The Archeology of Shamanism*. N. Price, editor, pp. 43-55. Routledge, London, UK.

DeVoto, B.
1981 *The Journals of Lewis and Clark*. Houghton Mifflin Company, Boston, MA.

Dewdney, S. and K. E. Kidd
1962 *Indian Rock Paintings of the Great Lakes*. University of Toronto Press, Toronto, Ontario.

Diaz-Granados, C. and J. R. Duncan
2000 *The Petroglyphs and Pictographs of Missouri*. University of Alabama Press, Tuscaloosa.

Dicken, S. N. and E. F. Dicken
1985 *The Legacy of Ancient Lake Modoc: A Historical Geography of the Klamath Lakes Basin*. Privately published. Distributed by University of Oregon Bookstore, Eugene and Shaw Stationary Company, Klamath Falls, OR.

Dixon, R.
1907 The Shasta. *American Museum of Natural History, Bulletin* 17(5):381-498.
1908 Some Shamans of Northern California. *Journal of American Folk Lore* 17:23-27.

Dobres, M. A.
1999 Book Reviews. *Visual Anthropology Review* 15(1):88-92.

Dornan, S. S.
1917 The Tati Bushmen (Masarwas) and their Language. *Journal of the Royal Anthropological Institution* 47:37-112.

Douglas, M.
1987 *Follow the Sun and Other Journeys*. Rigby, Adelaide, Australia.

Dowson, T. A.
1988 Revelations of Religious Reality: the Individual in San Rock Art. *World Archaeology* 20: 116-128.
1994 Reading Art, Writing History: Rock Art and Social Change in Southern Africa. *World Archaeology* 25: 332-344.

Driver, H. E.
1937 Cultural Element Distributions: VI, Southern Sierra Nevada. *University of California Anthropological Records* 1(2):53-154. Berkeley.
1939 Cultural Element Distributions: X, Northwest California. *University of California Anthropological Records* 1(6). Berkeley.
1941 Cultural Element Distributions: XVI, Girls' Puberty Ceremonies in North America. *University of California Anthropological Records* 6(2). Berkeley.

1969   *Indians of North America.* (Second edition, revised). University of Chicago Press, Chicago, IL.
Drucker, P.
1937   Culture Element Distributions: V, Southern California. *University of California Anthropological Records* 1(1):1-52.
DuBois, C. G.
1908   The Religion of the Luiseño Indians of Southern California. *University of California Publications in American Archaeology and Ethnology* 8(3):69-186. Berkeley.
Duff, W.
1956   Prehistoric Stone Sculpture of the Fraser River and Gulf of Georgia. *Anthropology in British Columbia* 5:15-151.
1983   The World is as Sharp as a Knife: Meaning in Northern Northwest Coast Art. In *Indian Art Traditions of the Northwest Coast*, R. L. Carlson, editor, pp. 47-66. Archaeology Press, Department of Archaeology, Simon Fraser University, Burnaby, British Columbia.
Durkheim, E.
1915   *The Elementary Forms of the Religious Life.* Translated by J.W. Swain. Unwin, London, UK.
Dusenberry, J. V.
1959   Visions Among the Pend d'Oreille Indians. *Ethnos* 24(1-2):52-57.
Eliade, M.
1964   *Shamanism: Archaic Techniques of Ecstasy.* Princeton University Press, Princeton, NJ.
Elkin, A.P.
1949   The Origin and Interpretation of Petroglyphs in South-east Australia. *Oceania* 20(2):119-157.
England, N.
1968   *Music Among the Zu'/'wã-si of South West Africa and Botswana.* Unpublished Ph.D. thesis, Harvard University, Cambridge, MA.
Ertani, L.
n.d.   *Bote de Al Camonega.* Esine, Italia.
Evans, M., R. Stoffle, and S.L. Pinel
1993   *Petroglyph National Monument Rapid Ethnographic Assessment Project, Final Report.* Bureau of Applied Research in Anthropology, University of Arizona, Tucson.
Ewers, J. C.
1958   *The Blackfeet: Raiders of the Northwestern Plains.* University of Oklahoma Press, Norman.
Farina, P.
2000   "La Rosa Camuna" nell'arte Rupestre della Valcamonica. *Notizie Archeologiche Bergomensi* 6:185-205, Bergamo, Italia.
Faulkner, C. H. (editor)
1986   *The Prehistoric Native American Art at Mud Glyph Cave.* University of Tennessee Press, Knoxville.

Fedele, F.
1995   Il Contesto Rituale delle Stele Calcolitiche Camuno-Valtellinesi: gli Scavi di Ossimo (Valcamonica). *Notizie Archeologiche Bergomensi*, 2:37-66, Bergamo, Italia.

Feliks, J.
1998   The Value of Interpretive Approaches in Archaeology. *Rock Art Research* 15(2):128-134.

Fell, B.
1976   *America B.C.* Times Books, New York
1982   *Bronze Age America*. Little, Brown and Company, Boston, MA

Fénies, J.
1965   *Spéléologie et Médecine*. Collection de Médecine Légale et de Toxicologie Médicale. Masson, Paris, France.

Fewkes, J. W.
1895   The Tusayan New Fire Ceremony. *Boston Society of Natural History Proceedings* 26:422-458.

Forde, C. D.
1931   Ethnography of the Yuma Indians. *University of California Publications in American Archaeology and Ethnology* 28(4):83-278. Berkeley.

Fossati, A.
1991   L'età del Ferro nelle Incisioni Rupestri della Valcamonica. In *Immagini di una Aristocrazia dell'età del Ferro nell'arte Rupestre Camuna*. R. La Guardia, editor, pp. 11-71, Milano, Italia.

1992   Alcune Rappresentazioni di "Oranti" Schematici Armati del Bronzo Finale nell'arte Rupestre della Valcamonica. *Appunti* 19:45-50, Circolo Culturale Ghislandi, Breno, Italia.

1993a   *Il Mondo dei Camunni. L'arte Rupestre della Valcamonica*. Valcamonica Preistorica, 4, Cerveno, Italia.

1993b   Deer in European Rock Art. In *Deer in Rock art of India and Europe*. G. Camuri, A. Fossati, and Y. Mathpal, editors, pp. 75-117, New Delhi, India.

1995   Cronologia ed Interpretazione. In *Rupe Magna: La Roccia Incisa più Grande delle Alpi*. A. Arcà, A. Fossati, E. Marchi, and E. Tognoni, editors, pp. 99-109. Quaderni del Parco, 1, Sondrio, Italia.

1998   Cronologia ed Interpretazione di Alcune Figure Simboliche nell'arte Rupestre del IV Periodo Camuno. *Notizie Archeologiche Bergomensi*, 5, 1996, Bergamo, Italia.

2001a   The Rock Art of the Iceman: The Petroglyphs of Valcamonica, Italy. *Screenings: Newsletter of the Oregon Archaeological Society* 50(5):3-5.

2001b   Discovery of Rock Paintings in Valcamonica, in 2° Convegno Internazionale di Archeologia Rupestre. "Archeologia e Arte Rupestre. L'Europa. Le Alpi. La Valcamonica." *Atti del Convegno di Studi, Darfo-Boario Terme 2-5 Ottobre 1997*:263-265, Milan, Italia.

2002a   Rock Art of the Columbia Plateau: Impressions of an Unforgettable Meeting. *Screenings: Newsletter of the Oregon Archaeological Society* 51(12):4-5.

2002b Landscape Representations on Boulders and Menhirs in the Valcamonica-Valtellina Area, Alpine Italy. In *European Landscapes of Rock Art*, G. Nash and C. Chippindale, editors, pp. 93-115, London, UK.

Foster, D.
1999 Imperfect Justice: The Modoc War Crimes Trial of 1873. *Oregon Historical Quarterly* 100:246-287.

Francfort, H. P.
1998 Central Asian Petroglyphs: Between Indo-Iranian and Shamanistic Interpretations. In *The Archaeology of Rock-Art*. C. Chippindale and P.S.C. Taçon, editors, pp. 302-318. Cambridge University Press, Cambridge, UK.

Francis, J. E.
2005 Pictographs, Petroglyphs, and Paradigms: Rock Art in North American Archaeology. In *Discovering North American Rock Art.* Lawrence L, Loendorf, Christopher Chippindale, and David S. Whitley, editors, pp 181-195. The University of Arizona Press, Tucson.

Francis, J. E. and L. L. Loendorf
2002 *Ancient Visions: Petroglyphs and Pictographs of the Wind River and Bighorn Country, Wyoming and Montana.* University of Utah Press, Salt Lake City.

Frazer, J.G.
1994 *The Golden Bough* [abridged edition]. Oxford University Press, New York.

Fredlund, G., L. Sundstrom, and R. Armstrong
1996 Crazy Mule's Maps of the Upper Missouri, 1877-1880. *Plains Anthropologist* 41:5-27.

Freer, S.
2001 The Handprints at CA-RIV-114: A Forensic and Anthropometric Study. *American Indian Rock Art* 27:319-332.

Gaioni, G.
1990 *Leggende di Val Camonica e Val di Scalve*. Brescia, Italia.

Garfield, V. and P. Wingert
1966 *The Tsimshian Indians and Their Arts.* University of Washington Press, Seattle.

Garlake, P.
2001 Sub-Saharan Africa. In *Handbook of Rock Art Research*. D.S. Whitley, editor, pp.637-664. AltaMira Press, New York.

Gatschet, A. S.
1877-1892 Miscellaneous papers and notes collected from the Klamath and Modoc Tribes. Bureau of American Ethnology documents 610, 1995, 2019, 2849, 2975, 3686, and 3990, Washington, D.C.

1890 *The Klamath Indians of Southwestern Oregon*. U. S. Geographic and Geological Survey of the Rocky Mountain Region, Contributions to North American Ethnology, 2.

Gaussen, J.
1964 *La Grotte Ornée de Gabillou (près Mussidan, Dordogne)*. Imprimerie Delmas, Bordeaux, France.

Gayton, A. H.
1930 Yokuts-Mono Chiefs and Shamans. *University of California Publications in American Archaeology and Ethnology* 24:361-420. Berkeley.
1948 Yokuts and Western Mono Ethnography. *University of California Anthropological Records* 10:1-290. Berkeley.

Gayton, A. H. and S. Newman
1940 Yokuts and Western Mono Myths. *University of California Anthropological Records* 5:1-110. Berkeley.

Gell, A.
1998 *Art and Agency: an Anthropological Theory.* Oxford University Press, Oxford, UK.

Gibeault, A. and R. Uhl
1998 De l'outil à l'œuvre d'art: l'invention de la Symbolisation. In *Le Propre de l'Homme. Psychanalyse et Préhistoire.* F. Sacco and G. Sauvet, editors, pp. 12-40. Delachaux & Niestlé, Paris, France.

Gifford, E. W.
1931 *The Kamia of the Imperial Valley.* Smithsonian Institute, Bureau of American Ethnology Bulletin 97. Washington, D.C.
1933 The Cocopa. *University of California Publications in American Archaeology and Ethnology* 31(5):257-334. Berkeley.

Gillespie, D.
1982 The Artist as Scientist. In *Aboriginal Art at the Top.* P. Cook and J. Altman, editors, pp. 17-20. Maningreda Arts and Crafts, Maningreda, N.T., Australia.

Gilreath, A. and W. R. Hildebrandt
2003 *Rock Art Variability Within the Coso Range.* Paper presented in SAA Rock Art Interest Group-Sponsored Symposium "Methods in Rock Art Analysis." Sixty-eighth Annual Meeting of the Society for American Archaeology, April 11, Milwaukee, WI.

Goddard, P.
1903 Life and Culture of the Hupa. *University of California Publications in American Archaeology and Ethnology* 1(1):1-88. Berkeley.
1904 Hupa Texts. *University of California Publications in American Archaeology and Ethnology* 1(2). Berkeley.

Gould, S. J.
1998 The Sharp-eyed Lynx Outfoxed by Nature. *Natural History* 6/98:23-27, 69-73.

Grant, C., J. W. Baird, and J. K. Pringle
1968 *Rock Drawings of the Coso Range.* Maturango Museum, China Lake, CA.

Green, E. and E. Holmes
2001 Kohta Circus: A Mesoamerican Connection. *American Indian Rock Art* 27:293-299.

Greenberg, J. H.
1963 *The Languages of Africa.* Mouton, The Hague, Netherlands.

Grinnell, G. B.
1874   Field notes from the Black Hills Expedition, July 11, 1874. George Bird Grinnell Collection, Braun Research Library, Southwest Museum, Los Angeles, CA.
1923   *The Cheyenne Indians: Their History and Ways of Life.* (two volumes) Yale University Press. [Reprinted 1972 by University of Nebraska Press, Lincoln.]
1926   *By Cheyenne Campfires.* Yale University Press, New Haven, CT.

Guenther, M.
1999   *Tricksters and Trancers: Bushman Religion and Society.* Indiana University Press, Bloomington.

Gunn, R. G.
1992   Bulajang - A Reappraisal of the Archaeology of an Aboriginal Religious Cult. In *State of the Art, Regional Rock Art Studies in Australia and Melanesia.* J. McDonald and I. P. Haskovec, editors, pp. 174-194. Occasional Aura Publication, 6.

Hamayon, R.
1990   *La Chasse à l'âme. Esquisse d'une Théorie du Chamanisme Sibérien.* Société d'Ethnologie, Université de Paris X, Paris, France.
1997   La Transe d'un Préhistorien: à Propos du Livre de Jean Clottes et David Lewis-Williams. *Les Nouvelles de l'Archéologie* 67:65-67.

Hammond-Tooke, W. D.
1981   *Boundaries and Belief: The Structure of a Sotho Worldview.* Witwatersrand University Press, Johannesburg, South Africa.

Hann, D.
2002   Rhythm on the Rocks: Trance and Petroglyph Production. Paper presented at the 67th Annual Meeting of the Society for American Archaeology, March 22, 2002. Denver, CO.

Hann, D., J.D. Keyser, and P. Cash Cash
2004   Columbia Plateau Rock Art: A Window to the Spirit World. In *Ethnography and Western North American rock art.* D.S. Whitley, editor (in press). AltaMira Press, Walnut Creek, CA.

Harrington, J. P. (editor)
1934   A New Original Version of Boscana's Historical Account of the San Juan Capistrano Indians of Southern California. *Smithsonian Miscellaneous Collections* 92(4). Smithsonian Institution, Washington, D.C.
1978   Annotations, in *Chinigchinich: An Historical Account of the Indians of the Mission of San Juan Capistrano Called the Acagchemem Tribe*, by G. Boscana, pp. 91-228. Malki Museum, Banning, CA.
n.d.a   Unpublished Luiseño notes, cited in Oxendine 1980.
n.d.b   Papers: Northern and Central California—Yokuts. National Anthropological Archives, Smithsonian Institution, Washington, D.C.
n.d.c   Papers: Southern California and Great Basin—Mojave. National Anthropological Archives, Smithsonian Institution, Washington, D.C.

Hascovec, I.P. and H. Sullivan
1989   Reflections of an Aboriginal artist. In *Animals into art.* H. Morphy, editor, pp. 57-74. Unwin, London, UK.

Hayden, N. L.
2001   Yavapai Cosmology: Early Timekeepers in the Prescott Area, Arizona. *American Indian Rock Art* 27:253-260.
Hays-Gilpin, K.
2002   Wearing a Butterfly, Coming of Age: A 1500 Year Old Pueblo Tradition. In *Children in the Prehistoric Puebloan Southwest.* K. A. Kamp, editor, pp. 196-210. University of Utah Press, Salt Lake City.
2004   *Ambiguous Images: Gender and Rock Art.* AltaMira Press, Walnut Creek, CA.
Hawley, F.
1937   Kokopelli, of the Prehistoric Southwestern Pueblo Pantheon. *American Anthropologist* n.s. 39:644-646.
Hedges K.
1970   An Analysis of Diegueño Pictographs. M.A. thesis, Department of Anthropology, San Diego State College, San Diego, CA.
1973   Rock Art in Southern California. *Pacific Coast Archaeological Society Quarterly* 9(4):1-28.
1992   Shamanistic Aspects of California Rock Art. In *California Indian Shamanism*, L.J. Bean, editor, pp. 67-88. Ballena Press, Menlo Park, CA.
1993   Places to See and Places to Hear: Rock Art and Features of the Sacred Landscape. In *Time and Space: Dating and Spatial Considerations in Rock Art Research.* J. Steinbring, A. Watchman, P. Faulstich, and P. S. C. Taçon, editors, pp.121-127. Occasional AURA Publication No. 8, Melbourne, Australia.
2001   Traversing the Great Gray Middle Ground: An Examination of Shamanistic Interpretation of Rock Art. *American Indian Rock Art* 27:123-136.
2002   Rock Art Styles in Southern California. *American Indian Rock Art* 28:25-40.
Heizer, R. F.
1953   Sacred Rain Rocks of Northern California. *University of California Archaeological Survey Report* 20. Berkeley.
Heizer, R. F. and M. A. Baumhoff
1962   *Prehistoric Rock Art of Nevada and Eastern California.* University of California Press, Berkeley.
Helvenston, P. A. and P. G. Bahn
2002   *Desperately Seeking Trance Plants: Testing the "Three Stages of Trance" Model.* RJ Communications, New York.
Henshaw, H.W.
n.d.   Unpublished Luiseño notes, cited in Oxendine 1980.
Hill, B. and R. Hill
1975   *Indian Petroglyphs of the Pacific Northwest.* University of Washington Press, Seattle.
Hill, J. N. and R. Nolasquez (editors)
1973   *MULU'WETAM: The First People, Cupeño Oral History and Language.* Malki Museum, Banning, CA.

Hill, K. C.
1992 A Serrano Gazetteer. Unpublished manuscript on file at Santa Barbara Museum of Natural History, Santa Barbara, CA.

Hill-Tout, C.
1978 *The Salish People, Volume III: The Mainland Halkomelem.* Talonbooks, Vancouver, British Columbia.

Hines, D. M.
1992 *Ghost Voices: Yakima Indian Myths, Legends, Humor, and Hunting Stories.* Great Eagle Publishing, Issaquah, WA.
1993 *Magic in the Mountains: The Yakima Shaman: Power and Practice.* Great Eagle Publishing, Issaquah, WA.

Hobson, J.A.
1994 *The Chemistry of Conscious States: Toward a Unified Model of the Brain and the Mind.* Little, Brown and Company, Boston, MA.

Hoebel, E. A.
1978 *The Cheyennes: Indians of the Great Plains.* Holt, Rinehart and Winston, New York.

Holmes, E. and P. A. Cramer
2002 Legends, Links, and Likenesses: Mesoamerican Symbols in Southern Nevada Rock Art. *American Indian Rock Art* 28:181-192.

Hooper, L.
1920 Cahuilla Indians. *University of California Publications in American Archaeology and Ethnology* 16(6):315-380. Berkeley.

How, M. W.
1962 *The Mountain Bushmen of Basutoland.* Van Schaik, Pretoria, South Africa.

Howard, J. H.
1965 *The Ponca Tribe.* Bureau of American Ethnology Bulletin 195, Washington, D.C.

Huffman, T. N.
1989 Ceramics, Settlements and Late Iron Age Migrations. *The African Archaeological Review* 7:155-182.

Hultkrantz, Å.
1979 *The Religions of the American Indians.* Translated by Monica Setterwall. University of California Press, Berkeley, Los Angeles, and London.
1981 *Belief and Worship in Native North America.* Syracuse University Press, Syracuse, NY.
1989 The Place of Shamanism in the History of Religions. In *Shamanism: Past and Present.* M. Hoppál and O.J. von Sadovszky, editors, pp. 43-51. Fullerton, Budapest-Los Angeles.
1995 Le Chamanisme, une Tradition Spirituelle Multimillénaire. In *Les Populations Traditionnelles. Continuité et Changement dans le Monde Contemporain.* G. Burenhult, editor, pp. 166-167. Bordas, Paris, France.

Hunger, H.
1983 Ritual Coiton as a Sacred Marriage in the Rock Art of North America. *American Indian Rock Art* 9:1-9.

Hunn, E. S.
1990 Nch'i-Wána, "The Big River": Mid Columbia Indians and Their Land. University of Washington Press, Seattle.

Hyde, G. E.
1968 Life of George Bent. University of Oklahoma Press, Norman.

Hyland, J. R.
1997 Image, Land, and Lineage: Hunter-Gatherer Archaeology in Central Baja California, Mexico. Unpublished Ph.D. Dissertation, University of California Department of Anthropology, Berkeley.

Inglis, J.
1998 Spirit in the Stone. Horsdal and Schubart, Victoria, British Columbia.

Inverarity, R. B.
1967 Art of the Northwest Coast Indians. University of California Press, Berkeley and Los Angeles.

Irwin, L.
1994 The Dream Seekers: Native American Visionary Traditions of the Great Plains. University of Oklahoma Press, Norman.

Jacobsthal, P.
1938 Celtic Rock-carvings in Northern Italy and Yorkshire. The Journal of Roman Studies, XXVIII.

Jett, S.C.
1986 Observations Regarding Chartkoff's California "Rock Feature Complex". American Antiquity 51: 615-616.

Jolly, P.
1986 A First Generation Descendant of the Transkei San. South African Archaeological Bulletin 41:6-9.

Jonaitis, A.
1988 From the Land of the Totem Poles. The Northwest Coast Indian art collection at the American Museum of Natural History. American Museum of Natural History, New York.
1991 From the Land of the Totem Poles. The Northwest Coast Indian art collection at the American Museum of Natural History. (Reprint of 1988 publication with corrections.) American Museum of Natural History, New York.

Jones, T. E. H.
1981 The Aboriginal Rock Paintings of the Churchill River. Saskatchewan Museum of Natural History, Regina.

Katz, R.
1982 Boiling Energy: Community-Healing Among the Kalahari !Kung. Harvard University Press, Cambridge, MA.

Katz, R., M. Biesele, and V. St. Denis
1997 Healing Makes our Hearts Happy: Spirituality and Cultural Transformation Among the Kalahari Ju/'hoansi. Inner Traditions, Rochester, VT.

Kehoe, A. B.
1996 Eliade and Hultkrantz: the European Primitivism Tradition. American Indian Quarterly 20:377–392.

2000 *Shamans and Religion: An Anthropological Exploration in Critical Thinking.* Waveland Press, Prospect Heights, IL.

Kellogg, R., M. Knoll, and J. Kugler
1965 Form-similarity Between Phosphenes of Adults and Preschool Children's Scribblings. *Nature* 2008:1129-1130.

Kelly, W. H.
1977 Cocopa Ethnography. *University of Arizona Anthropological Papers* 29. Tucson.

Kennedy, D. and R. Bouchard
1998a Lillooet. In *Handbook of North American Indians, Volume 12: Plateau.* D. E. Walker, Jr., editor, pp. 174-190. Smithsonian Institution, Washington, D.C.
1998b Northern Okanagan, Lakes and Colville. In *Handbook of North American Indians, Volume 12: Plateau.* D. E. Walker, Jr., editor, pp. 238-252. Smithsonian Institution, Washington, D.C.

Keyser, J. D.
1977 Writing-On-Stone: Rock Art on the Northwestern Plains. *Canadian Journal of Archaeology* 1:15-80.
1979 The Plains Indian War Complex and the Rock Art of Writing-On-Stone, Alberta, Canada. *Journal of Field Archaeology* 6:41-48.
1987 A Lexicon for Historic Plains Indian Rock Art: Increasing Interpretive Potential. *Plains Anthropologist* 32(115):43-71.
1990 Tsagiglalal—She Who Watches: Rock Art as an Interpretable Phenomenon. *Journal of Interpretation* 14(2):S1-S4
1991 A Thing to Tie on the Halter: An Addition to the Plains Rock Art Lexicon. *Plains Anthropologist* 36(136):261-267.
1992 *Indian Rock Art of the Columbia Plateau.* University of Washington Press, Seattle and London.
1996 Painted Bison Robes: The Missing Link in the Biographic Art Lexicon. *Plains Anthropologist* 41:29-52.
2005 Leader of the Pack: Government Sponsorship of Rock Art Research. In *Discovering North American Rock Art.* Lawrence L, Loendorf, Christopher Chippindale, and David S. Whitley, editors, pp 217-227. The University of Arizona Press, Tucson.

Keyser, J. D. and P. Cash Cash
2002 A Carved Quirt Handle from the Warm Springs Reservation: Northern Plains Biographic Art on the Columbia Plateau. *Plains Anthropologist* 47(180):51-59.

Keyser, J. D. and M. Cowdrey
2004 Ethnographic Clues to the Interpretation of Plains Biographic Rock Art. In *The Ethnography of Rock Art.* D. Whitley, editor, AltaMira Press, Walnut Creek, CA.

Keyser, J. D. and M. A. Klassen
2001 *Plains Indian Rock Art.* University of Washington Press, Seattle.
2003 Every Detail Counts: More Additions to the Plains Biographic Rock Art Lexicon. *Plains Anthropologist* 48(184):7-20.

Keyser, J. D. and G. C. Knight
1976 The Rock Art of Western Montana. *Plains Anthropologist* 21:1-12.

Keyser, J. D. and M. Mitchell
2000 Red Rock Ledge: Plains Biographic Rock Art in the Picketwire Canyonlands, Southeastern Colorado. *Southwestern Lore* 66(2):22-37.
2001 Decorated Bridles: Horse Tack in Plains Biographic Rock Art. *Plains Anthropologist* 46(176):196-210.

Keyser, J. D., C. Pedersen, G. M. Bettis, G. Poetschat, and H. Hiczun
1998b Owl Cave. *Oregon Archaeological Society Publication* 11:81-109, Portland.

Keyser, J. D. and G. Poetschat
2002 Rock Art of the Lower Columbia River: A Multi-disciplinary Recording Project. Paper presented at the 67th Annual Meeting of the Society for American Archaeology, March 22, 2002. Denver, CO.
2004 The Canvas as the Art: Landscape Analysis of the Rock-Art Panel. *The Landscapes of Rock Art*. C. Chippendale and G. Nash, editors, pp.118-130. Cambridge University Press, Cambridge, UK.

Keyser, J. D., G. Poetschat, P. Cash Cash, D. Hann, H. Hiczun, R. Malin, C. Pedersen, C. Poetschat, and B. Tandberg
1998a The Butte Creek Sites: Steiwer Ranch and Rattlesnake Shelter. *Oregon Archaeological Society Publication* 11:1-80, Portland.

Keyser, J. D. and L. Sundstrom
1984 *Rock Art of Western South Dakota*. South Dakota Archaeological Society Special Publication 8, Sioux Printing, Inc. Sioux Falls.

Keyser, J. D. and M. W. Taylor
2002 *Visions On Stone: Rock Art of the Columbia Plateau*. Oregon Archaeological Society, Portland.

Keyser, J. D., M. W. Taylor, and G. R. Poetschat
2004 Echoes of the Ancients: *Rock Art of the Dalles-Deschutes Region*. Oregon Archaeological Society Publication 14, Portland.

Keyser, J. D. and D. S. Whitley
2000 A New Ethnographic Reference for Columbia Plateau Rock Art: Documenting a Century of Vision Quest Practices. *International Newsletter on Rock Art* 25:14-20.
2006 Sympathetic Magic in Western North American Rock Art. *American Antiquity* 71(1):3-26.

Klassen, M.
1998 Icon and Narrative in Transition: Contact-period Rock-art at Writing-On-Stone, Southern Alberta, Canada. In *The Archaeology of Rock-Art*. C. Chippindale and P. Taçon, editors, pp. 42-72. Cambridge University Press, Cambridge, UK.

Klassen, M. A., J. D. Keyser, and L. L. Loendorf
2000 Bird Rattle's Petroglyphs at Writing-On-Stone: Continuity in the Biographic Rock Art Tradition. *Plains Anthropologist* 45:189-201.

Klug, L.
1999 *Local Patterns in Mid-Columbia Plateau Rock Art: A Preliminary Investigation*. Paper presented at the 52nd Northwest Anthropological Conference.

2002   New Insights on Priest Rapids Petroglyphs. Paper presented at the 67th Annual Meeting of the Society for American Archaeology, March 22, 2002. Denver, CO.

Krause, H. and G. D. Olson
1974   *Prelude to Glory.* Brevet Press and Center for Western Studies, Augustana College, Sioux Falls, SD.

Kroeber, A. L.
1906   Notes [to Rust 1906] *American Anthropologist* 8:31-32.
1908a   Ethnography of the Cahuilla Indians. *University of California Publications in American Archaeology and Ethnology* 8(2):29-68. Berkeley.
1908b   Notes on the Luiseño. *University of California Publications in American Archaeology and Ethnology* 8(3):174-186. Berkeley.
1925   *Handbook of the Indians of California.* Bulletin 78, American Bureau of Ethnology. Washington, D.C.
1957   Ad Hoc Reassurance Dreams. Ethnographic Interpretations 1-6. *University of California Publications in American Archaeology and Ethnology* 47(2):205-208. Berkeley.

Kuykendall, G. P.
1889   A Graphic Account of the Religions or Mythology of the Indians of the Pacific Northwest, including a History of their Superstitions, Marriage Customs, Moral Ideas and Domestic Relations, and their Conception of a Future State, and the Re-habiliment of the Dead. In *History of the Pacific Northwest: Oregon and Washington,* vol. 2. E. Evans, editor, pp. 60-95. North Pacific History Company. Portland, OR.

La Barre, W.
1972   *The Ghost Dance.* Unwin, London,UK.
1980   *Culture in Context: Selected Writings of Weston La Barre.* Duke University Press, Durham, NC.

Laeng, G.
1914   Cemmo (Capo di Ponte). *Guida d'Italia del Touring Club Italiano, Piemonte, Lombardia e Canton Ticino.* Page 595. Milano, Italia.

Lame Deer, J. F., and R. Erdoes
1972   *Lame Deer: Seeker of Visions.* Simon and Schuster, New York.

Laming-Emperaire, A.
1962   *La Signification de l'art Rupestre Paléolithique.* Picard, Paris, France.

Landes, R.
1968   *The Mystic Lake Sioux: Sociology of the Mdewakantonwan Santee.* University of Wisconsin Press, Madison.

LaPointe, J.
1976   *Legends of the Lakota.* The Indian Historian Press, San Francisco, CA.

Layman, W. D.
1986   The Rock Art of Rock Island Rapids: A Historical Overview. *American Indian Rock Art* 11:77-87.

Layton, R.
1992   *Australian Rock Art: a New Synthesis.* Cambridge University Press, Cambridge, UK.

1995 Rereading Rock Art: Text and Discourse. In *Perceiving rock art: Social and Political Perspectives*. K. Helskog and B. Olsen, editors, pp. 217-227. Novus Forlag, Oslo, Norway.
2000a Intersubjectivity and Understanding Rock Art. *Australian Archaeology* 51:48-53.
2000b Shamanism, Totemism and Rock Art ; *Les Chamanes de la Préhistoire* in the Context of Rock Art Research. *Cambridge Archaeological Journal* 10/1:69-186.

Leakey, M.
1983 *Africa's Vanishing Art: The Rock Paintings of Tanzania*. Hamish Hamilton/Rainbird, London, UK.

Lee, G., W. D. Hyder, and A. Benson
1988 *The Rock Art of Petroglyph Point and Fem Cave- Lava Beds National Monument*. Lava Beds National Monument, Tulelake, CA.

Lee, R. B.
1968 The Sociology of !Kung Bushman Trance Performance. In *Trance and Possession States*. R. Prince, editor, pp. 35-54. R. M. Bucke Memorial Society, Montreal, Quebec.
1979 *The !Kung San: Men, Women and Work in a Foraging Society*. Cambridge University Press, Cambridge, UK.

Leechman, D., M. Hess, and R. L. Fowler
1955 Pictographs in Southwestern Alberta. *National Museum of Canada, Annual Report, Bulletin* 136:36-53. Ottawa, Ontario.

Leen, D.
1988 *An Inventory of Hells Canyon Rock Art*. Technical Report submitted to U. S. Forest Service, USDA, Enterprise, OR.
1990 Archaeological Resources Protection Act Inventory, Hells Canyon 1989. Unpublished manuscript on file at Hells Canyon National Recreation Area Office, Enterprise, OR.
1991 Hells Canyon ARPA Monitoring. Unpublished manuscript on file at Hells Canyon National Recreation Area Office, Enterprise, OR.

Lemaire, C.
1993 *Rêves Éveillés. L'âme Sous le Scalpel*. Les Empêcheurs de Penser en Rond, Paris, France.

Lerman, N. H.
1954 Okanogan (Salish) Ethnology. Field Notes and Manuscript. Melville Jacobs Collection, University of Washington Library Archives. Seattle, WA.

Leroi-Gourhan, A.
1977 Le Préhistorien et le Chamane. *L'Ethnographie* 74-75, N° Spécial *Études Chamaniques*:19-25.

Lévi-Strauss, C.
1973 *Anthropologie Structurale II*. Plon, Paris, France.

Lewis, E. H.
1980 *Wo'Wakita, Reservation Recollections*. Center for Western Studies, Augustana College, Sioux Fall, SD.

Lewis, I. M.
1971   *Ecstatic Religion: An Anthropological Study of Spirit Possession and Shamanism.* Penguin, Harmondsworth, UK.

Lewis, T. H.
1886   Ancient Rock Inscriptions in Eastern Dakota. *American Naturalist* 20:423-425.
1887   Incised Boulders in the Upper Minnesota Valley. *American Naturalist* 21:639-642.

Lewis-Williams, J. D.
1981   *Believing and Seeing: Symbolic Meanings in Southern San Rock Paintings.* Academic Press, London, UK.
1986   The Last Testament of the Southern San. *South African Archaeological Bulletin* 41(143):10-11.
1987   Beyond Style and Portrait: A Comparison of Tanzanian and Southern African Rock Art. In *Contemporary Studies on Khoisan* 2. R. Vossen and K. Keuthmann, editors, pp. 93-139. Helmut Buske Verlag: Hamburg, Deutschland.
1991   Wrestling with Analogy: A Problem in Upper Paleolithic Art Research. *Proceedings of the Prehistoric Society*, 57(1):149-162.
1992a   Ethnographic Evidence Relating to 'Trance' and 'Shamans' Among Northern and Southern Bushmen. *South African Archaeological Bulletin* 45:126-136.
1992b   *Vision, Power and Dance: the Genesis of a Southern African Rock Art Panel.* (Fourteenth Kroon Lecture) Stichting Nederlands Museum voor Anthropologie en Praehistorie, Amsterdam.
1994   Rock Art and Ritual: Southern Africa and Beyond. *Complutum* 5:277-289.
1995   Modeling the Production and Consumption of Rock Art. *South African Archaeological Bulletin* 50:143-154.
1996   'A Visit to the Lion's House': the Structure, Metaphors and Sociopolitical Significance of Nineteenth-century Bushman Myths. In *Voices From the Past: /Xam Bushmen and the Bleek and Lloyd Collection.* J. Deacon and T. A. Dowson, editors, pp. 122-141. Witwatersrand University Press, Johannesburg, South Africa.
1997   Prise en Compte du Relief Naturel des Surfaces Rocheuses dans l'art Pariétal Sud-africain et Paléolithique Ouest-européen: Étude Culturelle et Temporelle Croisée de la Croyance Religieuse. *L'Anthropologie* 101:220-237.
1998   Quanto?: The Issue of 'Many Meanings in Southern African San rock Art Research. *South African Archaeological Bulletin* 53: 86-97.
1999   *Stories that Float from Afar: Ancestral Folklore of the /Xam San.* David Philip, Cape Town.
2001   Southern African Shamanistic Rock Art in its Social and Cognitive Contexts. In *The Archaeology of Shamanism.* N. Price, editor, pp. 17-39. Routledge, London, UK.
2002   *The Mind in the Cave.* Thames and Hudson, London, UK.

2003   *Images of Mystery: Rock Art of the Drakensberg*. Double Story, Cape Town. (French edition: *Art Rupestre en Afrique du Sud: Mystérieuses Images du Drakensberg*. Le Seuil, Paris)

Lewis-Williams, J. D. and M. Biesele
1978   Eland Hunting Rituals Among Northern and Southern San Groups: Striking Similarities. *Africa* 48:117-134.

Lewis-Williams, J. D. and J. Clottes
1998a   Shamanism and Upper Paleolithic Art: A Response to Bahn. *Rock Art Research* 15(1):46-50.
1998b   The Mind in the Cave – The Cave in the Mind: Altered Consciousness in the Upper Paleolithic. *Anthropology of Consciousness*, 9(1):13-21.

Lewis-Williams, J. D. and T. A. Dowson
1988   The Signs of all Times: Entoptic Phenomena in Upper Palaeolithic Rock Art. *Current Anthropology*, 29(2):201-245.
1989   *Images of Power: Understanding Bushman Rock Art*. Southern Book Publishers, Johannesburg, South Africa.
1990   Through the Veil: San Rock Paintings and the Rock Face. *South African Archaeological Bulletin* 45:5-16.
1992   Art Rupestre San et Paléolithique Supérieur: Le Lien Analogique. *L'Anthropologie*, 96/4:769-790.

Lewis-Williams, J. D. and D. G. Pearce
2003   Southern Africa San Rock Painting a Social Intervention: an Epistemological and Methodological Study of Rain-making Images. In Press. *South African Archaeological Bulletin*.
2004   *San Spirituality: Roots, Expressions, Consequences*. In Press. AltaMira Press, Walnut Creek, CA.

Libby, O. G.
1998   *The Arikara Narrative of Custer's Campaign and the Battle of the Little Bighorn*. University of Oklahoma Press, Norman [reprint of 1920 edition published as Volume 6 of the North Dakota Historical Collections].

Loeb, E. M.
1926   Pomo Folkways. *University of California Publications in American Archaeology and Ethnology* 19(2). Berkeley.

Loendorf, L.
1994   Finnegan Cave: a Rock Art Vision Quest Site in Montana. In *Shamanism and Rock Art in North America*. S. A. Turpin, editor, pp. 124-137. Rock Art Foundation Inc., Special Publication 1, San Antonio, TX.

Loftin, J. D.
1991   *Religion and Hopi Life in the Twentieth Century*. Indiana University Press, Bloomington.

Lorblanchet, M.
1999   Michel Lorblanchet: Pourquoi l'art est-il Apparu? *La Recherche* 326:107-109.

Lorblanchet, M. and A. Sieveking
1997   The Monsters of Pergouset. *Cambridge Archaeological Journal* 7/1:37-56.

Loring, M. J. and L. Loring
1983   *Pictographs and Petroglyphs of the Oregon Country*. Institute of Archaeology, University of California, Los Angeles.
1996   *Pictographs & Petroglyphs of the Oregon Country: Parts I & II* [second edition]. Institute of Archaeology, University of California, Los Angeles.

Loubser, J. H. N.
2001   *Condition and Management Assessment of Ten Selected Rock Art Sites within the Kondoa-Irangi Conservation Area, Central Tanzania*. Report submitted to ICCROM, Rome, Italy.
2002   *Tripping On the Snake, or, On a Quest for Visions Forgotten: An Assessment of Selected Rock Art Sites in the Hells Canyon National Recreation Area*. Technical Report submitted by New South Associates to the Hells Canyon National Recreation Area, Enterprise, OR.

Loubser J. H. N., J. Allan, and T. Hudson.
2004   Rock Art, Archaeology and Ethnography in the Deep South. In *Ethnography and Western North American rock art*. D.S. Whitley, editor (in press). AltaMira Press, Walnut Creek, CA.

Loubser J. H. N. and J. Brink.
1992   Unusual Paintings of Wildebeest and a Zebra-Like Animal from North-Western Lesotho. *Southern African Field Archaeology* 1:103-107.

Loubser, J. H. N. and G. Laurens
1994   Depictions of Domestic Ungulates and Shields: Hunter/Gatherers and Agro-Pastoralists in the Caledon River Valley Area. In *Contested Images: Diversity in Southern African Rock Art Research*. T. A. Dowson and J. D. Lewis-Williams, editors, pp.83-118. Witwatersrand University Press, Johannesburg, South Africa.

Loubser, J. H. N. and D. S. Whitley
1999   *Recording Eight Places with Rock Imagery: Lava Beds National monument, Northern California*. Three Volumes. Report on File, Lava Beds National Monument, Tulelake, CA.

Loubser J. H. N. and P. C. Zietsman.
1994   Rock Painting of Postulated *Brunsvigia* sp. (Amaryllidaceae) at Thaba Bosiu, Western Lesotho. *South African Journal of Science* 90: 611-612.

Lowie, R. H.
1924   Notes on Shoshonean Ethnography. *American Museum of Natural History, Anthropological Papers* 20:185-314.

Ludlow, W., Captain
1875   *Report of a Reconnaissance of the Black Hills of Dakota, Made in the Summer of 1874*. US Government Printing Office, Washington, D.C.

Lundy, D.
1974   *The Rock Art of the Northwest Coast*. Master's Thesis, Simon Fraser University, Burnaby, British Columbia.
1983   Styles of Coastal Rock Art. In *Indian Art Traditions of the Northwest Coast*. R. L. Carlson, editor, pp, 99-120. Archaeology Press, Department of Archaeology, Simon Fraser University, Burnaby, British Columbia.

MacDonald, G.
1983   Prehistoric Art of the Northern Northwest Coast. In *Indian Art Traditions of the Northwest Coast*. R. L. Carlson, editor, pp. 99-120. Archaeology Press, Department of Archaeology, Simon Fraser University, Burnaby, British Columbia.

Macintosh, N. W. G.
1977   Beswick Creek Two Decades Later: a Reappraisal. In *Form in Indigenous Art*. P. Ucko, editor, pp. 256-274. Aboriginal Studies Press, Canberra, Australia.

Mallery, G.
1893   *Picture-Writing of the American Indians*. Bureau of American Ethnology, Smithsonian Institution, 10th Annual Report. [Reprinted 1972 by Dover Publications, New York.]

Malotki, E.
1998   The Owl: A Shamanistic Motif in the Archaic Rock Art Iconography of the Palavayu Anthropomorphic Style, Northeastern Arizona. *American Indian Rock Art* 29:1-18.
2000   *Kokopelli: The Making of an Icon*. University of Nebraska Press, Lincoln.
2003   Liminal Animals in the Archaic/Basketmaker II Rock Art Iconography of the Palavayu Anthropomorphic Style (PASTYLE), Arizona. *American Indian Rock Art* 29:139-154.

Malouf, C. I. and T. White
1953   The Origin of Pictographs. *Montana State University Anthropology and Sociology Papers* 15:30-31.

Mandt, G.
1995   Alternative Analogies in Rock Art Interpretation: The West Norwegian Case. In *Perceiving Rock Art: Social and Political Perspectives*. K. Helskog and B. Olsen, editors, pp. 263-291. Novus forlag, Oslo, Norway.

Marriott, A. and C. K. Rachlin
1968   *American Indian Mythology*. Harper and Row Publishers, Inc., New York

Marro, G.
1930   La Nuova Scoperta di Incisioni Preistoriche in Valcamonica. (Nota prima). *Atti della Reale Accademia delle Scienze di Torino*, 65.

Marshall, L. J.
1969   The Medicine Dance of the !Kung Bushmen. *Africa* 39: 347-381.
1976   *The !Kung of Nyae Nyae*. Harvard University Press, Cambridge, MA.
1999   *Nyae Nyae !Kung: Beliefs and Rites*. Peabody Museum, Harvard University, Cambridge, MA.

Martineau, L.
1973   *The Rocks Begin to Speak*. KC Publications, Las Vegas, NV.

Maurer, E. M.
1992   *Visions of the People: A Pictorial History of Plains Indian Life*. Minneapolis Institute of Arts, Minneapolis, MN.

McClure, R. H.
1979 The Tsagiglalal Motif in Rock Art of the Lower Columbia River. *American Indian Rock Art* 5:173-189.
1980 Anthropomorphic Motifs and Style in Plateau Rock Art. Paper Presented at the 33rd Annual Northwest Anthropological Conference, Bellingham, Washington, March 27-29.
1981 Paired Anthropomorphs of Central Washington. *American Indian Rock Art* 6:36-47.
1984 *Rock Art of the Dalles-Deschutes Region: A Chronological Perspective.* Master of Arts Thesis, Washington State University, Pullman, Washington.

McGee, W. J.
1897 *The Siouan Indians.* Bureau of American Ethnology Annual Report 15.

McGlone, W. R., P. M. Leonard, J. L. Guthrie, R. W. Gillespie, and J. P. Whittall, Jr.
1993 *Ancient American Inscriptions: Plow Marks or History?* Early Sites Research Society, Sutton, MA.

McKay, D.
1889 The Origin of the Horse in Oregon. *McKay Papers.* Umatilla County Library, Pendleton, OR.

McLane, A. R. and O. Frock
2001 The Star Burst Solar Site, Pah Rah Range, Washoe County, Nevada. *American Indian Rock Art* 27:221-226.

McNeil, L.
2001 On "Ghost Dancing the Grand Canyon". *Current Anthropology* 42:277-278.

Meade, E.
1971 *Indian Rock Carvings of the Pacific Northwest.* Gary's Publishing Ltd., Sidney, British Columbia.

Meigs, P. C.
1939 The Kiliwa Indians of Lower California. *Ibero-Americana* 15.

Mercer, Bill
2005 *People of the River: Native Arts of the Oregon Territory.* University of Washington Press, Seattle.

Merlan, F.
1989 The Interpretive Framework of Wardaman Rock Art: a Preliminary Framework. *Australian Aboriginal Studies* 1989(2):14-24.

Michaelis, H.
1981 Willowsprings: A Hopi Petroglyph Site. *Journal of New World Archaeology* 4(2):2-23.

Miller, J.
1998 Middle Columbia River Salishans. In *Handbook of North American Indians*, volume 12. D. E. Walker, Jr., editor, pp.253-270. Smithsonian Institution, Washington, D.C.

Minor, R.
1975 Known Origins of Rock Paintings of Southwestern California. *Pacific Coast Archaeological Society Quarterly* 9(4):29-36.

Minthorn, G.
1930 Cayuse Interlinear Texts. Collected by Morris Swadesh, ms. notebooks in the American Philosophical Society Library, Philadelphia.

Mitchell, M.
2002 *Protohistoric Rock Art in the Arkansas River Basin: Integrating Archaeology, Rock Art and Ethnohistory*. Paper presented at the 67th Annual Meeting of the Society for American Archaeology, Denver, CO.

Mohen, J. P. and Y. Taborin
1998 *Les Sociétés de la Préhistoire*. Hachette, Paris, France.

Mönnig, H. O.
1967 *The Pedi*. Van Schaik, Pretoria, South Africa.

Morandini, D. A.
1927 *Folklore di Valcamonica. Leggende, Tipi, Usi e Costumi*. Breno, Italia.

Mulvaney, K.
1996 What to do on a Rainy Day. Reminiscences of Mirriuwung and Gadjerong artists. *Rock Art Research* 13:3-20.

Munn, N. D.
1973 *Walbiri Iconography: Graphic Representation and Cultural Symbolism in a Central Australian Society*. Cornell University Press, Ithaca, New York.

North Dakota Writers' Project, Works Project Administration
1938 *North Dakota: A Guide to the Northern Prairie State*. Knight Printing, Fargo, ND.

Norton, S. S. M.
1910 A Description of the Modderpoort Neighborhood One Hundred Years Ago. *South African Journal of Science* 6:114-117.

Oetting, A. C.
1989 *Villages and Wetlands Adaptations in the Northern Great Basin: Chronology and Land Use in the Lake Abert-Chewaucan Marsh Basin-- Lake County, Oregon*. University of Oregon Anthropological Papers 41. Eugene.
1990 *The Malheur Lake Survey: Lacustrine Archaeology in the Harney Basin, Central Oregon*. Heritage Research Report 96. Eugene, OR

O'Connor, J. T.
2002 The Nampaweap Site Petroglyphs—Stars, Sex and Piñon Nuts? *American Indian Rock Art* 28:193-206.

Odegaard, N. and K. Hays-Gilpin
2002 Technology of the Sacred: Painted Wood and Basketry in the Southwest. In *Traditions, Transitions, and Technologies: Themes in Southwestern Archaeology, Proceedings of the 2000 Southwest Symposium*, S. Schlanger, editor, pp. 307-331. University of Colorado Press, Boulder.

Oliva, M.
1996 Mladopaleolithicky hrob Brno II Jako Prispevek k Pocatkum Smananismu (Upper Paleolithic Grave Brno II as a Contribution to the Origins of Shamanism). *Archeologické Rothledy* XLVIII:353-383. Praha, Czech Republic.

Olson, J.
1999   Cultural Resource Protection Submits Claim to Ancient Meteorite. *Smoke Signals*, November 15, 1999, Grand Ronde Tribal Newspaper, Grande Ronde, OR.

Olson, L. and L. L. Loendorf
2002   *Tolar Petroglyph Site*. Paper presented at the 67th Annual Meeting of the Society for American Archaeology, Denver, CO.

Oregonian, The
1916   Indian Tells Story of City Hall Rock. *The Oregonian*, Monday, January 24, Page 3. Portland, OR.

Orpen, J. M.
1874   A Glimpse Into the Mythology of the Maluti Bushmen. *Cape Monthly Magazine* (n.s.) 9(49):1-13.

Over, W. H.
1943   *Indian Picture Writing in South Dakota*. University of South Dakota Museum, Vermillion.

Oxendine, J.
1980   The Luiseño Girls' Ceremony. *Journal of California and Great Basin Anthropology* 2:37-50.

Pace, D.
1968   Vestigia di Culto Arcaico su Rupi del Territorio Grosino. *Bollettino della Società Storica Valtellinese*, 21:14-30.

Panofsky, E.
1962   *Studies in Iconology*. Harper & Row, New York.

Park, W.
1938   *Shamanism in Western North America: A Study in Cultural Relationships*. Northwestern University Press, Evanston, IL.

Parker, H.
1966   *The Historic Valley of Temecula: The Early Indians of Temecula*. Librito No. 1, Paisano Press, Balboa Island, CA.

Parkman, B.
1986   Cupule Petroglyphs in the Diablo Range, California. *Journal of California and Great Basin Anthropology* 8:246-259.
1993   Creating Thunder: The Western Rain Making Process. *Journal of California and Great Basin Anthropology* 15:90-110.

Parsons, M. L.
1987   Plains Indian Portable Art as a Key to Two Texas Historic Rock Art Sites. *Plains Anthropologist* 32(117):257-274.

Pasotti, M.
1965   Incisioni Rupestri sul Lago di Garda. *Bolletino del Centro Camuno di Studi Preistorici* 65:65-72, Capo di Ponte, Italia.

Patencio, F.
1943   *Stories and Legends of the Palm Springs Indians*. Palm Springs Desert Museum, Palm Springs, CA.

Patterson, C.
2001   On "Ghost Dancing the Grand Canyon." *Current Anthropology* 42:278-279.

Penney, D. W.
1992 *Art of the American Indian Frontier: The Chandler-Pohrt Collection.* University of Washington Press, Seattle.

Perlès, C.
1992 André Leroi-Gourhan et le Comparatisme. *Les Nouvelles de l'Archéologie* 48/49:46-47.

Perrin, M.
1995 *Le Chamanisme.* Que Sais-Je ? P.U.F., Paris, France.

Peterson, M. S.
1978 *Prehistoric Mobile Stone Sculpture of the Lower Columbia River Valley.* Master of Arts Thesis, Portland Sate University, Portland, OR.

Petter, R.
1915 *English-Cheyenne Dictionary.* Kettle Falls, WA.

Phillips, A.
2002 Flute Players, Flayed Scalps, and Big Horn Sheep: Water-related Imagery on the Sand Island Petroglyph Panel, Southeastern Utah. Paper presented at the 2002 American Rock Art Research Association annual meeting, DuBois, WY.

Plinius
1998 *Naturalis Historia, III.* Edition Les Belles Lettres, Paris, France.

Poetschat, G., J. D. Keyser, and T. E. Fifield
2002 Pictograph Cave in Southeast Alaska: Expanding our Cultural Understanding of the Rock Art. *American Indian Rock Art* 28:83-93.

Poetschat, G., J. D. Keyser, B. Tandberg, H. Hiczun, and P. McCoy
2003 The Beaver Bowl: A Shaman's Petroglyph in the Northwest Coast Art Tradition. *American Indian Rock Art* 29:33-42

Priuli, A.
1983 *Incisioni Rupestri nelle Alpi.* Priuli e Verlucca Editori, Ivrea, Italia.

Quinlan, A.
2000 The Ventriloquist's Dummy: A Critical Review of Shamanism and Rock Art in Far Western North America. *Journal of California and Great Basin Anthropology* 22:92-108.

Ragazzi, G.
1995 Danza Armata e Realtà Ctonia nel Repertorio Iconografico Camuno dell'età del Ferro. *Notizie Archeologiche Bergomensi* 2:235-247, Bergamo, Italia.

Rajnovich, G.
1994 *Reading Rock Art: Interpreting the Indian Rock Paintings of the Canadian Shield.* Natural Heritage/Natural History, Inc., Toronto, Ontario.

Ranck, G.
1926 Tribal Lore of Wishram Indians Rich in Tradition of Columbia. *The Sunday Oregonian,* February 7. Portland, OR.

Randolph, J. E. and M. Dahlstrom
1977 Archaeological Test Excavations at Bernard Creek Rockshelter. *University of Idaho Anthropological Research Manuscript Series* No. 42. Moscow, ID.

Ray, D.J.
1967 *Eskimo Masks: Art and Ceremony.* University of Washington Press, Seattle.

Ray, V.
1932 The Sanpoil and Nespelem: Salishan Peoples of Northeastern Washington. *University of Washington Publications in Anthropology* 5.

1942 Cultural Element Distributions: XXII, Plateau. *University of California Anthropological Records* 8(2). Berkeley.

1963 *Primitive Pragmatism: The Modoc Indians of Northern California.* University of Washington Press, Seattle.

Reichel-Dolmatoff, G.
1967 Rock Paintings of the Vaupes: an Essay of Interpretation. *Folklore Americas* (University of California Los Angeles), 27(2):107-113.

1978 Drug-induced Optical Sensations and Their Relationship to Applied Art Among Some Colombian Indians. In *Art in Society: Studies in Style, Culture, and Aesthetics.* M. Greenhalgh and V. Megaw, editors, pp. 289-304. Duckworth, London.

Renault, P.
1995-1996 Fantômes et Maisons Hantées. *Les Cahiers Zététiques*, 5:11-21.

Richards, L. G.
1935 Mystery of Ancient Carved Lava Boulder Unsolved. *The Sunday Oregonian*, June 30. Portland, OR.

Riddle, J.
1890 Unpublished letters to Albert Gatschet. Bureau of American Ethnology document number 3743.

Ripoll López S., E. Ripoll Perelló, and H. Collado Giraldo
1999 *Maltravieso. El Santuario Extremeño de las Manos.* Junta de Extremadura, Consejería de Cultura, Museo de Cáceres, Cáceres, España.

Ritter, E.
1994 Scratched Rock Art Complexes in the Desert West: Symbols for Socio-Religious Communication. In *New Light on Old Art: Recent Advances in Hunter-Gatherer Rock Art Research.* D. S. Whitley and L. L. Loendorf, editors, pp. 51-66. Institute of Archaeology, University of California at Los Angeles

Robert-Lamblin, J.
1996 Les Derniéres Manifestations du Chamanisme au Groenland Oriental. *Boréales* 66/69:115-130.

1997 Les Chamanes du Groenland Oriental: Éléments Biographiques et Généalogiques. *Études Inuits* 21(1-2):269-292.

Rodee, H. D.
1965 The Stylistic Development of Plains Indian Painting and Its Relationship to Ledger Drawings. *Plains Anthropologist* 10:218-232.

Rosman, A. and P. Ruebel
1990 Structural Patterning in Kwakiutl Art and Ritual. *Man* 25:620-639.

Ross, A.
1967 *Pagan Celtic Britain.* London, UK.

Rossi, F.
1987   *La Valcamonica Romana, Ricerche, e Studi*. Brescia, Italia.
Roulette, B. R.
2001   *Results of a Cultural Resources Study of the Fisher Landing Parcels, Vancouver, Clark County, Washington*. Applied Archaeological Research Report No. 219. Portland, OR.
Rubin, R.
1999   *Naked Against the Rain: The People of the Lower Columbia River 1770-1830*. Far Shore Press, Portland, OR.
Ruby, R. H. and J. A. Brown
1976   *The Chinookan Indians: Traders of the Lower Columbia River*. University of Oklahoma Press, Norman.
Sahlins, M.
1985   *Islands of History*. Chicago University Press, Chicago, IL.
Salzer, R. J.
1987   Preliminary Report on the Gottschall Site (47IA80). *Wisconsin Archaeologist* 68:419-472.
Sampson, C. G.
1985   *Nightfire Island: Later Holocene Lake/Marsh Adaptation on the Western Edge of the Great Basin*. University of Oregon Anthropological Papers 33. Eugene.
Sansoni, U.
1993   Medioevo sulla Roccia. *Archeologia Viva*, 40:32-47.
Sansoni, U., S. Lentini, and A. Marretta
2001   *Il Segno Minore. Arte Rupestre e Tradizione nella Bassa Valcamonica (Pisogne e Piancamuno)*. Archivi 14, Capo di Ponte, Italia.
Sauvet, G. and G. Tosello
1998   Le Mythe Paléolithique de la Caverne. In *Le Propre de l'Homme*. F. Sacco and G. Sauvet, editors, pp. 55-90. Delachaux & Niestlé, Lausanne, Suisse, éd.
Schaafsma, P.
1994   Trance and Transformation in the Canyons: Shamanism and Early Rock Art on the Colorado Plateau. In *Shamanism and Rock Art in North America*. S. A. Turpin, editor, pp. 45-71. Rock Art Foundation Inc., Special Publication 1, San Antonio, TX.
Schefer, J.-L.
1997   L'Art paléolithique. Préliminaires Critiques. *Les Cahiers du Musée National d'art Moderne*:5-33.
Schiffman, L. H.
1994   *Reclaiming the Dead Sea Scrolls: Their True Meaning for Judaism and Christianity*. Anchor Bible Reference Library, Philadelphia, PA.
Schlegel, A.
1977   Male and Female in Hopi Thought and Action. In *Sexual Stratification: A Cross-cultural View*. A. Schlegel, editor, pp. 245–269. Columbia University Press, New York.

Schlesier, K. H.
1987   *The Wolves of Heaven: Cheyenne Shamanism, Ceremonies, and Prehistoric Origins*, University of Oklahoma Press, Norman and London.

Schoolcraft, H. R.
1851-1857   *Historical and Statistical Information Respecting the History, Condition, and Prospects of the Indian Tribes of the United States.* (six volumes)   United States Government, Bureau of Indian Affairs, Philadelphia, PA.

Schuck, W. P.
1958   The 'Whoosit' at Five Mile Locks. *Screenings: Newsletter of the Oregon Archaeological Society* 7(3):3.

Schult, M. J.
1979   *Where Buffalo Roam.* Badlands Natural History Association, Interior, SD.

Scott, S., J. D. Keyser, and J. H. N. Loubser
2000   The Hellgate Pictographs: Shamanism and Ritual in West-Central Montana. *Archaeology In Montana* 41(1):31-52.

Seaman, N. G.
1946   *Indian Relics of the Pacific Northwest.* Binfords & Mort, Portland, Oregon.

Sébillot, P.
1990   *Riti Precristiani nel Folklore Europeo.* Milano, Italia.

Seidelman, H. and J. Turner
1994   *The Inuit Imagination: Arctic Myth and Sculpture.* Thames and Hudson, London, UK.

Simmons, L. W.
1942   *Sun Chief: The Autobiography of a Hopi Indian.* Yale University Press, New Haven, CT.

Simonnet, G., L. Simonnet, and R. Simonnet
1991   Le Propulseur au Faon de Labastide (Hautes-Pyrénées). *Bulletin de la Société Préhistorique Ariège-Pyrénées* XLVI:133-143.

Simonnet, R.
1996   Les Techniques de Représentation dans la Grotte Ornée de Labastide (Hautes-Pyrénées). In *Pyrénées préhistoriques, arts et sociétés.* H. Delporte and J. Clottes, editors, pp. 341-352. Actes du 118° Congrès des Sociétés historiques et scientifiques, 25-29 October 1993, Éditions du CTHS, Paru, Paris, France.

Sioux Falls [South Dakota] Argus-Leader
ca. 1931 "Indian Says Carved Rock in State Done by Members of Tribe," photocopy of undated clipping in author's possession.

Slifer, D.
2000   *The Serpent and the Sacred Fire. Fertility Images in Southwest Rock Art.* Museum of New Mexico Press, Sante Fe.

Smith, G. and M. Lerch
1984   Cupule Petroglyphs in Southern California. *San Bernardino Museum Quarterly* 32.

Smith, C.R. and D. Lee
2002   Pictographs of the Volcanic Tableland, Inyo and Mono Counties, California. *American Indian Rock Art* 27:201-210.

Smits, L. G. A.
1983   Rock Paintings in Lesotho: Site Characteristics. *South African Archaeological Bulletin* 38:62-76.

Sparkman, P. S.
1908   The culture of the Luiseño Indians. *University of California Publications in American Archaeology and Ethnology* 8(4):187-234. Berkeley.

Spier, L.
1930   Klamath Ethnography. *University of California Publications in American Archaeology and Ethnology* 30(1):1-338. Berkeley.

Spier, L. and E. Sapir
1930   Wishram Ethnography. *University of Washington Publications in Anthropology* 3(3):151-300. Seattle.

Spinden, H. J.
1908   The Nez Percé. *Memoirs of the American Anthropological Association*, 2, part 3.

Sprague, J. and G. Grasse
2001   Lizard Cave: A Possible Solar Marker at CA-KER-5525. *American Indian Rock Art* 27:227-235.

Stands in Timber, J. and M. Liberty
1967   *Cheyenne Memories*. University of Nebraska Press, Lincoln.

Stanford, W. E.
1910   Statement of Silayi, With Reference to His Life Among the Bushmen. *Transactions of the Royal Society of South Africa* 1:435-440.

Steinbring, J.
1998   Account of P. G. Bahn, *The Cambridge illustrated History of prehistoric Art,* In *Rock Art Research* 18/1:52.

Stephen, A.
1936   *The Hopi Journals of Alexander Stephen.* E. C. Parsons, editor. Columbia University Press, New York.

Stern, T.
1966   *The Klamath Tribe: A People and Their Reservation*. University of Washington Press, Seattle.

1998   Cayuse, Umatilla, and Walla Walla. In *Handbook of North American Indians: Volume 12, Plateau*. D. E. Walker, Jr., editor, pp. 395-419. Smithsonian Institution, Washington, D.C.

Stevens, E. T.
1974   *Alaskan Petroglyphs and Pictographs*. Master of Arts Thesis, University of Alaska, Fairbanks.

Stevenson, M. C.
1887   The Religious Life of the Zuni Child. *Fifth Annual Report of the Bureau of American Ethnology for the Years 1883–1884*:533–555. Smithsonian Institution, Washington, D.C.

1904 The Zuni Indians: Their Mythology, Esoteric Fraternities, and Ceremonies, *Twenty-third Annual Report of the Bureau of American Ethnology*:3–634. Smithsonian Institution, Washington, D.C.

Steward, J. H.
1929 Petroglyphs of California and Adjoining States. *University of California Publications in American Archaeology and Ethnology* 24(2). Berkeley.
1937 Petroglyphs of the United States. *Smithsonian Institution, Annual Report for 1936*:405-425.
1942 The Direct Historical Approach to Archaeology. *American Antiquity* VII:337-343.
1943 Culture Element Distributions: XXIII, Northern and Gosiute Shoshoni. *University of California Anthropological Records* 8(3):263-392. Berkeley.

Stewart, K. M.
1977 Mojave Indian Ghosts and the Land of the Dead. *The Masterkey* 51(1):14-21.

Stoffle, R. W., L. Loendorf, D. E. Austin, D. B. Halmo, and A. Bulletts
2000 Ghost Dancing in the Grand Canyon. Southern Paiute Rock Art, Ceremony and Cultural Landscapes. *Current Anthropology* 41:11-38.

Stoffle. R. W., M. Nieves Zedeño, and D. B. Halmo
2001 *American Indians and the Nevada Test Site: A Model of Research and Cooperation.* U.S. Government Printing Office, Washington, D.C.

Stone, R.
1982 *First Encounters: Indian Legends of Devils Tower.* Sand Creek Printing, Belle Fourche, SD.

Stow, G. W.
1930 *Rock Paintings in South Africa.* Methuen, London, UK.

Strong, E.
1958 Effigy Bowl. *Screenings: Newsletter of the Oregon Archaeological Society* 7(10):1.
1959a *Stone Age on the Columbia River.* Binfords & Mort Publishers, Portland, Oregon.
1959b *Wakemap Mound: A Stratified Site on the Columbia River.* Oregon Archaeological Society, Publication 1, Portland, OR.
1960 The John Krussow Collection. *Screenings: Newsletter of the Oregon Archaeological Society* 9(1):1-2.

Strong, W. D.
1929 Aboriginal Society in Southern California. *University of California Publications in American Archaeology and Ethnology* 26. Berkeley.
1935 *An Introduction to Nebraska Archaeology*, Smithsonian Miscellaneous Collections 93(20), Washington, D.C.

Strong, W. D. and W. Egbert Schenck
1925 Petroglyphs Near The Dalles of the Columbia River. *American Anthropologist* 27(1):76-90.

Strong, William D., W. E. Schenck, and J. H. Steward
1930 Archaeology of The Dalles-Deschutes Region. *University of California Publications in American Archaeology and Ethnology* 29(1):1-154. Berkeley.

Sturtevant, W. C.
1974 *Boxes and Bowls: Decorated Containers by Nineteenth-Century Haida, Tlingit, Bella Bella, and Tsimshan Indian Artists.* Smithsonian Institution Press, Washington, D.C.

Sundstrom, L.
1989a *Rock Art of the Southern Black Hills: A Contextual Approach.* PhD Dissertation, Department of Anthropology, University of Kansas. University Microfilms International, Ann Arbor, MI.
1989b Archaic Hunting Practices Depicted in a Northwestern Plains Rock Art Style. *Plains Anthropologist* 34:149-169.
1990 *Rock Art of the Southern Black Hills: A Contextual Approach.* Garland Publishing, Inc., New York.
1996 *The Material Culture of Ludlow Cave, Custer National Forest, Harding County, South Dakota: A NAGPRA Evaluation.* Custer National Forest, Billings, MT.
2002 Steel Awls for Stone Age Plainswomen: Rock Art, Religion, and the Hide Trade on the Northern Plains. *Plains Anthropologist* 47:99-119.
2003 *Storied Stone: Rock Art of the Black Hills Country.* University of Oklahoma Press, Norman.

Sundstrom, L. and J. D. Keyser
1998 Tribal Affiliation of Shield Petroglyphs from the Black Hills and Cave Hills, *Plains Anthropologist* 43:225-238.

Swartz, B. K. Jr.
1978 *Klamath Basin Petroglyphs.* Ballena Press, Menlo Park, CA.

Taborin, Y.
2000 Les Interprétations de l'art Paléolithique. *Archéologia* 366:52-61.

Taçon, P. S. C.
1983 An analysis of Dorset Art in Relation to Prehistoric Culture Stress. *Inuit Studies* 7(1):41-65.
2001 Australia. In *Handbook of Rock Art Research*, D. S. Whitley, editor, pp.530-575. AltaMira Press, Walnut Creek, CA.

Taçon, P. S. C. and C. Chippindale
1998 An Archaeology of Rock-Art Through Informed Methods and Formal Methods. In *The Archaeology of Rock-Art.* C. Chippindale and P. S. C. Taçon, editors, pp. 1-10. Cambridge University Press, Cambridge, UK.

Taylor, M. and J. Keyser
2003 The Columbia Plateau Scratched Style: A Preliminary Interpretation. *American Indian Rock Art* 29:11-20.

Tcherter, E.
1997 Lectures et Documents. *Ardèche Archéologie* 14:63.

Teit, J. A.
1896 A Rock Painting of the Thompson River Indians, British Columbia. *Bulletin of the American Museum of Natural History* 8(12):227-230.

1900 The Thompson Indians of British Columbia. *American Museum of Natural History, Memoir 2, Publications of the Jesup North Pacific Expedition* 1(4):163-392.
1906 The Lillooet Indians. *American Museum of Natural History, Publications of the Jesup North Pacific Expedition* 2(5).
1909 The Shuswap. *Memoir of the American Museum of Natural History* 4: pp. 584-594.
1918 Notes on Rock Paintings in General, 1918. Unpublished Manuscript, Glenbow Alberta Institute Archives.
1930 The Salishan Tribes of the Western Plateau. *Bureau of American Ethnology* Annual Report 45:23-396.

Ten Raa, E.
1969 Sandawe Prehistory and the Vernacular Tradition. *Azania* 4:91-103.
1971 Dead Art and Living Society: A Study of Rock Paintings in Social Context. *Mankind* 8:42-58.

Thackeray, A. I.
1983 Dating the Rock Art of Southern Africa. *South African Archaeological Society Goodwin Series* 4:21-26.

Thomas, E. H.
1970 *Chinook: A History and Dictionary of the Northwest Coast Trade Jargon.* Binfords & Mort Publishers, Portland, OR. (Reprint of original 1935 edition)

Thomas, E. M.
1959 *The Harmless People.* Penguin, Harmondsworth, UK.

Thwaites, R. G.
1905 *The Original Journals of Lewis and Clark.* The Arthur F. Clark Co, New York.

Tilley, C.
1999 Why Things Matter: Some Theses on Material Forms. *Mind and Body* 315-339.

Titiev, M.
1939 The Story of Kokopele. *American Anthropologist* n.s. 41:91-98.

Townsend, J. K.
1839 Narrative of a Journey Across the Rocky Mountains, to the Columbia River, and A Visit to the Sandwich Islands, Chili, &c. with A Scientific Appendix. In *Early Western Travels 1748-1846* Vol. XXI. R. G. Thwaites, editor, pp. 349-364. Henry Perkins, Philadelphia, PA.

Trippel, E. J.
1889 The Yuma Indians. *Overland Monthly*, 2nd series, 13:561-584.

True, D. L.
1954 Pictographs of the San Luis Rey Basin, California. *American Antiquity* 20:68-72.

True, D. L. and M. Baumhoff
1981 Pitted Rock Petroglyphs in Southern California. *Journal of California and Great Basin Anthropology 3:257-268.*

Tsuru, D.
1998   Diversity of Ritual Spirit Performances Among the Baka Pygmies in Southeastern Cameroon. *African Study Monographs, supplement* 25:47-84.

Turner, D.
1973   The Rock Art of Bickerton Island. *Oceania* 43(4):286-325.

Turner, V.
1967   *The Forest of Symbols: Aspects of Nedembu Ritual.* Cornell University Press, Ithaca, NY.

Turney-High, H. H.
1937   *The Flathead Indians of Montana.* American Anthropological Association, Memoirs 48.
1941   Ethnography of the Kutenai. *American Anthropological Association Memoirs* 48.

Turpin, S. A.
1994   On a Wing and a Prayer: Flight Metaphors in Pecos River Art. In *Shamanism and Rock Art in North America.* S. A. Turpin, editor, pp. 73-102. Rock Art Foundation Inc., Special Publication 1, San Antonio, TX.
2001   Archaic North America. In *Handbook of Rock Art Research.* D.S. Whitley, editor, pp.361-413. AltaMira Press, New York.

United States Court of Claims
1927   *The Yankton Sioux v. the United States*, evidence for the plaintiff.

Valentin, B.
1999   Compte Rendu de J. Clottes, 1998, *Voyage en Préhistoire,* La Maison des Roches. *La Recherche* 326:102-103. Paris, France.

Van Der Vliet, V.
1974   Growing Up in Traditional Society. In *TheBantu-Speaking Peoples of Southern Africa.* W. D. Hammond-Tooke, editor, pp.211-245. Routledge, London, UK.

Van de Kimmenade, M.
1936   'Les Sandawe'. *Anthropos* 31:395-416.

Van Warmelo, N. J.
1932   *Contributions Towards Venda History, Religion and Tribal Ritual.* Ethnological Publication, 3. Government Printer, Pretoria, South Africa.

Vazeilles, D.
1991   *Les Chamanes, Maîtres de l'univers.* Editions du Cerf, Paris, France.

Vialou, D.
1998   *L'Art des Grottes.* Scala. Paris, France.

Villaverde Bonilla, V.
1994   *Arte Paleolítico de la Cova del Parpalló. Estudio de la Colección de Plaquetas y Cantos Grabados y Pintados.* Diputació de València, Valencia, España.

Vinnicombe, P.
1976   *People of the Eland: Rock Paintings of the Drakensberg Bushmen as a Reflection of their Life and Thought.* University of Natal Press, Pietermaritzburg, South Africa.

Vitebsky, P.
1995   *The Shaman. Voyages of the Soul, Trance, Ecstasy, and Healing from Siberia to the Amazon.* Little, Brown and Company, Boston, MA.
1997   What is a Shaman? *Natural History* 3/97:34-35.
Voegelin, C. F. (editor)
1959   Melville Jacobs' Field Notes: *Clackamas Chinook Texts Part 2*, International Journal of American Linguistics 25:2: part II: 99
Voegelin, E. W.
1938   Tubatulabal Ethnography. *University of California Anthropological Records* 2(1):1-90.
Walker, D. E., Jr.
1991   Protection of American Indian Sacred Geography. In *Handbook of American Indian Religious Freedom.* C. Vecsey, editor, pp. 100-115. Crossroad Publishing Company, New York.
Walker, J. R.
1980   *Lakota Belief and Ritual.* R. J. DeMallie and E. A. Jahner, editors. University of Nebraska Press, Lincoln.
Walker, N. J.
1987   The Dating of Zimbabwean Rock Art. *Rock Art Research* 4(2):137-148.
Walsh, R.
1989   What is a Shaman: Definition, Origin and Distribution. *The Journal of Transpersonal Psychology* 211:1-11.
Wardwell, A.
1996   *Tangible Visions: Northwest Coast Indian Shamanism and Its Art.* The Monacelli Press, Inc. New York.
Waterman, T. T.
1910   The Religious Practices of the Diegueño Indians. *University of California Publications in American Archaeology and Ethnology* 8(6):271-358. Berkeley.
Wedel, W. R.
1938   *The Direct-Historical Approach in Pawnee Archaeology.* Smithsonian Miscellaneous Collections 97(7), Washington, D.C.
Wellman, K. F.
1979   *A Survey of North American Indian Rock Art.* Akademische Druck-und Verlagsanstalt, Graz, Austria.
Wendt, W. E.
1976   'Art Mobilier' from the Apollo 11 Cave, South West Africa's Oldest Dated Works of Art. *South African Archaeological Bulletin* 31:5-11.
Werner, R. H. (editor)
1995   *Field Inventory, Mapping, and National Register District Evaluation: Miller Island (3 Volumes).* Report on file with the Columbia River Gorge National Scenic Area, Hood River, OR.
White, R. C.
1963   Luiseño Social Organization. *University of California Publications in American Archaeology and Ethnology* 48:91-194. Berkeley.
White, R.
1997   Structure, Signification and Culture. Different logics of representation and their archaeological implications. *Diogenes* 180, Vol. 45/4:97-113.

Whitley, D. S.
1992 Shamanism and rock art in far western North America. *Cambridge Archaeological Journal* 2:89-113.
1994a Shamanism, Natural Modeling and the Rock Art of Far Western North America. In *Shamanism and Rock Art in North America.* S. Turpin, editor, pp.1-43 Rock Art Foundation, San Antonio, TX.
1994b Ethnography and Rock Art in the Far West: Some Archaeological Implications. In *New Light on Old Art: Recent Advances in Hunter-Gatherer Rock Art Research.* D. S. Whitley and L. L. Loendorf, editors, pp. 81-94. Institute of Archaeology, University of California at Los Angeles.
1996 *A Guide to Rock Art Sites: Southern California and Southern Nevada.* Mountain Press Publishing, Missoula, MT.
1998 Finding Rain in the Desert: Landscape, Gender, and Far Western North American Rock Art. In *The Archaeology of Rock-Art.* C. Chippindale and P.S.C. Taçon, editors, pp. 11-29, Cambridge University Press, Cambridge, UK.
2000a *Les Chamanes de Californie. Le Monde des Amérindiens.* Le Seuil, Paris, France.
2000b *The Art of the Shaman: Rock Art of California.* University of Utah Press, Salt Lake City.
2001 Response to Quinlan. *Journal of California and Great Basin Anthropology* 23:108-128.
2003 What Is Hedges Arguing About? *American Indian Rock Art* 29:83-104.

Whitley, D. S., R. I. Dorn, J. M. Simon, R. Rechtman, and T. K. Whitley
1999 Sally's Rockshelter and the Archaeology of the Vision Quest. *Cambridge Archaeological Journal* 9:221-247.

Whitley, D. S. and L. L. Loendorf
1994 Off the Cover and Into the Book. In *New Light on Old Art: Recent Advances in Hunter-Gatherer Rock Art Research.* D. S. Whitley and L. L. Loendorf, editors, pp. xi-xx. Institute of Archaeology, University of California at Los Angeles.

Whitley, D. S. and J. H. N. Loubser
n.d. *Mulwas*: Pictographs of Lava Beds National Monument. (Manuscript in preparation).

Whitley, D. S., J. H. N. Loubser, and D. Hann
2004 Friends in Low Places: Rock Art and Landscape on the Modoc Plateau. In *Pictures in Place: Landscapes of Rock-Art.* C. Chippindale and G. Nash editors, pp. 217-238. Cambridge University Press, Cambridge, UK.

Wilbert, J.
1987 *Tobacco and Shamanism in South America.* Yale University Press, New Haven, CT.

Willey, G. R., and J. A. Sabloff
1980 *A History of American Archaeology* (second edition). Freeman, San Francisco, CA.

Wilson, G. L.
1928 *Hidatsa Eagle Trapping.* Anthropological Papers of the American Museum of Natural History, Vol. 30, Part 4.

Wingert, P. S.
1952 *Prehistoric Stone Sculpture of the Pacific Northwest.* Portland Art Museum, Portland, OR.

Winthrop, R. H., K. R. Winthrop, and D. J. Gray
1995 Rock Feature Sites on the Mt. Hood National Forest: An Inventory and Evaluation. Unpublished report on file, Mt. Hood National Forest, Gresham, OR.

Wissler, C.
1912 *Societies and Ceremonial Associations of the Oglala Division of the Teton-Dakota.* American Museum of Natural History Anthropological Paper 11(1).

Wolff, C. F.
1987 *I Monti Pallidi. Leggende delle Dolomiti.* Bologna, Italia.

Womack, Mary
1967 Emics, Etics, "Ethics" and Shamans. *American Anthropological Society Anthropology News,* pg. 7.

Woodward, J. A.
1982 *The Ancient Painted Images of the Columbia Gorge.* Acoma Books, Ramona, CA.

Wormington, H. M., and R. G. Forbis
1965 *An Introduction to the Archaeology of Alberta, Canada.* Denver Museum of Natural History Proceedings 11.

Yates, R. and A. Manhire
1991 Shamanism and Rock Paintings: Aspects of the Use of Rock Art in the South-West Cape, South Africa. *South African Archaeological Bulletin* 46:3-11.

York, A., R. Daly, and C. Arnett
1993 *They Write Their Dreams on the Rock Forever. Rock Writings in the Stein River Valley of British Columbia.* Talonbooks, Vancouver, British Columbia.

Young, M. J.
1988 *Signs From the Ancestors: Zuni Cultural Symbolism and Perceptions of Rock Art.* University of New Mexico Press, Albuquerque.

Zigmond, M.
1977 The Supernatural World of the Kawaiisu. In *Flowers of the Wind: Papers on Ritual, Myth and Symbolism in California and the Southwest.* T.C. Blackburn, editor, pp. 9-95. Ballena Press, Socorro, NM.
1980 *Kawaiisu Mythology: An Oral Tradition of South-Central California.* Ballena Press, Socorro, NM.
1981 Kawaiisu Ethnobotany. University of Utah Press, Salt Lake City.

INDEX

-A-
ancestral spirits, in rock art, 46-47, 76-78, 239
-B-
biographic art, 3, 5, 63, 69, 143-155
British Columbia, 7, 171, 221, 226
-C-
Captain Jack, 190, 198
Chauvet Cave, *119, 131,* 136, 328, 329
Columbia Plateau, 1-3, 5-7, 9, 90, 141, 143-153, 161, 164, 167, 177, 200-221, 223, 226, 240-246, 295, 315-326, 328, 330, 331
Columbia River, 1, 6, 9, 24, 89, 143-156, 159-175, 199. 204, 209, 216, 219, 220, 240-242, 293, 324, 327
coup count, 67, 145-147, 155
cupules, 89, 160, 168, 169, 210, 261ff, 274, 295, 310-315, 319-321, 323, 326
-D-
dance, as shown in rock art, 32ff, 258, 279, 288; trance dance, 32-34, 192, 212, 217, 231, 234
Donald McKay, 20, 151-152, 156-157. (*See also* Yakima Scouts)
double woman, 57-59, 61-63, 70
-E-
entoptics, 91-93, 95-99, 218, 219, 221, 247, 249, 251, 252, 305, 310, 323
ethnography, use in rock art interpretation, 2-7, 30-33, 38, 42-47, 49, 61-71, 75ff, 91, 92, 108-110, 129, 135, 155, 176, 178-180, 187, 189, 200, 211, 214, 216, 217, 219, 231, 245, 282-292, 295-318; direct ethnographic approach, 52ff
-F-
flute player, 286-292
-G-
Great Basin, 4, 141, 176, 177, 196, 202, 208, 282, 295, 310-315, 318, 319
-H-
hallucinogens, related to rock art, 16, 50, 112, 117, 122, 123, 134, 296, 304, 306; hallucinogenic character of caves, 126, 249-251
handprints, in rock art, 77, 131, 236, 237, 262, 297, 298, 304, 320-322
horse, arrival to Columbia Plateau, 143-156

Horse Thief Lake State Park, 17, 165, 202, 207
hunting imagery, in rock art, 41, 82, 90, 91, 94, 258, 282
-I-
Indian doctor, 13, 51, 89, 170, 173-174, 189, 323. (*See also* Twatees, shamans, medicine man, sorcerer)
-K-
Klamath Basin, 176-199, 240, 242, 245
Kokopelli, 289-291. (*See also* flute player)
-L-
ledger Art, 63
-M-
McKay, (*See also* Donald McKay)
medicine bundle, 62
medicine man, 13, 17, 26, 62, 64, 89, 141, 169, 233; special sites: medicine man's cave, 187; women's medicine cave, 188. (*See also* Indian doctor, shaman, sorcerer, Twatees)
mobiliary art, 6, 8, 102-103, 119, 125-126, 139, 158-160, 164-167, 172
Modoc, 176-199, 241, 245
mortuary rituals, 13, 200, 221, 240
mountain sheep, in rock art, 44-45, 84, 141, 222, 246, 290-291, 329
-N-
neuropsychology, neuropsychological model, 96, 112, 115, 117, 135, 220, 221, 249ff, 305, 316
Nez Perce, 1, 5, 143, 153, 156, 213, 214, 223, 251
-O-
offerings, at rock art sites, 15, 60, 66, 72, 87, 219, 283, 318
oral tradition. (*See also* ethnography, and rock art, oral traditions relating to)
-P-
Pacific Northwest, 6, 160, 167, 177
Petroglyph Canyon, 174, 175
petroglyphs, 6, 7, 12, 18, 51, 56, 58, 60, 61, 65-67, 155, 158-172, 178, 184, 189, 197, 198, 202, 255, 256, 260, 283, 284, 290, 293, 300, 307, 315, 317-319, 323, 324, 326, 330. (*See also* rock art)
pictographs, 7, 11, 12, 65, 82, 83, 147, 148, 150, 154, 155, 158, 178, 196, 197, 202, 242, 297-300, 304-307, 311-316, 321-326, 330-332; binders, 15; as witnessing mythic events, 22-25, 77-81, 143-144. (*See also* rock art)
pigments, 14-15, 20, 86, 88, 159, 166, 167, 195, 200, 221, 222, 227, 230, 233- 236, 238, 240, 243, 245-247, 306, 312, 331; in mortuary ritual, 13
Plains, 3, 4, 7, 51, 52, 54, 58, 63, 64, 155, 156, 158, 221, 223, 251, 282, 310. (*See also* rock art, North American Plains)

INDEX

-R-

robe art, 63

rock art, Africa, 6, 97, 108, 225-240; as part of initiation rites, 89, 90, 121, 255, 258, 270, 295-326; as public art, 22, 23, 238, 247, 268; as sorcery, 32, 76, 233, 247, 307, 323; associated with Ghost Dance, 22, 85-92; at water sources, 17, 18, 25. 26, 55, 58, 80, 263, 270, 285; Australia, 5, 73-93; by those seeking spirit power, 12, 20, 89, 182, 183, 208, 214-219, 234, 243, 244, 253, 285, 304, 305; by young people during puberty rites, 6, 11, 15, 27, 39, 81ff, 88ff, 169, 182, 193, 238, 243, 286, 288, 295-326; California, 4, 6, 25, 89, 176, 226, 240-242, 295-315; changing at different times, 64; Columbia Plateau, field trip to and discussion of sites, 11-27, 80-85, 143-153, 172, 200-220, 240-246, 315-318, 324-326; destruction of, 107; early use of ethnography for interpretation, 2-6, 42, 79, 83, 91, 101, 176-192, 200, 225, 308; Europe, 5, 100-142, 240, 254-278; fertility rituals, 4, 219, 262, 273-276, 281, 285-289, 291, 310-315; gender, 6, 38, 39, 45-47, 56ff, 62, 193-194, 286ff, 293; interacting with surface irregularities, 41, 207, 208, 223, 229, 234, 236, 264; made by shamans, 34, 82, 88, 89, 119, 130, 134, 158, 186, 189, 211-221, 226, 234, 239-240, 244-246, 247, 252-253, 307, 310, 323; made by spirits, 62, 63, 325; made by women, 63, 67, 268-270, 297ff, 312, 316ff; North American Plains, 54, 64, 67, 69, 158; Northwest Coast, 6, 80-85, 158-175; not necessarily all shamanic, 88ff, 320; oral tradition relating to, 2, 4, 5, 8, 86, 87, 89, 147, 152, 236, 264, 275, 283, 285, 287, 290; Paleolithic, 5, 100-136, 139, 140, 248, 256, 276; Parpallo Cave with continuous rock art tradition, 120-121; sexual imagery, 6, 286-289; site itself is sexual image, 121; solar aspect, 4, 183, 187, 256, 258, 271, 272, 276-278, 284; South Africa, 5, 7, 30-48; Southwest US, 3, 4, 6, 7, 85-87, 282-294; Valcamonica, 6, 254-278

-S-

sacred geography, 3, 23, 176-199, 311, 317

Sahaptin, 1, 5, 143-153

San (South African Bushmen), 7, 30-48, 91, 108-109, 228-240

shaman, 32-35, 38-43, 46, 47, 51, 80-83, 93, 106, 112, 123-124, 130-132, 134, 174, 186, 187, 189, 212-213, 219, 231, 244, 247, 296, 307, 310, 312, 317, 318, 320, 323, 328, 330; Columbia Plateau shaman, 6, 212, 317; Klamath shaman, 244; Mojave shaman, 98; woman as shaman, 82-83, 212, 231, 244. (*See also* Indian doctor, medicine man, sorcerer, Twatees)

shamanic, 38-43, 46, 85, 88-91, 106, 108, 116-117, 126, 135, 187; distinction between shamanic and shamanistic, 226, 240, 246, 247, 295, 320

"Shamanic Wars," conflict over shamanism as explanation for rock art, 135
shamanism, 74, 80, 87, 88, 107, 109-115, 124-125, 129, 138, 139, 141, 183, 211ff, 231ff
shamanistic, 90, 104, 108, 110-111, 127, 129, 246, 282
She Who Watches, (*See also* Tsagiglalal)
shield bearing warrior, 149, 150, 155, 284
shield design, 63
snake, in rock art, 41, 76, 94, 234, 266, 286, 304-306, 321-322, 330
Snake River, location of rock art, 24, 207, 240, 241, 331
sorcerer, 32, 117-118, 226, 246; (*See also* Indian doctor, medicine man, rock art as sorcery, shaman, Twatees)
Spilyay Tymoo, 2, 327-332
spirituality, 42, 43, 81, 108
spirit power, 21, 56, 137, 140, 169, 182, 183, 187, 188, 208, 216, 217, 219. (*See also* rock art, by those seeking spirit power)
Steiwer Ranch, 5, 144, 145, 150, 241
stone sculpture, 159-175
stone plaquettes, 121, 122
Swallowing Monster, 19-20, 22-23, 27
sympathetic magic, 47, 88, 292
synecdoche 7, 34-35

-T-

tahmanawis, 21, 89, 157, 168-175, 252-253
therianthrope, 106, 112, 117-125
totemism, 74-91, 129, 290, 303, 308
tobacco, 16, 17, 167, 294, 297, 299-303, 322; as offering at rock art, 87
tracks, animal, in rock art, 55, 57-58, 60, 63, 65, 81, 84
trance, 52, 112-115, 117, 118, 123, 124, 130, 171, 187, 214; in rock art, 32ff, 92, 216, 231; death as metaphor for, 47, 91; induced by cave environments, 126, 249-252. (*See also* dance, trance dance)
Tsagiglalal (She Who Watches), 17-18, 25, 98, 158, 163, 172
Twatees, 13, 16, 174

-V-

vision quest, 12, 16-17, 20-21, 27, 34, 40, 62-65, 67, 69, 80ff, 81-84, 98, 114, 125, 130, 134, 168, 182, 183, 187, 188, 192, 200, 205, 211, 214, 219, 221, 222, 215, 243-246, 295, 310, 315-319, 324, 325, 328, 330
vulvaform, 58, 60, 66, 67, 69, 205. (*See also* sexual imagery in rock art)

-Y-

Yakima scouts, 20, 157
Yakima War, 157, 169

CONTRIBUTING AUTHORS

Jean Clottes is recognized worldwide as a rock art researcher and expert. A Knight of the French Legion of Honor, he has written numerous books on the Paleolithic cave art of France. Most recently he has published major works on Cosquer and Chauvet caves.

Phillip Cash Cash is a Nez Perce-Cayuse tribal traditionalist and scholar. While he is pursuing a PhD in linguistics at Arizona State University he has published several articles on Columbia Plateau rock art. His paper in this volume was presented at the Society for American Archaeology meetings in 2000—the first such presentation ever in a native North American Language.

J. David Lewis-Williams is Professor Emeritus and Senior Mentor in the Rock Art Research Institute at the University of Witwatersrand, Johannesburg, South Africa. In his long and distinguished career he has published extensively on the rock art of South Africa and the European Paleolithic. His most recent books include *The Shamans of Prehistory* (with Jean Clottes) and *The Mind in the Cave*.

Linea Sundstrom is a rock art researcher working primarily in the Northern Plains. She has written extensively about the rock art of South Dakota. Her most recent book is *Storied Stone: Rock Art of the Black Hills Country*.

Robert Layton is a professor of anthropology at the University of Durham, England, specializing in rock art ethnography. Much of his work concerns Australia. He is the author of The *Anthropology of Art* and *Australian Rock Art: A New Synthesis*.

James D. Keyser is currently a rock art researcher for the US Forest Service. He has written extensively about rock art on the Northern Plains, Columbia Plateau, and Northwest Coast regions of North America. He is the author of *Indian rock Art of the Columbia Plateau, Plains Indian Rock Art* (with Michael A. Klassen), *The Five Crows Ledger: Biographic Warrior Art of the Flathead Indians*, and *Art of the Warriors: Rock Art of the American Plains*.

Contributing Authors   379

George Poetschat has been an archaeological volunteer for twenty years with the Oregon Archaeological Society. He has co-authored numerous articles and monographs on rock art from Alaska, Washington, Oregon, and Wyoming. His most recent publications are *Echoes of the Ancients: Rock Art of The Dalles-Deschutes Region* and *Warrior Art of Wyoming's Green River Basin: Biographic Petroglyphs Along the Seedskadee*.

Michael W. Taylor has been an archaeological volunteer with the Oregon Archaeological Society for ten years. He has written extensively on rock art of the Pacific Northwest. His most recent publications are the co-authored volumes *Echoes of the Ancients: Rock Art of The Dalles-Deschutes Region* and *Visions on Stone: Rock Art of the Columbia Plateau*.

Johannes H. N. Loubser is a research archaeologist and rock art conservator working the southeastern United States. He has published research on the rock art of Africa, the southeastern United States, the Columbia Plateau, and Baja California. His most recent book is *Archaeology: The Comic*.

Angelo Fossati is a rock art researcher with Le Orme Dell'Uomo in Valcamonica Italy, and a professor at the Catholic University in Brescia, Italy. He has written extensively on rock art in the European Alps. Recent publications include *Rupe Magna: La Roccia Incisa piu Grande delle Alpi* and *Archeologia e Arte Rupestre: L'Europa, Le Alpi, La Valcamonica*.

Kelley Hayes-Gilpin is currently professor of anthropology at Northern Arizona University. Her research is focused on gender issues and southwestern rock art. She is the author of *Ambiguous Images: Gender and Rock Art*.

David S. Whitley is a California rock art researcher widely known throughout the United States and Europe. His research focuses on rock art and shamanism in western North America. Recent books include *Art of the Shaman: The Rock Art of California* and *The Handbook of Rock Art Research*.

Don Hann is forest archaeologist on the Malheur National Forest in central Oregon. He has co-authored several articles on Klamath Basin and Columbia Plateau rock art and is currently conducting master's thesis research on pictograph sites in the upper John Day River basin.

Contributing Authors

Helen Hiczun has been an archaeological volunteer with the Oregon Archaeological Society for more than ten years. She is co-author of published research on the Butte Creek and Owl Cave rock art sites.

Betty Tandberg has been an archaeological volunteer with the Oregon Archaeological Society for more than ten years. She is co-author of a monograph on the Butte Creek rock art sites.

Pat McCoy has been an archaeological volunteer with the Oregon Archaeological Society for more than ten years. This is her first publication in archaeology.

Gordon Bettles is a member of the Klamath Tribe and currently a graduate student in anthropology at the University of Oregon. He has a deep interest in traditional Klamath culture and has worked with Don Hann in transcribing the Klamath-Modoc field notes of Jeremiah Curtin.